Learning to Solve Complex Scientific Problems

Edited by

David H. Jonassen
University of Missouri

Lawrence Erlbaum Associates
Taylor & Francis Group

New York   London

Cover design by Katherine Houghtaling Lacey.

Cover artwork by Morgan Gibbs Colston. Father Figure, 2002; paraffin crayon on paper, 46 × 30 cm, private collection.

Lawrence Erlbaum Associates
Taylor & Francis Group
270 Madison Avenue
New York, NY 10016

Lawrence Erlbaum Associates
Taylor & Francis Group
2 Park Square
Milton Park, Abingdon
Oxon OX14 4RN

© 2007 by Taylor & Francis Group, LLC
Lawrence Erlbaum Associates is an imprint of Taylor & Francis Group, an Informa business

Printed in the United States of America on acid-free paper
10 9 8 7 6 5 4 3 2 1

International Standard Book Number-13: 978-0-8058-6062-7 (Softcover) 978-0-8058-6061-0 (Hardcover)

Library of Congress Cataloging-in-Publication Data

Irony in language and thought : a cognitive science reader / edited by Herbert L.
    Colston and Raymond W. Gibbs, Jr.
        p. cm.
    Includes bibliographical references and index.
    ISBN 978-0-8058-6062-7 (pbk. : alk. paper) -- ISBN 978-0-8058-6061-0 (alk. paper)
    -- ISBN 978-1-4106-1668-5 (e-book)
    1. Irony. I. Colston, Herbert L. II. Gibbs, Raymond W. III. Title.

P301.5.I73I76 2007
809'.918--dc22   2006037734

Visit the Taylor & Francis Web site at
http://www.taylorandfrancis.com

and the LEA Web site at
http://www.erlbaum.com

Contents

Cover design by Kathryn Houghtaling Lacey.

Lawrence Erlbaum Associates
Taylor & Francis Group
270 Madison Avenue
New York, NY 10016

Lawrence Erlbaum Associates
Taylor & Francis Group
2 Park Square
Milton Park, Abingdon
Oxon OX14 4RN

© 2007 by Taylor & Francis Group, LLC
Lawrence Erlbaum Associates is an imprint of Taylor & Francis Group, an Informa business

Printed in the United States of America on acid-free paper
10 9 8 7 6 5 4 3 2 1

International Standard Book Number-13: 978-0-8058-5919-5 (Softcover) 978-0-8058-5918-8 (Hardcover)

Library of Congress Cataloging-in-Publication Data

Learning to Solve Complex Scientific Problems / edited by David H. Jonassen.
      p. cm.
   Includes bibliographical references and index.
   ISBN 978-0-8058-5918-8 -- 0-8058-5918-7 (cloth : alk. paper)
   ISBN 978-0-8058-5919-5 -- 0-8058-5919-5 (pbk. : alk. paper)
   ISBN 978-1-4106-1623-4 -- 1-4106-1623-1 (e book)
      1. Science--Study and teaching (Higher). 2. Problem solving--Studying and teaching (Higher). 3. Problem-based education. 4. Science--Methodology. I. Jonassen, David H., 1947-

Q181.L4959 2007
507.6--dc22

2006021873

Visit the Taylor & Francis Web site at
http://www.taylorandfrancis.com

and the LEA Web site at
http://www.erlbaum.com

June 19, 2007

Dear Customer:

Thank you for your purchase of *Learning to Solve Complex Scientific Problems*,
by David H. Jonassen.

The correct Library of Congress Cataloging-in-Publication Data appears on the
other side of this page.

We sincerely regret any inconvenience this may have caused you. Please let us
know if we can be of any assistance regarding this title or any other titles that
Taylor & Francis publishes.

Best regards,

Taylor & Francis

#ER9231/0-8058-5918-7(hb)
#ER9232/0-8058-5919-5(pb)

Introduction

Virtually every scientist (pure scientist, engineer, mathematician, applied scientist, social scientist, and even technician-hereafter scientist) is hired, retained, and rewarded for solving problems. Problem solving is implicit in the very nature of all science. In everyday life and professional workplaces, scientists expend most of their intellectual effort solving problems. For years, reports have validated the importance of problem solving in the workplace. For instance, the report of the Secretary's Commission on Achieving Necessary Skills (1991), What Work Requires of Schools: A SCANS Report for America 2000, states that problem solving is an essential thinking skill for workers. The Accreditation Board for Engineering Technology (ABET, 2005) specifies the abilities to identify, formulate, and solve engineering problems as essential learning outcomes for any engineering program. The National Council of Teachers of Mathematics claimed the following: "Learning to solve problems is the principal reason for studying mathematics" (NCTM, 2000, p. 1). "If the United States is to maintain its economic leadership and sustain its share of high-technology jobs, it must prepare the engineers of tomorrow for future technological and societal changes and to acquire new knowledge quickly and apply it to emerging problems," said Wayne Clough, Chair of the Committee on the Engineer of 2020 (National Academy of Engineering, 2004). Scientists solve problems (technicians troubleshoot; engineers design products, processes, or systems; scientists research).

Although the need for skilled problem solvers has never been greater, there is a growing disconnect between the need for problem solvers and our educational capacity to prepare them. Among the myriad impediments, the most significant is the incongruence between workplace problems and the kinds of problems students learn to solve in their education programs. We know that workplace problems are ill structured, with multiple goals, multiple solution methods, unanticipated problems, no explicit means for determining appropriate actions, and distributed skills (Jonassen, Strobel, & Lee, 2006).

However, the most common kind of problem solved in scientific education is the story (word) problem, which is well structured. Those problems possess correct solutions, convergent solution paths, and require limited conceptual understanding. When learning to solve story problems in mathematics, science, and engineering, students learn to translate relations about unknowns into equations, solve the equations to find the value of the unknowns, and check the values found to see if they satisfy the original problem. This incongruence is explored in chapter 1.

There are many reasons for the incongruence between workplace and educational problem solving. One, we do not adequately understand the complex, collaborative, dynamic, and distributed nature of 21st century workplace problem solving. Problems are typically distributed among diverse workers in complex, multifaceted teams, each with their own social, cultural, historical, political, economic, and organizational entailments. Challenges of the 21st century workplace also require scientists to employ and master a variety of tools to represent the complexity of modern problems.

Second, because of a lack of industry experience in solving workplace problems, many kindergarten through 12th-grade and university faculty are inadequately prepared to teach students how to solve complex and ill-structured workplace problems. And these skills were not modeled in their own academic preparation. To prepare workplace problem solvers, faculty members must learn how to represent and solve workplace-like problems to teach those skills.

Third, relatively little research has focused on ill-structured, workplace problem solving. Rather, most of the research on problem solving has addressed story problems, with less research on the ill-structured problems such as design, systems analysis, diagnosis, and decision making.

This volume resulted from a grant from the National Science Foundation to construct a proposal for a Science of Learning Center focused on scientific problem solving. That effort aggregated a distinguished group of scientists, engineers, cognitive scientists, psychologists, and learning scientists who were committed to pursuing a research agenda about scientific problem solving. We were committed to conducting theory-driven research on how scientists solve problems. No group or organization has ever undertaken the comprehensive and systematic study of scientific problem solving. Unfortunately, our proposal was not funded. However, as a group of committed researchers, we have pursued a number of other funding opportunities and collaborative research and publications, including this volume.

Because creating a workforce of effective problem solvers is so essential to our ability to be competitive in today's global economy, we offer this as a state-of-the-art volume of problem-solving issues, while addressing the needs for continuing research in part III.

The collaborators in this effort fall naturally into two camps: cognitive scientists (including cognitive psychologists, educational psychologists, learning scientists, informatics-hereafter cognitive scientists) and scientists (pure scientists, engineers, applied scientists). This volume contrasts cognitive perspectives on problem solving that focus on knowledge representation and human information processing with research efforts by scientists to change their pedagogies. We believe that there continue to be great opportunities for synergies among these communities.

In part I, the cognitive scientists explicate not only the nature of problem solving but also how problems are represented by the problem solvers and how perception, attention, memory, and various forms of reasoning impact the management of information and the search for solutions. In chapter 1, I explicate the affective and cognitive attributes of scientific problems that make them complex and difficult to solve. I describe external problem factors, including structuredness, contextualization, complexity, and dynamicity. Based on those attributes, I describe a number of different kinds of problems, including story, rule using and rule induction, decision making, troubleshooting, policy, and design problems along with dilemmas. A variety of factors internal to the problem solver also make scientific problems complex, including domain knowledge, experience, reasoning skills, and epistemological development.

In chapter 2, Joachim Funke and Peter Frensch, two of the most widely published scholars in problem solving, revisit the findings of their volume, Complex Problem Solving: The European Perspective (1995), after a decade of subsequent research. European scientists have been examining complex problem solving more diligently than most of us. They examine the unpredictable relation between intelligence and problem solving. They focus on implicit learning more than global attributes, such as intelligence. More importantly, they focus their attention on future research, while debunking cognitive myths surrounding problem solving, taking a decidedly more social, emotional, and distributed perspective.

Among the psychological factors most affected by problem solving is working memory, the ability to keep enough of the elements of the problem space active in memory. In chapter 3, Jodi Price, Richard Catrambone, and Randall Engle examine the relation of working memory to problem solving. Clearly, the more complex the problem, the more demands are placed on working memory. Based on well-established principles of cognitive load theory, they provide guidelines that will reduce cognitive load, support working memory, and improve learning to solve problems.

Working memory is also important, because so many problems require that learners perform multiple tasks simultaneously. In chapter 4, Fred Oswald, Zach Hambrick, and Andrew Jones describe various task performance options used by learners, including baseline and emergency performances. They report a study in which they searched for individual difference predictors of multitasking ability. General intelligence was the strongest and most consistent predictor of both kinds of performance, whereas neuroticism was negatively related to baseline performance and conscientiousness was negatively related to emergency performance. Their research lays the foundation examining strategies to support learner performance in complex multitasking scenarios.

In chapter 5, Peter Cheng and Rossano Barone address one of the most vexing of issues related to ill-structured problems: How to represent the complexity of most everyday problems. Cognitive scientists have long assumed that the ways that problems are represented to learners naturally map onto learners' mental representations of problems; however, representations have seldom captured the informational or conceptual complexity of problems. Cheng and Barone describe the rationale and empirical research on a representational epistemic approach to representation design in the context of bakery scheduling. This approach begins by conceptually defining the taxonomy of entities within the domain by identifying their properties; temporal, structural, functional, and formal relations among them; and methods for evaluating those relations. These entities and relations are represented as different types of icons. They show how these visual representations enhance mental models, problems solving, learning, and system development.

Very few scientists ever solve problems individually in the workplace. Rather, scientists work in complex, constantly evolving work teams. In chapter 6, Michael A. Rosen, Stephen M. Fiore, and Eduardo Salas examine work teams from a cultural, biological, evolutionary perspective called memetics. They apply this novel memetic perspective to knowledge growth and sharing among team members and how expertise emerges from teams. Teams culturally evolve (mutate) over time. Yet they inherit knowledge sharing methods over time. This evolutionary framework for studying teams is original and illuminative.

In the first six chapters, cognitive scientists address the relations of a number of individual psychological differences and processes and complex problem solving. In part II of this volume, a number of scientific academics describe how they have applied those lessons from cognitive science to better prepare their student to solve complex scientific problems. In the context of science and engineering education, their efforts are innovative and sometimes risky. Our hope is that their ideas will stimulate more innovation in science and engineering education.

In chapter 7, Craig Ogilvie describes how he uses multifaceted (complex) problems in his physics classes to develop deeper and better structured conceptual knowledge and metacognitive skills to strengthen students' personal epistemologies. He uses paired worked examples (see chap. 3) and concept maps to emphasize problem categories and causal relations. The lessons that he has learned in his classes are generalizable to all science and engineering education classrooms.

To solve complex scientific problems, learners must distinguish relevant from irrelevant information and then integrate large amounts of information into a coherent model. Limitations in short-term memory and working memory (see chap. 3) complicate this integration process. In chapter 8, Sarah Ryan, John Jackman, Piyamart Kumsaikaew, Veronica Dark, and Sigurdur Olafsson describe those limitations along with the Problem Solving Learning Portal that they have constructed to scaffold difficulties in information acquisition and use. They show how their industrial engineering students use the portal for data mining and problem solving and conclude by identifying research issues related to information use.

In chapter 9, Gary L. Gray and Francesco Costanzo describe a new, conceptual approach to teaching dynamics called Interactive Dynamics. Interactive Dynamics starts with authentic problems that are solved in teams. Students use computer-based tools and hands-on laboratory experiences to concretize the dynamics concepts. Conceptual instruction is integrated throughout the process. Additionally, they report on the development and validation of an assessment tool, the Dynamics Concept Inventory, which assesses students' conceptual understanding of dynamics content.

The Holy Grail of problem-solving instruction is transfer. That is, can students who learn how to solve a kind of problem transfer that skill to new and different problems. In chapter 10, N. Sanjay Rebello, Lili Cui, Andrew G. Bennett, Dean A. Zollman, and Darryl J. Ozimek contrast the traditional conception of transfer (transfer to new context) with two contemporary conceptions (preparation for future learning and actor oriented transfer) of transfer. They then review some of their extensive research on transferring problem solving between domain (calculus to physics, trigonometry to physics) in terms of these conceptions.

In chapter 11, John Jackman, Sarah Ryan, Sigurdur Olafsson, and Veronica J. Dark take an alternative view on representing complex problems (see chap. 5), focusing on representing the problem space. They contrast different approaches for searching through the problem space to find crucial information. They then demonstrate how to represent well structured problems and introduce the concept of a metaproblem space to represent complex ill-structured problems in the Problem Solving Learning Portal (also described in chap. 8). They conclude by identifying research issues that will occupy their efforts in the future.

Based on their engineering experience, Madara Ogot and Gül E. Okudan have developed a theory of inventive problem solving that can be used to support learning how to design, the most common kind of problem solving that engineers perform. They articulate a four-stage design process supplemented by 40 design principles. They then demonstrate how their theory can be applied to different engineering problems.

Following up chapter 6 on the memetic conception of teamwork, Alok Bhandari, Larry Erickson, Marie Steichen, and William Jacoby describe ways of helping students become more productive members of interdisciplinary design teams. They examine how interdisciplinary teams work in industry and how to prepare learners to engage in many of those activities, exemplifying their recommendations in case studies. Finally, they describe ways of assessing and evaluating team performance in design classes.

In chapter 14, Barbara Bogue and Rose M. Marra address gender issues in science and engineering classrooms. They begin by representing gender equity issues as an important problem in education. They recommend a number of strategies for rectifying that problems, including selecting problems that are more meaningful to women, support collaborative learning (at which women are typically more successful than men) and social interdependence, and promoting self-efficacy among women. Their recommendations are based on many years of research on gender equity issues.

As indicated before, part I includes chapters by cognitive scientists which explicate cognitive processes in learning to solve problems. Part II of this volume includes descriptions of pedagogical approaches that have been tried by science and engineering faculty members. However, there are many more questions that remain unanswered than are answered by all of these chapters. Parts I and II raise a number of issues that need to be addressed if we are to better prepare science and engineering students to become better workplace problem solvers. In part III, Randall Engle, Peter Cheng, Edwardo Salas and I articulate the questions that we believed should guide problem-solving research in the future. These questions resulted from our deliberations and collaborations on the National Science Foundation proposal. In that work, we identified five research themes, including cognitive processes that are required in progressing from novice to expert problem solver, how learners construct mental models and engage in conceptual change as they progress from novice to expert, how we should represent problems to learners, how individual differences impact those learning processes, and how learners should collaborate and distribute cognitive responsibility for problem solving among team members. We also describe a number of assessment issues that must be resolved before we can conduct broad-based research on problem solving. Part III represents our challenge to ourselves and other researchers committed to problem solving. At some future date, I hope that we have resolved many of these research questions.

NOTE

The material in this volume is based on work supported by the National Science Foundation under Grant No. 0350305. Any opinions, findings, and conclusions or recommendations expressed in this material are those of the authors and do not necessarily reflect the views of the National Science Foundation.

REFERENCES

Accreditation Board for Engineering and Technology. (2005). *Criteria for accrediting engineering programs*. Baltimore, MD: Engineering Accreditation Commission. (Available from http://www.abet.or/criteria_eac.html)

Clough, W. (2004). *The engineer of 2020: Visions of engineering in the new century*. Washington, DC: National Academy of Engineering.

Frensch, P. A., & Funke, J. (1995). *Complex problem solving: The European perspective*. Hillsdale, NJ: Lawrence Erlbaum Associates.

Jonassen, D. H., Strobel, J., & Lee, C. B. (2006). Everyday problem solving in engineering: Lessons for engineering educators. *Journal of Engineering Education*, *95*(2), 1–14.

Secretary's Commission on Achieving Necessary Skills. (1991). What work requires of schools: A SCANS report for America 2000. Washington, DC: U.S. Department of Labor.

NCTM. (2000). *Yearbook of the National Council of Teachers of Mathematics*. Reston, VA: National Council of Teachers of Mathematics.

About the Authors

Rossano Barone is a Research Fellow in the Representation and Cognition Group, Department of Informatics, University of Sussex. His academic background is in psychology and cognitive science. He has worked in academic research for several years on projects concerned with the design of external representations to support problem solving. His other research interests involve with cognitive models of diagrammatic reasoning.

Dr. Alok Bhandari is an Associate Professor of Civil Engineering at Kansas State University (KSU). He teaches undergraduate, graduate, and distance education courses in environmental engineering. He is the coordinator of KSU's New Faculty Institute and a recipient of the CAREER award from the National Science Foundation (NSF). He serves as Associate Editor of the *Journal of Environmental Engineering* and the *Practice Periodical of Hazardous, Toxic and Radioactive Waste Management*.

Dr. Andrew G. Bennett works on the effective use of technology for teaching mathematics. He serves on the editorial board of the MAA Journal for Online Mathematics and its Applications and the MAA subcommittee on Curriculum Reform and the First Two Years and has been an organizer of several award-winning projects for developing effective programs for teacher education. He has won over a half-dozen teaching awards for both undergraduate and graduate instruction, including, in 2001, the Commerce Bank Award for Outstanding Undergraduate Instruction in the College of Arts and Sciences. He has recently received NSF grants for work in using data-mining with online homework to better understand how students learn.

Barbara Bogue is a renowned expert in retention issues for underrepresented students in engineering, career development, and program development. She has developed courses and projects aimed at providing a foundation in self-efficacy and competence for underrepresented engineering students, codeveloped and copresents workshops aimed at faculty ability to enhance the learning environment foundation and development of systemic assessment, and codeveloped the FacultyfortheFuture.org. She has received the Presidential Award for Excellence in Science, Mathematics and Engineering Mentoring and the WEPAN Founder's Award.

Dr. Richard Catrambone has published extensively in the areas of problem solving, instructional design, and human–computer interaction. His research has been funded by Office of Naval Research, Air Force Office for Scientific Research (AFOSR), the German-American TransCoop program, and other organizations. He has developed a task analysis approach for determining what learners need to know that provides a valuable tool for designing teaching and training materials. His research and teaching have been mutually beneficial: he is the recipient of Georgia Tech's Class of 1940 W. Howard Ector Outstanding Teacher Award which recognizes the most outstanding teacher at the institute.

Dr. Peter C.-H. Cheng is a leading figure in research on diagrammatic and other representational systems. He publishes in the fields of Cognitive Science, Human Computer Interaction and Science, and Mathematics Education. He is a member of the governing board of the Cognitive Science Society and a member of the editorial board of reviewers of the *Cognitive Science* journal. In 1994, the Human Factors and Ergonomics Society awarded him the Jerome H. Ely Award for the best article in the 2003 volume of the *Human Factors* journal.

Dr. Francesco Costanzo has been committed to the improvement of engineering education for many years. This commitment has been expressed in a number of activities. He and Gary Gray are under contract with McGraw-Hill Publishing to develop the next generation of sophomore-level mechanics textbooks (the subject matter of these books represents the largest market of the undergraduate engineering textbook market). As described in their chapter, these textbooks include several unique features that build on the research literature in student learning such as a problem-centered approach to new material, presentation of concepts and conceptual questions, systematic development of universal problem strategies in engineering mechanics. These features were developed as part of a result of two initiatives: an NSF proof-of-concept grant entitled "Instructional Materials for Engineering Mechanics Using Problem-Based Learning" and the development of Interactive Dynamics, a studio-based sophomore-level engineering dynamics course that was taught in experimental sections at The Pennsylvania State University. Under the auspices of the NSF sponsored Foundation Coalition, he has also participated in the development of the Dynamics Concept Inventory test for the assessment of conceptual understanding in Engineering dynamics.

Lili Cui is lecturer in the Physics Department at the University of Maryland, Baltimore County. Her doctoral dissertation at Kansas State University in the area of physics education research focused on transfer from mathematics to physics. Particularly, her research focuses on examining how students transfer their learning from calculus to physics. Her research has highlighted the factors that impede transfer of learning between these two domains as well as proposed a theoretical framework that would help examine transfer in solving well-structured and ill-structured problems.

Dr. Veronica J. Dark is completing a term as Associate Editor for the Psychonomic Society Journal of Memory & Cognition, where she handled submissions regarding individual differences in cognition. Her research in attention and working memory examines how expectation and knowledge influence which aspects of the environment are selected into awareness. She also examines individual differences in working memory and problem solving, particularly differences in the cognitive processes in gifted youth.

Dr. Randall W. Engle has published extensively on the nature of individual differences in cognition and particularly ability to control attention and conditions under which this ability is important to cognitive tasks. He is currently involved with studies on the effects of sleep deprivation and fatigue on attention control, learning, and problem solving. His work has been funded by AFOSR and National Institute of Child Health and Human Development.

Larry E. Erickson is Professor of Chemical Engineering and Director of the Center for Hazardous Substance Research at Kansas State University. He has participated in team teaching two multidisciplinary design/project courses, and he has worked with multidisciplinary research teams. His current research interests include design education and problem solving by multidisciplinary teams.

Dr. Stephen M. Fiore is an assistant professor in the University of Central Florida's (UCF) Cognitive Sciences Program and director of the Consortium for Research in Adaptive Distributed Learning Environments at UCF's Institute for Simulation and Training and Team Performance Laboratory. He earned his PhD degree (2000) in Cognitive Psychology from the University of Pittsburgh, Learning Research and Development Center. He maintains a multidisciplinary research interest that incorporates aspects of cognitive, social, and organizational psychology in the investigation of learning and performance in individuals and teams. He is co-Editor of a recent volume on Team Cognition as well as currently co-editing a volume on Distributed Training. Dr. Fiore has published in the area of learning, memory, and problem solving at the individual and the group level. As Principal Investigator, Co-Principal Investigator, or Senior Personnel he has helped to manage nearly $4 million in research funding from organizations such as the National Science Foundation, the Transportation Security Administration, the Office of Naval Research, and the Air Force Office of Scientific Research.

Dr. Peter A. Frensch publishes primarily in the areas of problem solving, expertise and skill acquisition, and implicit learning. He has received more than a dozen grants funding his research, is Editor of the international journal Psychological Research, and was recently elected president of the XXIXth International Congress of Psychology to be held in Berlin, Germany, in 2008. His contribution to the SSL project focuses on exploring the cognitive mechanisms underlying the acquisition of problem-solving expertise.

Dr. Joachim Funke represents European research on complex problem solving, is German national advisor for problem-solving assessment, and has research experience with computer simulations. He does basic and applied research on thinking and problem solving. He has received grants from the German National Science Foundation, European Community, and other institutions.

Dr. Gary L. Gray does research on the dynamics of mechanical systems, nanomechanics, and the improvement of learning and instruction in sophomore level engineering mechanics courses. He has received funding from NSF to develop problem-based materials for sophomore-level engineering mechanics and he is, under the auspices of the NSF-sponsored Foundation Coalition, leading the development of a nationwide Dynamics Concept Inventory test for the assessment of conceptual understanding in engineering dynamics. In addition, he has, in the past, taught a studio-based sophomore-level dynamics course at The Pennsylvania State University. As a result of all of these efforts, he is under contract with McGraw-Hill Publishing to develop the next generation of engineering statics and dynamics textbooks. These textbooks include several unique features that build on the research literature in student learning, such as the following: a problem-centered approach to new material; explicit teaching and testing of concepts; contemporary and relevant problems; and systematic development of universal problem strategies in engineering mechanics.

Dr. Zachary Z. Hambrick studies individual differences in higher-level cognition, and in particular, the role of working memory in complex cognitive activities such as problem solving and language comprehension. Dr. Hambrick received the 2001 James McKeen Cattell Award from the New York Academy of Sciences and is currently an assistant professor of Psychology at Michigan State University. Dr. Hambrick's work has appeared in journals such as *Journal of Experimental Psychology: General*, *Psychological Bulletin*, *Cognitive Psychology*, and *Memory & Cognition*.

Dr. John Jackman has recently received an NSF grant for his work leading to the development of the Engineering Learning Portal. He publishes on the product development process, manufacturing systems, and engineering learning environments for problem solving. His research has addressed the need for understanding the effects of engineering activities on the development of new products. He is currently investigating how engineers use and create information during the development process to improve their productivity and reduce development time. Dr. Jackman is a recipient of the A. D. Welliver Fellowship for his work in manufacturing systems. He has served as Department Editor of Enterprise Computing for the IIE Transactions journal. He currently serves as director of Graduate Education for the Department of Industrial and Manufacturing Systems Engineering at Iowa State University.

Dr. William A. Jacoby is a hands-on engineering educator who is looking forward to testing problem-solving hypotheses in his classrooms and laboratories. Six years of experience as a BS-level chemical engineer in industry (prior to graduate school) provides a view from both sides of the fence. His research is highly interdisciplinary and he is interested in incorporating interdisciplinary activities in the teaching environment.

Dr. David H. Jonassen is Distinguished Professor of Education at the University of Missouri where he teaches in the areas of Learning Technologies and Educational Psychology. Since earning his doctorate in educational media and experimental educational psychology from Temple University, Dr. Jonassen has taught at The Pennsylvania State University, University of Colorado, the University of Twente in the Netherlands, the University of North Carolina at Greensboro, and Syracuse University. He has published 29 books and numerous articles, papers, and reports on text design, task analysis, instructional design, computer-based learning, hypermedia, constructivist learning, cognitive tools, and technology in learning. He has consulted with businesses, universities, public schools, and other institutions around the world. His current research focuses on problem solving.

Dr. L. Andrew Jones is a personnel research scientist in the Institute for Selection and Classification, Navy Personnel Research, Studies, and Technology Division, Bureau of Naval Personnel. His research experience includes work on a Navy job qualification algorithm, a job preference inventory, and his current work with sailor multitasking. He is a retired Navy lieutenant commander with over 25 years experience in shipboard operations and human resource management. He earned his Ph.D. in human resource management in 2004 from Capella University in Minneapolis, Minnesota.

Piyamart Kumsaikaew is a PhD candidate in Industrial Engineering at Iowa State University. She obtained a BS in Computer Engineering from King Mongkut's Institute of Technology Ladkrabang and a MS in Industrial Engineering from Iowa State University. She is currently conducting research on cognitive engineering methods in problem-solving environments.

Dr. Rose M. Marra is an expert in assessment, evaluation, engineering education, and diversity issues in engineering. She is PI for an NSF Program for Gender Equity grant where she has worked with five partner institutions to develop assessment tools for women in engineering programs and is currently working to expand their application to engineering diversity programs in general. She has also served as assessment and evaluation expert on numerous other engineering-related grants.

Dr. Craig A. Ogilvie is a recognized leader in both nuclear physics and in the teaching of problem-solving skills in large enrollment physics classes. His nuclear physics research focuses on recreating in the laboratory the matter that filled the universe a microsecond after the Big Bang. In this work he is a leading member of the PHENIX collaboration at the Relativistic Heavy Ion Collider, New York. PHENIX has approximately 500 scientists from 11 countries and Professor Ogilvie is responsible for the U.S.-side of a $8.6 million upgrade to this experiment. He is also renowned for his teaching of problem-solving skills in large enrollment physics classes by having students work in small groups on tough, multifaceted problems that they cannot apply plug-n-chug techniques to solve. This work is now being adapted to other disciplines. He has received numerous awards and grants for innovative use of technology to support problem solving.

Dr. Madara Ogot publishes on engineering education, innovative design, and optimization methods. He has received NSF funding for establishment of a scholarship or mentorship program for engineering students from underrepresented groups and for introduction of multimedia tools into the engineering curriculum, as well as several National Atmospheric and Space Administration grants for research in stochastic optimization methods.

Dr. Gül E. Okudan is the Co-PI on the NSF funded Integrating Systematic Creativity to Engineering Curriculum, and the PI of Air Force Research Laboratory funded Understanding Expert Designer's Strategies for Complex, Information Rich System Design. She has been awarded National Regulatory Commision's Research Associateship for 4 consecutive years (2002–2005). Her research work focuses on understanding various facets of engineering design problem solving (e.g., tolerance for ambiguity, gender orientation of the design task, sources and patterns of information integration to design, and transfer of learning in solid modeling) and developing software tools to aid designers.

Dr. Sigurdur Olafsson has expertise in knowledge discovery and data mining as well as a background in the field of operations research. He is a pioneer in the interdisciplinary area of operations research and data mining and recently edited the first journal issue focused on this emerging area. He has been elected to leadership roles in numerous professional organizations, including the American Society for Engineering Education, and his education research has been funded by the NSF. His research interests include data mining for formative assessment and intelligent tutoring, and their application in solving ill-structured engineering problems.

Dr. Frederick L. Oswald has expertise in individual differences within student-learning and employment contexts. Currently his work with the College Board seeks to develop new measures as potential supplements in college admissions. He also has a number of applied projects, including a lab-based and field-based project with Detroit Energy examining multitasking in managers of electrical power grids.

Darryl J. Ozimek is an instructor in the Physics Department at Duquesne University. His masters research at Kansas State University in the area of physics education research focused on transfer from mathematics to physics. Particularly, his research focused on examining how students transfer their learning from trigonometry to physics. His research has demonstrated the need for a dynamic perspective of transfer to examine transfer between these two domains and the factors that both facilitate and impede transfer.

Jodi Price is a doctoral student at the Georgia Institute of Technology. Her research is concerned with metacognition and strategy use in younger and older adults. Specifically, her work explores whether there are age-related differences in the ability to learn with task experience that interactive imagery is a more effective strategy than rote repetition for memorizing paired associates. Currently she is conducting a series of experiments examining whether manipulations that improve younger adults' ability to accurately predict and postdict their recall performance for each type of strategy will also improve older adults' metamemory judgments.

Dr. N. Sanjay Rebello has 10 years experience in physics education research and curriculum development. His research focuses on modeling student understanding and transfer of learning. In 2004, he received the Presidential Early Career Award for Scientists & Engineers. Research funded through Dr. Rebello's NSF CAREER grant focuses on student learning and transfer between the classroom and real-world contexts and the factors that mediate students' sense-making processes.

Michael A. Rosen is a PhD student in the Applied Experimental and Human Factors Psychology program at the University of Central Florida and has been a graduate research assistant at the Institute for Simulation and Training since the fall of 2004. His research interests include individual and team decision making, human–computer interaction, and team performance.

Dr. Sarah Ryan received an NSF CAREER award to study stochastic dynamic models for managing manufacturing and service systems and to implement active learning methods in operations research courses. Her interest in the science of learning engineering problem solving grew out of an ongoing collaborative project to improve student problem-solving skills by engaging them with realistic engineering problems mediated by an online environment.

Dr. Eduardo Salas is Trustee Chair and Professor of Psychology at the University of Central Florida. He has coauthored over 300 journal articles and book chapters, has edited 13 books, serves on 10 editorial boards, and currently is Editor of *Human Factors* journal. He is an international recognized scholar on teamwork, team decision making, simulation-based training, and training effectiveness. He has received over $5 million dollars in grants from Department o Defense, Federal Aviation Association, and the industry. He is a Fellow of Division 14 (recipient of the Division's applied research award) and 21 (recipient of Division's Taylor award for contributions to the field; member of Division 19) of American Psychological Association and a Fellow of the Human Factors and Ergonomics Society. He has over 15 years of managing and directing large research and development projects.

Dr. E. Marie Steichen is Codirector of the Environmental Engagement and Empowerment Office (E3), Assistant Professor, and Senior Evaluator for the Institute for Civic Discourse and Democracy at Kansas State University. Her research and work in engagement focus on processes by which students and communities are empowered as problem solvers. Additional empowerment work involves environmental justice issues on tribal lands, university education, and civic engagement of youth. Dr. Steichen has been a Senior Program Evaluator for local, national, and international programs for 9 years, conducting Empowerment Evaluations and Appreciative Inquiry in Evaluation in a variety of contexts.

Dr. Dean A. Zollman is University Distinguished Professor and Head of Physics at Kansas State University. He has been a leader in the use of contemporary technology in the teaching of physics and conducts research on how students transfer knowledge and develop mental models when learning and solving problems in physics. His awards include the NSF Director's Award for Distinguished Teaching Scholars, the Carnegie Foundation's Research University Professor of the Year, and the American Association of Physics Teachers' Millikan Medal. Dean Zollman's current funded research includes the investigations of mental models that students build about the application of physics to medical imaging and cross-cultural explorations of students' models of microscopic properties of matter. He is also developing technology-based systems to aid new physics teachers and to teach pre-professional students about applications of quantum physics to medical diagnosis.

Part I

COGNITIVE SCIENCE VIEWS
OF PROBLEM SOLVING

Chapter 1

What Makes Scientific Problems Difficult?

David H. Jonassen
University of Missouri

PROLOGUE: PROBLEMS AS COGNITION AND AFFECT

This chapter and this volume address problem solving from cognitive and scientific perspectives. How do science/technology/engineering/mathematics (STEM) students and workers have to think as they collaborate to solve the myriad scientific problems they experience throughout work and life? The emphases are largely cognitive.

However, problems also elicit affective responses that make problem solving, as a topic, very problematic. These affective responses are important, because (I have discovered that) many professionals, including STEM workers and academics, prefer not to consider or contemplate problems, despite the fact that they are being paid to solve problems. They prefer to consider problems as opportunities. This aversion to problem solving results, in part I believe, from the affective connotations of the concept "problem." Thesauri list synonyms of problem, such as dilemma, quandary, obstacle, predicament, difficulty, all of which have heavy affective connotations. Indeed, problems often do represent predicaments, and problems are often difficult. However, whether problems represent opportunities or obstacles, they need to be addressed in the research and practice of science in all of its quadrants (Stokes, 2000) because STEM workers are hired, retained, and rewarded for solving problems. Therefore, it is important to

STEM educators to better prepare students to seize opportunities or wrestle with dilemmas to solve important scientific problems.

The cognitive perspective on problems, on the other hand, considers a problem as "a question to be solved." That is the spirit in which this chapter and this volume address problems. STEM students and workers are constantly faced with questions to be solved. They need to learn how to solve them.

WHAT IS A PROBLEM?

A problem, from a traditional, information-processing perspective, consists of sets of initial states, goal states, and path constraints (Wood, 1983). The problem is to find a path through the problem space that starts with initial states passing along paths that satisfy the path constraints and ends in the goal state. Unfortunately this conception describes only well-structured problems. For most everyday, ill-structured problems, the goal states and path constraints are often unknown or are open to negotiation, and there are no established routes through path constraints toward the goal state. Information-processing models of problem solving are inadequate for representing the situated, distributed, and social nature of problem solving. As problems become more ill-structured, their solutions become more socially and culturally mediated (Kramer, 1986; Roth & McGinn, 1997). What becomes a problem arises from the interaction of participants, activity, and context.

A problem has two important attributes. First, a problem is a situated unknown, a question to be answered in some context. "Problems become problems when discrepancies are noted, when contradictions are experiences so that at least a temporary state of disequilibrium is reached" (Arlin, 1989, p. 230). Situations vary from algorithmic math problems to vexing and complex social problems, such as environmental sustainability. Second, finding or solving for the unknown must have some social, cultural, or intellectual value. "Problems become problems when there is a 'felt need' or difficulty that propels one toward resolution" (Arlin, 1989, p. 230). That is, someone believes that the question is worth answering. If no one perceives a need to answer the question, there is no problem. This latter attribute may expel most formal, in-school problems from the class of real problems because students often do not perceive a need to find the unknowns to problems posed in schools. However, because their teachers do perceive such a need, they are normally regarded as problems.

Problem solving as a process also has two critical attributes. First, problem solving requires the mental representation of the problem in the situation in the world. Human problem solvers construct mental representations of the problem, known as the problem space, the set of symbolic structures (the states of space), and the set of operators over the space (Newell, 1980; Newell & Simon, 1972). Once again, those states of space are easily identifiable in well-structured problems; however, they are much more difficult to identify for ill-structured problems (see chap. 10, this volume). Problem spaces may be externalized as formal models or may be represented using a variety of tools, but it is the mental construction of the problem space that is the most critical for problem solving. Until the problem solver constructs a model of the problem in its context, a viable solution is unlikely. Second, problem solving requires some activity-based manipulation of the problem space. Problem solvers act on the problem space to generate and test hypotheses and solutions.

Problems and the methods and strategies used by individuals and groups to solve them, both in the everyday and classroom worlds, vary dramatically. Smith (1991) categorized factors that influence problem solving as external and internal. Internal factors are related to the personal characteristics of the problem solver, such as prior experience, prior knowledge, or strategies used. External factors are those related to the nature of the problem as encountered in the world. Problem solving usually varies both externally (the problem as it exists in the world) and internally. Figure 1.1 depicts internal factors (nature of the problem solver) and external factors (nature of the problem, context, and problem representation) and the attributes of each and the interactions among them. Figure 1.1 provides a graphic organizer of this chapter. I first describe external problem factors and later explicate some internal factors that are important to problem solving.

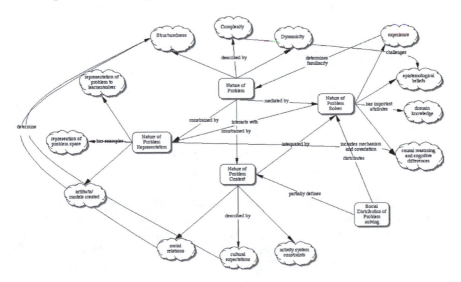

Figure 1.1.   Dimensions of problems.

EXTERNAL FACTORS

Problems, as they are encountered in the world, differ in several important ways. Bassok (2003) described two important external attributes of problems, abstraction and continuity. Abstraction refers to the representation of the content and context of a problem that either facilitates or impedes analogical transfer of one problem to another. Most classroom problems are more abstract than most everyday problems, which are embedded in various contexts. Continuity of the problem is the degree to which attributes of problems remain the same or change over time (described later as dynamicity). High continuity problems are more easily solved and transferred.

The primary reason for distinguishing among different kinds of problems is the assumption that solving different kinds of problems calls on distinctly different sets of skills (Greeno, 1980). Solving different kinds of problems entails different levels of certainty and risk (Wood, 1983). If solving different kinds of problems requires different sets of skills, then learning to solve different kinds of problems will require different forms of instruction. To better understand how problems differ in terms of required processing, I describe four primary, external characteristics of problems: structuredness and situatedness, contextual factors, complexity, and dynamicity.

External Factor: Structuredness and Situatedness of Problem

The most descriptive dimension of problem solving is structuredness. Problems vary along a continuum form well-structured to ill-structured (Arlin, 1989; Jonassen, 1997; Newell & Simon, 1972). It is important to note that structuredness represents a continuum, not a dichotomous variable. Although well-structured problems tend to be associated with formal education and ill-structured problems tend to occur in the everyday world, that is not necessarily the case. The most commonly encountered problems, especially in formal educational contexts, are well-structured problems. These are typically found at the end of textbook chapters, well-structured problems which present all of the information needed to solve the problems in the problem representation; they require the application of a limited number of regular and circumscribed rules and principles that are organized in a predictive and prescriptive way; and they have knowable, comprehensible solutions where the relations between decision choices and all problem states are known or are probabilistic (Wood, 1983). These problems have also been referred to as transformation problems (Greeno, 1978) that consist of a well-defined initial state, a known goal state, and constrained set of logical operators.

Ill-structured problems, on the other hand, are the kinds of problems that are encountered in everyday life and work, so they are typically emergent and not self-contained. Because they are not constrained by the content domains being studied in classrooms, their solutions are not predictable or convergent. Ill-structured problems usually require the integration of several content domains, that is, they are usually interdisciplinary in nature. Workplace engineering problems, for example, are ill-structured because they possess conflicting goals, multiple solution methods, nonengineering success standards, nonengineering constraints, unanticipated problems, distributed knowledge, collaborative activity systems, and multiple forms of problem representation (Jonassen, Strobel, & Lee, 2006). Ill-structured problems appear ill-defined because one or more of the problem elements are unknown or not known with any degree of confidence (Wood, 1983); they possess multiple solutions, solution paths, or no solutions at all (Kitchner, 1983); they possess multiple criteria for evaluating solutions, so there is uncertainty about which concepts, rules, and principles are necessary for the solution and how they are organized; and they often require learners to make judgments and express personal opinions or beliefs about the problem. Everyday, ill-structured problems are uniquely human interpersonal activities (Meacham & Emont, 1989) because they tend to be relevant to the personal interest of the problem solver who is solving the problem as a means to further ends.

Although information processing theories averred that "in general, the processes used to solve ill-structured problems are the same as those used to solve well structured problems" (Simon, 1978, p. 287), more recent research in situated and everyday problem solving makes clear distinctions between thinking required to solve well-structured problems and ill-structured problems. Allaire and Marsiske (2002) found that measures that predict well-structured problem solving could not predict the quality of solutions to ill-structured, everyday problems among elderly people. "Unlike formal problem solving, practical problem solving cannot be understood solely in terms of problem structure and mental representations" (Scribner, 1986, p. 28), but rather include aspects outside the problem space, such as environmental information or goals of the problem solver. Hong, Jonassen, and McGee (2003) found that solving ill-structured problems in an astronomy simulation called on different skills than well-structured problems, including metacognition and argumentation. Argumentation is a social and communicative activity that is an essential form of reasoning in solving ill-structured, everyday problems. Jonassen and Kwon (2001) showed that communication patterns in teams differed when solving well-structured and ill-structured problems. Finally, groups of students solving ill-structured economics problems produced more extensive arguments than when solving well-structured problems because of the importance of generating and supporting alternative solutions when solving ill-structured problems (Cho & Jonassen, 2002). Clearly more research is needed to substantiate these differences, yet it appears that well-structured and ill-structured problem solving engage different intellectual skills.

The structuredness of problems is significantly related to the situatedness of problems. That is, well-structured problems tend to be more abstract and decontextualized, relying more on defined rules and less on context. On the other hand, ill-structured problems tend to be more embedded in and defined by the everyday or workplace situation, making them more subject to belief systems that are engendered by social, cultural, and organizational drivers in the context (Jonassen, 2000; Meacham & Emont, 1989; Smith, 1991). The role of problem context is described next.

External Factor: Role of Problem Context

In everyday problems that tend to be more ill-structured, context plays a much more significant role in the cognitive activities engaged by the problem (Lave, 1988; Rogoff & Lave, 1984). The context in which problems are embedded becomes a significant part of the problem and necessarily part of its solution (Wood, 1983). Well-structured problems, such as story problems (described later), embed problems in shallow story contexts that have little meaning or relevance to learners. Workplace engineering problems are made more ill-structured because the context often creates unanticipated problems (Jonassen et al, 2006). Very ill-structured problems, such as design problems, are so context-dependent that the problems have no meaning outside the context in which they occur.

The role of context defines the situatedness of problems. Situatedness is concerned with the situation described in the problem (Hegarty, Mayer, & Monk, 1995). Rohlfing, Rehm, and Goecke (2003) defined situatedness as a specific situation in which problem-solving activity occurs, contrasting it with the larger, more stable context that supplies certain patterns of behavior and analysis for situations with which to be confronted. Any situation may be constrained by several, overlapping contexts. That is why everyday problems are often more difficult to solve, yet they are more meaningful. Situativity theorists claim that when ideas are extracted from an authentic context, they lose meaning. The problem solver must accommodate multiple belief systems embedded in different contexts.

External Factor: Complexity

According to Meacham and Emont (1989), problems vary in terms of complexity (how clearly the problem's initial and goal states are identified). Complexity is an interaction between internal and external factors. Problem-solving complexity is a function of how the problem solver interacts with the problem, determined by the difficulty problem solvers experience as they interact with the problem, importance (degree to which the problem is significant and meaningful to a problem solver), and urgency (how soon the problem should be solved). The choices that problem solvers make regarding these factors determines how difficult everyday problems are to solve. Ill-structured problems are more difficult to solve, in part because they tend to be more complex. The more complex that problems are, the more difficulty students have to choose the best solution method (Jacobs, Dolmans, Wolfhagen, & Scherpbier, 2003). Also, problem solvers represent complex problems in different ways that lead to different kinds of solutions (Voss, Wolfe, Lawrence, & Engle, 1991).

At the base level, problem complexity is a function of external factors, such as the number of issues, functions, or variables involved in the problem; the number of interactions among those issues, functions, or variables; and the predictability of the behavior of those issues, functions, or variables. Although complexity and structuredness invariably overlap, complexity is more concerned with how many components are represented implicitly or explicitly in the problem, how those components interact, and how consistently they behave. Complexity has direct implications for working memory requirements as well as comprehension. The more complex a problem, the more difficult it will be for the problem solver to actively process the components of the problem. Most well-structured problems, such as textbook math and science problems, are not very complex. They involve a constrained set of factors or variables. Although ill-structured problems tend to be more complex, well-structured problems can be extremely complex and ill-structured problems fairly simple. For example, chess is a very complex, well-structured problem, and selecting what to wear from our closets (at least for me) is a simple ill-structured problem. Complexity is clearly related to structuredness, although it is a sufficiently independent factor to warrant consideration.

Complexity can also be described in terms of the processing required to solve the problem. For example, Wood (1983) suggested that there are three kinds of problem complexity: component complexity, coordinative complexity, and dynamic complexity. Component complexity describes the number of distinct acts required to solve the problems along with the diversity of kinds of information needed to perform these acts. Coordinative complexity described the variety of relations among problem-solving acts. Dynamic complexity describes changes in those relations over time. I see dynamicity as a separate external factor, described next.

External Factor: Dynamicity

With everyday or workplace problems, it is often difficult to determine what the problem is because problems change in light of new developments

(Roth & McGinn, 1997). That is, many problems are dynamic, because their conditions or contexts change over time, converting them into different problems.

KINDS OF PROBLEMS

The characteristic of my work on problem solving that distinguishes it from previous research efforts is the underlying assumptions that there are different kinds of problems. Jonassen (2000) identified 11 kinds of problems, including logic problems, algorithms, story problems, rule-using problems, decision making, troubleshooting, diagnosis-solution problems, strategic performance, policy analysis problems, design problems, and dilemmas. That typology represents a developmental theory or problem solving. How discrete each kind of problem is, or whether additional kinds of problems exist, is not certain. I briefly describe some of the kinds of problems that are germane to scientific problem solving.

Story Problems

In an attempt to make problem solving more meaningful, textbook authors, teachers, and professors most often employ story problems. These can be found at the backs of textbook chapters in virtually every science, mathematics, and engineering textbook in existence. Traditional methods for solving story problems require learners to (a) represent the unknowns by letters, (b) translate relations about unknowns into equations, (c) solve the equations to find the value of the unknowns, and (d) verify values found to see if they fit the original problem (Rich, 1960). Unfortunately, it is the unsuccessful problem solvers who base their solution plans on the numbers and keywords that they select from the problem (Hegarty et al., 1995). This linear process implies that solving problems is a procedure to be memorized, practiced, and habituated and that emphasizes answer getting, not meaning making (Wilson, Fernandez, & Hadaway, 2001), so transferring that process to new contexts is very difficult for learners because they focus too closely on surface features or recall familiar solutions from previously solved problems (Woods et al., 1997). They fail to understand the principles and the conceptual applications underlying the performance, so they are unable to transfer the ability to solve one kind of problem to problems with the same structure but dissimilar features. Jonassen (2003a) has articulated a model for designing technology-enhanced story problem-solving environments, including a set identifier, situational model, structural model builder, equation builder, and different representations of problem outcomes. The environment integrates qualitative and quantitative problem representations and requires that learners construct a conceptual model of the problem that integrates the situational (story) content with an understanding of the semantic structure of the problem based on the science principles.

Rule-Using and Rule Induction Problems

Many problems have correct solutions but multiple solution paths or multiple rules governing the process. They tend to a have clear purpose or goal that is constrained but not restricted to a specific procedure or method. Using an online search system to locate scientific literature or using a search engine to find scientific information on the World Wide Web are examples of rule-using problems. The purpose is clear: find the most relevant information sources in the least amount of time. That requires selection of search terms, constructing effective search arguments, implementing the search strategy, and evaluating the utility and credibility of information found. Schacter, Chung, and Dorr (1998) found that students rarely employ systematic search strategies and spend little to no time planning their searches. This is the rule-oriented essence of searching. Given that there are multiple search strategies that are possible, rule-using problems can become decidedly more ill-structured. Many problems require that learners induce rules to solve problems. Qualitative analysis labs in chemistry provide students unknown compounds on which they conduct numerous tests to discover the identity of the compound. Doing so requires that they induce rules that describe the behavior of various reagents. These are generally perceived as more difficult problems than applying rules, although the level of experienced difficulty depends on individual differences in cognition.

Decision-Making Problems

Decision-making problems usually require that problem solvers select maximal solutions from a set of alternative solutions based on a number of selection criteria. Those criteria may be provided the problem solver(s), or the solver(s) may have to identify the most relevant criteria. Scientific businesses daily solve many decision-making problems, such as selecting a new part vendor or other contractor, determining inventory levels, selecting appropriate testing methods, or awarding prizes for research. Although these problems typically require selecting one solution, the number of decision factors to be considered in deciding among those solutions as well as the weights assigned to them can be very complex. Decision problems usually require comparing and contrasting the advantages and disadvantages of alternate solutions. Decisions are justified in terms of the weight of those factors.

Troubleshooting Problems

Troubleshooting is one of the most common forms of everyday problem solving. Although troubleshooting is most commonly associated with technician level jobs (maintaining complex communications and avionics equipment, repairing computer equipment), professionals also engage in troubleshooting faulty systems (e.g., engineers identify faults in chemical processes, physicians or psychotherapists diagnose medical or psychological problems). Although troubleshooting is most commonly taught as a procedure, it requires a combination of domain and system knowledge (conceptual models of the system including system components and interactions, flow control, fault states, fault characteristics, symptoms, contextual information, and probabilities of occurrence); troubleshooting strategies such as search-and-replace, serial elimination, and space splitting; and fault testing procedures. These skills are integrated and organized by the troubleshooter's experiences. As troubleshooters gain experience, their knowledge becomes indexed by those experiences rather than by any conceptual models of domain knowledge. Jonassen and Hung (2006) have articulated a research-based model for designing troubleshooting learning environments that include a multilayered conceptual model of the system, a simulator for hypothesis generation and testing, and a case library of stories from other troubleshooters.

Policy Problems

Engineering problems that are embedded are complex, multifaceted situations. What makes these problems difficult to solve is that it is not always clear what is the problem In a recent qualitative study, we found that workplace engineering problems are very ill-structured because the problem solvers experience conflicting goals; multiple solution methods; nonengineering success criteria; social, environmental, and regulatory constraints; unanticipated problems; and knowledge distributed among engineering and nonengineering personnel (Jonassen, Strobel, & Lee, 2006). These problem facets cannot be addressed using engineering processes. Rather, they represent policy issues that must be addressed in significantly different ways. Because defining the problem space is more ambiguous, policy problems are more ill-structured. These are the most common types of problems solved in professional contexts. Policy problems require the solver to articulate the nature of the problem and the different perspectives that impact the problem before suggesting solutions (Jonassen, 1997). They are more contextually bound than any kind of problem considered so far. That is, their solutions rely on an analysis of contextual factors. Classical situated case problems also exist in international relations, such as "… given low crop productivity in the Soviet Union, how would the solver go about improving crop productivity if he or she served as Director of the Ministry of Agriculture in the Soviet Union" (Voss & Post, 1988, p. 273). International relations problems involve decision making and solution generation and testing in a political context. Justifying decisions is among the most important processes in solving case problems.

Design Problems

Perhaps the most ill-structured kind of problem is design. Whether it be an electronic circuit, a mechanical part, or a new manufacturing system, design requires applying a great deal of domain knowledge with a lot of strategic knowledge resulting in an original design. Design problems are among the most complex and ill-structured of all problems (Jonassen, 2000). Despite the apparent goal of finding an optimal solution within determined constraints, design problems usually have vaguely defined or unclear goals with unstated constraints. They possess multiple solutions, with multiple solution paths. Perhaps the most vexing part of design problems is that they possess multiple criteria for evaluating solutions, and these criteria are often unknown. Ultimately, the designer must please the client, however, the criteria for an acceptable design are usually unstated. Design problems often require the designer to make judgments about the problem and defend them or express personal opinions or beliefs about the problem, so ill-structured problems are uniquely human interpersonal activities (Meacham & Emont, 1989). Generic design processes include articulating the problem space, specifying functional requirements, applying prior knowledge, analyzing constraints, selecting a solution, constructing a model or artifact, and optimizing the solution. Because design is so domain or context specific, these processes assume many different forms. Design literature comes from product design, architectural design, engineering design, and instructional design. Each literature base begins with different assumptions and prescribes different processes and methods. Designing a bridge and designing a chemical process are so different that they share little knowledge and skills in common.

Dilemmas

Scientists and engineers often become embroiled in social or ethical dilemmas. Creating a biochemical product that is profitable but environmentally injurious represents a dilemma. Dilemmas may be the most ill-structured and unpredictable, often because there is no solution that will ever be acceptable to a significant portion of the people affected by the problem. Usually there are many valuable perspectives on the situation (economic, political, social, ethical, etc.), however none compels an acceptable solution to the crisis. The situation is so complex and unpredictable, that no best solution can ever be known. That does not mean that there are not many solutions, which can be attempted with variable degrees of success; however, none will ever meet the needs of the majority of people or escape the prospects of catastrophe. Dilemmas are often complex, social situations with conflicting perspectives, and they are usually the most vexing of problems.

Discrete Problems Versus Problem Aggregates. The problem types just described are conveyed as discrete problems. Although discrete problems are most commonly solved in formal educational institutions, everyday and professional problems typically are aggregates of problems to be solved. Problems in the workplace are rarely discrete, and the parameters of the problems are not easily isolated. Jonassen, Strobel, and Lee (2006) found that most engineering problems consisted of numerous better-structured problems, each of which had to be solved in some sequence. Problem aggregates are problem clusters related to the same work activities. For example, developing a computer system requires solving a host of design, troubleshooting, and case problems. Starting a business likewise represents myriad decision-making problems. Problems in everyday and professional contexts are generally problem aggregates, so when analyzing any problem context, it is necessary to identify both the problem aggregates and the problems that constitute the problem aggregate.

NATURE OF PROBLEM REPRESENTATION

The difficulty in solving problems is also a function of how they are represented to the learner or problem solver. Early research showed that the way that problems are represented to a problem solver influences how problems are solved. There are three characteristics of problem displays: the form of information item, the organization of items into structures, and the sequences of items or groups (Kleinmutz & Schkade, 1993). Problem information can assume three different forms: numerical, verbal, or pictorial. That information can be organized into meaningful structures, including groups, hierarchies, or patterns, such as tables or matrices. There are many ways to sequence the problem information. For example, matrix representations of information are superior to other groupings, graphs, and sentences because they clearly define needed information, suggest orders of operations, and provide consistency checks for partial solutions (Schwartz, 1971; Schwartz & Fattaleh, 1973). Diagrams (flowcharts) have also produced better performance than verbal representations, especially for more complex problems (Mayer, 1976). Carroll, Thomas, and Malhotra (1980) found that spatial layouts of isomorphic design problems resulted in better performances and shorter solution times than temporal representations. It seems that spatial reorganization of information facilitates some of the cognitive activities that are required to solve problems.

As opposed to classroom problems, problems "in the wild" (in the workplace or everyday situations) are more difficult to solve because the problems are embedded in the larger culture, organization, and social dynamics of the problem context. Relevant information about the problem must be disambiguated from the surrounding context. For everyday problems, we are more concerned with how problem solvers mentally represent problems and how different technologies can be used to externalize those mental representations because "problem solving must begin with the conversion of the problem statement into an internal representation" (Reimann & Chi, 1989, p. 165).

Mental problem representation is important because the problem must be related to domain knowledge to construct a meaningful internal representation that can be manipulated (Larkin, 1985), and because individuals choose to represent problems in ways that make more sense to them. Problem spaces are mentally constructed by selecting and mapping specific relations from a problem domain onto the problem (McGuinness, 1986). These mappings facilitate different kinds of cognitive processing. Some mappings onto mental problem representations reduce the number of mental steps, and so facilitate problem solving. There are three kinds of knowledge represented in mental problem representations: naïve, qualitative scientific, quantitative scientific (Ploetzner & Spada, 1993). Naïve representations are replete with misconceptions so should not be considered further. Qualitative knowledge specifies the concepts and abstractions in a problem situation, the conditions under which concepts and abstractions can be applied, the physical objects referred to, the attributes and values objects possess, and other concepts to which objects are related. Quantitative representations are those that make use of mathematical formalisms to represent the problem. Students often fail to transfer classroom problems because they are taught only to represent the problem quantitatively. However, when solving scientific problems, qualitative problem representations are necessary prerequisites to learning quantitative representations (Ploetzner, Fehse, Kneser, & Spada, 1999).

Another line of research has examined how to directly affect learners' problem representations by providing them with tools (e.g., concept mapping, expert systems, systems modeling; see Jonassen, 2006a) that model different kinds of qualitative representations. Practicing engineers, for example, use multiple forms of problem representation, such as drawing, spreadsheets, computer-assisted design documents, mathematical models, and so on (Jonassen et al, 2006). Tools that constrain and scaffold problem representations are more likely to affect the cognitive representations they develop than the ways in which the problems are represented to the learners. When learners internalize the tool, they begin to think in terms of it. Internal and external representations are equal partners in a representation system, each with separate functions (Zhang & Norman, 1994). External representations activate perceptual processes while internal representations activate cognitive processes. Together, the representations are reciprocal and symbiotic. That is, external representations cannot function independently of internal cognition and vice versa. Space restriction prevent an explication of the use of cognitive tools for representing problems (see Jonassen, 2003b, for a more complete discussion).

INTERNAL FACTORS

Solving problems, simple or complex, engages a variety of cognitive skills, which are necessarily mediated by numerous individual differences. Those differences include different forms of intelligence, cognitive capacities, and personality characteristics (Jonassen & Grabowski, 1993). Numerous researchers have attempted to isolate the most important differences. For example, Arlin (1989) claimed that intensity, temporality, and familiarity were most predictive attributes of problem-solving abilities. Intensity refers to the level of motivation and effort that a problem solver invests in the problem based on the appeal or interest of the problem to the problem solvers. Temporality refers to the ability of the problem solver to remember similar problem encountered in the past thereby requiring fewer cognitive resources to solve. Familiarity is the level of experiences that the problem solver has had with similar problems. Very familiar problems require relatively automated processing. Treating problems similarly enables the problem solver to distinguish various types of problems and more efficiently use previously applied solutions. Although there are hundreds of individual differences that have been researched that may affect problem-solving ability, the three primary individual differences that mediate the ability of learners or practitioners to solve ill-structured problems (I believe) are prior domain knowledge, prior experience in solving similar problems, and cognitive skills (especially causal reasoning, analogical reasoning, and epistemological beliefs).

Domain Knowledge

Cognitive researchers agree that the learner's prior domain knowledge is among the most important determinants of problem-solving ability (Greeno, 1980; Hayes, 1989; Rittle-Johnson & Alibali, 1999). However, all of that research was conducted using well-structured problems. With ill-structured problems, it is not just quantity of knowledge possessed by problem solvers, but also the quality. To solve ill-structured problems, problem solvers must possess better integrated conceptual frameworks for domain knowledge that accommodate multiple perspectives, methods, and solutions. Here problem-solving research should be well informed by conceptual change research. Learners synthesize more complex and integrated conceptual models of the world from naïve understandings that have been challenged by conflicting information (Vosniadou, 1992). Well-developed conceptual models stress the importance of conceptually oriented instruction and experiences used to prepare problem solvers.

It is also important to note that domain knowledge is almost never sufficient to solve problems (Roth & McGinn, 1997). Problem-solving skills also rely on experience, reasoning skills, and epistemological development.

Experience

Experience is the most common metric for identifying expertise (Smith, 1991). Recall of historical information is the most frequent strategy for failure diagnosis (Konradt, 1995). Experts' first search for and reuse prior experiences when solving problems, where symptoms observed in previous situations are collected and compared with those in similar and current situations. Bereiter and Miller (1989) found that problem solvers base their problem identification on their beliefs about the cause once a discrepant symptom is found. Those beliefs are based on historical information (i.e., experience). They also found that the most common reason for taking a particular action during troubleshooting is to test for the most common problem based on experience. Physicians, for example, shorten their diagnostic process by applying their historical knowledge (known as illness scripts) of specific fault tendencies in recognizing patterns of symptoms.

Experiences are phenomenological and are normally conveyed through stories. For examples, when troubleshooting complex systems, technicians tell stories because "the hardest part of diagnosis is making sense out of a fundamentally ambiguous set of facts, and this is done through a narrative process to produce a coherent account" (Orr, 1996, p. 186). Therefore, Jonassen and Hung (2006) recommended the use of case libraries of stories about how experienced problem solvers have solved similar problems. Case libraries, based on principles of case-based reasoning, represent one of the most powerful forms of instructional support for ill-structured problems such as troubleshooting (Jonassen & Hernandez-Serrano, 2002). Hernandez-Serrano and Jonassen (2003) found that students who accessed experts' stories of similar product development problems outperformed control group learners on prediction, inference, explanation, and inference questions. Case libraries provide viable substitutes for experience when learning to solve ill-structured problems.

Thinking and Reasoning Skills

The underlying assumption of my work is that different kinds of problem solving entail different kinds of cognition: different knowledge, different forms of knowledge representation, and different thinking skills. It is impossible to isolate and explicate all of the thinking processes entailed by every kind of problem in every context. However, the two most important cognitive processes that enable problem solvers to learn from their prior problem-solving experiences are analogical reasoning and causal reasoning (Jonassen, 2006b). The dominant theory of analogical reasoning is structure mapping theory (Gentner, 1983), where mapping the structure of the prior problem to the problem being solved independent of the surface objects is required for learning from experience. To do so, those surface features (which attract the attention of poor problem solvers) must be discarded. Then the higher order, systemic relations must be compared on a one-to-one basis in the example and the problem. Learning by drawing structural comparisons across two examples (analogical encoding) has been shown to be the most effective method for reasoning by analogy (Gentner, Loewenstein, & Thompson, 2003).

The cognitive process that underlies all scientific thinking is causal reasoning (Keil, 1989), what Hume (1739/2000) called "the cement of the universe." Relations among the conceptual entities in every scientific domain are primarily causal. To make predictions, draw inferences or implications, or explain phenomena in every scientific domain, learners must understand the cause–effect relations among the phenomena in that domain.

Deep understanding of causal relations requires the ability to convey multiple attributes of causality. Some of those attributes (temporal succession, direction, valency, probability, duration, immediacy, and reciprocity) describe the extent of covariation between cause and effect (Jonassen & Ionas, in press). Covariational understanding models the degree or extent to which one element consistently affects another, which is expressed quantitatively in terms of probabilities or covariance. Understanding of causal mechanisms refers to people's beliefs about the transmission of causal influence, that is, what are the mechanisms or basic processes that take place between cause and effect in which a force of causal power is transmitted from the cause to the effect (Ahn & Kalish, 2000), that is, what is the underlying mechanism of causality. Mechanistic attributes include process, conjunction and disjunction, and necessity and sufficiency. These attributes require qualitative conceptual understanding of the mechanisms that mediate causal relations. These multiple attributes explain why qualitative representations of the problem space are so important.

Epistemological Development

Also known as intellectual maturity, epistemic beliefs, and intellectual development, epistemological development describes one's beliefs about the meaning of epistemological constructs, such as knowledge and truth and how those beliefs change over time (Hofer & Pintrich, 1997). There are several stage theories for describing learners' levels of epistemological development, including epistemological reflection (Baxter-Magolda, 1987), reflective judgment (King & Kitchener, 2002), and Perry's (1970) levels of intellectual development. Although the theories differ in detail and scope, they suggest a common pattern of development that progresses from simple, black–white thinking, through an exploration of multiple perspectives, to complex, relativistic thinking.

Although epistemological development of learners and problem solvers probably does not mediate understanding of and performance on well-structured problems, most researchers believe that they play an important role in solving ill-structured problems (Wood, Kitchener, & Jensen, 2002). Dunkle, Schraw, and Bendixen (1995) found that performance in solving well-defined problems is independent of performance on ill-defined tasks, because ill-defined problems engaged a different set of epistemological development. Because ill-structured problems require accommodation of different perspectives and the use of argumentation (Hong, Jonassen, & McGee, 2003), generating solutions for ill-structured problems requires higher levels of epistemological development.

SUMMARY

The purpose of this chapter was to describe the attributes that make scientific problem solving complex. Problem solving pervades everyday and workplace experiences, so students must learn how to become better problem solvers. Becoming better problem solvers is a complicated process because of the complex nature of problems and problem solving. Problems as they are experienced vary according to their structuredness and situatedness, the nature of the domains and contexts in which they occur, the complexity of the problem characteristics, and the dynamism exhibited by those characteristics. Based primarily on the structuredness attributes, several different kinds of problems that are common to scientific settings are described, including story problems, rule-using problems, decision making, troubleshooting, policy analysis, design problems, and dilemmas.

Problems are difficult to solve based on how they are experienced by or represented to the problem solver. Well-structured problems can be improved by the ways that they are represented to learners. Ill-structured problems are more difficult because problem elements must be disambiguated from the problem context and mentally represented by the problem solver. Cognitive tools may be used effectively to help problem solvers to externally integrate problem elements and domain knowledge.

Problem solving is also mediated by a number of internal, mental attributes of the problem solver, including prior domain knowledge, problem-solving experience, reasoning skills, and epistemological development.

Understanding these attributes when describing problems and problem contexts will help us to better prepare students to become more effective problem solvers.

REFERENCES

Ahn, W., & Kalish, C. W. (2000). The role of mechanism beliefs in causal reasoning. In F. C. Keil & R. A. Wilson (Eds.), *Explanation and cognition* (pp. 199–225). Cambridge, MA: MIT Press.

Allaire, J. C., & Marsiske, M. (2002). Will- and ill-defined measures of everday cognition relationship to older adults' intellectual ability and functional status. *Psychology and Aging, 17*(1), 101–115.

Arlin, P. K. (1989). The problem of the problem. In J. D. Sinnott (Ed.), *Everyday problem solving: Theory and applications* (pp. 229–237). New York: Praeger.

Bassok, M. (2003). Analogical transfer in problem solving. In J. E. Davidson & R. J. Sternberg (Eds.), *The psychology of problem solving* (pp. 343–369). New York: Cambridge University Press.

Baxter-Magolda, M. B. (1987). Comparing open-ended interviews and standardized measures of intellectual development. *Journal of College Student Personnel, 28*, 443–448.

Bereiter, S. R., & Miller, S. M. (1989). A field study of computer-controlled manufacturing systems. *IEEE Transactions on Systems, Man, and Cybernetics, 19*, 205–219.

Carroll, J. M., Thomas, J. C., & Malhotra, A. (1980). Presentation and representation in design problem solving. *British Journal of Psychology, 71*, 143–153.

Cho, K. L., & Jonassen, D. H. (2002). The effects of argumentation scaffolds on argumentation and problem solving. *Educational Technology: Research & Development, 50*(3) 5–22.

Dunkle, M. E., Schraw, G., & Bendixen, L. D. (1995, April). *Cognitive processes in well-defined and ill-defined problem solving.* Paper presented at the annual meeting of the American Educational Research Association, San Francisco, CA.

Gentner, D. (1983). Structure mapping: A theoretical framework for analogy. *Cognitive Science, 77*, 155–170.

Gentner, D., Loewenstein, J., & Thompson, L. (2003). Learning and transfer: A general role for analogical encoding. *Journal of Educational Psychology, 95*, 393–408.

Greeno, J. (1978). Natures of problem-solving abilities. In W. Estes (Ed.), *Handbook of learning and cognitive processes* (pp. 239–270). Hillsdale, NJ: Lawrence Erlbaum Associates.

Greeno, J. (1980). Trends in the theory of knowledge for problem solving. In D. T. Tuma & F. Reif (Eds.), *Problem solving and education: Issues in teaching and research* (pp. 9–23). Hillsdale, NJ: Lawrence Erlbaum Associates.

Hayes, J. R. (1989). *The complete problem solver* (2nd ed.). Hillsdale, NJ: Lawrence Erlbaum Associates.

Hegarty, M., Mayer, R. E., & Monk, C. A. (1995) Comprehension of arithmetic word problems: A comparison of successful and unsuccessful problem solvers. *Journal of Educational Psychology, 87,* 18–32.

Hernandez-Serrano, J., & Jonassen, D. H. (2003). The effects of case libraries on problem solving. *Journal of Computer-Assisted Learning, 19,* 103–114.

Hofer, B. K., & Pintrich, P. R. (1997). The development of epistemological theories: Beliefs about knowledge and knowing and their relation to learning. *Review of Educational Research, 67,* 88–140.

Hong, N. S., Jonassen, D. H., & McGee, S. (2003). Predictors of well-structured and ill-structured problem solving in an astronomy simulation. *Journal of Research in Science Teaching, 40,* 6–33.

Hume, D. (2000). *A treatise of human nature* (D. F. Norton & M. J. Norton, Eds.). Oxford, England: Oxford University Press. (Original work published 1739)

Jacobs, A. E. J. P., Dolmans, D. H. J. M., Wolfhagen, I. H. A. P., & Scherpbier, A. J. J. A. (2003). Validation of a short questionnaire to assess the degree of complexity and structuredness of *PBL* problems. *Medical Education, 37*(11), 1001–1007.

Jonassen, D. H. (1997). Instructional design model for well-structured and ill-structured problem-solving learning outcomes. *Educational Technology: Research and Development, 45*(1), 65–95.

Jonassen, D. H. (2000). Toward a design theory of problem solving. *Educational Technology: Research & Development, 48*(4), 63–85.

Jonassen, D. H. (2003a). Designing research-based instruction for story problems. *Educational Psychology Review, 15,* 267–296.

Jonassen, D. H. (2003b). Using cognitive tools to represent problems. *Journal of Research in Technology in Education, 35,* 362–381.

Jonassen, D. H. (2006a). Modeling with technology: Mindtools for conceptual change (3rd ed.). Columbus, OH: Merrill/Prentice Hall.

Jonassen, D. H. (2006b). Facilitating case reuse during problem solving. *Technology, Instruction, Cognition, and Learning, 3,* 51–62.

Jonassen, D. H., & Grabowski, B. L. (1993). *Handbook of individual differences, learning and instruction.* Hillsdale, NJ: Lawrence Erlbaum Associates.

Jonassen, D. H., & Hernandez-Serrano, J. (2002). Case-based reasoning and instructional design: Using stories to support problem solving. *Educational Technology: Research and Development, 50*(2), 65–77.

Jonassen, D. H., & Hung, W. (2006). Learning to troubleshoot: A new theory-based design architecture. *Educational Psychology Review, 18,* 77–144.

Jonassen, D. H., & Ionas, I. G. (in press). Learning to reason causally. *Educational Technology: Research & Development.*

Jonassen, D. H., & Kwon, H. I. (2001). Communication patterns in computer-mediated vs. face-to-face group problem solving. *Educational Technology: Research and Development, 49*(1), 35–52.

Jonassen, D. H., Strobel, J., & Lee, C. B. (2006). Everyday problem solving in engineering: Lessons for engineering educators. *Journal of Engineering Education, 95,* 1–14.

Keil, F. C. (1989). *Concepts, kinds, and cognitive development.* Cambridge, MA: MIT Press.

King, P. M., & Kitchener, K. S. (2002). The reflective judgment model: Twenty years of research on epistemic cognition. In B. K. Hofer & P. R. Pintrich (Eds.), *Personal Epistemology: The psychology of beliefs about knowledge and knowing* (pp 37–62). Mahwah: NJ, Lawrence Erlbaum Associates.

Kitchener, K. S. (1983). Cognition, metacognition, and epistemic cognition: A three-level model of cognitive processing. *Human Development, 26,* 222–232.

Kleinmutz, D. N., & Schkade, D. A. (1993). Information displays and decision processes. *Psychological Science, 4,* 221–227.

Konradt, U. (1995). Strategies of failure diagnosis in computer-controlled manufacturing systems. *International Journal of Human Computer Studies, 43,* 503–521.

Kramer, D. A. (1986). A life-span view of social cognition. *Educational Gerontology, 12,* 277–289.

Larkin, J. H. (1985). Understanding, problem representation, and skill in physics. In S. F. Chipman, J. W. Segal, & R. Glaser (Eds.), *Thinking and learning skills: Research and open questions* (Vol. 2, pp. 141–160). Hillsdale, NJ: Lawrence Erlbaum Associates.

Lave, J. (1988). *Cognition in practice: Mind, mathematics and culture in everyday life.* Cambridge, England: Cambridge University Press.

Mayer, R. E. (1976). Comprehension as affected by structure of problem representation. *Memory & Cognition, 4,* 249–255.

McGuinness, C. (1986). Problem representation: The effects of spatial arrays. *Memory & Cognition, 14,* 270–280.

Meacham, J. A., & Emont, N. C. (1989). The interpersonal basis of everyday problem solving. In J. D. Sinnott (Ed.), *Everyday problem solving: Theory and applications* (pp. 7–23). New York: Praeger.

Newell, A. (1980). Reasoning, problem solving, and decision process: The problem space as a fundamental category. In R. Nickerson (Ed.), *International symposium on attention and performance VIII* (pp. 693–718). Hillsdale, NJ: Lawrence Erlbaum Associates.

Newell, A., & Simon, H. (1972). *Human problem solving.* Englewood Cliffs, NJ: Prentice Hall.

Orr, J. E. (1996). *Talking about machines: An ethnography of a modern job.* Ithaca, NY: Cornell University Press.

Perry, W. G. (1970). *Intellectual and ethical development in the college years: A scheme.* New York: Holt, Rinehart & Winston.

Ploetzner, R., Fehse, E., Kneser, C., & Spada, H. (1999). Learning to relate qualitative and quantitative problem representations in a model-based setting for collaborative problem solving. *Journal of the Learning Sciences, 8,* 177–214.

Ploetzner, R., & Spada, H. (1993). Multiple mental representations of information in physics problems. In G. Strube & K. F. Wender (Eds.), *The cognitive psychology of knowledge* (pp. 285–312). Amsterdam: Elsevier.

Reimann, P., & Chi, M. T. H. (1989). Human expertise. In K. J. Gilhooly (Ed.), *Human and machine problem solving* (pp. 161–191). New York: Plenum.

Rich, B. (1960). *Schaum's principles of and problems of elementary algebra.* New York: Schaum's.

Rittle-Johnson, B., & Alibali, M. W. (1999). Conceptual and procedural knowledge of mathematics: Does one lead to the other? *Journal of Educational Psychology, 91,* 175–189.

Rogoff, B., & Lave, J. (1984). *Everyday cognition: Its development in social context.* Cambridge, MA: Harvard University Press.

Rohlfing, K. J., Rehm, M., & Goecke, K. U. (2003). Situatedness: The interplay between context(s) and situation. *Journal of Cognition and Culture, 3,* 132–156.

Roth, W. M., & McGinn, M. K. (1997). Toward a new perspective on problem solving. *Canadian Journal of Education, 22,* 18–32.

Schacter, J., Chung, G. K. W. K., & Door, A. (1998). Children's Internet searching on complex problems: Performance and process analyses. *Journal of the American Society for Information Science, 49,* 840–849.

Schwartz, S. H. (1971). Modes of representation and problem solving: Well evolved is half solved. *Journal of Experimental Psychology, 91,* 347–350.

Schwartz, S. H., & Fattaleh, D. L. (1973). Representation in deductive problem solving: The matrix. *Journal of Experimental Psychology, 95,* 343–348.

Scribner, S. (1986). Thinking in action: some characteristics of practical thought. In R. J. Sternberg & R.K. Wagner (Eds.), *Practical intelligence: Nature and origins of competence in the everyday world* (pp. 13–30). Cambridge, England: Cambridge University Press.

Simon, D. P. (1978). Information processing theory of human problem solving. In D. Estes (Ed.), *Handbook of learning and cognitive process.* Hillsdale, NJ: Lawrence Erlbaum Associates.

Smith, M. U. (1991). A view from biology. In M. U. Smith (Ed.), *Toward a unified theory of problem solving* (pp. 1–20). Hillsdale, NJ: Lawrence Erlbaum Associates.

Stokes, D. E. (1997). *Pasteur's quadrant: Basic science and technological innovation.* Washington, DC: Brookings Institution Press.

Vosniadou, S. (1992). Knowledge acquisition and conceptual change. *Applied Psychology: An International Review, 41,* 347–357.

Voss, J. F., & Post, T. A. (1989). On the solving of ill-structured problems. In M. T. H. Chi, R. Glaser, & M. J. Farr (Eds.), *The nature of expertise.* Hillsdale, NJ: Lawrence Erlbaum Associates.

Voss, J. F., Wolfe, C. R., Lawrence, J. A., & Engle, J. A (1991). From representation to decision: An analysis of problem solving in international relations. In R. J. Sternberg & P. A. Frensch (Eds.), *Complex problem solving: Principles and mechanisms* (pp. 119–158). Hillsdale, NJ: Lawrence Erlbaum Associates.

Wilson, J. W., Fernandez, M. L., & Hadaway, N. (n.d). *Mathematical problem solving.* Retrieved September 22, 2005, from http://jwilson.coe.uga

Wood, P., Kitchener, K., & Jensen, L. (2002). Considerations in the design and evaluation of a paper-and-pencil measure of epistemic cognition. In B. K. Hofer & P. R. Pintrich (Eds.), *Personal epistemology: The psychology and beliefs about knowledge and knowing* (pp. 277–294). Mahwah, NJ: Lawrence Erlbaum Associates.

Wood, P. K. (1983). Inquiring systems and problem structure: Implications for cognitive development. *Human Development, 26,* 249–265.

Woods, D. R., Hrymak, A. N., Marshall, R. R., Wood, P. E., Crowe, C. M., Hoffman, T. W., et al.. (1997).Developing problem-solving skills: The McMaster problem solving program. *Journal of Engineering Education, 86,* 75–92.

Zhang, J., & Norman, D. (1994). Representations in distributed cognitive tasks. *Cognitive Science, 18,* 87–122.

Chapter 2

Complex Problem Solving: The European Perspective—10 Years After

Joachim Funke
University of Heidelberg, Germany

Peter A. Frensch
Humboldt University, Berlin, Germany

Twelve years have passed since the publication of *Complex Problem Solving: The European Perspective* (Frensch & Funke, 1995a). In the volume, most of the prominent European researchers in the area of *complex problem solving* (CPS) summarized the—then current—state of the field in this relatively young and exciting area of study. As many readers know, CPS is a term that was introduced about 30 years ago in Germany by Dietrich Dörner (1975). *Komplexes Problemlösen* (which is the original German term) established not only a new type of problem to be studied, a type that differed from "simple" problem solving in terms of complexity, temporal dynamics, and other attributes, but also a new method, namely, the use of computer-simulated microworlds.

Since the publication of *Complex Problem Solving: The European Perspective* (Frensch & Funke, 1995a), the young field's most pressing questions and preferred answers have changed. In this chapter, we focus on some of the issues that have been at the center of attention in the CPS literature during the past 12 years (see also Funke, 1999, 2006). The chapter is divided into four parts. In the first part, we briefly redescribe the historic roots of modern research on CPS and establish a working definition of the concept. In the second part, we discuss one specific issue that has been of interest in the CPS community lately, namely, the question to what extent, if at all, CPS performance might be related to intelligence. We discuss some of the older, and much of the most recent, research that has been concerned with exploring the link between intelligence and CPS. In doing so, we differentiate between explicit and implicit CPS. In the third part, we focus on the question to what extent, if at all, CPS can be empirically distinguished from "simple" problem solving, and if there are domain specific or domain general principles at work. In the final part of the chapter, we present and discuss 10 myths about CPS that we believe very much hampers scientific progress in the area at the present time.

THE EUROPEAN PERSPECTIVE
ON COMPLEX PROBLEM SOLVING

As pointed out by Frensch and Funke (1995b), researchers in the area of human problem solving have often been quite inconsistent in their use of terms such as *problem, problem solving,* and *intelligence.* Although perhaps understandable, different uses of the same term seriously undermine scientific progress. Because the definition of a term affects the choice of experimental tasks and methods, and thus, ultimately affects the conclusions to be drawn (Frensch & Funke, 1995b), we make an attempt in this section to delineate what exactly we mean when we talk about "problems" in general and "complex problems" in particular. First, however, we give a brief historical overview of complex problem-solving research.

Simple and Complex Problems

Beginning with the early experimental work of the Gestaltists in Germany (e.g., Duncker, 1935), and continuing through the 1960s and early 1970s, research on problem solving was typically conducted with relatively simple laboratory tasks (e.g., Duncker's "X-ray" problem, 1935; Ewert & Lambert's "disk" problem, 1932, later known as "Tower of Hanoi") that were novel to research participants (e.g., Mayer, 1992). Simple novel tasks were used for a variety of reasons: They had clearly defined optimal solutions, they were solvable within a relatively short time frame, research participants' problem-solving steps could be traced, and so on. The underlying assumption was, of course, that simple tasks, such as the "Tower of Hanoi," capture the main properties of "real" problems, and that the cognitive processes underlying participants' solution attempts on simple problems were representative of the processes engaged in when solving "real" problems. Thus, simple problems were used for reasons of convenience and generalizations to more complex problems were thought possible. Perhaps the best known and most impressive example of this line of research is the work by Newell and Simon (1972).

However, beginning in the 1970s, researchers became increasingly convinced that empirical findings and theoretical concepts derived from simple laboratory tasks were not easily generalizable to more complex, real-life problems. Even worse, it appeared that the processes underlying CPS in different domains were different from each other (Sternberg, 1995). These realizations have led to rather different responses in North America and Europe.

In North America, initiated by the work of Herbert Simon on learning by doing in semantically rich domains (e.g., Anzai & Simon, 1979; Bhaskar & Simon, 1977), researchers began to investigate problem solving separately in different natural knowledge domains (e.g., physics, writing, chess playing), thus relinquishing on their attempts to extract a global theory of problem solving (e.g., Sternberg & Frensch, 1991). Instead, researchers frequently focused on the development of problem solving within a certain domain, that is, on the development of expertise (e.g., Anderson, Boyle, & Reiser, 1985; Chase & Simon, 1973; Chi, Feltovich, & Glaser, 1981). Areas that have attracted rather intensive attention in North America include such diverse fields as reading, writing, calculation, political decision making, managerial problem solving, lawyers' reasoning, mechanical problem solving, problem solving in electronics, computer skills, game playing, and even personal problem solving.

In Europe, two main approaches have surfaced, one initiated by Donald Broadbent (1977; see Berry & Broadbent, 1995) in Great Britain and the other one started by Dietrich Dörner (1975, 1980; see also Dörner & Wearing, 1995) in Germany. The two approaches have in common an emphasis on relatively complex, semantically rich, computerized laboratory tasks that are constructed to be similar to real-life problems. The approaches differ somewhat in their theoretical goals and methodology (see Buchner, 1995, for a more detailed comparison). The tradition initiated by Broadbent emphasizes the distinction between cognitive problem-solving processes that operate under awareness versus outside of awareness, and typically employs mathematically well-defined computerized systems. The tradition initiated by Dörner, on the other hand, is interested in the interplay of cognitive, motivational, and social components of problem solving, and utilizes very complex computerized scenarios that contain up to 2,000 highly interconnected variables (e.g., Dörner, Kreuzig, Reither, & Stäudel's, 1983, LOHHAUSEN project).

With the aforementioned considerations in mind, it is not surprising that there exists a wide variety of definitions of the term CPS that have relatively little in common (e.g., Frensch & Funke, 1995b). Any general conclusion regarding CPS, however, and any theoretical model of CPS can only be meaningful if all agree on what constitutes a problem and what constitutes CPS. For the remainder of this chapter we define CPS as follows:

> Complex problem solving occurs to overcome barriers between a given state and a desired goal state by means of behavioral and/or cognitive, multi-step activities. The given state, goal state, and barriers between given state and goal state are complex, change dynamically during problem solving, and are intransparent. The exact properties of the given state, goal state, and barriers are unknown to the solver at the outset. CPS implies the efficient interaction between a solver and the situational requirements of the task, and involves a solver's cognitive, emotional, personal, and social abilities and knowledge. (Frensch & Funke, 1995b, p.18)

INTELLIGENCE AND COMPLEX PROBLEM SOLVING

In this section, we review some of the research on the relation between CPS and intelligence that has mainly been conducted in the past 15 years. In the relevant studies, intelligence was assessed by traditional intelligence tests or specific subtests. The assumption underlying this research is that a person's IQ score reflects some global and relatively stable intellectual ability that might be associated with CPS. In our review, we distinguish CPS that is dependent on the intended actions of a problem solver (i.e., explicit problem solving) and problem solving that occurs, more or less, outside the realm of intention (i.e., implicit problem solving). For both types of CPS, we ask to what extent individual differences in CPS competence might be tied to individual differences in intelligence (for a more extensive discussion of this issue, see Wenke & Frensch, 2003).

Explicit Complex Problem Solving

With few exceptions, the tasks used to assess complex explicit problem solving competence consist of dynamic scenarios presented on a computer, with the number of (independent exogenous and interconnected endogenous) variables ranging from 3 to about 2,000. The scenarios are described to research participants with the more or less clearly specified goal to optimize some aspects of the scenario's output (for a review, see Funke, 1995, 2006).

Perhaps surprisingly, empirical support for a relation between intelligence and problem solving ability is poor. Typically, the reported correlations are low or even zero, at least when the problem situation is intransparent or the goal to be achieved is poorly specified (for detailed reviews, see Kluwe, Misiak, & Haider, 1991, as well as Beckmann & Guthke, 1995). The probably best-known study producing zero correlations was conducted by Dörner and colleagues (1983) in the early 1980s using the

LOHHAUSEN system. Participants' task was to "take care of the future prosperity" of a small town called LOHHAUSEN over a simulated 10-year period. About 2,000 variables were involved in this system (e.g., number of inhabitants, earnings of the industry, etc.). Participants interacted with the system through an experimenter. Problem-solving competence on this task did not correlate with the Raven's Advanced Progressive Matrices (APM; Raven, Court, & Raven, 1980) scores, and it did not correlate with scores on the Culture Fair Intelligence Test (Cattell & Weiss, 1980).

Results such as these have been interpreted and discussed quite controversially by different groups of researchers. One group of researchers (e.g., Dörner & Kreuzig, 1983; Putz-Osterloh, 1981) has argued that zero correlations between problem-solving competence and general intelligence reflect the fact that traditional IQ measures tend to be ecologically less valid than CPS measures. More specifically, these researchers claim that in dynamic scenarios (a) the goals are often ill specified, (b) information needs to be actively sought after, and (c) semantic and contextual embeddedness (i.e., a meaningful cover story) is almost always present, and that traditional intelligence tests do not measure the intellectual abilities (such as the so-called operative intelligence; Dörner, 1986) required for successful problem-solving performance in highly complex and ecologically valid environments.

According to a second group of researchers (e.g., Funke, 1983, 1984; Kluwe et al., 1991), low correlations between IQ and CPS are due to methodological and conceptual shortcomings. Kluwe et al. (1991) have pointed out, for instance, that it is impossible to derive valid indicators of problem-solving performance for tasks that are not formally tractable and thus do not possess a mathematically optimal solution. Indeed, when different dependent measures are used in studies with the same scenario (i.e., TAILORSHOP; e.g., Funke, 1983; Putz-Osterloh, 1981; Süß, Kersting, & Oberauer, 1991, 1993), then the empirical findings frequently differ for different dependent variables.

Second, the reliability of the performance indexes is often low (e.g., Funke, 1983, 1984; Kluwe et al., 1991), ranging between .2 to .7, depending on the dependent variable used (see, e.g., Müller, 1993; Putz-Osterloh & Haupts, 1989; Strohschneider, 1986). Other quite serious methodological criticisms concern the narrow sampling of IQ in most of the studies mentioned earlier (e.g., Funke, 1991), and the different ecological validity of the scenarios.

However, the empirical picture is far more complicated and less clear than might have been suggested thus far. Although zero correlations between test intelligence and complex problem-solving competence are frequently obtained, this is not always the case. For example, Putz-Osterloh (1981; Putz-Osterloh & Lüer, 1981) has argued that the relation between global intelligence and complex problem-solving competence is mediated by the transparency of the problem-solving task. Like Dörner et al. (1983), Putz-Osterloh (1981) failed to find significant correlations between problem-solving competence and the APM in an intransparent experimental condition with the TAILORSHOP scenario, a scenario simulating a small company in which shirt production and sales are controlled via purchasing raw materials and modifying the production capacity in terms of the number of workers and machines. Participants' goal in the study was to maximize the company's profit, either in a transparent condition, in which they had access to a diagram depicting the relations between the system variables, or in an intransparent condition in which no diagram was shown.

Putz-Osterloh (1981, see also Putz-Osterloh & Lüer, 1981; Hörmann & Thomas, 1989) found a statistically reliable relation ($Tau = .22$) between IQ and problem-solving competence (operationalized by the number of months with increasing capital assets) in the transparent experimental condition (but see Funke, 1983, for different results).

A different moderator variable affecting the link between global intelligence and complex problem-solving competence has been suggested by Strohschneider (1991). The author, using the MORO system in which participants are asked to improve the living conditions of nomads in the Sahel zone, manipulated the specificity of the to-be-attained goals (cf. Burns & Vollmeyer, 2002). In the specific-goal condition, participants were asked to reach specified values on critical variables (e.g., number of cattle, number of inhabitants, etc.). In the unspecific-goal condition, the participants' task was to take actions that guaranteed long-term improvements of the MORO living conditions.

In the unspecific-goal condition, problem-solving performance did not correlate with general intelligence as measured by the Berlin Intelligence Structure test (BIS, Jäger, 1982; Jäger, Süß, & Beauducel, 1997); however, substantial correlations (up to $r = -.59$) were found in the specific-goal condition.

Yet another variable affecting the relation between global intelligence and complex problem-solving ability may be the semantic context of a problem-solving task. Hesse (1982) investigated the impact of the semantic embeddedness of the problem-solving task on the relation between IQ and CPS. In the semantic condition, participants were asked to solve the DORI problem, a computerized system involving ecological variables and relations. In the semantic-free condition, a system with an isomorphic problem structure but without the cover story and without meaningful variable names was presented to the participants. In addition, transparency was manipulated in the same way as had been done in the Putz-Osterloh (1981) experiment described earlier. Hesse (1982) obtained moderate correlations between problem-solving performance and APM scores only in the semantic-free condition ($r = .38$ and $r = .46$ for the transparent and the intransparent condition, respectively).

On the whole, the empirical findings described earlier do not support a strong link between global intelligence and complex problem-solving competence when goal specificity and transparency are low and when the semantic content is rich; the link appears to be somewhat stronger when the intelligence-testing conditions more closely resemble the problem-solving testing conditions. We agree with Kluwe et al. (1991) that, on the basis of these results, it cannot be determined whether low correlations are due to invalid intelligence testing (i.e., their failure to assess real-world intellectual abilities necessary for dealing with complexity), or are due to a lack of reliability of the CPS measures. The heterogeneity of the scenarios and IQ tests used further complicates the interpretation of the existing results.

In the research reviewed next, IQ subtests such as the ones that are inherent in the BIS or learning-test scores were correlated with CPS performance. For example, Süß et al. (1991, 1993; see also Hussy, 1991) had problem solvers work on an intransparent version of the TAILORSHOP. The authors hypothesized that to successfully control this system, problem solvers need to infer the relations among critical variables and need to deduce meaningful goals and actions. Therefore, reasoning ability, as assessed by the BIS-factor K (processing capacity, capturing the ability to recognize relations and rules and to form logical inferences in figure series, number series, and verbal analogies), was assumed to be the single best predictor of problem-solving ability. This is indeed what the authors found. Overall problem-solving performance correlated substantially with K ($r = .47$). In addition, knowledge (specific system knowledge as well as general economic knowledge) was found to be a predictor of problem solving as well (see also Putz-Osterloh, 1993).

Similar findings have been reported by Hörmann and Thomas (1989) who administered the TAILORSHOP under two different transparency conditions. When problem solvers' system knowledge, as assessed by a questionnaire, was high, then the K-factor (indicating capacity, $r = .72$) and the G-factor (indicating memory performance, $r = .54$) correlated with CPS performance in the intransparent condition, whereas the B-factor (indicating processing speed, $r = .77$) was the best predictor in the transparent condition. However, when system knowledge was not considered, then significant correlations only emerged in the transparent condition.

A different "componential" approach has been taken by Beckmann (1994; for a comprehensive overview, see Beckmann & Guthke, 1995). Beckmann and colleagues argued that successful problem-solving performance involves the ability to learn from success and failure. The authors therefore used learning tests (e.g., Guthke & Beckmann, 2003) that assess problem solvers' learning potential, in addition to the reasoning subtests of traditional intelligence tests (Intelligence Structure Test; Amthauer, Brocke, Liepmann, & Beauducel, 2001, and Learning Test Battery "Reasoning," LTS 3; Guthke, Jäger, & Schmidt, 1983) to predict problem-solving performance and knowledge acquisition. Diagrams for which the relevant relations need to be filled in are used to assess the latter. The authors' six-variable system is based on a linear equation system, and was administered in either an abstract MACHINE version or in a semantically meaningful version (CHERRY-TREE, for which water supply, warmth, etc., had to be manipulated to control the growth of cherries, leaves, and beetles).

In the abstract MACHINE version, problem solvers acquired substantial system knowledge, and learning-test scores correlated substantially with the system knowledge measure as well as with problem-solving performance measures, whereas traditional intelligence subtest scores only correlated (albeit to a smaller degree) with problem-solving performance. In contrast, in the CHERRYTREE version, problem solvers did not demonstrate system knowledge and test scores did not (regardless of type) correlate with problem-solving performance. Interestingly, the two experimental groups (i.e., MACHINE vs. CHERRYTREE) did not differ in terms of the quality of their CPS performance, that is, in their control of the system. This and similar results have led several researchers (e.g., Berry & Broadbent, 1984) to propose different modes of learning and of problem solving; we return to this issue in the next section when we discuss implicit problem solving.

To summarize, when specific intelligence components are correlated with problem-solving performance in complex systems and when the problem solving goals are clearly specified, then moderate to substantial correlations are obtained, even under intransparent task conditions. The most important intelligence components predicting problem-solving competence appear to be processing capacity-reasoning ability and learning potential. Semantic content appears to be an important mediator of the relation between abilities and CPS, implying that the content may activate prior knowledge and affect the problem representation. Furthermore, inconsistent results have been obtained regarding the relation between system knowledge (i.e., knowledge about the relations among variables) and problem-solving performance.

Implicit Complex Problem Solving

Some recent findings with artificial grammar learning, sequence learning, and CPS tasks all suggest that people are capable of successfully solving problems even when they are not able to verbally express the knowledge they are utilizing (e.g., Frensch & Rünger, 2003). Such findings have led some researchers (e.g., Berry & Broadbent, 1984, 1987; Nissen &

Bullemer, 1987; Reber, 1967, 1969) to propose independent learning systems that might underlie performance in a problem-solving task, an explicit learning system and an implicit learning system. The former is thought to be based on deliberate hypothesis testing, to be selective with respect to what is learned, and to lead to consciously accessible and verbalizable knowledge. Implicit learning, on the other hand, has been characterized as involving "the unselective and passive aggregation of information about the co-occurrence of environmental events and features" (Hayes & Broadbent, 1988, p. 251). Thus, implicit learning is assumed to take place irrespective of the intention to learn, to not rely on hypothesis testing, and to lead to implicit (tacit) knowledge that cannot or can only partially be accessed (Frensch, 1998). Furthermore, it has been argued (Reber, Walkenfield, & Hernstadt, 1991; see also Anderson, 1998) that implicit learning is an evolutionary older, less variable, and more robust ability, suggesting that problem-solving performance that is based on implicit learning might not be correlated with intelligence.

Reber et al. (1991) were among the first to empirically explore the relation between implicit learning and intelligence. The authors compared participants' performance on an "explicit" letter series completion task (i.e., requiring an explicit search for underlying rules) with implicit learning (i.e., a well-formedness judgment) following an artificial grammar learning task. Reber et al. were able to show that series completion, but not implicit learning, was associated with global intelligence. During the learning phase of the artificial grammar learning task, participants were instructed to memorize letter strings produced by a finite state grammar. They were informed about the existence of rules underlying the strings only after the learning phase had ended, that is, before the test phase took place. During the test phase, participants were asked to judge whether a given string corresponded to the rules (i.e., well-formedness task). To ensure a common metric for the series completion task and the well-formedness task, performance on the series completion task was assessed via two-choice response alternatives. In addition, participants were required to explain their choices.

Reber et al. (1991) found relatively small individual differences on the well-formedness task as compared to much larger individual differences on the series completion task. This result could be corroborated by a re-analysis of former studies (e.g., Reber, 1976) in which implicit versus explicit learning was manipulated by varying the instruction for the artificial grammar task.

More to the point and much more interesting was the fact that Reber et al. (1991) could show that participants' Wechsler Adult Intelligence Scale scores ($M = 110$, $SD = 21.2$) correlated only weakly and nonsignificantly with performance on the well-formedness task ($r = .25$). The intercorrelation between the two tasks did not reach significance ($r = .32$). Thus, implicit learning did not correlate significantly with IQ.

Recently, McGeorge, Crawford, and Kelly (1997) replicated and extended the earlier findings from Reber et al. (1991) in interesting ways. First, a factor analysis showed that although the correlation between performance on the implicit task and overall IQ was not significant ($r = .12$), there was a small but statistically reliable correlation between implicit learning and the Perceptual Organization factor ($r = .19$). Interestingly, this factor is the one most clearly associated with fluid intelligence. Second, there were no differences in performance on the implicit task with increasing age.

Furthermore, Maybery, Taylor, and O'Brien-Malone (1995) found that performance on an implicit contingency detection task was not related to IQ ($r = .02$ and $.04$ for children in Grades 1–2 and 6–7, respectively). Also, the children in these studies showed no association between their success on the implicit task and actual verbalized knowledge of the contingency tested ($r = .05$ for both groups). Interestingly, the low correlations between implicit learning and IQ seem not to have been due to lack of variation in implicit functioning. That is, there were individual differences in implicit learning but these were not related to the differences obtained on the IQ measure. Also of interest is the fact that performance on the implicit tasks increased systematically with age.

Unfortunately, in more recent work, Fletcher, Maybery, and Bennett (2000) were not able to replicate their earlier findings. Comparing 20 children with intellectual disability (mean mental age = approximately 5.8 years) with intellectually gifted children (mean mental age = approximately 12.4 years) of similar chronological age (approximately 9.5 years), the authors found that implicit learning varied with intellectual level. It is unclear why the earlier and the more recent findings using essentially the same methodology yielded conflicting results.

In a somewhat different and yet related area of research, Ellis and colleagues have found that individuals identified as retarded often display intact incidental learning. In the first of their studies, Ellis, Katz, and Williams (1987) found that mildly retarded adolescents, normal children, and normal adults were all equivalent in incidental learning of location. As with the studies discussed earlier, individual differences were obtained but were unrelated to gross measures of high-level cognitive functioning.

Ellis and Allison (1988) painted a more complex picture. Incidental learning of frequency of occurrence was equivalent for mildly retarded adolescents and college students, but only for visual information. Although many individuals with a diagnosis of retardation displayed normal incidental learning of verbal-semantic material, several such individuals did not. The findings suggest that uncontrolled, unintentional learning processes show little age and IQ variation when visual-spatial or noncomplex materials are used, but that individual differences might emerge in processing of verbal or complex materials. Anderson (1998) has recently reviewed research into related phenomena, arguing that variation in IQ is associated primarily with variations in mechanisms that are amenable to conscious control and reflection.

On the whole, an empirical relation between complex implicit problem solving and intelligence is usually not obtained. The typically obtained null findings are nevertheless interesting because they point to the possibility that implicit and explicit problem-solving competence might rely on different intellectual abilities.

ISSUES FOR FUTURE RESEARCH

In this section of the chapter we address two issues that have begun to attract the interest of researchers in the CPS community and might well guide much of the future research in the area: (a) the question of whether CPS is a construct that is independent of other cognitive abilities, and (b) the question of the domain specificity of strategies and representations.

Is There an Independent Construct of CPS?

One of the interesting questions of this research is the following: is there an independent construct of CPS or are there only "normal" problem-solving processes operating on complex environments? The question can also be posed this way: are the CPS processes of such a kind that a new quality of problem solving is reached, or do we have only an extension on the task dimension with respect to complexity but not on the level of cognitive processes?

A recent study by Wittmann and Süß (1999) addressed this question and asked for the cognitive prerequisites of CPS. In an extensive data collection, 136 students from Mannheim University worked on three microworlds over the course of 3 days. Each microworld was performed twice with changed starting values: (a) a simulation called POWERPLANT (Wallach, 1998), (b) the Berlin version of the famous TAILORSHOP (Süß & Faulhaber, 1990), and (c) the economic microworld LEARN (Millin;, 1996), which—similar to LOHHAUSEN—consists of over 2,000 variable. Additionally, all participants took the BIS-4 (Jäger, Süß, & Beauduce , 1997) and worked on nine tasks of a test battery for working memory capacity (Oberauer & Süß, 1996).

It turned out that for all three microworlds, the processing capacity (as measured with the BIS-4) was a substantial predictor of problem-solving quality. But just as influential was the system-specific knowledge. Both predictors explained around 30% each of the variance of the aggregated CPS scores. "Speed of information processing" was with 5% explained variance without importance. Also, working memory capacity explained variance above processing capacity. Wittmann and Süß (1999) as well as Süß (1999) drew the conclusion from these results that, in principle, CPS might be seen as a construct of its own right, but that at the same time, the effects could be explained by referring to intelligence and domain-specific knowledge.

Considering the study and the interpretation arrived at by the authors, the question still remains if there exists a unique capacity for solving complex problems. If there indeed exist differences between simple and CPS, then one must be able to demonstrate a distinctive feature that separates the one from the other. This has not been demonstrated yet in terms of cognitive processes, but only in terms of different task descriptions.

An empirical argument against a separate ability of CPS comes from Süß (2001, p. 127 f.). He summarized several of his own microworld studies in which he regularly assessed intelligence and knowledge. According to his analyses, most of the CPS variance could be explained by these two indicators—therefore, he argued that we do not need a construct like CPS besides intelligence and knowledge.

A different view is implied by recent PISA results (the international study on student achievements). In the German national extension of PISA, computer simulated microworlds have been used in addition to an intelligence test and other more conventional problem-solving instruments (see Klieme, Funke, Leutner, Reimann, & Wirth, 2001). It turned out in multidimensional scaling analyses that the conventional problem solving is located close to analytical reasoning, but knowledge acquisition and system control based on parameters from a finite state automaton which served as microworld constitute a separate dimension independent of test intelligence. This result could be interpreted as supporting the assumption of an independent construct.

From our view, the question about an independent CPS construct remains open until precise process models of CPS activities are presented that differ from models for simple problems. Today, we can only be certain that CPS research introduced new tasks to the problem solver, tasks that have not been analyzed before. Whether different cognitive abilities are necessary which lead to different processes cannot be answered today.

Domain Specificity of Strategies and Representations

What determines the mental representation of a problem? The assumption that structural features of a problem (i.e., type of dependencies between variables, time horizon, requested information processing, etc.) are important has been rejected by studies with so-called "problem isomorphs." Such isomorphs are structurally equivalent versions of one and the same problem in different "clothes." Early research by Kotovsky, Hayes, and Simon (1985) has shown that isomorph problems produce different types of representation and—as a consequence—also different solution strategies. Such isomorphs have been used for complex problems by Funke (1992; ALTOEL) and Beckmann (1994; KIRSCHBAUM). As was the case with simple problems, the different versions of the same complex problem produce significant differences with respect to the acquired knowledge about the problem. These results demonstrate the massive effects of context: it seems that problem solving—in the same way as other cognitive functions—is highly driven by semantic embedding and knowledge. The idea of an abstract context-independent capacity for solving problems of a certain structure is not supported by this research.

Newell, Shaw, and Simon (1959) attracted much attention with their "general problem solver" (GPS). They believed at that time that GPS could be a universal procedure which, independent of domains, would solve every problem. Nowadays, we see the restrictions of the GPS more clearly, two of them being the most important:

1. GPS is not as general as one might think because it works only for the small class of well-defined problems. The urgent problems to mankind are ill-defined problems which cannot be solved by algorithms but which need ethical and moral considerations as guiding principles.
2. GPS has ignored domain-specific knowledge and domain-specific strategies, which play an important role in our daily problem-solving activities. To describe problem solving as a procedure which solves problems independent of their context was a fascinating idea but the ignorance of accumulated knowledge and its use by intelligent problem solvers turns out to be a deficit of that approach.

SOME MYTHS OF RESEARCH ON THINKING AND PROBLEM SOLVING

With the advent of CPS research, we are sailing into new ports of our scientific world, but with us on board remain some of the unsolved research questions and also some of the myths of traditional research. Following, we present our list of the top 10 assumptions that currently seriously undermine progress in the area of CPS research because they are not discussed broadly and because they have the status of implicit beliefs—the reason why we call them myths:

1. *Thinking and problem solving occur (solely) in the head*—Isn't it true that we need our brain for problem solving? For sure, without the brain, goal-directed problem solving would never happen. But the real process

requires an interaction with the environment (the scissors metaphor used by Herbert Simon) and it remains fair to request research about the ecology of thinking (Graumann, 2002), which is present in the recent approach of ecological rationality (see Gigerenzer & Selten, 2001).

2. *The more complex the problem, the more complex the cognitive activities for problem solving*—This is an assumption, which was questioned as early as 1908 by Karl Bühler. What operations will be used on the stage of problem solving is not only determined by the type of problem but also by the intended operations. For example, the unbelievable capacity of a mental calculator, who computes in his head and within a minute the 137. root of a number consisting of 1,000 places, needs no new concepts to explain this enormous performance. As Bredenkamp (1990) could demonstrate, even the reader of this chapter would be able to do that—at least in principle, if he or she is willing to train extensively on certain procedures and to have the table of logarithms available by heart. The message is this: It is a very complex task but the cognitive procedures behind the scene are very normal.

3. *Thinking and problem solving are cognitive activities that have little or nothing to do with emotion*—The divergence of cognition and emotion as two different areas of psychological research has been a historical fact, which we have to overcome as soon as possible. It is not true that we deal with either cognition or with emotion. A huge amount of research demonstrates the strong interaction between the two areas. Problem solving in complex domains has much to do with emotion regulation; emotions trigger the way problems are tackled (Fiedler, 2001; Forgas, 2001; Schwarz, 2000; Spering, Wagener, & Funke, 2005).

4. *Problem solving is a universal domain-independent ability*—The assumption of a universal domain-independent ability was part of the early research program called "information processing approach." The idea of a domain-independent ability was fascinating but as empirical evidence showed that cognition is a highly domain-specific enterprise.

5. *Thinking and problem solving occurs by the use of rules*—It is true that a lot of problem solving and thinking can be reconstructed as a series of rules which are followed by the problem solver. In certain environments, the use of plans will be helpful and lead to the goal. But there are other situations in which the control of action is more triggered by the events and the environment than by following a fixed plan. "Situated cognition" (Clark, 1997; Hutchins, 1995) makes the point that thinking does not occur solely in the head but partly also in the word. This has been demonstrated in more detail in point 1. The assumption of rule-based processing is standard in so-called production systems, which are used for cognitive modeling (e.g., ACT-R from Anderson & Lebiere, 1998). On the other hand, there exist connectionist systems, which completely

resist the use of symbolic representations (for a review, see Medler, 1998). It is true that modeling of problem solving by means of production rules might be the first choice, as has been done by Wallach (1998). But even complex processes of planning can be successfully conceived of as connectionistic networks (Schenck, 2001). Also, PSI theory (Dörner et al., 2002) is based completely on a connectionistic approach.

6. *Simple problem solving can be analyzed experimentally, complex problem solving not because of its system character*—Complex systems have a lot of connections within and between the different subsystems. On the first view, a systematic testing of the different functions and their interactions seems to not be possible. But nevertheless, the highly skilled art of system analysis allows it, even with complex systems to localize and diagnose disturbances as well as latent functions.

7. *One needs many participants to identify the small effects, which are important for thinking and reasoning*—Indeed it is necessary to have many observations if the expected effect size is small. On the other side, if one has a strong theory, even a single participant would be enough to falsify a universal hypothesis. For research on thinking and problem solving, this fact implies the following: Single cases cannot only be used for the generation of hypothesis (Kluwe, 1995) but under given conditions they can also be used for hypothesis testing.

8. *Problem solving and thinking (especially complex problem solving) could not be learned*—Especially in the context of complex requirements, the pedagogics of CPS seem not to work well. You cannot easily teach "critical thinking" (Dauer, 1989; Halpern, 1989). But with computer-simulated microworlds, one can use fast motion and slow motion to allow for a precise observation of consequences. As Dörner (1989, p. 305) argued, the use of different time scales allows for multiple learning by means of "symphony of requirements." This argument goes as follows: if you make many experiences on different time scales with different scenarios, you will learn a lot about actions and their consequences. To play is always a good preparation for the real thing. With the use of computer-simulated microworlds, it never was more easy to have these experiences available.

9. *The use of brain imaging allows new insights into the active brain. Therefore, traditional cognitive theories will be replaced by neurological concepts*—It is true that the potential of brain imaging has been increased tremendously (Posner & Raichle, 1994). The expectations are set to watch the brain life in action. Will we be listening to the brain if it is working on complex problems? And if it will be possible, what could be seen? Op de Beeck, Wagemans, and Vogels (2001) wrote the following in their critical review: "… if one wants to construct a cognitive model of behavior, then a mere localization of these processes is not that important (con-

trary to its importance for neuropsychology). For a cognitive scientist, it is important which cognitive processes are involved in a task and how these a computed, but it does not matter where they are computed ..." (p. 344).

The old discussion about the right level of analysis started by Marr (1982) in the context of his work on artificial intelligence models of seeing has to be remembered here. Also, the controversial debate around connectionistic versus symbolic approaches is related to that issue (see Broadbent, 1985; McClelland, 1988; McClelland & Rumelhart, 1985; McCloskey, 1991). Do new insights about neural structures really shed new light on theories which are formulated on a much more abstract level of analysis? The answer is also, in the case of brain imaging techniques, similar as in the debates about connectionistic systems: It is an interesting issue how the brain realizes certain activities but the finally important questions are on a more abstract level and cannot be answered by insights on this deep level. The ghost of a "new phrenology" (Uttal, 2001) will hopefully sleep in his box.

10. *CPS is an intercultural stable component of human cognition*—This last point relates to the cultural boundedness of cognitive processes in general and of problem solving in special (see Nisbett 2003; Nisbett & Norenzayan, 2002). Especially in the context of CPS, a lot of interesting results from cross-cultural studies are available today (Strohschneider, 1996, 2001; Strohschneider & Güss, 1998, 1999). Culturally bound problem-solving styles are the expression of cultural boundedness of thinking and problem solving, which we should accept more intensively in the interest of our own survival.

SUMMARY AND CONCLUSIONS

The study of CPS by means of computer-simulated scenarios is indeed a huge extension of traditional research on thinking and problem solving. The results from the last decade provide a deeper understanding of the behavior of human actors in complex situations. But even today we have no final answers to key questions like trainability. The fundamental idea—to simulate reality and to watch actors in their problem-solving activities—has become a fundamental part of modern psychology. It was a basic idea at the beginning of the 20th century when German working psychologists used the idea of work specimens as diagnostic approach, which they called "Psychotechnik." It is time for us to keep this idea running in the 21st century.

The first goal of this chapter was to discuss to what extent, if indeed at all, individual differences in complex problem-solving competence are related to individual differences in intelligence. Two forms of problem solving were distinguished: explicit problem solving, that is, problem solving that is controlled by a problem solver's intentions; and implicit problem solving, that is, automatic or nonconscious CPS.

Our main conclusions are as follows. First, there exists no convincing empirical evidence that would support a relation, let alone a causal relation, between complex explicit or implicit problem-solving competence, on the one hand, and global intelligence on the other hand. It is important to emphasize that this conclusion is one that is based on a lack of evidence, not necessarily a lack of theoretical relation. That is, we do not deny the theoretical possibility that a relation between global intelligence and CPS competence might exist; we argue only that there exists no convincing empirical evidence that would support such a relation. Nevertheless, the evidence reviewed in this chapter is consistent with a wealth of empirical findings on the relation between intelligence and simple problem solving which suggests that even when a relation between intelligence and problem-solving competence is obtained, it is quite modest in size (e.g., Sternberg, 1982).

Second, however, there exists a considerable amount of empirical data suggesting that specific components of intelligence, such as processing capacity, might be related to specific components of explicit CPS. To what extent a similar conclusion might be warranted for implicit CPS remains to be seen; the available research has, thus far, not addressed this specific question.

On the whole then, the available evidence suggests that the global concepts of intelligence and problem solving are not related, but that specific subcomponents of intelligence and explicit problem solving might share variance. The existing empirical evidence does not speak, unfortunately, to the issue of whether subcomponents of intelligence predict subcomponents of problem solving or whether the opposite causal relation holds; the empirical designs used up to now simply cannot answer this question.

REFERENCES

Amthauer, R., Brocke, B., Liepmann, D., & Beauducel, A. (2001). *Intelligenz-Struktur-Test 2000 R* [Assessment of Intelligence Structure]. Göttingen, Germany: Hogrefe.

Anderson, J. R., Boyle, C. B., & Reiser, B. J. (1985). Intelligent tutoring systems. *Science, 228*, 456–462.

Anderson, J. R., & Lebiere, C. (Eds.). (1998). *The atomic components of thought*. Mahwah, NJ: Lawrence Erlbaum Associates.

Anderson, M. (1998). Individual differences in intelligence. In K. Kirsner, C. Speelman, M. Maybery, A. O'Brien-Malone, M. Anderson, & C. MacLeod (Eds.), *Implicit and explicit processes* (pp. 171–185). Mahwah, NJ: Lawrence Erlbaum Associates.

Anzai, K., & Simon, H. A. (1979). The theory of learning by doing. *Psychological Review, 86*, 124–140.

Beckmann, J. F. (1994). *Lernen und komplexes Problemlösen. Ein Beitrag zur Konstruktvalidierung von Lerntests* [Learning and problem solving. A contribution to validate learning potential tests]. Bonn, Germany: Holos.

Beckmann, J. F., & Guthke, J. (1995). Complex problem solving, intelligence, and learning ability. In P. A. Frensch & J. Funke (Eds.), *Complex problem solving. The European perspective* (pp. 3–25). Hillsdale, NJ: Lawrence Erlbaum Associates.

Berry, D. C., & Broadbent, D. E. (1984). On the relationship between task performance and associated verbalizable knowledge. *Quarterly Journal of Experimental Psychology, 36A,* 209–231.

Berry, D. C., & Broadbent, D. E. (1987). The combination of explicit and implicit learning processes in task control. *Psychological Research, 49,* 7–15.

Berry, D. C., & Broadbent, D. E. (1995). Implicit learning in the control of complex systems. In P. A. Frensch & J. Funke (Eds.), *Complex problem solving. The European perspective* (pp. 3–25). Hillsdale, NJ: Lawrence Erlbaum Associates.

Bhaskar, R., & Simon, H. A. (1977). Problem solving in semantically rich domains: An example from engineering thermodynamics. *Cognitive Science, 1,* 193–215.

Bredenkamp, J. (1990). Kognitionspsychologische Untersuchungen eines Rechenkünstlers [Cognitive studies of a mathematical genius]. In H. Feger (Ed.), *Wissenschaft und Verantwortung. Festschrift für Karl Josef Klauer* (pp. 47–70). Göttingen, Germany: Hogrefe.

Broadbent, D. E. (1977). Levels, hierarchies, and the locus of control. *Quarterly Journal of Experimental Psychology, 29,* 181–201.

Broadbent, D. E. (1985). A question of levels: Comments on McClelland and Rumelhart. *Journal of Experimental Psychology: General, 114,* 189–192.

Buchner, A. (1995). Basic topics and approaches to the study of complex problem solving. In P. A. Frensch & J. Funke (Eds.), *Complex problem solving. The European perspective* (pp. 27–63). Hillsdale, NJ: Lawrence Erlbaum Associates.

Bühler, K. (1908). Antwort auf die von W.Wundt erhobenen Einwände gegen die Methode der Selbstbeobachtung an experimentell erzeugten Erlebnissen [Response to W. Wundt's objections to the method of self-observation of experimentally generated experiences]. *Archiv für die Gesamte Psychologie, 12,* 93–112.

Burns, B. D., & Vollmeyer, R. (2002). Goal specificity effects on hypothesis testing in problem solving. *Quarterly Journal of Experimental Psychology, 55A,* 241–261.

Cattell, R. B., & Weiss, R. H. (1980). *Culture Fair Intelligence Test, Scale 3 (CFT3).* Göttingen, Germany: Hogrefe.

Chase, W. G., & Simon, H. A. (1973). Perception in chess. *Cognitive Psychology, 4,* 55–81.

Chi, M. T. H., Feltovich, P. J., & Glaser, R. (1981). Categorization and representation of physics problems by experts and novices. *Cognitive Science, 5,* 121–152.

Clark, A. (1997). *Being there. Putting brain, body, and world together again.* Cambridge, MA: MIT Press.

Dauer, F. W. (1989). *Critical thinking. An introduction to reasoning.* New York: Oxford University Press.

Dörner, D. (1975). Wie Menschen eine Welt verbessern wollten [How people wanted to improve a world]. *Bild der Wissenschaft, 12,* 48–53.

Dörner, D. (1980). On the difficulty people have in dealing with complexity. *Simulation & Games, 11,* 87–106.

Dörner, D. (1986). Diagnostik der operativen Intelligenz [Assessment of operative intelligence]. *Diagnostica, 32,* 290–308.

Dörner, D. (1989). *Die Logik des Mißlingens. Strategisches Denken in komplexen Situationen* [The logic of failure. Recognizing and avoiding error in complex situations]. Hamburg, Germany: Rowohlt.

Dörner, D., Bartl, C., Detje, F., Gerdes, J., Halcour, D., Schaub, H., et al. (2002). *Die Mechanik des Seelenwagens. Eine neuronale Theorie der Handlungsregulation* [The mechanics of the soul wagon. A neuronal theory of action regulation]. Bern, Switzerland: Huber.

Dörner, D., & Kreuzig, H. W. (1983). Problemlösefähigkeit und Intelligenz [Problem solving and intelligence]. *Psychologische Rundschau, 34,* 185–192.

Dörner, D., Kreuzig, H. W., Reither, F., & Stäudel, T. (1983). *Lohhausen. Vom Umgang mit Unbestimmtheit und Komplexität* [Lohhausen. On dealing with uncertainty and complexity]. Bern, Switzerland: Huber.

Dörner, D., & Wearing, A. (1995). Complex problem solving: Toward a (computersimulated) theory. In P. A. Frensch & J. Funke (Eds.), *Complex problem solving: The European perspective* (pp. 65–99). Hillsdale, NJ: Lawrence Erlbaum Associates.

Duncker, K. (1935). *Zur Psychologie des produktiven Denkens* [On productive thinking]. Berlin, Germany: Springer.

Ellis, N. R., & Allison, P. (1988). Memory for frequency of occurrence in retarded and nonretarded persons. *Intelligence, 12,* 61–75.

Ellis, N. R., Katz, E., & Williams, J. E. (1987). Developmental aspects of memory for spatial location. *Journal of Experimental Child Psychology, 44,* 401–412.

Ewert, P. H., & Lambert, J. F. (1932). The effect of verbal instructions upon the formation of a concept. *Journal of General Psychology, 6,* 400–413.

Fiedler, K. (2001). Affective states trigger processes of assimilation and accomodation. In L. L. Martin & G. L. Clore (Eds.), *Theories of mood and cognition: A user's guidebook* (pp. 85–98). Mahwah, NJ: Lawrence Erlbaum Associates.

Fletcher, J., Maybery, M. T., & Bennett, S. (2000). Implicit learning differences: A question of developmental level? *Journal of Experimental Psychology: Learning, Memory, and Cognition, 26,* 246–252.

Forgas, J. P. (2001). The Affect Infusion Model (AIM): An integrative theory of mood effects on cognition and judgment. In L. L. Martin & G. L. Clore (Eds.), *Theories of mood and cognition: A user's guidebook* (pp. 99–134). Mahwah, NJ: Lawrence Erlbaum Associates.

Frensch, P. A. (1998). One concept, multiple meanings. On how to define the concept of implicit learning. In M. A. Stadler & P. A. Frensch (Eds.), *Handbook of implicit learning* (pp. 47–104). Thousand Oaks, CA: Sage.

Frensch, P. A., & Funke, J. (Eds.). (1995a). *Complex problem solving: The European perspective.* Hillsdale, NJ: Lawrence Erlbaum Associates.

Frensch, P. A., & Funke, J. (1995b). Definitions, traditions, and a general framework for understanding complex problem solving. In P. A. Frensch & J. Funke (Eds.), *Complex problem solving. The European perspective* (pp. 3–25). Hillsdale, NJ: Lawrence Erlbaum Associates.

Frensch, P. A., & Rünger, D. (2003). Implicit learning. *Current Directions in Psychological Science, 12,* 13–17.

Funke, J. (1983). Einige Bemerkungen zu Problemen der Problemlöseforschung oder: Ist Testintelligenz doch ein Prädiktor? [Some remarks on the problems of problem solving research or: Does test intelligence predict control performance?]. *Diagnostica, 29,* 283–302.

Funke, J. (1984). Diagnose der westdeutschen Problemlöseforschung in Form einiger Thesen [Assessment of West German problem solving research]. *Sprache & Kognition, 3,* 159–172.

Funke, J. (1991). Solving complex problems: Exploration and control of complex systems. In R. J. Sternberg & P. A. Frensch (Eds.), *Complex problem solving: Principles and mechanisms* (pp. 185–222). Hillsdale, NJ: Lawrence Erlbaum Associates.

Funke, J. (1992). *Wissen über dynamische Systeme: Erwerb, Repräsentation und Anwendung* [Knowledge about dynamic systems: Acquisition, representation, and use]. Berlin, Germany: Springer.

Funke, J. (1995). Experimental research on complex problem solving. In P. A. Frensch & J. Funke (Eds.), *Complex problem solving: The European perspective* (pp. 243–268). Hillsdale, NJ: Lawrence Erlbaum Associates.

Funke, J. (Ed.). (1999). Themenheft komplexes problemlösen [Special issue on complex problem solving]. *Psychologische Rundschau, 50*(4).

Funke, J. (2006). Komplexes Problemlösen [Complex problem solving]. In J. Funke (Ed.), *Denken und Problemlösen* (pp. 375–446). Göttingen, Germany: Hogrefe.

Gigerenzer, G., & Selten, R. (2001). Rethinking rationality. In G. Gigerenzer & R. Selten (Eds.), *Bounded rationality. The adaptive toolbox* (pp. 1–12). Cambridge, MA: MIT Press.

Graumann, C. F. (2002). The phenomenological approach to people-environment studies. In R. B. Bechtel & A. Churchman (Eds.), *Handbook of environmental psychology* (pp. 95–113). New York: Wiley.

Guthke, J., & Beckmann, J. F. (2003). Dynamic assessment with diagnostic programs. In R. J. Sternberg, J. Lautrey & T. I. Lubart (Eds.), *Models of intelligence* (pp. 227–242). Washington, DC: American Psychological Association.

Guthke, J., Jäger, C., & Schmidt, I. (1983). Lerntestbatterie "Schlussfolgerndes Denken" [Learning test battery "reasoning"]. Berlin: Psychodiagnostisches Zentrum.

Halpern, D. F. (1989). *Thought and knowledge. An introduction to critical thinking.* Hillsdale, NJ: Lawrence Erlbaum Associates.

Hayes, N. A., & Broadbent, D. E. (1988). Two modes of learning for interactive tasks. *Cognition, 28,* 249–276.

Hesse, F. W. (1982). Effekte des semantischen Kontexts auf die Bearbeitung komplexer Probleme [Effects of semantic context on problem solving]. *Zeitschrift für Experimentelle und Angewandte Psychologie, 29,* 62–91.

Hörmann, J. J., & Thomas, M. (1989). Zum zusammenhang zwischen intelligenz und komplesem problemlösen [On the relationship between intelligence and complex problem solving]. *Sprache & Kognition, 8,* 23–31.

Hussy, W. (1991). Komplexes Problemlösen und Verarbeitungskapazität [Complex problem solving and processing capacity]. *Sprache & Kognition, 10,* 208–220.

Hutchins, E. (1995). *Cognition in the wild.* Cambridge, MA: MIT Press.

Jäger, A. O. (1982). Mehrmodale klassifikation von intelligenzleistungen [Multimodal classification of intelligent performance]. *Diagnostica, 28,* 195–225.

Jäger, A. O., Süß, H.-M., & Beauducel, A. (1997). *Berliner Intelligenzstrukturtest. BIS-Test, Form 4* [Berlin Intelligence Structure Test, Manual]. Göttingen, Germany: Hogrefe.

Klieme, E., Funke, J., Leutner, D., Reimann, P., & Wirth, J. (2001). Problemlösen als fächerübergreifende kompetenz. Konzeption und erste resultate aus einer schulleistungsstudie [Problem solving as crosscurricular competence. Conceptual framework and first results from a study on school achievement]. *Zeitschrift für Pädagogik, 47,* 179–200.

Kluwe, R. H. (1995). Single case studies and models of complex problem solving. In P. A. Frensch & J. Funke (Eds.), *Complex problem solving: The European perspective* (pp. 269–291). Hillsdale, NJ: Lawrence Erlbaum Associates.

Kluwe, R. H., Misiak, C., & Haider, H. (1991). Systems and performance in intelligence tests. In H. Rowe (Ed.), *Intelligence: Reconceptualization and measurement* (pp. 227–244). Hillsdale, NJ: Lawrence Erlbaum Associates.

Kluwe, R. H., Schilde, A., Fischer, C., & Oellerer, N. (1991). Problemlöseleistungen beim umgang mit komplexen systemen und intelligenz [Problem solving performance when interacting with complex systems and intelligence]. *Diagnostica, 37*, 291–313.

Kotovsky, K., Hayes, J. R., & Simon, H. A. (1985). Why are some problems hard? Evidence from Tower of Hanoi. *Cognitive Psychology, 17*, 248–294.

Marr, D. (1982). *Vision. A computational investigation into the human representation and processing of visual information.* New York: W. H. Freeman.

Maybery, M., Taylor, M., & O'Brien-Malone, A. (1995). Implicit learning: Sensitive to age but not IQ. *Australian Journal of Psychology, 47*, 8–17.

Mayer, R. E. (1992). *Thinking, problem solving, cognition* (2nd ed.). New York: Freeman.

McClelland, J. L. (1988). Connectionist models and psychological evidence. *Journal of Memory and Language, 27*, 107–123.

McClelland, J. L., & Rumelhart, D. E. (1985). Distributed memory and the representation of general and specific information. *Journal of Experimental Psychology: General, 114*, 159–188.

McCloskey, M. (1991). Networks and theories: The place of connectionism in cognitive science. *Psychological Science, 2*, 387–395.

McGeorge, P., Crawford, J. R., & Kelly, S. W. (1997). The relationships between psychometric intelligence and learning in an explicit and an implicit task. *Journal of Experimental Psychology: Learning, Memory, & Cognition, 23*, 239–245.

Medler, D. A. (1998). A brief history of connectionism. *Neural Computing Surveys, 1*, 61–101.

Milling, P. (1996). Modelling innovation processes for decision support and managing simulation. *System Dynamics Review, 12*, 211–234.

Müller, H. (1993). *Komplexes problemlösen: Reliabilität und wissen* [Complex problem solving: Reliability and knowledge]. Bonn, Germany: Holos.

Newell, A., & Simon, H. A. (1972). *Human information processing.* Englewood Cliffs, NJ: Prentice Hall.

Newell, A., Shaw, J. C., & Simon, H. A. (1959). A general problem-solving program for a computer. *Computers and Automation, 8*, 10–16.

Nisbett, R. E. (2003). *The geography of thought. How Asians and Westerners think differently … and why.* New York: Free Press.

Nisbett, R. E., & Norenzayan, A. (2002). Culture and cognition. In H. Pashler & D. Medin (Eds.), *Steven's handbook of experimental psychology. Third edition. Vol. 2: Memory and cognitive processes* (pp. 561–597). New York: Wiley.

Nissen, M. J., & Bullemer, P. (1987). Attentional requirements of learning: Evidence from performance measures. *Cognitive Psychology, 19*, 1–32.

Oberauer, K., & Süß, H.-M. (1996). Working memory starship. Computerbasierte testbatterie zur diagnostik der arbeitsgedächtniskapazität [Computer based test battery for the assessment of working memory]. Mannheim, Germany: Universität Mannheim, Lehrstuhl Psychologie II.

op de Beeck, H., Wagemans, J., & Vogels, R. (2001). Can neuroimaging really tell us what the human brain is doing? The relevance of indirect measures of population activity. *Acta Psychologica, 107*, 323–351.

Posner, M. I., & Raichle, M. E. (1994). *Images of mind*. New York: Freeman.

Putz-Osterloh, W. (1993). Strategies for knowledge acquisition and transfer of knowledge in dynamic tasks. In G. Strube & K.-F. Wender (Eds.), The cognitive psychology of knowledge (pp. 331–350). Amsterdam: Elsevier Science Publishers.

Putz-Osterloh, W. (1981). Über die beziehung zwischen testintelligenz und problemlöseerfolg [On the relationship between test intelligence and success in problem solving]. *Zeitschrift für Psychologie, 189*, 79–100.

Putz-Osterloh, W., & Haupts, I. (1989). Zur reliabilität und Validität computergestützter diagnostik komplexer organisations— und entscheidungsstrategien [On the reliability and validity of computerbased assessment of complex organizational and decision strategies]. *Untersuchungen des Psychologischen Dienstes der Bundeswehr, 24*, 5–48.

Putz-Osterloh, W., & Lüer, G. (1981). Über die Vorhersagbarkeit komplexer problemlöseleistungen durch ergebnisse in einem intelligenztest [On the predictability of complex problem solving performance by intelligence test scores]. *Zeitschrift für Experimentelle und Angewandte Psychologie, 28*, 309–334.

Raven, J. C., Court, J., & Raven, J., Jr. (1980). *Advanced Progressive Matrices (APM)*. Weinheim, Germany: Beltz.

Reber, A. S. (1967). Implicit learning of artificial grammars. *Journal of Verbal Learning and Verbal Behavior, 77*, 317–327.

Reber, A. S. (1969). Transfer of syntactic structure in synthetic languages. *Journal of Experimental Psychology, 81*, 115–119.

Reber, A. S. (1976). Implicit learning and tacit knowledge. *Journal of Experimental Psychology: Human Learning and Memory, 2*, 88–94.

Reber, A. S., Walkenfield, F. F., & Hernstadt, R. (1991). Implicit and explicit learning: Individual differences and IQ. *Journal of Experimental Psychology. Learning, Memory, and Cognition, 17*, 888–896.

Schenck, W. (2001). *A connectionist approach to human planning*. Retrieved March 11, 2005, from http://www.ub.uni-heidelberg.de/archiv/1428

Schwarz, N. (2000). Emotion, cognition, and decision making. *Cognition and Emotion, 14*, 433—440.

Spering, M., Wagener, D., & Funke, J. (2005). The role of emotions in complex problem-solving. *Cognition and Emotion, 19*, 1252–1261.

Sternberg, R. J. (1982). Reasoning, problem solving, and intelligence. In R. J. Sternberg (Ed.), *Handbook of human intelligence* (pp. 225–307). Cambridge, MA: Cambridge University Press.

Sternberg, R. J. (1995). Expertise in complex problem solving: A comparison of alternative conceptions. In P. A. Frensch & J. Funke (Eds.), *Complex problem solving: The European perspective* (pp. 295–321). Hillsdale, NJ: Lawrence Erlbaum Associates.

Sternberg, R. J., & Frensch, P. A. (Eds.). (1991). *Complex problem solving: Principles and mechanisms*. Hillsdale, NJ: Lawrence Erlbaum Associates.

Strohschneider, S. (1986). Zur Stabilität und Validität von Handeln in komplexen Realitätsbereichen [On the stability and validity of complex problem-solving behavior]. *Sprache & Kognition, 5*, 42–48.

Strohschneider, S. (1991). Problemlösen und Intelligenz: Über die Effekte der Konkretisierung komplexer Probleme [Complex problem solving and intelligence: On the effects of problem concreteness]. *Diagnostica, 37*, 353–371.

Strohschneider, S. (Ed.). (1996). *Denken in Deutschland: Vergleichende Untersuchungen in Ost und West* [Thinking in Germany: A comparison between East and West Germany]. Bern, Switzerland: Huber.

Strohschneider, S. (2001). *Kultur — Denken — Strategie. Eine Indische Suite* [Culture — thinking — strategy. An Indian suite]. Bern, Switzerland: Huber.

Strohschneider, S., & Güss, D. (1998). Planning and problem solving: Differences between Brazilian and German students. *Journal of Cross-Cultural Psychology, 29,* 695–716.

Strohschneider, S., & Güss, D. (1999). The fate of the Moros: A cross-cultural exploration of strategies in complex and dynamic decision making. *International Journal of Psychology, 34,* 235–252.

Süß, H.-M. (1999). Intelligenz und komplexes Problemlösen — Perspektiven für eine Kooperation zwischen differentiell-psychometrischer und kognitionspsychologischer Forschung [Intelligence and complex problem-solving. Perspectives for a cooperation between differential-psychometric and cognition-psychological research]. *Psychologische Rundschau, 50,* 220–228.

Süß, H.-M. (2001). Prädikative Validität der Intelligenz im schulischen und außerschulischen Bereich [Predictive validity of test intelligence for school and non-school purposes]. In E. Stern & J. Guthke (Eds.), *Perspektiven der Intelligenzforschung. Ein Lehrbuch für Fortgeschrittene* (pp. 89–108). Lengerich, Germany: Pabst Science Publishers.

Süß, H.-M., & Faulhaber, J. (1990). Berliner Version der Schneiderwerkstatt. PC Simulationsprogramm [Berlin version of Tailorshop]. Berlin, Germany: Freie Universität Berlin, Fachbereich Erziehungs- und Unterrichtswissenschaften, Institut für Psychologie.

Süß, H. M., Kersting, M., & Oberauer, K. (1991). Intelligenz und Wissen als Prädiktoren für Leistungen bei computersimulierten komplexen Problemen [Intelligence and knowledge as predictors of performance in solving complex computer-simulated problems]. *Diagnostica, 37,* 334–352.

Süß, H.-M., Kersting, M., & Oberauer, K. (1993). Zur Vorhersage von Steuerungsleistungen an computersimulierten Systemen durch Wissen und Intelligenz [Predicting control performance in computersimulated systems by means of knowledge and intelligence]. *Zeitschrift für Differentielle und Diagnostische Psychologie, 14,* 189–203.

Uttal, W. R. (2001). *The new phrenology.* Cambridge, MA: MIT Press.

Wallach, D. (1998). *Komplexe Regelungsprozesse. Eine kognitionswissenschaftliche Analyse* [Complex control processes. A cognitive science analysis]. Wiesbaden, Germany: Deutscher Universitäts-Verlag.

Wenke, D., & Frensch, P. A. (2003). Is success or failure at solving complex problems related to intellectual ability? In J. E. Davidson & R. J. Sternberg (Eds.), *The psychology of problem solving* (pp. 87–126). Cambridge: Cambridge University Press.

Wittmann, W. W., & Süß, H.-M. (1999). Investigating the paths between working memory, intelligence, knowledge and complex problem solving: Performances via Brunswik-symmetry. In P. L. Ackerman, P. C. Kyllonen, & R. D. Roberts (Eds.), *Learning and individual differences: Process, trait, and content* (pp. 77–108). Washington, DC: American Psychological Association.

Chapter 3

When Capacity Matters: The Role of Working Memory in Problem Solving

Jodi Price, Richard Catrambone, and Randall W. Engle
Georgia Institute of Technology

Each day we are faced with problem-solving tasks, many of which are dependent on working memory (WM) capacity, which we broadly define as the capacity for controlled processing (Engle & Kane, 2004). Take, for example, the seemingly simple task of selecting new furniture. This problem-solving task would seem to have very little to do with WM capacity at first glance. However, visualizing and deciding whether the chosen furniture will fit in the allotted space taps WM capacity as it requires holding an image of the space in mind while mentally juggling and moving the selected furniture within the imaged space. Similarly, the act of mentally calculating whether one can afford the more expensive furniture again utilizes WM capacity as one must hold a series of numbers in mind while performing additional mathematical operations before reaching a decision. Thus it becomes apparent that even a task such as selecting new furniture uses WM capacity and fits within Baddeley and Logie's (1999) notion of WM, which they defined as the following:

> … multiple specialized components of cognition that allow humans to comprehend and mentally represent their immediate environment, to retain information about their immediate past experience, to support the acquisition of new knowledge, to solve problems, and to formulate, relate, and act on current goals. (p. 28)

Tasks such as selecting new furniture rarely seem overly complex and yet other tasks that also rely on WM processing can be cognitively overwhelming. This raises the question of why two tasks, equally dependent on WM capacity, can seem disproportionately difficult. The purpose of this chapter is to address this issue by providing a brief history of WM research while detailing the real-world implications of WM capacity limitations and discussing what WM capacity is and is not related to as well as when WM capacity should be expected to matter. Finally, we discuss how this relates to problem solving and detail a line of problem-solving research specifically designed to address what we currently know about WM capacity limitations.

HISTORY OF WORKING MEMORY RESEARCH

To understand why WM capacity might be expected to play a role in some tasks but seem irrelevant in others, it is necessary to address how the WM system is presumed to operate. One of the most influential models of WM was put forth by Baddeley and Hitch (1974; see also Baddeley, 1986, 2001; Baddeley & Hitch, 1994). The Baddeley and Hitch (1974) model focused and expanded on the short-term store in Atkinson and Shiffrin's (1968) "modal" model and proposed that short-term memory (STM) acts as a WM system that is responsible for temporarily maintaining and manipulating a limited amount of information to support the performance of a variety of cognitive tasks (e.g., comprehension, learning, and reasoning; Baddeley, 1986).

The three components that comprise the WM system in the Baddeley and Hitch (1974) model are a supervisory system, called the central executive, and two specialized temporary memory slave systems, the visuospatial sketchpad and the articulatory loop. In its supervisory role, the central executive oversees and coordinates the two slave systems, switches the focus of attention, and activates information previously stored in long-term memory (LTM; Baddeley & Logie, 1999). In this sense, the central executive is very similar to Norman and Shallice's (1986) supervisory attentional system. The task of temporarily maintaining information is handled by the two slave systems which are believed to briefly store information by either creating images, in the case of the visuospatial sketchpad, or utilizing rehearsal processes, in the case of the articulatory loop (Baddeley & Logie, 1999).

OTHER WAYS OF CONCEPTUALIZING WORKING MEMORY

Other approaches to WM have been proposed since Baddeley and Hitch's (1974) model. Consistent with the Baddeley and Hitch model are multistore, distributed processing models which assume that different components handle different aspects or types of processing (e.g., Bayliss,

Jarrold, Gunn, & Baddeley, 2003; Carlson, Khoo, Yaure, & Schneider, 1990; Carlson, Sullivan, & Schneider, 1989). Such models are contrasted by those that conceptualize WM as a unitary construct (Colom & Shih, 2004; Engle & Kane, 2004; Kyllonen & Christal, 1990). For example, Engle and Kane (2004) viewed the WM system as a single store in which controlled attention and related processes keep a limited amount of information from LTM activated above threshold. Debates about the unitary versus multidimensional nature of WM thus reflect differences in opinion about how information is processed and maintained in WM. Such distinctions constitute only one way to differentiate among different models of WM.

Another basis for distinguishing among the different views of WM is whether WM capacity is conceptualized as being domain and task specific or something that may be generalized across many domains and tasks. Researchers such as Daneman and Carpenter (1980, 1983) suggested that WM capacity is domain specific and that WM capacity tasks will only have predictive validity when they tap specific skills necessary in the criterion task (Hambrick & Engle, 2003). Others such as Engle and colleagues (e.g., Hambrick & Engle, 2002, 2003; Hambrick, Kane, & Engle, 2005; Kane et al., 2004) argued that, although the coding formats are specific to language or visual and spatial domains, the supervisory attention aspect of WM is domain general. They suggested that measures of WM capacity tap information processing capabilities that are useful in many tasks, thus accounting for the ability of WM capacity to predict performance in a wide variety of domains and tasks.

ASSESSING WORKING MEMORY CAPACITY

WM capacity is typically assessed using measures that combine the storage component of STM tasks with an additional requirement of simultaneous processing of other information. For example, Daneman and Carpenter's (1980) reading span measure requires participants to read and comprehend a series of two to seven sentences before being asked to recall the final word of each sentence. Turner and Engle's (1989) operation span task also requires the maintenance of words or letters while solving a series of simple math problems. One's reading or operation span (i.e., capacity) is the number of words one can correctly recall while correctly answering questions about the sentences or solving the math problems, respectively. In general then, these tasks assess how much information one can maintain in an active state while processing other information. The processing component in WM capacity tasks is believed to tap the central executive or ability to control attention, and is what distinguishes STM from WM capacity tasks (Engle, Tuholski, Laughlin, & Conway, 1999). Therefore those with higher WM spans (i.e., those that can maintain more items in an active state) are assumed to have more attentional resources or greater ability to control their attentional focus relative to those who score lower on these WM span measures (Feldman Barrett, Tugade, & Engle, 2004).

TO WHAT IS WORKING MEMORY CAPACITY RELATED?

WM capacity, as reflected by scores in operation span, reading span, and other measures of WM capacity, has been found to be related to performance in a variety of tasks (Hambrick & Engle, 2003) such as reading and language comprehension (Daneman & Carpenter, 1980; Daneman & Merikle, 1996; Engle, Cantor, & Carullo, 1992; Engle, Nations, & Cantor, 1990; Turner & Engle, 1989), learning to spell (Ormrod & Cochran, 1988), and learning a new vocabulary (Daneman & Green, 1986).

WM capacity tasks have been found to predict such cognitive tasks as taking lecture notes (Kiewra & Benton, 1988), storytelling (Pratt, Boyes, Robins, & Manchester, 1989), writing (Benton, Kraft, Glover, & Plake, 1984), logic learning (Kyllonen & Stephens, 1990), comprehending and following directions (Engle, Carullo, & Collins, 1991), as well as the ability to effectively navigate in a hypertext learning environment (Lee & Tedder, 2003).

That WM capacity is predictive of performance in so many cognitive tasks has raised questions about the relation between WM capacity and intelligence, specifically fluid intelligence (Colom & Shih, 2004; Colom, Rebollo, Palacios, Juan-Espinosa, & Kyllonen, 2004; Conway, Cowan, Bunting, Therriault, & Minkoff, 2002; Mackintosh & Bennett, 2003; Schweizer & Moosbrugger, 2004), which Cattell (1963) proposed reflects the basic capacity to reason and solve novel problems. Engle, Tuholski, et al. (1999) used exploratory and confirmatory factor analyses as well as structural equation modeling to examine the nature of the constructs of STM, WM, and fluid intelligence and concluded that STM and WM are distinct, yet highly related constructs. However, despite the relatedness of STM and WM, only WM was found to relate to fluid intelligence. That WM capacity tasks involve an attention component that STM tasks do not led the authors to suggest that the link between WM capacity and fluid intelligence constructs is the ability to maintain an active representation, particularly in the face of interference or distraction (Engle, Tuholski, et al., 1999). Thus the ability to control attention is the component of WM capacity that is important to higher order functioning (Engle, Kane, & Tuholski, 1999).

WHEN DOES WORKING MEMORY CAPACITY MATTER (AND WHEN IS IT IRRELEVANT)?

The previous discussion of the many things to which WM capacity is related highlights the fact that WM capacity will matter in tasks requiring the simultaneous processing and storage of information. Engle, Kane, and Tuholski (1999) suggested that because WM capacity reflects the capability for controlled processing, only tasks or situations that encourage or demand controlled attention should yield individual differences in task performance. They specified seven contexts in which individual differences in WM capacity are likely to be observed:

1. When task goals may be lost unless actively maintained in WM.
2. When actions competing for responding or response preparation must be scheduled.
3. When conflict among actions must be resolved to prevent error.
4. When there is value in maintaining some task information in the face of distraction and interference.
5. When there is value in suppressing or inhibiting information irrelevant to the task.
6. When error monitoring and correction are controlled and effortful.
7. When controlled, planful search of memory is necessary or useful (p. 104).

Many of these contexts are present in tasks commonly used in psychology experiments and instructional settings. For example, category fluency tasks require individuals to say as many exemplars from a given category as possible without providing redundant answers. To do so individuals must maintain the category name (i.e., context 1) while conducting a controlled, planful search of memory (i.e., context 7), and keep a running list of items that have and have not been produced (i.e., context 4) so they can inhibit items already said (i.e., context 5) to prevent redundant responses (i.e., context 6). These same contexts are also apparent in classrooms when instructors discuss a concept and then ask students to provide examples of that concept (e.g., "What are some examples of sedimentary rocks?").

In another popular task, the Stroop (1935) task, individuals view colored bars and color words printed in opposing ink colors (e.g., the word *red* printed in green ink) and are asked to say the ink color (rather than the word) as quickly as possible. To successfully complete the Stroop task, individuals must maintain the goal of saying the ink color (i.e., context 1) while inhibiting the automatic tendency to read the word (i.e., contexts 2 and 5) to prevent erroneous responses (i.e., contexts 3 and 6).

Consistent with the Engle Kane, and Tuholski (1999) suggestion that these contexts can be expected to yield individual differences in WM capacity, Kane and Engle (2003) found that in the Stroop task, low span individuals were less able to inhibit the more automatic response (e.g., reading the word rather than saying the ink color of the word) than high span participants. Similarly, Kane, Bleckley, Conway, and Engle (2001) found that in an antisaccade task, which required individuals to ignore a flashing light in the periphery to instead view stimuli that appeared in the opposite direction of the flashing light, low span individuals were less likely than high span participants to inhibit the automatic response (e.g., attending to the flashing light in the periphery) to achieve the goal-directed response of identifying a pattern masked letter that appeared in the opposite direction of the flashing light.

Cantor and Engle (1993) also found WM capacity-related differences in the ability to inhibit responses. They presented participants with unrelated sentences containing a subject paired with different predicates and then gave participants a speeded recognition test. Response times on the recognition test increased for both high and low WM span individuals as the number of predicates a single subject was paired with (i.e., FAN size) increased, but the increase in response times was much greater for the low than high span individuals. Cantor and Engle attributed the low spans' relatively higher response times to their having greater difficulty inhibiting previously associated subject-predicate pairs.

Similar differences in high and low WM capacity individuals have been found in tasks that require other types of controlled processing. Rosen and Engle (1997) examined the ability of their participants to use controlled versus automatic processing to overcome retroactive interference (i.e., the interference that occurs when newer material hinders memory for older items) in a category fluency task and found that high WM capacity individuals showed greater immunity to retroactive interference than the low WM span participants. Feldman Barrett et al. (2004) suggested that controlled processing depends on the central executive component of WM and "occurs when attention is applied in a goal-directed, top-down, or endogenous fashion" (p. 555). They further posited that the reason individual differences in WM capacity play a role in tasks that require the suppression or inhibition of automatically processed information is because controlled processing is necessary to suppress or inhibit this information.

Studies examining the relation between WM capacity and things such as stereotype threat, life stressors, and prejudice also provide support for the notion that WM capacity and controlled processing are necessary to suppress or inhibit task-irrelevant information. Schmader and Johns (2003) explicitly and implicitly activated stereotype threat, "the phenomenon whereby individuals perform more poorly on a task when a relevant stereotype or stigmatized social identity is made salient in the performance situation" (p. 440), and found that women and Latinos were more likely to experience a reduction in Operation span scores when placed in stereotype threat conditions, relative to control conditions. Schmader and Johns also found that WM capacity mediated the effects of stereotype threat on women's math performance and suggested that stereotype threat reduces

WM capacity because individuals utilize attentional resources, which would otherwise be devoted to task performance, to suppress the negative stereotypes. A similar explanation was offered by Klein and Boals (2001) for why life event stress was found to reduce functional WM capacity and result in lower Operation span scores. Klein and Boals attributed stressed individuals' lower scores to their devoting attentional resources to suppressing or inhibiting thoughts about the stressful event(s) rather than to their performance on the WM capacity task.

WM capacity and its role in inhibiting responses can also explain why prejudiced individuals showed reduced Stroop task performance after participating in interracial, but not same-race interactions. Richeson and Shelton (2003) measured implicit and explicit racial prejudice and then examined response modulation and behavioral control, two indicators of self-regulation believed to rely on attentional capacity, in participants asked to interact with interracial or same-race individuals before completing a Stroop task. The researchers hypothesized and found that prejudiced individuals exercised greater self-regulation during interracial interactions, relative to those in same-race interactions or less prejudiced individuals, which in turn hurt their performance on the Stroop task. Richeson and Shelton explained these findings in terms of WM capacity and executive control by suggesting that because self-regulation in interracial interactions and performance on the Stroop task involved the same attentional resources, prejudiced individuals exercising greater self-regulation were more likely to exhaust WM capacity and have fewer attentional resources left to devote to performance on the Stroop task.

A series of experiments examining "choking under pressure" (Beilock & Carr, 2005; Beilock, Kulp, Holt, & Carr, 2004; Gimmig, Huguet, Caverni, & Cury, 2005) provides additional evidence that external sources of pressure (e.g., stereotype threat, life stressors, and interracial interactions) can strain WM capacity resources and result in reduced problem-solving performance. Beilock and colleagues (2004, 2005) presented modular arithmetic problems that varied in how much they taxed WM capacity, in both low and high pressure situations, to low and high WM span individuals and asked them to indicate the "truth" of the problems. To solve modular arithmetic problems (e.g., $62 \equiv 18$ [mod 4]), one must subtract the middle number from the first (i.e., $62 - 18$), divide the difference by the last number (i.e., $44 \div 4$), and then declare the statement "true" if the resulting dividend is a whole number. Problems containing numbers larger than 20 or requiring borrow operations were classified as having higher WM demand relative to problems with smaller numbers that did not require borrowing (e.g., $5 \equiv 3$ [mod 2]). Participants completed several practice problems and a low-pressure test, which participants viewed as more practice problems, before being given a scenario designed to create a high pressure environment and completing the high-pressure test. Beilock and Carr (2005) found that high WM span participants outperformed their lower WM span counterparts on the high WM demand problems, but only in the low pressure test. The low spans' disadvantage disappeared in the high pressure test because their level of performance did not decrease under pressure whereas the high spans' performance did. Beilock and Carr suggested that this somewhat counterintuitive finding, that high pressure situations emphasizing WM capacity are more detrimental to high than low WM span individuals' performance, reflects the inability of high WM spans to use the WM-taxing strategies in high pressure situations that foster their performance in low pressure situations due to pressure tapping and reducing available WM capacity resources. Gimmig et al. (2005) offered a similar explanation for the choking under pressure they observed on the Raven's Standard Progressive Matrices task in which individuals are given increasingly difficult patterns with one missing piece and asked to decide which of eight pieces will complete the pattern. Consistent with the Beilock and Carr results, Gimmeg et al. found that high pressure situations hurt high more than low WM spans' performance on the complex, but not the easier items. Engle and colleagues (Kane & Engle, 2000, 2002; Rosen & Engle, 1997) have also reported similar counterintuitive findings of dual task conditions hurting high more than low WM span individuals' performance (e.g., on verbal fluency and proactive interference tasks; i.e., tasks in which older items interfere with memory for newer items).

Together these studies highlight the role of controlled processing in task performance, as each fits one or more of the Engle, Kane, and Tuholski (1999) criteria of situations in which WM capacity should be important. Situations and tasks that do not fit these criteria are cases where WM capacity should be less important if not completely irrelevant. For example, WM capacity should be less important after extensive practice at a task because, with practice, performance of the task becomes more automatic and less dependent on controlled processing (i.e., automaticity develops). Reber and Kotovsky (1997) presented evidence to support the notion that practice and expertise serve to reduce the role of WM capacity in task performance. They found that WM load initially slowed the implicit learning of how to solve the Balls and Boxes puzzle task, but that after the task was learned, WM load no longer had an effect on problem-solving performance.

Also consistent with the notion that task experience influences how much controlled attention is necessary is another set of experiments conducted by Beilock and colleagues (Beilock & Carr, 2001; Beilock, Carr, MacMahon, & Starkes, 2002). Beilock et al. (2002) found that novel sensorimotor skills (e.g., golf putting and soccer ball dribbling) were performed better in skill-focused conditions in which participants had to attend to a particular component of how they were performing the sensorimotor task (e.g., noting the completion of one's golf swing in putting; noting which side of the foot was being used to dribble a soccer ball), relative to dual-task conditions that required monitoring something unrelated to the sensorimotor skill (e.g., attending to and noting different auditory tones). Conversely, expert golfers and soccer players performed better under dual-task than in skill-focused conditions. Beilock et al. suggested that the skill-focused condition resulted in better performance for novices (and experts constrained to be novices in the soccer dribbling task by using a nondominant foot), because in the early stages of skill acquisition, greater attentional control is necessary and few attentional resources are left to devote to dual-task performance. However, dual-task conditions resulted in better performance in experts for whom it is counterproductive to attend to a component of a skill (as the skill-focused conditions required), because doing so takes proceduralized skills that occur essentially outside of WM capacity and breaks them back down into smaller, independent units that must each be processed in a step-by-step attention-demanding way, similar to the way processing occurs early in skill acquisition. These findings that WM capacity demands are reduced as skill level increased are consistent with Ackerman's (1988) theory of complex skill acquisition which suggests that early task performance will be influenced by general fluid intelligence (e.g., domain-specific perceptual speed) whereas later task performance will be driven by psychomotor abilities. Thus varying levels of task experience can be expected to require varying levels of WM capacity, regardless of whether one is dealing with cognitive or sensorimotor tasks.

By considering the various tasks and constructs to which WM capacity is related and the conditions under which WM capacity can be expected to exert its influence, it becomes apparent that there are many more situations in which WM capacity matters than in which it does not. Ericsson and Delaney (1999) argued that "WM is so central to human cognition that it is hard to find activities where it is not involved" (p. 259). For example, all novel problem-solving tasks or novel task components are likely to require controlled processing until practiced. Because WM capacity can be expected to influence initial task performance, it becomes necessary to address how WM capacity affects problem solving. In the sections that follow, we discuss what implications WM research has for problem solving and detail a line of research that has incorporated what we currently know about WM capacity limitations into instructional design.

IMPLICATIONS OF WORKING MEMORY RESEARCH FOR PROBLEM SOLVING

The discussion up to this point demonstrates that WM capacity can be expected to influence problem-solving performance for tasks or situations that require controlled processing, particularly those involving interference from previous problem-solving situations. This suggests that both instructional methods and the design of instructional materials should consider the role of WM capacity in problem solving. Two major efforts have been seen in this regard, with the introduction of Sweller's (1989) cognitive load theory (CLT) and Mayer's (2001) cognitive theory of multimedia learning. Each of these theories is based on the goal of designing instructional materials in such a way so as to reduce the learner's WM load and thereby increase understanding.

COGNITIVE LOAD THEORY

In 1989, Sweller introduced CLT, which takes what we know about the structures and functions of the human cognitive architecture and incorporates this knowledge into a set of guidelines about how best to present information to maximize learning. These guidelines are based on assumptions about the roles of LTM, WM, and WM capacity in how people learn, as well as assumptions about different factors that serve to increase or decrease various types of cognitive load (i.e., the amount of mental capacity being used; Sweller, 1989).

The Human Cognitive Architecture

CLT assumes that humans have a very limited WM capacity, but a large LTM. CLT adopts Baddeley's (1986) multicomponent model of WM, with the central executive, visuospatial sketchpad, and phonological rehearsal loop, and suggests that under certain conditions, WM capacity might be increased by utilizing both slave systems (visual and verbal) simultaneously rather than relying on one or the other (Tindall-Ford, Chandler, & Sweller, 1997). Increasing WM capacity is important because Sweller (1989) argued that, contrary to Miller's (1956) notion that we can handle five to nine items in WM, in reality humans are only capable of dealing with two to three items simultaneously if the items must be processed rather than just held in WM. If the items that are being processed in WM interact with each other in any way then this will require additional WM capacity and will serve to reduce further the number of elements or items that can be dealt with at the same time. CLT therefore posits that instructional materials can compensate for WM capacity limitations by taking advantage of our large LTM (Sweller, van Mërrienboer, & Paas, 1998).

LTM plays an important role in CLT by providing a way to overcome WM capacity limitations via the creation and storage of schemas. Schema formation allows many complex knowledge elements to be stored in LTM and worked on within WM as a single unit rather than many individual pieces of knowledge, thus bypassing WM capacity limitations and allowing more processing to occur. Schemas help organize and store the information in LTM, but also play a major role in the development of skilled performance, as individuals combine several lower level schemas into one higher level schema to ultimately build increasing numbers of increasingly complex schemas (Sweller et al., 1998). The notion that the way in which information is encoded in WM and stored in LTM (e.g., in the form of schemas) can interact to influence the development of skilled performance is consistent with models of WM that emphasize the contribution of LTM to everyday skilled performance (e.g., Ericsson & Kintsch's, 1995, long-term working memory model; see also Ericsson & Delaney, 1999).

Schema Construction and Working Memory Cognitive Load

Although schemas are stored in LTM, they are constructed based on controlled processing that occurs in WM (Sweller, 1989). CLT assumes that the effort one must exert to process the information in WM will depend both on the load that is imposed by the difficulty of the material itself, the *intrinsic* cognitive load, which is presumably unaffected by design manipulations, as well as the unnecessary or *extraneous* cognitive load imposed by poorly designed materials, which can be reduced by creating better instructional materials. *Germane* cognitive load can also be altered by design considerations, but reflects the effort that contributes to the construction of schemas. CLT therefore suggests that instructional materials should be designed to reduce extraneous cognitive load so as to free up capacity to apply toward germane cognitive load (Sweller et al., 1998).

The three types of cognitive load are additive in nature and combine to determine how difficult schema construction and ultimately learning will be for different types of instructional materials. Although both extraneous and germane cognitive load can be affected by design considerations, the intrinsic cognitive load imposed by materials depends on how many elements must be processed simultaneously in WM as well as how much element interactivity there is. When the elements can be learned or dealt with in isolation (e.g., solving a problem such as "Amy is shorter than Bobby. Bobby is shorter than Cory. Cory is shorter than Darren—Who is the shortest?"), there is low element interactivity and low cognitive load relative to materials or tasks that contain elements that must be processed simultaneously in WM to be understood (e.g., solving a problem such as "Amy, Bobby, Cory, and Darren are taking turns driving on a road trip. Each will drive one time and must drive in the following order—Amy must drive before Cory but after Darren. Darren must drive before Cory but after Bobby.—Who is the last to drive?"). Note that although both examples involve the same four people and are overly simplified examples of the analytical reasoning problems one might see in graduate or law school admissions tests, there is low element interactivity in the first problem because each comparison can be processed in isolation, whereas high element interactivity exists in the second problem because the driving orders must be processed and compared at the same time in WM to determine the answer to the problem. Similarly, Sweller and Chandler (1994) noted that learning a new language involves both low element interactivity (e.g., learning individual vocabulary words) and high element interactivity (e.g., learning how to combine multiple words to form a syntactically correct sentence). Therefore, regardless of whether the learning domain is reasoning or language, as in our examples, or math, science, engineering, or technology, learners presented with materials low in element interactivity might be able to manage higher levels of extraneous cognitive load relative to those given materials high in element interactivity. The more element interactivity there is, the more important it is that extraneous cognitive load is reduced so that overall cognitive load is kept manageable for the learner (Sweller et al., 1998).

Determining what amount of cognitive load should be manageable for a learner and what constitutes too much is a difficult proposition, however. The difficulty centers on the fact that one cannot estimate the level of element interactivity in instructional materials without taking into account the learners because what constitutes a large number of interacting elements for one person might be a single element for someone with more expertise. Intrinsic cognitive load thus depends not only on the nature of the materials, but also the expertise of the learners (Sweller et al., 1998).

Schema Automation and Expertise

One aspect that contributes to experts being able to handle higher item interactivity than novices is the process of schema automation. As discussed earlier in this chapter in the context of when WM capacity is irrelevant (or at least less important), automaticity occurs after extensive practice and allows familiar components of tasks to be carried out with minimal cognitive effort. This serves to free WM capacity, making it possible to perform unfamiliar tasks at levels that otherwise might be impossible were conscious processing necessary for all of the task components. So what initially is a schema with high item interactivity might, with practice, become automatized to the point that the schema is processed with little to no load on the WM system, thus freeing the learner to focus on other aspects of the task. In keeping with this idea, Ericsson and Kintsch (1995) suggested that preexisting domain knowledge can ease encoding and processing demands on WM when dealing with domain-relevant information. Results from a study conducted by Hambrick and Engle (2002) are also consistent with the idea that domain knowledge and WM capacity interact to determine how much element interactivity can be managed. They tested low and high WM capacity individuals' preexisting knowledge about baseball before presenting them with simulated radio broadcasts of baseball games such as the following excerpt:

> Gabriel Garcia, the number seven hitter in the lineup, is next to bat ... . Now Lawson delivers—and there goes the runner, and a groundball is hit into right field. That was perfect execution. The batter holds up at first base with a single, and here comes the throw to third base. The runner slides head first—and he's safe ... . Sam Philipe is the next batter of the inning ... .

The baseball task had high element interactivity as evinced by the number and types of things participants were instructed to keep track of while listening to the games (e.g., the number of outs, the score, which bases were occupied by which players), as well as the types of questions contained in the memory and comprehension tests (e.g., to correctly answer who struck out, which player was on third, and the score at the end of the inning required participants to simultaneously track, process, and update WM as changes occurred for multiple players in the game). Hambrick and Engle (2002) found that those with preexisting knowledge about baseball were better equipped to track changes in the games, as indicated by their test scores, but that WM capacity also influenced memory performance, regardless of the level of preexisting domain knowledge. These findings support the notion that schemas and domain knowledge (i.e., expertise) can serve to free up WM resources that are otherwise occupied in novices, thus enabling individuals with greater knowledge or greater WM capacity to handle more item interactivity (Sweller et al., 1998).

Although issues of expertise and schema automation create problems for calculating acceptable levels of cognitive load a priori, Paas and van Mërrienboer (1993) have created an a posteriori computation method in which performance and cognitive load values are converted to z scores to allow comparison of the mental efficiency of different instructional conditions. High task performance combined with low mental effort yields scores indicative of high-instructional efficiency whereas low task performance with high mental effort indicates low-instructional efficiency. Paas, Tuovinen, Tabbers, and Van Gerven (2003) suggested that this computational method provides a way to meaningfully interpret participants' cognitive load ratings in terms of their actual performance and thus compare different instructional design methods across a variety of tasks. The usefulness of such a tool becomes apparent when one considers that the major goal of CLT is to provide guidelines for the development of instructional methods that are high in instructional efficiency (Sweller et al., 1998). This goal is also the basis for Mayer's (2001) cognitive theory of multimedia learning.

MAYER'S (2001) COGNITIVE THEORY
OF MULTIMEDIA LEARNING

Mayer's (2001) cognitive theory of multimedia learning is based on the assumption that the human information processing system has two different channels, one for processing visual and pictorial information and the other for auditory and verbal processing, each of which has limited processing capabilities. The model assumes that active learning requires the learner to select and organize relevant words and images from text-narrations and illustrations before integrating them with prior knowledge. These assumptions of the cognitive theory of multimedia learning are the basis for several principles that Mayer argued should guide the design of multimedia instructional materials (i.e., those using both words [printed or spoken text] and pictures [e.g., static or dynamic graphics, illustrations, graphs, video, etc.]). These principles from Mayer's theory combine with suggestions derived from Sweller's (1989) CLT to yield a set of guidelines about how best to design and present instructional materials.

GUIDELINES FOR DESIGNING AND PRESENTING
INSTRUCTIONAL MATERIALS

The guidelines that stem from Mayer's (2001) cognitive theory of multimedia learning and Sweller's (1989) CLT are empirically based suggestions about the content, format, and presentation methods one should use when designing and presenting materials to yield better learning. Following, we summarize these suggestions by stating each guideline and then detailing the supporting research.

Guideline 1: Give Learners Problems That Do Not Specify a Goal State

This first guideline represents what Sweller et al. (1998) called the goal-free effect (also known as the no-goal effect or the reduced goal-specificity effect), which reflects the finding that giving learners problems that do not specify a goal state (i.e., goal-free problems) alters how the learners go about trying to solve them. Sweller et al. (1998) suggested that goal-free problems result in better schema acquisition and lower extraneous cognitive load because rather than trying to figure out and keep in mind differences between the current and goal problem states, as one might do using means-ends analysis in conventional problems, learners given goal-free problems tend to adopt a strategy of finding any operator that can be applied to the current problem state, and, in so doing, end up with the identical result obtained by those using the more cognitively overwhelming means-ends analysis. Sweller, Mawer, and Ward (1983) found that students given goal-free problems were superior to students given conventional kinematics and geometry problems in terms of schema construction. Similar results favoring goal-free problems have also been found using biology (Vollmeyer, Burns, & Holyoak, 1996) and trigonometry materials (Owen & Sweller, 1985).

In keeping with the idea that means-ends analysis results in greater WM load than goal-free problems, Ayres (1993) found that students given conventional two-step geometry problems made more errors at the subgoal phase than at the goal phase and rated their WM load highest at the subgoal phase because of the need to consider multiple elements in the problem at that point.

At odds with Ayres's findings, however, are the results of a series of studies conducted by Catrambone (1996, 1998) in which he examined the effect of manipulations designed to increase subgoal formation on problem-solving performance. Catrambone consistently found that learners given worked examples incorporating manipulations (e.g., labels and captions) designed to elicit self-explanation and subgoal formation had superior (i.e., more accurate) problem-solving performance, as assessed by near and far transfer tests, relative to those given worked examples without labels or captions.

Recently, Catrambone (2004) extended this line of work to examine the effect of labeling subgoals on cognitive load ratings. Participants were given paper-based study materials in the domain of physics mechanics and asked to study two worked examples after studying brief reviews of Newton's second law and trigonometry. Catrambone manipulated between-participants whether the subgoals were labeled or not in the two physics worked examples and collected cognitive load ratings once during the study phase and three times during the test phase (after completion of the near, medium, and far transfer test problems, respectively) to determine if highlighting subgoals would result in better performance, but perhaps at the expense of greater cognitive load either during training or testing. Contrary to Ayres (1993), Catrambone found that using labels designed to aid subgoal learning resulted in superior test performance on the medium and far transfer problems (ceiling effects were observed in both conditions on the near transfer problems) and lower cognitive load ratings during training and testing. This discrepancy in findings might be due to Ayres using conventional problems versus Catrambone's use of worked examples (i.e., the worked example effect) rather than subgoals per se.

Guideline 2: Give Learners Worked Examples Rather Than Conventional Problems to Solve

The finding that studying worked examples can be more beneficial than actually solving conventional problems has been called the worked example effect by Sweller et al. (1998). The advantage of worked examples seems to be due to the fact that worked examples help focus the learners' attention on the pertinent problem states and solution steps in the problem whereas conventional problems tend to result in the learner using means ends analysis (Sweller et al., 1998). Paas and van Mërrienboer (1994) found that students who studied geometry worked examples had higher transfer performance, lower extraneous cognitive load, and better schema construction than those given conventional problems. Moreover, using their mental efficiency computation method, Paas and van Mërrienboer found higher instructional efficiency in the worked examples condition than in the conventional problem condition. Sweller and Cooper (1985; see also Cooper & Sweller, 1987) found similar effects with algebra worked examples. Because worked examples have been found to be effective instructional tools, an ever-increasing body of research exists examining how to design good worked examples, a topic the next guideline addresses.

Guideline 3: Avoid Forcing the Learner to Integrate Separate Pieces of Information

This guideline is based on what Sweller et al. (1998) called the split-attention effect and is derived directly from the worked example effect. It is based on the finding that worked examples that force the learner to integrate separate pieces of information to understand the material can result in more cognitive load than studying well-integrated worked examples. The split attention effect occurs when the same worked example with physically integrated material results in superior performance and reduced cognitive load relative to studying nonintegrated worked examples (Sweller et al., 1998). Work by Tarmizi and Sweller (1988) provides an example of the split attention effect in that they initially failed to obtain the worked example effect and only observed it after switching from conventional (i.e., nonintegrated) geometry examples to examples in which the information was well integrated.

Similar in nature and rationale to the split attention effect (Sweller et al., 1998) are Mayer's (2001) spatial and temporal contiguity principles. The spatial contiguity principle suggests that students learn better and experience less cognitive load when corresponding words and pictures are presented near rather than far from each other on the page or screen (Moreno & Mayer, 1999). The temporal contiguity principle addresses the timing rather than the location of information presentation and states that students learn better and experience less cognitive load when corresponding words and pictures are presented simultaneously rather than sequentially because it obviates the need to hold multiple things in memory for processing. The split attention effect, spatial, and temporal contiguity principles combine to suggest that instructional materials should be designed to prevent the learner from having to try to hold in memory and integrate multiple pieces of information. However, if complete integration of materials cannot be addressed by location or spacing methods, it might be possible to deal with nonintegrated materials using dual modality presentation methods, a topic addressed by the fourth guideline.

Guideline 4: Present Materials Using Both Visual and Auditory Methods

Sweller et al. (1998) suggested that presenting materials both visually and auditorially can help compensate for split attention conditions when, for example, two pieces of visual information that would normally need to be physically integrated for understanding are instead combined by using both visual and auditory WM. Sweller et al. (1998) called this the modality effect, which is said to have occurred if presenting some information visually and some information auditorially results in better performance than using either the visual or auditory channel alone. Mayer (2001) suggested that the reason individuals learn better when two modalities are used rather than only one (e.g., an animation plus narration as opposed to an animation with on screen text), is because combining animations with narration utilizes both the visual and the verbal channels, whereas animations combined with on-screen text must both rely on the visual channel, which increases the likelihood that the visual channel will become overloaded and ignores the processing capacity available in the auditory channel. Experiments conducted by Mousavi, Low, and Sweller (1995) and Tindall-Ford et al. (1997) provided support for the modality effect in that both found lower cognitive load ratings when both audio and visual instructions were used than when only visual instructions were used, but only when the materials were high in element interactivity. The fact that the modality effect all but disappeared with low element interactivity materials supports the Sweller et al. (1998) claim that reductions in extraneous cognitive load via better designed instructional materials are most crucial when materials already have high intrinsic cognitive load.

Mayer (2001) argued that dual modality presentations not only help prevent WM overload, but are also more likely to induce learners to create verbal and pictorial mental models that may then be integrated for increased learning. This integration of the verbal and pictorial mental models might be facilitated due to the reduction of the effective WM load, through the use of multiple channels as suggested by CLT (Sweller et al., 1998). Mayer has named the improved learning that occurs when materials are presented with words and pictures, as opposed to words alone, the multimedia principle and cited multiple experiments in which he and his colleagues (e.g.,

Mayer & Anderson, 1991, 1992; Mayer & Gallini, 1990) have found that words and pictures resulted in better learning than words alone. Together the modality and multimedia principles suggest that combining visual and auditory presentation methods can serve to reduce WM load and increase learning. However, the benefits of dual modality presentations only hold true if the information presented in the two channels is not redundant and if extraneous, unnecessary information is removed from the materials to allow learners to focus on the relevant information. This caveat is the basis of the fifth guideline.

Guideline 5: Avoid Redundant and Irrelevant Sources of Information When Designing Instructional Materials

Sweller et al. (1998) and Mayer (2001) suggested that presenting learners with redundant information or multiple sources of information that are self-contained and can be used without reference to each other can result in WM overload and reduced learning. For example, learners given an animation and narration have been found to learn more than those given an animation, narration, and text because the additional text in the latter case is redundant with the narration and runs the risk of overloading the visual channel (Mayer, 2001). The redundancy effect is said to have occurred when students not given redundant information perform better and report lower cognitive load than students presented redundant information. However, what is redundant information for one individual (e.g., an expert) might be necessary for another (e.g., a novice) to understand a diagram or worked example. For example, McNamara, Kintsch, Singer, and Kintsch (1996) found redundancy effects for experienced learners but not for novice learners, which aligns with the Beilock et al. (2002) observation that "experienced performers suffer more than novices from conditions that call their attention to individual task components or elicit step-by-step monitoring and control" (p. 14). Once again, this suggests that it is necessary to consider the learners' level of knowledge when designing instructional materials.

Although the redundancy effect reflects the need to avoid duplicate sources of information, Mayer's (2001) coherence principle suggests detrimental effects on WM load and learning can also occur if instructional materials include extraneous information (e.g., interesting but irrelevant words, pictures, music, and sounds). Mayer suggested that the inclusion of irrelevant pictures or sounds only serves to increase WM load as well as the likelihood that the learner will fail to notice the important aspects of the lesson because his or her attention has been drawn away by this other interesting, but irrelevant, information (Moreno & Mayer, 2000). A series of four experiments conducted by Mayer, Heiser, and Lonn (2001) yielded consistent support for redundancy and coherence effects.

Such findings detail the need to develop well-designed materials that highlight the important information without drawing attention to other, unimportant or redundant information that can reduce learning and increase cognitive load. Mayer's (2001) individual differences principle suggests, however, that some types of learners are more likely to benefit from well-designed materials than others. Mayer posited that it is more important for instructional materials to be designed well for low knowledge individuals who lack the knowledge base that would allow them to compensate for poorly designed materials, than for high knowledge individuals, who may draw on their larger body of knowledge to make sense of the lesson. On the other hand, the principle states that design effects will not benefit low spatial learners who will be using all their WM capacity to hold images in WM, leaving no additional WM capacity resources to integrate the visual and verbal representations, but will help high spatial ability learners who will have enough WM capacity to handle both maintenance and integration. For these reasons, well-designed visual and verbal materials are expected to benefit low knowledge, high spatial ability learners more than high knowledge, low spatial ability learners (Mayer, 2001). So again we see that knowledge and ability levels interact with design and presentation methods to influence overall levels of WM (cognitive) load and learning.

An additional factor that interacts with design and presentation methods to influence learning is type of practice. Consistency in practice can facilitate learning but may also increase the likelihood of proactive interference (Woltz, Gardner, & Gyll, 2000). For example, Luchins's (1942) classic water jug experiment demonstrated that individuals given a series of arithmetic computation problems requiring the same sequence of water jug manipulations to obtain the correct answer had difficulty switching to a new sequence of operations to solve transfer problems. Woltz, Gardner, and Bell (2000) also observed proactive interference, or what they called *einstellung* or negative near transfer effects, in a number reduction tasks, when learners were given consistent practice with possible rule sequences necessary to solve the problems. Functional fixedness, the inability to view or use common objects in new ways (Maier, 1930, 1931), and strong-but-wrong errors, which occur when learners incorrectly apply well-practiced skills (Reason, 1990), ar other examples of proactive interference that may occur after consistent practice. These examples of proactive interference in problem solving a represent cases where consistent practice can have detrimental effects and WM capacity should be necessary to overcome the interference to produce accurate problem solving and transfer performance.

Sweller et al. (1998) suggested that one way to overcome these problems and enhance transfer performance is to give learners variability in practice. Variability in practice, whether the variability stems from the context in which the task is performed or how the task is presented, results in learners being better able to transfer what they have learned to novel tasks. Such variability produces an apparent paradox, however, because variability results in higher cognitive load ratings during practice than if type of practice is held constant, yet the variability results in better transfer performance. Paas and van Mërrienboer (1994) explained this paradox in terms of germane and extraneous cognitive load by hypothesizing and finding an interaction between the two types of cognitive load. They found that if extraneous cognitive load was high, then having variability during practice increased germane cognitive load to the point where learning and transfer performance were impaired. However, if extraneous cognitive load was low, then it was beneficial to transfer training to have variability during practice.

Together these five guidelines yield multiple ways to reduce WM load and increase learning by designing instructional materials that reduce extraneous cognitive load caused by poorly designed materials, thus freeing up WM to handle more germane cognitive load and schema construction. That each of these guidelines yields testable hypotheses has resulted in a large body of problem-solving research based wholly or in part on Sweller's (1989) CLT and Mayer's (2001) cognitive theory of multimedia learning. For example, aspects of the variability effect can be found in the research examining the effects of scaffolding on problem-solving ability. Renkl, Atkinson, Maier, and Staley's (2002; see also Atkinson, Renkl, & Merrill, 2003; Renkl & Atkinson, 2003) use of scaffolding to gradually move the learner from studying worked examples to eventually having the learner solve conventional problems represents one way of manipulating the variability of practice. By moving learners from worked examples to solving conventional problems after practice, the Renkl et al. (2002) scaffolding work also capitalizes on the worked example effect and the notion put forth by CLT (Sweller et al., 1998), that what is appropriate for novices might be inappropriate or redundant once expertise is achieved in a problem-solving domain. Thus multiple aspects of the Sweller et al. (1998) and Mayer (2001) theories play a role in scaffolding.

INTEGRATING WORKING MEMORY AND PROBLEM-SOLVING RESEARCH

Mayer's (2001) multimedia design principles, Sweller's (1989) CLT instructional design principles, and the body of research each has inspired are an important first step in integrating what we know about WM capacity limitations into instructional design methods. However, examination of the WM and problem-solving-instructional design literatures suggests several gaps and areas for future empirical research that should be addressed. For example, it seems that greater emphasis must be placed on explicating when and how expertise can be expected to interact with WM capacity and the different instructional design methods to influence learning. CLT (Sweller, 1989) addresses the role of schemas and automaticity, both of which are components of expertise, in overcoming WM limitations and element interactivity, and Mayer's (2001) individual differences principle suggests that novices are more likely to benefit from well-designed instructional materials than experts. However, neither theory leads to direct predictions about how their principles are likely to interact with varying levels of knowledge or WM capacity to influence learning other than to suggest that instructional design methods that benefit novices might prove detrimental to experts (Kalyuga, Ayres, Chandler, & Sweller, 2003; see also Kalyuga, Chandler, & Sweller, 1998; Kalyuga & Sweller, 2004). This lack of specificity is problematic in light of Hambrick and Engle's (2002) finding that domain knowledge and WM capacity each accounted for unique and varying levels of variance in the ability to recall information about simulated baseball games. This suggests it is not sufficient to know how much an individual knows about a topic or whether an individual has low or high WM capacity because each can be expected to contribute to task performance in a different way. Therefore, a clear delineation of which principles are effective for different knowledge and WM capacity levels will ultimately be needed before the CLT (Sweller, 1989; Sweller et al., 1998) and multimedia design (Mayer, 2001) principles can be maximally effective and useful for students and instructors.

A second issue that warrants further examination is how external and internal sources of pressure combine with WM capacity to influence performance, and whether any of the previously described design guidelines can be used to offset such sources of pressure. The WM research examining choking under pressure in math (Beilock & Carr, 2005; Beilock et al., 2004), life stressors (Klein & Boals, 2001), prejudice (Richeson & Shelton, 2003), stereotype threat (Schmader & Johns, 2003), and the problem-solving research investigating the effects of different aspects of instructional materials (e.g., number of elements and element interactivity) known to "pressure" and reduce WM capacity, all suggest that pressure can have deleterious effects on WM capacity or problem-solving performance. More disconcerting is the finding that pressure is most likely to negatively affect high WM capacity individuals who, under less stressful, less WM-demanding situations, would have superior problem-solving performance, relative to those with low WM capacity (Beilock & Carr, 2005). As Beilock and Carr (2005) noted, such findings have serious implications for the validity and interpretation of performance scores collected under highly stressful situations (e.g., Scholastic Assessment Test, Graduate Record Exam, Law School Admission Test, etc.) and raise questions about what scores on such measures represent (e.g., domain knowledge,

WM capacity, the effect of pressure on WM capacity). Questions such as these highlight the need for additional research into the various types of cognitive load (i.e., intrinsic, extraneous, and germane), the pressure each one induces (separately and together), and whether the multimedia design or CLT principles are in any way able to compensate for internal and external sources of pressure. For example, are there experimental manipulations that would "push" or alter intrinsic and germane cognitive load and how would such manipulations interact with WM capacity and situation-based pressure (see, e.g., Gerjets, Scheiter, & Catrambone, 2004)? Would training materials that emphasize learning subgoals increase germane cognitive load too much for a low WM span individual but be within acceptable WM load limits for a high span individual and would these acceptable limits vary as a function of internal and external sources of pressure (Catrambone, 2004)? In other words, do CLT (Sweller, 1989) and the cognitive theory of multimedia design (Mayer, 2001) need to include a "pressure principle" to account for the influence of pressure on WM capacity and problem-solving performance? Further research is necessary to see if the addition of such a principle is warranted.

Finally, although research has examined how CLT (Sweller, 1989) and multimedia design (Mayer, 2001) principles influence performance on cognitive tasks, it would seem worthwhile to also examine the usefulness of their application to the instruction of sensorimotor tasks. For example, would applying the principles stemming from the Sweller et al. (1998) modality and redundancy effects or Mayer's (2001) multimedia, spatial contiguity, and coherence principles to magazines, books, and videos designed to improve one's golf game result in one having a lower handicap? Although Ackerman's (1988) theory of complex skill acquisition and Beilock and colleagues' (Beilock & Carr, 2001; Beilock et al., 2002) findings of decreased reliance on controlled processing as sensorimotor skills develop suggest that the CLT (Sweller, 1989) and multimedia design (Mayer, 2001) principles might not apply once a skill has been acquired, it remains an empirical question whether the principles are useful in the "early" stages of sensorimotor skill acquisition.

These empirical questions will need to be addressed using a combination of methods, tasks, and manipulations commonly used in the WM and problem-solving literatures before we can definitively answer the question regarding when WM considerations can be expected to matter across different problem-solving tasks and learning environments. These literatures suggest a variety of factors that might influence WM capacity or problem-solving performance. However, until more research has been conducted to address the noted gaps, we are left with the speculation that, in problem solving and instructional design, WM capacity matters a lot, but research is needed to determine more precisely when it matters.

REFERENCES

Ackerman, P. L. (1988). Determinants of individual differences during skill acquisition: Cognitive abilities and information processing. *Journal of Experimental Psychology: General, 117*, 288–318.

Atkinson, R. C., & Shiffrin, R. M. (1968). Human memory: A proposed system and its control processes. In K. W. Spence & J. T. Spence (Eds.), *The psychology of learning and motivation: Advances in research and theory* (Vol. 2, pp. 89–195). New York: Academic.

Atkinson, R. K., Renkl, A., & Merrill, M. M. (2003). Transitioning from studying examples to solving problems: Effects of self-explanation prompts and fading worked-out steps. *Journal of Educational Psychology, 95*, 774–783.

Ayres, P. (1993). Why goal-free problems can facilitate learning. *Contemporary Educational Psychology,18*, 376–381.

Baddeley, A. D. (1986). *Working memory.* Oxford, England: Oxford University Press.

Baddeley, A. D. (2001). Is working memory still working? *American Psychologist, 56*, 849–864.

Baddeley, A. D., & Hitch, G. J. (1974). Working memory. In G. H. Bower (Ed.), *The psychology of learning and motivation: Advances in research and theory* (Vol. 8, pp.47–89). New York: Academic.

Baddeley, A. D., & Hitch, G. J. (1994). Developments in the concept of working memory. *Neuropsychology, 8*, 485–493.

Baddeley, A. D., & Logie, R. H. (1999). Working memory: The multiple-component model. In A. Miyake & P. Shah (Eds.), *Models of working memory: Mechanisms of active maintenance and executive control* (pp. 28–61). New York: Cambridge University Press.

Bayliss, D. M., Jarrold, C., Gunn, D. M., & Baddeley, A. D. (2003). The complexities of complex span: Explaining individual differences in working memory in children and adults. *Journal of Experimental Psychology: General, 132*, 71–92.

Beilock, S. L., & Carr, T. H. (2001). On the fragility of skilled performance: What governs choking under pressure? *Journal of Experimental Psychology: General, 130*, 701–725.

Beilock, S. L., & Carr, T. H. (2005). When high-powered people fail: Working memory and "choking under pressure" in math. *Psychological Science, 16*, 101–105.

Beilock, S. L., Carr, T. H., MacMahon, C., & Starkes, J. L. (2002). When paying attention becomes counterproductive: Impact of divided versus skill-focused attention on novice and experienced performance of sensorimotor skills. *Journal of Experimental Psychology: Applied, 8*, 6–16.

Beilock, S. L., Kulp, C. A., Holt, L. E., & Carr, T. H. (2004). More on the fragility of performance: Choking under pressure in mathematical problem solving. *Journal of Experimental Psychology, 133*, 584–600.

Benton, S. L., Kraft, R. G., Glover, J. A., & Plake, B. S. (1984). Cognitive capacity differences among writers. *Journal of Educational Psychology, 76*, 820–834.

Cantor, J., & Engle, R. W. (1993). Working memory capacity as long-term memory activation: An individual differences approach. *Journal of Experimental Psychology: Learning, Memory, and Cognition, 19*, 1101–1114.

Carlson, R. A., Khoo, B. H., Yaure, R. G., & Schneider, W. (1990). Acquisition of a problem-solving skill: Levels of organization and use of working memory. *Journal of Experimental Psychology: General, 119*, 193–214.

Carlson, R. A., Sullivan, M. A., & Schneider, W. (1989). Practice and working memory effects in building procedural skill. *Journal of Experimental Psychology: Learning, Memory, and Cognition, 15*, 517–526.

Catrambone, R. (1996). Generalizing solution procedures learned from examples. *Journal of Experimental Psychology: Learning, Memory, and Cognition, 22,* 1020–1031.

Catrambone, R. (1998). The subgoal learning model: Creating better examples so that students can solve novel problems. *Journal of Experimental Psychology: General, 127,* 355–376.

Catrambone, R. (2004, November). *Subgoal learning reduces cognitive load during training and problem solving.* Paper presented at the 45th annual meeting of the Psychonomic Society, Minneapolis, MN.

Cattell, R. B. (1963). Theory of fluid and crystallized intelligence: A critical experiment. *Journal of Educational Psychology, 54,* 1–22.

Colom, R., Rebollo, I., Palacios, A., Juan-Espinosa, M., & Kyllonen, P. C. (2004). Working memory is (almost) perfectly predicted by *g*. *Intelligence, 32,* 277–296.

Colom, R., & Shih, P. C. (2004). Is working memory fractionated onto different components of intelligence? A reply to Mackintosh and Bennett (2003). *Intelligence, 32,* 431–444.

Conway, A. R. A., Cowan, N., Bunting, M. F., Therriault, D. J., & Minkoff, S. R. B. (2002). A latent variable analysis of working memory capacity, short-term memory capacity, processing speed, and general fluid intelligence. *Intelligence, 30,* 163–183.

Cooper, G., & Sweller, J. (1987). The effects of schema acquisition and rule automation on mathematical problem-solving transfer. *Journal of Educational Psychology, 79,* 347–362.

Daneman, M., & Carpenter, P. A. (1980). Individual differences in working memory and reading. *Journal of Verbal Learning and Verbal Behavior, 18,* 450–466.

Daneman, M., & Carpenter, P. A. (1983). Individual differences in integrating information between and within sentences. *Journal of Experimental Psychology: Learning, Memory, and Cognition, 9,* 561–584.

Daneman, M., & Green, I. (1986). Individual differences in comprehending and producing words in context. *Journal of Memory and Language, 25,* 1–18.

Daneman, M., & Merikle, P. M. (1996). Working memory and comprehension: A meta-analysis. *Psychonomic Bulletin and Review, 3,* 422–433.

Engle, R. W., Cantor, J., & Carullo, J. J. (1992). Individual differences in working memory and comprehension: A test of four hypotheses. *Journal of Experimental Psychology: Learning, Memory, and Cognition, 18,* 972–992.

Engle, R. W., Carullo, J. J., & Collins, K. W. (1991). Individual differences in working memory for comprehension and following directions. *Journal of Educational Research, 84,* 253–262.

Engle, R. W., & Kane, M. J. (2004). Executive attention, working memory capacity, and a two-factor theory of cognitive control. In B. Ross (Ed.), *The psychology of learning and motivation,* (Vol. 44, pp. 145–199). New York: Academic.

Engle, R. W., Kane, M. J., & Tuholski, S. W. (1999). Individual differences in working memory capacity and what they tell us about controlled attention, general fluid intelligence, and functions of the prefrontal cortex. In A. Miyake & P. Shah (Eds.), *Models of working memory: Mechanisms of active maintenance and executive control* (pp. 102–134). New York: Cambridge University Press.

Engle, R. W., Nations, J. K., & Cantor, J. (1990). Is "working memory capacity" just another name for word knowledge? *Journal of Educational Psychology, 82,* 799–804.

Engle, R. W., Tuholski, S. W., Laughlin, J. E., & Conway, A. R. A. (1999). Working memory, short-term memory, and general fluid intelligence: A latent-variable approach. *Journal of Experimental Psychology: General, 128,* 309–331.

Ericsson, K. A., & Delaney, P. F. (1999). Long-term working memory as an alternative to capacity models of working memory in everyday skilled performance. In A. Miyake & P. Shah (Eds.), *Models of working memory: Mechanisms of active maintenance and executive control* (pp. 257–297). New York: Cambridge University Press.

Ericsson, K. A., & Kintsch, W. (1995). Long-term working memory. *Psychological Review, 102,* 211–245.

Feldman Barrett, L., Tugade, M. M.. & Engle, R. W. (2004). Individual differences in working memory capacity and dual-process theories of the mind. *Psychological Bulletin, 130,* 553–573.

Gerjets, P., Scheiter, K., & Catrambone, R. (2004). Designing instructional examples to reduce intrinsic cognitive load: Molar versus modular presentation of solution procedures. *Instructional Science, 32,* 33–58.

Gimmig, D., Huguet, P., Caverni, J. P., & Cury, F. (2005). *Choking under pressure and working memory capacity: When performance pressure reduces fluid intelligence (Gf).* Manuscript submitted for publication.

Hambrick, D. Z., & Engle, R. W. (2002). Effects of domain knowledge, working memory capacity, and age on cognitive performance: An investigation of the knowledge-is-power hypothesis. *Cognitive Psychology, 44,* 339–387.

Hambrick, D. Z., & Engle, R. W. (2003). The role of working memory in problem solving. In J. E. Davidson & R. J. Sternberg (Eds.), *The psychology of problem solving* (pp. 176–206). London: Cambridge University Press.

Hambrick, D. Z., Kane, M. J., & Engle, R. W. (2005). The role of working memory in higher-level cognition: Domain-specific versus domain-general perspectives. In R. J. Sternberg & J. E. Pretz (Eds.), *Cognitive intelligence: Identifying the mechanisms of the mind* (pp.104–121). London: Cambridge University Press.

Kalyuga, S., Ayres, P., Chandler, P., & Sweller, J. (2003). The expertise reversal effect. *Educational Psychologist, 38,* 23–31.

Kalyuga, S., Chandler, P., & Sweller, J. (1998). Levels of expertise and instructional design. *Human Factors, 40,* 1–17.

Kalyuga, S., & Sweller, J. (2004). Measuring knowledge to optimize cognitive load factors during instruction. *Journal of Educational Psychology, 96,* 558–568.

Kane, M. J., Bleckley, M. K., Conway, A. R. A., & Engle, R. W. (2001). A controlled-attention view of working-memory capacity. *Journal of Experimental Psychology: General, 130,* 169–183.

Kane, M. J., & Engle, R. W. (2000). Working-memory capacity, proactive interference, and divided attention: Limits on long-term memory retrieval. *Journal of Experimental Psychology: Learning, Memory, and Cognition, 26,* 336–358.

Kane, M. J., & Engle, R. W. (2002). The role of prefrontal cortex in working-memory capacity, executive attention, and general fluid intelligence: An individual-differences perspective. *Psychonomic Bulletin & Review, 9,* 637–671.

Kane, M. J., & Engle, R. W. (2003). Working memory capacity and the control of attention: The contributions of goal neglect, response competition, and task set to Stroop interference. *Journal of Experimental Psychology: General, 132,* 47–70.

Kane, M. J., Hambrick, D. Z., Tuholski, S. W., Wilhelm, O., Payne, T. W., & Engle, R. W. (2004). The generality of working-memory capacity: A latent-variable approach to verbal and visuospatial memory span and reasoning. *Journal of Experimental Psychology: General, 133,* 189–217.

Kiewra, K. A., & Benton, S. L. (1988). The relationship between information-processing ability and notetaking. *Contemporary Educational Psychology, 13,* 33–44.

Klein, K., & Boals, A. (2001). The relationship of life event stress and working memory capacity. *Applied Cognitive Psychology, 15,* 565–579.

Kyllonen, P. C., & Christal, R. E. (1990). Reasoning ability is (little more than) working-memory capacity? *Intelligence, 14,* 389–433.

Kyllonen, P. C., & Stephens, D. L. (1990). Cognitive abilities as determinants of success in acquiring logic skill. *Learning and Individual Differences, 2,* 129–160.

Lee, M. J., & Tedder, M. C. (2003). The effects of three different computer texts on readers' recall: Based on working memory capacity. *Computers in Human Behavior, 19,* 767–783.

Luchins, A. S. (1942). Mechanization in problem solving: The effect of *Einstellung. Psychological Monographs, 54*(6), 1–95.

Mackintosh, N. J., & Bennett, E. S. (2003). The fractionation of working memory maps onto different components of intelligence. *Intelligence, 31,* 519–531.

Maier, N. R. F. (1930). Reasoning in humans: I. On direction. *Journal of Comparative Physiological Psychology, 10,* 115–143.

Maier, N. R. F. (1931). Reasoning in humans: II. The solution of a problem and its appearance in consciousness. *Journal of Comparative Physiological Psychology, 12,* 181–194.

Mayer, R. E. (2001). *Multimedia learning.* New York: Cambridge University Press.

Mayer, R. E., & Anderson, R. B. (1991). Animations need narrations: An experimental test of a dual-condition hypothesis. *Journal of Educational Psychology, 83,* 484–490.

Mayer, R. E., & Anderson, R. B. (1992). The instructive animation: Helping students build connections between words and pictures in multimedia learning. *Journal of Educational Psychology, 84,* 444–452.

Mayer, R. E., & Gallini, J. K. (1990) When is an illustration worth ten thousand words? *Journal of Educational Psychology, 82,* 715–726.

Mayer, R. E., Heiser, J., & Lonn, S. (2001). Cognitive constraints on multimedia learning: When presenting more material results in less understanding. *Journal of Educational Psychology, 93,* 187–198.

McNamara, D., Kintsch, E., Singer, N. B., & Kintsch, W. (1996). Are good texts always better? Interactions of text coherence, background knowledge, and levels of understanding in learning from text. *Cognition and Instruction, 14,* 1–43.

Miller, G. A. (1956). The magical number seven, plus or minus two: Some limits on our capacity for processing information. *Psychological Review, 63,* 81–97.

Moreno, R., & Mayer, R. E. (1999). Cognitive principles of multimedia learning: The role of modality and contiguity. *Journal of Educational Psychology, 91,* 358–368.

Moreno, R., & Mayer, R. E. (2000). A coherence effect in multimedia learning: The case for minimizing irrelevant sounds in the design of multimedia instructional messages. *Journal of Educational Psychology, 92,* 117–125.

Mousavi, S. Y., Low, R., & Sweller, J. (1995). Reducing cognitive load by mixing auditory and visual presentation modes. *Journal of Educational Psychology, 87,* 319–334.

Norman, D. A., & Shallice, T. (1986). *Attention to action: Willed and automatic control of behavior* (Report No. 8006). San Diego: University of California Center for Human Information Processing.

Ormrod, J. E., & Cochran, K. F. (1988). Relationship of verbal ability and working memory to spelling achievement and learning to spell. *Reading Research & Instruction, 28*(1), 33–43.

Owen, E., & Sweller, J. (1985). What do students learn while solving mathematics problems? *Journal of Educational Psychology, 77,* 272–284.

Paas, F., Tuovinen, J. E., Tabbers, J., & Van Gerven, P. W. M. (2003). Cognitive load measurement as a means to advance cognitive load theory. *Educational Psychologist, 38,* 63–71.

Paas, F., & van Mërrienboer, J. J. G. (1993). The efficiency of instructional conditions: An approach to combine mental effort and performance measures. *Human Factors, 35,* 737–743.

Paas, F., & van Mërrienboer, J. J. G. (1994). Variability of worked examples and transfer of geometrical problem solving skills: A cognitive load approach. *Journal of Educational Psychology, 86,* 122–133.

Pratt, M. W., Boyes, C., Robins, S., & Manchester, J. (1989). Telling tales: Aging, working memory, and the narrative cohesion of story retellings. *Developmental Psychology, 25,* 628–635.

Reason, J. T. (1990). *Human error.* Cambridge, England: Cambridge University Press.

Reber, P. J., & Kotovsky, K. (1997). Implicit learning in problem solving: The role of working memory capacity. *Journal of Experimental Psychology: General, 126,* 178–203.

Renkl, A., & Atkinson, R. K. (2003). Structuring the transition from example study to problem solving in cognitive skill acquisition: A cognitive load perspective. *Educational Psychologist, 38,* 15–22.

Renkl, A., Atkinson, R. K., Maier, U. H., & Staley, R. (2002). From example study to problem solving: Smooth transitions help learning. *The Journal of Experimental Education, 70,* 293–315.

Richeson, J. A., & Shelton, J. N. (2003). When prejudice does not pay: Effects of interracial contact on executive function. *Psychological Science, 14,* 287–290.

Rosen, V. M., & Engle, R. W. (1997). The role of working memory capacity in retrieval. *Journal of Experimental Psychology: General, 126,* 211–227.

Schmader, T., & Johns, M. (2003). Converging evidence that stereotype threat reduces working memory capacity. *Journal of Personality and Social Psychology, 85,* 440–452.

Schweizer, K., & Moosbrugger, H. (2004). Attention and working memory as predictors of intelligence. *Intelligence, 32,* 329–347.

Stroop, J. R. (1935). Studies of interference in serial verbal reactions. *Journal of Experimental Psychology, 18,* 643–662.

Sweller, J. (1989). Cognitive technology: Some procedures for facilitating learning and problem solving in mathematics and science. *Journal of Educational Psychology, 81,* 457–466.

Sweller, J., & Chandler, P. (1994). Why some material is difficult to learn. *Cognition and Instruction, 12,* 185–233.

Sweller, J., & Cooper, G. A. (1985). The use of worked examples as a substitute for problem solving in learning algebra. *Cognition and Instruction, 2,* 59–89.

Sweller, J., Mawer, R., & Ward, M. (1983). Development of expertise in mathematical problem solving. *Journal of Experimental Psychology: General, 112,* 634–656.

Sweller, J., van Mërrienboer , J. J. G., & Paas, F. G. W. C. (1998). Cognitive architecture and instructional design. *Educational Psychology Review, 10,* 251–296.

Tarmizi, R., & Sweller, J. (1988). Guidance during mathematical problem solving. *Journal of Educational Psychology, 80,* 424–436.

Tindall-Ford, S., Chandler, P., & Sweller, J. (1997). When two sensory modes are better than one. *Journal of Experimental Psychology: Applied, 3,* 257–287.

Turner, M. L., & Engle, R. W. (1989). Is working memory capacity task dependent? *Journal of Memory and Language, 28,* 127–154.

Vollmeyer, R., Burns, B. D., & Holyoak, K. J. (1996). The impact of goal specificity on strategy use and the acquisition of problem structures. *Cognitive Science, 20,* 75–100.

Woltz, D. J., Gardner, M. K., & Bell, B. G. (2000). Negative transfer errors in sequential cognitive skills: Strong-but-wrong sequence application. *Journal of Experimental Psychology: Learning, Memory, and Cognition, 26,* 601–625.

Woltz, D. J., Gardner, M. K., & Gyll, S. P. (2000). The role of attention processes in near transfer of cognitive skills. *Learning and Individual Differences, 12,* 209–252.

Chapter 4

Keeping All the Plates Spinning: Understanding and Predicting Multitasking Performance

Frederick L. Oswald
David Z. Hambrick
Michigan State University

L. Andrew Jones
Navy Personnel Research, Studies, and Technology

As indicated by a recent Google® search with over 8,700,000 hits, *multitasking* is clearly a popular term today, perhaps because it (increasingly) captures the type of work and home environments found in modern society. The term also surfaces in the organizational research literature, often within the paradigm of a "changing world of work" (e.g., Ilgen & Pulakos, 1999), and in the cognitive psychology literature when discussing limitations or bottlenecks in human information processing (e.g., Tombu & Jolicoeur, 2005). But regardless of whether the context of a discussion on multitasking is colloquial or academic, the term appears to carry multiple definitions and therefore multiple implications. In some instances, multitasking implies cases where individuals are navigating the chaos of a situation. Cooking breakfast while watching a snippet of a news program on TV and holding a conversation with your children before they take the bus to school—all more or less at the same time—might be one example to which you can relate. In other instances, multitasking can imply the goal of efficiency in producing desired outcomes: A person answering e-mails and phone calls simultaneously may hope to perform more work in a given day than by performing both tasks in serial order. Finally, multitasking can be thought of as a trait: Some people seem to perform consistently well across a variety of multitasking situations, whereas others tend not to perform well at all and may benefit more from training interventions tailored to a specific problem. Our work is broader than any one definition or perspective on multitasking; it attempts to create a theoretical framework that encapsulates both individual and situational characteristics as they relate to multitasking, because in general, research evidences strong support for the influence of both individual and situational characteristics on human behavior (Hattrup & Jackson, 1996; Magnusson & Endler, 1977).

ORGANIZATION OF THE CHAPTER

The chapter is organized as follows: First, we offer a broad definition of multitasking performance and raise important considerations related to this definition. Second, we outline the many task and environmental characteristics that potentially influence multitasking performance in critical ways. Third, specific cognitive and noncognitive variables are identified as prime candidates for predicting multitasking performance, and specific research-based predictions follow. Fourth, related to the previous point, we summarize our initial empirical work on multitasking, based on college-student participants who engaged in a computerized task. Fifth, we conclude by suggesting several avenues for conducting future research on multitasking performance.

TOWARD A DEFINITION OF MULTITASKING

Our broad definition of multitasking performance is informed by several important contributions from the literature on job performance in organizations, a literature that has made meaningful advances over the past 15 years. *Job performance* has been defined, and widely accepted by scholars in organizational research, as behaviors within an individual's control that contribute to outcomes valued by the organization (Campbell, McCloy, Oppler, & Sager, 1993). Because this volume is concerned with problem-solving performance of students, let's apply this definition to the axample of grade point average (GPA), a common benchmark of student performance. GPA is a deficient measure with respect to this definition of job performance in two major ways. First, GPA tends to be a rather distal indicator of actual student performance (albeit a very important one). In other words, GPA is a performance measure that is subject to many factors out of a student's control, such as any caprices in how the instructor assigns grades, the performance of a student relative to other students in a particular class, and the type of questions that the instructor decided to select for a test. To the extent that factors such as these affect students or classrooms differently, GPA would be a distortion of actual levels of performance. Second, GPA by definition is an aggregate index, meaning it is possible that two students obtaining the same GPA underwent completely different routes in getting there. GPA is thus a global indicator of student performance that is likely to mask important content and processes related to actual student performance (Oswald, Schmitt, Kim, Ramsay, & Gillespe, 2004). Both of the aforementioned deficiencies apply to almost any other measure of performance, such as supervisory ratings of job performance.

Although it may never be possible to eliminate such deficiencies entirely, we have remained mindful of them in selecting our own measures of multitasking performance. It is important to acknowledge that external factors out of the individual's control may affect measures of multitasking performance, and these factors are distinct from multitasking performance itself. To the extent that such factors interact with individual multitasking performance, they should be measured and empirically taken into consideration. Although any practical and useful measure of multitasking performance may out of necessity reflect an aggregate of individual behaviors, it cannot aggregate too much without potentially sacrificing valuable information regarding these processes.

Determinants of Multitasking Performance

In addition to past research defining job performance as being tied directly to individual behavior, performance has been defined as a function of three—and only three—determinants (see Campbell, Gasser, & Oswald, 1996). These also apply to multitasking performance in a straightforward manner. The first determinant, *declarative knowledge*, refers to an individual's storehouse of performance-relevant facts, whereas the second determinant, *procedural knowledge*, refers to an individual's past behaviors that are related to performance, either directly or indirectly. Although declarative knowledge contains the building blocks for developing procedural knowledge, skilled performers who have procedural knowledge may not be able to articulate the declarative knowledge that contributes to their performance; they only do so retrospectively when asked, but not while actually performing (e.g., children who can snow ski, calculating prodigies who can instantly take cube roots of numbers). The third determinant, *motivation*, comprises the direction, frequency, and intensity of performance-related behavior. We know that high school students, for example, vary widely in their motivation levels. At any given point in time, students can choose to engage in solving a problem-solving task—or they can choose not to (direction). Across time, students can choose to revisit a task and keep working to make progress on it—or they can choose not to (frequency); and even when students are engaged in a task, they can concentrate and work hard on it—or they can choose not to (intensity). If it is an axiom that performance reflects behaviors in control of the individual, then changes in performance over time must occur through a shift in emphasis or proportions of these three determinants. For instance, declarative knowledge can surge when individuals undergo formal training, procedural knowledge can be shaped implicitly through feedback concerning performance successes and failures over time, and motivation can increase (or be reduced) by observing the performance of similar peers.

Defining Multitasking Performance

Refined definitions of job performance are relatively recent in the organizational literature, at least compared with the century-long scientific interest in complex task performance within workplace settings. Hugo Münsterberg, one of the forefathers of organizational psychology, was interested in individual differences as predictors of accidents in electric streetcar operators. In his creation of one of the first work simulations in an experimental setting, for use in personnel selection, he noted the following:

> The test of the method lies first in the fact that the tried motormen agreed that they really pass through the experiment with the feeling which they have on their car. The necessity of looking out in both directions, right and left, for possible obstacles, of distinguishing those which move toward the track from the many which move along the track, the quick discrimination among the various rates of rapidity, the steady forward movement of the observation point, the constant temptation to give attention to those which are still too far away or to those which are so near that they will cross the track before the approach of the car, in short, the whole complex situation with its demands on attention, imagination, and quick adjustment, soon brings them into an attitude which they themselves feel as identical with that in practical life. (Münsterberg, 1913, pp. 74–75)

Sarting with Münsterberg, we follow a long line of researchers who have demonstrated an interest in studying complex task performance, as we seek to understand and predict multitasking performance in real-world scenarios. We argue that evaluating whether a problem-solving or work environment is a true multitasking environment involves gathering information on three key points. Acquiring information relevant to these three points may be quite difficult, but is well worth any time devoted to them.

The first point seems almost circular at first glance: multitasking requires performing multiple tasks. This is simple enough, but what is a task, and what is the most appropriate way to make distinctions between one task and another? We argue that task distinctions should be made on the basis of the following features, or some combination thereof: (a) the physical nature of the tasks (e.g., different equipment is used or different processes are involved), (b) the real and perceived demands placed on individuals performing the tasks (e.g., what ability or personality characteristics predict performance in each task), (c) the outcomes of the tasks (e.g., performance outcomes on the tasks correlate less than 1.0 at the latent level), and (d) the performers' perceptions of the tasks as separable (e.g., expert performers might view many subtasks as one overall task, whereas novice performers may view the subtasks as separate tasks).

The second point is that multitasking performance does not simply require multiple tasks; performance requires a conscious shifting from one task to another. Tasks may appear simultaneous (e.g., listening to the radio while driving a car), but we argue that multitasking occurs when attention shifts across tasks. Whether such shifting is simple or difficult depends on the amount and type of attentional resources that are devoted to each task. Tasks that can be performed relatively automatically tend to rely on an individual's procedural knowledge and require fewer attentional resources (Ackerman, 1987; Hasher & Zacks, 1977); such tasks are therefore more amenable to easier and more coordinated task shifting than tasks that are unpredictable or whose rules are constantly changing.

The third point is that performance on multiple tasks, with shifts in attention, must occur over a short time span. To form a judgment about whether the time span across which tasks are performed is short, one might obtain (a) objective information, such as the length of time required in executing each task, the intervals in between transitioning from one task to another, or the number of instances per unit time that a performer returns to a specific task; and (b) subjective information, such as measures of individuals' perception of pace in moving from one task to another or by having incumbents with job experience rate the job environment comprising multiple tasks on the extent to which performance requires multitasking ability.

Given these three points we feel are essential to a definition of multitasking, there are many nonessentials. Here are but a few examples:

1. Multitasking individuals may or may not return to a task that was previously performed.
2. They may or may not complete the tasks in which they are engaged, although rewards for multitasking performance may often be contingent on completion of some or all of the tasks.
3. Tasks may or may not accomplish the same goals. In fact, some tasks may be viewed as distractions that cannot be avoided (see Table 4.1).

TABLE 4.1

Task Features in Individual Multitasking Performance

Task Characteristics

  Physical (modality, visual similarity)

  Psychological (pleasant, fatiguing)

  Complexity (simple vs. complex, detailed vs. general)

  Novelty (unique features, changing features)

Task Structure

  Number of tasks (many vs. few)

  Ordering (sequential vs. simultaneous)

  Interdependence (independent vs. interdependent)

  Importance of tasks (constant vs. variable importance, goal-relevant vs. distracting)

Task Timing

  Pace (self-driven vs. task-driven, predictable vs. unpredictable)

  Response demand (serial vs. parallel, alternating vs. random)

Task Control

  Task flexibility (able to be rearranged, restructured, or supplemented)

  Task execution (scripted vs. unscripted)

  Temporal presentation (simultaneous vs. serial)

  Task facilitators or limiters (e.g., signs or alarms that guide behavior, computer output that takes too long to read)

  Environmental facilitators or limiters (quiet vs. loud noise, adequate vs. dim lighting, no odors vs. strong odors)

Task Outcomes

  Feedback (content, structure, timing; specific task feedback or overall multitasking feedback)

  Reward (content, structure, timing; specific task reward or overall multitasking reward)

4. Individuals may perform tasks in what seems to be a simultaneous manner, particularly when they are cross-modal (e.g., visual and auditory; Wickens, Mountford, & Schreiner, 1981), or there may be more obvious shifting between tasks.

It is also theoretically interesting and practically important to note that the same multitasking situation can yield very different individual responses: What one person may perceive as interesting and exciting, another person may view as threatening and stressful. Empirical research could investigate how multitasking traits relate to a wide variety of important outcomes. For instance, individuals who enjoy—and thrive within—multitasking environments might deliberately construct their work and home environments to involve multitasking; conversely, individuals who tend to dislike and perform poorly at multitasking might instead structure their environments to facilitate concentration and execution of one task at a time. Both experimental and correlational research could fruitfully bring empirical evidence to bear on issues such as these.

RELATING MULTITASKING TO ABILITY, PERSONALITY, AND MOTIVATIONAL DETERMINANTS

The remainder of this chapter describes some preliminary results that led to a program of research in collaboration with the Navy Personnel Research, Studies, and Technology (NPRST) laboratory. The ultimate aim of this research is to measure multitasking performance in high-fidelity simulations of Navy jobs, such as radar monitoring, and to identify and operationalize relevant individual differences. However, as a starting point, we adopted a task that was designed by Elsmore (1994) to capture basic aspects of individual multitasking for many different jobs instead of a single job. This "synthetic work" task, illustrated in Figure 4.1, comprises four component tasks that are presented simultaneously. In *memory search* (upper left), after a set of letters is presented and then covered, participants must verify whether periodically presented probe letters were from this set; clicking the mouse arrow on the cover reveals the letter set again, but doing so carries a point penalty. In *arithmetic*, participants are to add two-digit or three-digit numbers together correctly. In *visual monitoring*, a needle moves

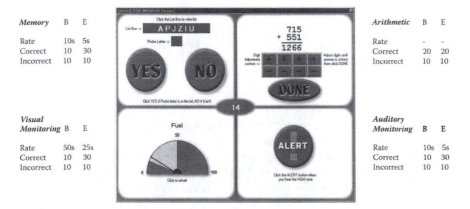

Figure 4.1.   Synthetic work: Tasks, rate, and payoffs in baseline (B) and emergency (E) conditions.

from right to left across a gauge, and the task is to click on the gauge and re-set the needle before it reaches zero; participants receive more points for the needle being as close to zero as possible, but they lose points propor-tional to the length of time the needle stays at zero. Finally, in *auditory moni-toring*, the task is to respond to a higher pitch target tone and to ignore a lower pitch distracter tone. Obviously, SynWin is not a simulation of any particular real-world task. However, from the standpoint of studying multitasking scientifically, key advantages of this platform are that task dif-ficulty and task payoffs can be flexibly altered and that it requires no special skills or prior knowledge.

Predictions

Research has established a strong relation between performance in multitasking paradigms and performance in standard tests of intelligence. In fact, evidence suggests that multitasking ability is highly related to general in-telligence (e.g., Brookings, 1990). Research has further established a strong re-lation between measures of general intelligence (g) and measures of working memory capacity, defined as the ability to store and process information simul-taneously. In fact, research has suggested that working memory is the central component underlying variation in g (e.g., Engle & Kane, 2004). Results of a study by Kane et al. (2004) are illustrative. In this study, participants completed six "complex span" tasks to assess working memory capacity. Each task was es-sentially a dual-task. For example, in a task called reading span, each trial con-sisted of a sentence-word pair. The task was to verify whether the sentence makes sense and to remember the word. In addition, participants completed 12 tests of abstract reasoning and spatial visualization to assess psychometric g. The major finding of this study was that a working memory factor comprising the complex span tasks correlated strongly with a g factor ($r > .60$).

On the basis of this evidence, we predicted that measures of cognitive ability would positively predict synthetic work performance. Of more inter-est was the possible contribution of noncognitive factors. Everyday observa-tion suggests that one factor that may predict success in environments that require multitasking (e.g., the workplace) is the ability to keep a "cool head"—particularly under time pressure. In more scientific terms, our speculation is that a critical determinant of multitasking success is the abil-ity to effectively regulate anxiety or arousal during task performance. This speculation stems out of an extensive literature documenting the relation between arousal and complex task performance (see Proctor & Dutta, 1995, for a review). The basic finding from that body of research was captured by the Yerkes-Dodson Law nearly 100 years ago: A "middle" level of arousal leads to optimal task performance; underarousal and overarousal lead to suboptimal task performance (Yerkes & Dodson, 1908; see Fig. 4.2).

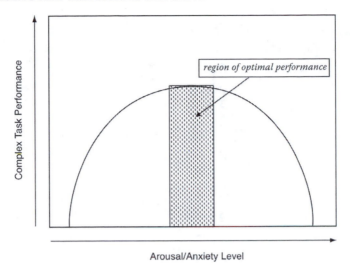

Figure 4.2.   Hypothetical anxiety-performance relation (Yerkes-Dodson Law).

We therefore predicted that measures assumed to reflect anxiety would also emerge as significant predictors of multitasking performance. More specifically, we hypothesized that neuroticism—a broad dimension of personality that encompasses susceptibility to experiencing anxiety—would predict individuals' performance in the synthetic work task, more so in the "routine" (or baseline) condition than in the "emergency" condition. This may seem counterintuitive at first glance, but under "emergency" conditions, multitasking is made more difficult by greatly increasing the pace of the component tasks, and thus everyone should be more anxious when multitasking—not just those higher in neuroticism. Thus, the correlation between neuroticism and performance should be negative in the routine condition and slightly negative or near-zero in the emergency condition.

These predictions motivate the rationale for the empirical study that follows. However, we should also point out that the ability and nonability variables targeted for this study are part of a more general conceptual model for predicting multitasking performance. Figure 4.3 illustrates the model that we are in the process of developing further. Here, the three major determinants of job performance reside at the center, serving as the prime mediators residing between individual multitasking performance—the dependent variable of interest—and a complement of ability and nonability variables that we have identified as theoretically relevant predictors. At its essence, our model is aligned with other integrative models of individual differences and performance that incorporate anxiety, motivation, person-

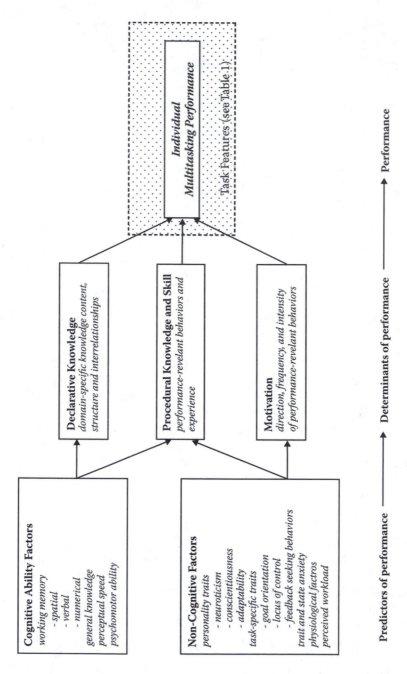

Figure 4.3. General conceptual model for individual multitasking performance.

ality, and other noncognitive factors as influences on complex task performance (e.g., Humphreys & Revelle, 1984; Kahneman, 1973; Kanfer & Ackerman, 1989). Also, an empirical study of job performance supports a similar model (McCloy, Campbell, & Cudeck, 1994).

METHOD

Participants

Participants were 125 undergraduate students recruited from introductory psychology courses at Michigan State University. Participants received course credit for volunteering their time; 68% of participants were women, 40% were freshmen, 27% were sophomores, 27% were juniors, and 6% were seniors or more advanced students. The mean age was 19.1 years, but most students (68%) were between 18 and 19 years of age. Regarding ethnicity, 75% of the sample was non-Hispanic White, 10% Asian, 7% African American, 4% Hispanic, with 4% classified as other or unidentified.

Materials and Procedure

Participants were tested in a laboratory setting in small proctored groups across two sessions, each session taking approximately 1.5 hr, and each session with small groups of 4 to 10 individuals being tested simultaneously. Tests and questionnaires relevant to this chapter are as follows.

Session 1. In Session 1, after completing a demographic questionnaire, participants completed two working memory tasks. In *operation span*, participants were presented with equation-word pairs such as *IS (12 / 3) + 3 = 6? DOG*. For each pair like this, the task was to indicate whether the equation was correct or incorrect, and also to remember the word. Following presentation of from two to six equation-word pairs, a recall prompt appeared, and the task was to report the words in the order in which they were presented. In *symmetry span*, each trial consisted of a matrix, with some cells filled, followed by an arrow. The task was to judge whether the pattern in the matrix was symmetrical along the vertical axis, and then to remember the direction of each arrow. Following presentation of from two to six matrix-arrow pairs, the task was to report the direction of the first arrow, the second arrow, and so forth.

After the working memory tasks, participants completed two perceptual speed tasks. In *letter comparison*, stimuli were pairs of letters separated by a line such as "XJK ___ XRK." Participants were to write S on the line if the pairs were the same or D if they were different. In *pattern comparison*, the task was the same, except that the stimuli were geometric patterns. In both tasks, the goal was to make as many comparisons as possible in 30 sec. Following these perceptual speed tasks were two abstract reasoning tests. In *matrix reasoning*, each item consisted of a 3 × 3 matrix in which each cell contained a pattern except the one in the lower right-hand corner; the task was to choose from among eight alternatives a pattern that made logical sense in the missing ninth cell. Eight min were allowed for 14 items. In *letter sets*, each item consisted of five sets of letters; the task was to infer the rule that made these letter sets similar and to identify the letter set that did not fit this rule. Eight min were allowed for 14 items.

Finally, following this set of cognitive tasks, participants completed 50 items from the International Personality Item Pool (IPIP) to measure five dimensions of personality: neuroticism, extraversion, openness, agreeableness, and conscientiousness. Each item was a statement such as "Get stressed out easily" or "Feel comfortable around people." The participants' task was to rate each item on how well it described them, using a 5-point scale.

Session 2. In Session 2, following task instructions and practice, participants performed nine 5-min blocks of the synthetic work task, called SynWin. Figure 4.1 illustrates the parameters for Blocks 1 to 5 (baseline blocks) and Blocks 6 to 9 (emergency blocks). As shown, in terms of points awarded for correct answers, the math task was emphasized in the baseline blocks, where by contrast the memory, auditory monitoring, and visual monitoring tasks were emphasized in the emergency blocks. It can also be seen that the overall pace of the task was faster in the emergency blocks than in the baseline blocks. Specifically, the interstimulus interval in the memory task and auditory task changed from 10 sec to 5 sec, and the pace of the needle in the visual monitoring task doubled, from 50 sec to 25 sec. For all blocks, the participant's total score was displayed in the center of the screen (see Fig. 4.1).

RESULTS AND DISCUSSION

Table 4.2 displays correlations among the ability and personality predictor variables. As expected, the cognitive ability variables correlated positively with each other, and when the variables were entered into a factor analysis, the first principal component accounted for a large proportion of the variance (36.5%). Thus, we created a unit-weighted composite variable reflecting psychometric *g* by averaging the *z* scores for the six variables. The

TABLE 4.2
Correlations Among Ability and Nonability Variables

	1	2	3	4	5	6	7	8	9	10	11
Ability											
1. Operation span	—										
2. Symmetry span	.37	—									
3. Letter comparison	.14	.14	—								
4. Pattern comparison	.23	.29	.39	—							
5. Matrix reasoning	.27	.34	.15	.19	—						
6. Letter sets	.32	.19	.27	.13	.11	—					
Personality											
7. Neuroticism	.05	.01	.07	.04	.01	-.07	—				
8. Extraversion	.04	.19	.03	.22	-.04	.05	-.27	—			
9. Openness	.16	.16	-.06	.25	.17	.08	-.18	.20	—		
10. Agreeableness	.08	.07	-.20	-.03	-.11	.14	-.16	.31	.18	—	
11. Conscientiousness	-.07	-.23	.00	-.07	-.09	-.03	-.14	.02	.02	.34	—

Note. Correlations with an absolute magnitude greater than .18 are statistically significant ($p < .05$).

pattern of correlations among the personality variables was in line with those found in previous research (e.g., De Fruyt & Mervielde, 1999).

Table 4.3 displays correlations among total scores from the nine synthetic work blocks. Not surprisingly, the correlations were uniformly positive: Participants who performed well in one block tended to perform well in the other blocks. However, it can also be seen that scores from baseline blocks (1–5) correlated more strongly with each other than with scores from the emergency blocks (6–9), and vice-versa. The implication of this finding is that there was a shift in factors underlying performance moving from the baseline blocks to the emergency blocks. To investigate this possibility more formally, we entered the total scores for each block into a factor analysis. The criterion for factor extraction was the scree plot, and we rotated the two factors extracted to an oblique solution, allowing the factors to correlate. Results are displayed in Table 4.4. As shown, Factor 1 was clearly interpretable as *baseline performance* and Factor 2 as *emergency performance*. Furthermore, consistent with the possibility that different factors contributed to variance across the two major phases of the task, the latent factors correlated only moderately ($r = .38$).

Once this was established, we correlated baseline and emergency factor scores with the ability and nonability variables described previously to see whether there was a shift in factors contributing to performance in the two phases. Results are displayed in Table 4.5. Confirming our first prediction, *g* was a positive predictor of performance under both conditions: baseline ($r = .25$) and emergency ($r = .36$). Furthermore, confirming our second prediction, neuroticism emerged as a significant predictor of baseline performance ($r = -.21$): Individuals low in neuroticism tended to outperform individuals high in neuroticism, and there was no evidence for an increased influence of neuroticism in the emergency blocks. In fact, neuroticism correlated essentially zero with emergency performance ($r = -.03$). There was, however, a significant negative correlation of conscientiousness with emergency performance ($r = -.24$), such that individuals high in conscientiousness tended to perform worse than individuals low in conscientiousness.

Not surprisingly, cognitive ability correlated positively with our multitasking performance task. We can only speculate at this point about specific processes captured by our tests of cognitive ability that were the most important contributors to multitasking performance, but one possibility stems from the research perspective that working memory capacity is the central component underlying general intelligence (see Kyllonen, 1996). More specifically, our thinking is that success in multitasking depends critically on active maintenance of what might be termed *control information*. In our empirical study, consider the case of performing the arithmetic task and then being interrupted by an alarm coming from the

TABLE 4.3
Correlations Among Total Scores From Synthetic Work Task

	1	2	3	4	5	6	7	8	9
Baseline Blocks									
1. Block 1	—								
2. Block 2	.85	—							
3. Block 3	.83	.93	—						
4. Block 4	.67	.78	.78	—					
5. Block 5	.44	.61	.63	.71	—				
Emergency Blocks									
6. Block 6	.30	.42	.37	.48	.40	—			
7. Block 7	.16	.31	.27	.35	.43	.80	—		
8. Block 8	.17	.26	.25	.34	.35	.75	.89	—	
9. Block 9	.12	.22	.19	.28	.39	.70	.85	.90	—

Note. Correlations with an absolute magnitude greater than .18 are statistically significant ($p < .05$). Baseline blocks = blocks 1–5, emergency blocks = blocks 6–9.

TABLE 4.4

Factor Analysis of Synthetic Work Total Scores

	Factor 1	Factor 2
Baseline Blocks		
Block 1	*.87*	−.12
Block 2	*.98*	−.03
Block 3	*.98*	−.06
Block 4	*.81*	.11
Block 5	*.60*	.20
Emergency Blocks		
Block 6	.19	*.74*
Block 7	.00	*.95*
Block 8	−.04	*.97*
Block 9	−.09	*.94*
Eigenvalue	5.02	2.43
Percentage of total variance	56	27

Note. Pattern matrix is displayed from an oblimin solution, where Factor 1 and Factor 2 correlate .38. Salient loadings (> .30) are in italics.

TABLE 4.5

Correlations of Predictor Variables With Baseline Performance Versus
Emergency Performance

Performance Block	g	N	E	O	A	C
Baseline	**.25**	*−.21*	.01	.13	.01	.00
Emergency	**.36**	−.03	.02	*.17*	−.08	**−.24**

Note. g = general cognitive ability; N = Neuroticism; E = Extraversion; O = Openness; A = Agreeableness; C = Conscientiousness. Boldface and italics indicate statistical significance at $p < .01$, and italics at $p < .05$.

auditory task. Given the view that working memory capacity reflects the capability to maintain task goals in an active state, particularly in the face of distraction or interference (Engle & Kane, 2004), then individuals with higher levels of working memory capacity should be better able to maintain in memory the goal of returning to the arithmetic task (e.g., "Go back to math") while responding to the auditory task than individuals with lower levels of working memory capacity.

The results presented here also suggest that important nonability factors underlie success (or failure) in multitasking. Neuroticism correlated negatively with performance in the baseline condition of the task, and as already discussed, one possible explanation for this finding is that people high in neuroticism are more likely to experience levels of anxiety that interfere with overall performance during multitasking than are people low in neuroticism. The correlation was nonsignificant in the "emergency" condition, where the pace doubled. In this condition, everyone was arguably more anxious and hence neuroticism across individuals was not as much of a predictor of performance. In the nonability domain, it is also interesting to note the negative correlation we obtained between conscientiousness and performance during the emergency blocks of the task. What might explain this result? One possibility is that those scoring higher on the conscientiousness measure tend to be more careful and deliberate in their work, and that these factors are actually detrimental to emergency task performance which demands rapid, reflexive responding.

Thus, we conclude that the promise of nonability factors in predicting multitasking performance has received empirical support in this study. Moreover, the amount of variance predicted by nonability factors meaningfully added to the prediction offered by ability factors. Because ability and personality correlations were very small in our study (i.e., g and conscientiousness correlated $-.09$, and g and neuroticism correlated $-.01$, with both correlations statistically nonsignificant), the prediction offered by personality variables was not redundant. This conclusion is in line with Ackerman, Kanfer, and Goff (1995) in their prediction of performance on an air traffic controller task from personality and ability measures, and also that of Schmidt and Hunter (1998), whose meta-analytic results support incremental validity for measures of employee integrity, above and beyond measures of cognitive ability.

CONCLUSIONS AND FUTURE DIRECTIONS

Our continued program of research seeks to make modest gains toward an important goal: to identify and better understand a critical set of task features and experimental manipulations that have practically and theoretically important influences on multitasking performance, and to link these features and manipulations to individual characteristics and behavioral processes that are cognitive, motivational, personality, and interest based. Given our start at a definition of multitasking performance as presented in this chapter, along with a broad conceptual framework adapted from the job performance literature, we and other researchers can continue our work in addressing many useful research questions related to multitasking performance. For example, what ability-related and non-ability-related strategies are most effective for dealing with demands of multitasking environments, and do certain groups—such as older adults (e.g., Salthouse, Hambrick, Lukas, & Dell, 1996), people with lower levels of working memory capacity (e.g., Sit & Fisk, 1999), or people with higher levels of neuroticism—profit more by adopting certain strategies than others? Or as another example, can physiological measures (e.g., heart rate as an index of anxiety) help refine our understanding of the processes through which personality traits (e.g., neuroticism) influence multitasking performance?

Research questions such as these can be investigated using advanced statistical techniques such as latent-growth curve modeling and hierarchical linear modeling. Statistically, these techniques can model multitasking performance and how it changes over time, while incorporating individual-difference measures as predictors of performance and performance change. Conceptual and statistical work in this area might increase our basic scientific understanding of multitasking. On a more practical note, we are pursuing this line of research to inform and improve personnel selection, classification, and training in applied settings, given multitasking-related jobs where workers must concurrently monitor multiple systems that are relatively independent of one another, and execute quick decision making and planning. Given the thrust of this volume, we also hope that the work presented here provides some insights related to ability and nonability predictors of student learning and performance.

ACKNOWLEDGMENTS

We thank the research group at the Skilled Performance Laboratory at Michigan State University: Sonia Ghumman, Nicole Moon, Elizabeth Oberlander, Sarah Pachulicz, and Emily Swensen. We also thank Ron Bearden, David Dickason, Geoff Fedak, and Jacqueline Mottern at the Navy Personnel Research, Studies, and Technology (NPRST) for their helpful discussions and input. This work was partially supported by a grant from the NPRST (Contract No. DAAD19–02–D–0001). All views contained herein are those of the authors and should not be interpreted as representing the official policies or endorsements, either expressed or implied, of NPRST or of the U.S. Government.

REFERENCES

Ackerman, P. L. (1987). Individual differences in skill learning: An integration of psychometric and information processing perspectives. *Psychological Bulletin, 102*, 3–27.

Ackerman, P. L., Kanfer, R., & Goff, M. (1995). Cognitive and noncognitive determinants and consequences of complex skill acquisition. *Journal of Experimental Psychology: Applied, 1,* 270–304.

Campbell, J. P., Gasser, M. B., & Oswald, F. L. (1996). The substantive nature of job performance variability. In K. R. Murphy (Ed.), *Individual differences and behavior in organizations* (pp 258–299). San Francisco: Jossey-Bass.

Campbell, J. P., McCloy, R. A., Oppler, S. H., & Sager, C. E. (1993). A theory of performance. In N. Schmitt & W. Borman (Eds.), *Personnel selection in organizations* (pp. 35–70). San Francisco: Jossey-Bass.

De Fruyt, F., & Mervielde, I. (1999). RIASEC types and big five traits as predictors of employment status and nature of employment. *Personnel Psychology, 52,* 701–727.

Elsmore, T. F. (1994). SYNWORK1: A PC-based tool for assessment of performance in a simulated work environment. *Behavior, Research Methods, Instruments, & Computers, 26,* 421–426.

Engle, R. W., & Kane, M. J. (2004). Executive attention, working memory capacity, and a two-factor theory of cognitive control. In B. Ross (Ed.), *The psychology of learning and motivation* (Vol. 44, pp. 145–199). New York: Elsevier.

Hasher, L. & Zacks, R. T. (1977). Automatic and effortful processes in memory. *Journal of Experimental Psychology: General, 108,* 356–388.

Hattrup, K., & Jackson, S. (1996). Learning about individual differences by taking situations seriously. In K. R. Murphy (Ed.), *Individual differences and behavior in organizations* (pp. 507–547). San Francisco: Jossey-Bass.

Humphreys, M. S., & Revelle, W. (1984). Personality, motivation, and performance: A theory of the relationship between individual differences and information processing. *Psychological Review, 91,* 153–184.

Ilgen, D. R., & Pulakos, E. D. (1999). Introduction: Employee performance in today's organizations. In D. R. Ilgen & E. D. Pulakos (Eds.), *The changing nature of performance* (pp. 1–20). San Francisco: Jossey-Bass.

Kanfer, R., & Ackerman, P. L. (1989). Motivational and cognitive abilities: An integrative/aptitude-treatment interaction approach to skill acquisition. *Journal of Applied Psychology, 74,* 657–690.

Kahneman, D. (1973). *Attention and effort.* Englewood Cliffs, NJ: Prentice Hall.

Kane, M. J., Hambrick, D. Z., Tuholski, S. W., Wilhelm, O., Payne, T. W., & Engle, R. W. (2004). The generality of working-memory capacity: A latent-variable approach to verbal and visuo-spatial memory span and reasoning. *Journal of Experimental Psychology: General, 133,* 189–217.

Kyllonen, P. C. (1996). Is working memory capacity Spearman's *g*? In I. Dennis & P. Tapsfield (Eds.), *Human abilities: Their nature and measurement* (pp. 49–75). Mahwah, NJ: Lawrence Erlbaum Associates.

Magnusson, D., & Endler, N. S. (1977). *Personality at the crossroads: Current issues in interactional psychology.* Hillsdale, NJ: Lawrence Erlbaum Associates.

McCloy, R. A., Campbell, J. P., & Cudeck, R. (1994). A confirmatory test of a model of performance determinants. *Journal of Applied Psychology, 79,* 493–505.

Münsterberg, H. (1913). *Psychology and industrial efficiency.* Boston: Houghton Mifflin.

Oswald, F. L., Schmitt, N., Kim, B. H., Ramsay, L. J., & Gillespie, M. A. (2004). Developing a biodata measure and situational judgment inventory as predictors of college student performance. *Journal of Applied Psychology, 89,* 187–207.

Proctor, R. W., & Dutta, A. (1995). *Skill acquisition and human performance.* Thousand Oaks, CA: Sage.

Salthouse, T. A., Hambrick, D. Z., Lukas, K. E., & Dell, T. C. (1996). Determinants of adult age differences on synthetic work performance. *Journal of Experimental Psychology: Applied, 2,* 305–329.

Schmidt, F. L., & Hunter, J. E. (1998). The validity and utility of selection methods in personnel psychology: Practical and theoretical implications of 85 years of research findings. *Psychological Bulletin, 124,* 262–274.

Sit, R. A., & Fisk, A. D. (1999). Age-related performance in a multiple-task environment. *Human Factors, 41,* 26–34.

Tombu, M., & Jolicoeur, P. (2005). Testing the predictions of a central capacity sharing model. *Journal of Experimental Psychology: Human Perception and Performance, 4,* 790–802.

Wickens, C. D., Mountford, S. J., & Schreiner, W. (1981). Multiple responses, task-hemispheric integrity, and individual differences in time-sharing. *Human Factors, 23,* 211–229.

Yerkes, R. M., & Dodson, J. D. (1908). The relation of strength of stimulus to rapidity of habit-formation. *Journal of Comparative Neurology and Psychology, 18,* 459–482.

Chapter 5

Representing Complex Problems: A Representational Epistemic Approach

Peter C-H. Cheng
Rossano Barone
University of Sussex

Understanding how to represent problems is a multidisciplinary endeavor. Cognitive science has shown the substantial impact that alternative forms of representation can have on the difficulty of solving problems (e.g., Kaplan & Simon, 1990; Kotovsky, Hayes, & Simon, 1985; Zhang, 1997). It has also provided explanations why certain forms of representation, such as diagrams, may confer substantial advantages on problem solvers (e.g., Cheng, 2004; Larkin & Simon, 1987). In computer science, the areas of information visualization and scientific visualization (e.g., Card, MacKinlay, & Shneiderman, 1999; Ware, 1999) have provided approaches to the design of displays that support the comprehension of large databases of information. Artificial intelligence has created systems that reason using diagrams, which gives theoretical insights into the nature of representations for problem solving (e.g., Glasgow, Narayanan, & Chandrasekaran, 1995). Studies in the area of human–computer interaction and human factors have provided guidelines for analysis and design of good notional systems and usable computer interfaces (e.g., Burns & Hajdukiewicz, 2004; Green, 1989). Psychology speaks to the design of effective representations for problem solving by informing us about the nature of underpinning human perceptual processes and cognitive processes (e.g., Kosslyn, 1989; Pinker, 1990).

Substantial advances have been made with respect to the representation of problems and the presentation of information within complex domains. However, our understanding of how to represent complex problems is still limited. The work on problem representations has tended to focus on relatively narrow domains, such as numeration systems (e.g., Zhang & Norman, 1994), or toy problems such as the mutilated checker board (e.g., Kaplan & Simon, 1990). Where work has focused on complex domains, it has tended to focus on the visualization of rich datasets to find hidden relations or patterns and often has little emphasis on problem solving more broadly conceived (e.g., Card et al., 1999; Ware, 1999).

The purpose of this chapter is to present the Representational Epistemic (REEP) approach to understanding and designing representations for complex problem domains. The approach was initially developed from studies on the role of alternative representations in scientific discovery (Cheng & Simon, 1995) and on the invention of novel diagrammatic systems to enhance conceptual learning in science and mathematics (Cheng, 2002; Cheng, 2003; Cheng & Shipstone, 2003). REEP has also been applied to the design of representations for event scheduling and personnel rostering (Barone & Cheng, 2004; Cheng, Barone, Cowling, & Ahmadi, 2002). We use the terms "representational" and "epistemic" for the approach because it focuses on the nature of representational systems to preserve the conceptual structure, or inherent system of knowledge, of the problem domain. A refinement to the approach is presented that involves theoretical advances that provide better definitions of key notions and a more coherent formulation of the REEP design principles.

Bakery production scheduling will be used as an example of a complex problem-solving domain throughout the chapter, to illustrate the key ideas underpinning the REEP approach and to explain how the design principles are applied. A problem-solving domain is defined as the problem-solving environment (e.g., bakeries) plus the range of tasks that are under consideration (e.g., production planning and scheduling). The application of the REEP approach to this domain is part of the ROLLOUT project, which has been found to improve bakery scheduling practices and training. The project involves a consortium of 10 commercial partners including a membership-based research organization, plant (factory scale) bakery companies, supermarket chains with in-store bakeries, and bakery equipment manufacturers. The project has conducted detailed studies of bakery scheduling knowledge and problem-solving strategies. The REEP approach has been used to design a novel graphical representation for bakery planning and scheduling—the ROLLOUT diagram. The ROLLOUT diagram has been used as the interface for a software tool that allows schedules to be modified through the interactive manipulation of the representation. Figure 5.1 shows a screen snapshot of the tool setup to model an in-store bakery of a

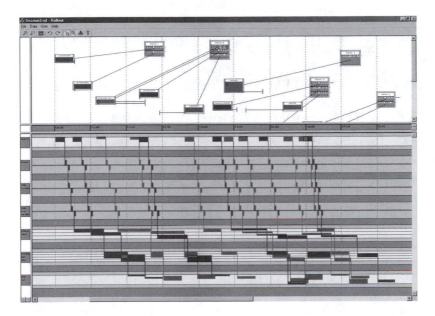

Figure 5.1.   The ROLLOUT diagram for bakery scheduling.

supermarket. The effectiveness of ROLLOUT has been established using empirical evaluation, with favorable comparisons to familiar tabular representations and spreadsheet tools. The project studied real bakers in a range of trials, including the following: laboratory experiments using realistic schedules and a range of problem-solving tasks, evaluations in a training bakery configured as a simulation of a real bakery requiring real-time rescheduling of production, and trials of ROLLOUT in a real working bakery. Some of the outcomes are summarized by Cheng et al. (2006) and full details are reported elsewhere. The outcomes of all the trials demonstrate that ROLLOUT is at least as effective as conventional approaches, and usually superior. Bakery schedulers can quickly learn to use ROLLOUT successfully with minimal training. The success of ROLLOUT then in turn provides further evidence of the utility and benefits of the REEP approach to representation design.

The next section of this chapter considers the challenges to the design of effective representations for complex problems by discussing the various ways in which a problem domain may be complex. This provides a number of challenges that representations for complex domains must satisfy to be effective for complex problem solving. Next the REEP approach is described to explain the key concepts and how the design principles can be applied, with bakery scheduling and ROLLOUT providing examples. The penultimate section discusses the advantages of representations designed using the REEP approach and specifically addresses how these benefits can be used to tackle the challenges of complex problem solving. The final section is a concluding summary.

WHAT MAKES PROBLEMS COMPLEX?

First, there are sources that arise from the inherent nature of the domain in which problem solving is occurring. Second, the process of problem solving can itself be complex in various ways; and third, the individual doing the problem solving brings with him or her a set of issues related to the variability of knowledge and experience. Each of these issues is considered in turn while drawing on examples from our adopted bakery scheduling problem domain.

Complexity of Information and Concepts

Solving problems in a domain typically requires the problem solver to have declarative or conceptual knowledge of that domain. That knowledge may be complex in many ways that directly impacts on how it is possible to represent the domain.

A domain can be complex because it involves many different types of entities, each with numerous properties or attributes, and each of those in turn can possess many different possible values. Products and equipment are two obvious examples. The product attributes include the following: type (e.g., loaf, stick, bun, roll, bloomer, doughnut), dough or mix recipe (e.g., white, wholemeal, brown, whole grain), weight (e.g., 800 g, 400 g), decoration or coating (e.g., split, poppy seeds, flour dusted, "Tiger"), proof duration, baking duration, and so forth. Equipment attributes include the following: type (e.g., mixer, divider, prover, oven), configuration (e.g., rack oven, deck oven), capacity (e.g., maximum number of items of each product type), and process type (e.g., bulk versus piece-wise or conveyor-based).

At a more abstract level, potential complexity arises when many concepts are essential to understanding a domain. In bakery scheduling, many of these concepts are common notions found in all scheduling tasks, such as deadline, start time, process duration, delay, and capacity. Others have more specific interpretations. Bakery process stages are particular types of baking operations such as mixing, dividing, molding, proving, baking, and cooling. A process step is the occurrence of one process stage for one product. A batch is the production of a single product and a run is the production of a sequence of batches. An order is a group of products with a common deadline, perhaps destined for a single customer.

Large amounts of data are another source of complexity. A bakery may manufacture hundreds of products in a day. Each product will have multiple process steps and each step will have several parameters. Hence, many thousands of pieces of information are potentially relevant. To solve problems, the relations among such pieces of information must be considered, which brings into consideration combinatoric issues when dealing with all potentially relevant relations.

Another sense in which a domain may be complex is in relation to the different classes of concepts, or ontologies, that must be used to reason about a domain. Each of these perspectives contain hierarchies of concepts and relations, but problem solving will require interrelations among the perspectives to be maintained. Hence, there is complexity due to the existence of tangled networks of concepts to be navigated and manipulated during problem solving. For example, in bakery scheduling, it is critical to relate temporal information (such as process durations, start times, and deadlines) with assignment information about what products are being processed in which equipment.

Conceptual complexity also arises when a domain involves different levels of abstraction and various levels of granularity, or scale. Problem solving is more difficult when one has to successfully apply general laws or principles to specific concrete cases, in addition to reasoning about just one level or the other. Similarly, when there are different scales at which things must be considered, this makes problem solving harder because things at different levels of granularity must be interrelated. In bakery scheduling, considerations range from the small scale, such as individual process steps for a single product, through to the large scale level comprising sequences of runs of multiple products.

There are many different manifestations of informational and conceptual complexity. The design of a representation for problem solving in a complex domain will need to support the amount, variety, and interrelatedness of the information and concepts of the domain. Deciding what information and knowledge to make explicit and how to coherently structure the presentation are major challenges of the designer of representations.

Complexity of the Task and the Solution Process

To solve problems in complex domains requires the means to process the information of the domain. Newell and Simon's (1972) classical account of well-structured problem solving provides an initial basis for considering the ways in which information processing may be complex. The established theory that problem solving is a process of heuristic search through a problem space identifies ways in which problem solving may vary in complexity. The elementary operators to transform one meaningful problem state to the next may be elaborate. Problem solving may be more complex if the average branching factor of the problem space is large, which in turn may be due to the availability of a wide range of operators or multiple ways in which a given set of operators can be applied to a state. Similarly, problem solving will be more complex when, on average, long sequences of operators are required to move from the initial to the goal state. In addition to the complexity due to breadth and depth of the problem space, complexity arises from the heterogeneity of the search, in terms of the tortuousness of the goal hierarchy needed for problem solving.

Many of the tasks of bakery scheduling have these characteristics of complex problems. Schedulers use many different criteria to assess the quality of a schedule, for example: the meeting of deadlines or matching of customer demand profile, the overall production time used, how efficiently equipment has been used, the number of changes of dough type or equipment settings, sufficient inclusion of staff breaks. The problem space is often broad and deep, because there are typically many options for when a product can be scheduled and many consequences follow from each option. For example, if an extra production run is to be inserted into an existing schedule, this can be done by displacing planned mixes. However, if any of the subsequent runs is near their deadline, they will in turn have to be brought forward, which in turn requires further rescheduling.

Moving beyond the classical theory of well-structured problem solving, there are other ways in which problem solving can be considered complex. Ill-structured problems (Simon, 1973) are more complex than well-structured problems, because some part of the definition or processing of the problem space is absent. For instance, the lack of a mechanistic means to test whether a goal state has been found means that it would be difficult to know whether problem solving has been successful and so can stop. Ill-structured problems will require a superordinate problem space to be invoked to fill in the absent aspects before a solution in the given problem space can be found (Simon, 1973). An example in bakery scheduling is knowing when a satisfactory schedule has been produced. This requires considerations at a higher level than the schedule itself and involves considerations of what criteria to use to make such judgments. Some problems cannot adequately be described in terms of the search of a single problem space, but are more coherently modeled as the search of multiple spaces, with the outcomes of the searches in each space mutually constraining the search in the other spaces (e.g., Klahr & Dunbar, 1988; Simon & Lea, 1974). At its most general, bakery scheduling may be considered as complementary searches of two spaces: (a) the space of possible sequences of runs assembled from similar products from different orders, and (b) the space of possible assignment of products to items of equipment at specific times. Decisions about what products can be put together into runs will be constrained by how much free capacity has been left from previous assignments, which in turn will depend on previously assembled and assigned runs.

One of the goals for the designer of representations is to mollify the impact of these forms of complexity. Representations may be created that support the process of searching the breadth and depth of the problem spaces by providing additional representational tools that record and make explicit the problem states actually examined. When there are multiple problem spaces, the designer may provide automatic links between the information in multiple representations to aid mapping between the spaces (e.g., Cheng, 1999; Scaife & Rogers, 1996).

The Human Factor

Focusing on the people doing the problem solving brings a further set of complicating factors. The level of expertise of a problem solver will differentially impact on their ability to solve a problem in different circumstances, which in turn raises a further set of issues for the designer of representations to consider. Novices and experts will have different requirements from a representation because of the amount of knowledge and the way it is encoded in memory. In addition to being limited, the novices' knowledge will be more declarative and will require conscious effort to apply it to specific problem cases. In contrast, experts' knowledge will be broad and deep. Some of their knowledge is in the form of rich perceptual chunks and schemas, with associated actions, which allows the swift recognition of problem states and applications of operations to improve those states. Other knowledge may be in the form of sophisticated mental models that capture intricate structural constraints concerning aspects of the domain, that allow them to mentally simulate problem scenarios and to read-off and interpret consequences.

Novice bakery schedulers will require support in recognizing significant problem situations and need help in inferring what actions to perform and the potential consequences. Expert bakery schedulers have well-rehearsed rules for creating and revising schedules, but they also use heuristics to manage the complexity of the problem; for example, by reducing variability of processing times across products and by building in gaps between runs to serve as contingency buffers in case problems occur. This suggests that their mental models are rather crude and are not suited to detailed reasoning about the interactions between sequences of production runs.

Other sources of complexity related to the problem solvers themselves are negative transfer and psychological biases. Negative transfer occurs when knowledge from one area of expertise is incorrectly applied in a different problem-solving domain (VanLehn, 1989). An example is our everyday knowledge of scheduling that is typically concerned with the scheduling of events or travel, which is not applicable to the scheduling of conveyor-based processes in bakeries. Psychological or cognitive biases are revealed when people's reasoning about simple situations fail to match the ideal of logic and mathematics (e.g., Evans, 1989). From our studies of bakery schedulers, it appears that they prefer to schedule forward rather backward in time. To populate a schedule, the common strategy is to allocate batches from a given point working forward to the future and to see how much time is left before the deadline. Only in special cases is the strategy of allocating backward from the deadline used. This may be due to a temporal cognitive bias that favors the making of assignments forward in time, which is perhaps more natural than thinking about things ordered backward in time.

Novice–expert differences are sometimes considered in the design of interfaces and displays, with the presumption that simplified versions should be provided for novices. The issues of avoiding negative transfer and preventing cognitive biases are not well addressed by the literature on the design of representations. Creating an effective representation for the basic requirements of problem solving is usually such a challenge that these secondary issues are not tackled. Nevertheless, a complete approach to the design of representations needs to be able to deal with these aspects of user complexity.

Clearly there are many things that make the representation of complex problems a challenge, including informational and conceptual complexity, task and solution process complexity, and complexity arising from the nature of users. The next section introduces an approach to the design of representations that aims to address difficulties for problem solving that arise from these sources of complexity by designing effective representations.

REPRESENTATIONAL EPISTEMIC APPROACH TO REPRESENTATION DESIGN

The central idea of the REEP approach is to design representations that preserve the conceptual structure of the domain in the design of the structure of the representational system. It is claimed that representations created to directly encode the system of knowledge that underpins the problem-solving domain will provide a whole range of small- and large-scale benefits for cognition and complex problem solving. The benefits are discussed in the section following this one. This section presents a revision of the REEP approach, which clarifies and extends our previous theoretical formulation. Previously, the design guidelines were couched in terms of semantic transparency and syntactic plasticity characteristics, which were posed as desirable properties that a representation should possess (Cheng, 2002, 2003; Cheng et al., 2002). However, that account was problematic, because the definition of these characteristics lacked precision, and being characteristics, it was not clear how they could be fully operationalized for the process of design.

The revision of the REEP approach has, in part, been driven by the need to deal with the complexities of the bakery scheduling domain. The approach is now centered on the notion of conceptual dimensions. The elaboration of the nature of conceptual dimensions and the interrelations among them provides an analysis of the system of knowledge that is to be preserved by the design of the representation. In turn, the principles for designing a representation are specified in terms of intrarelations among parts of each conceptual dimension and in terms of interrelations across sets of representational dimensions. The idea of conceptual dimensions is first introduced. Then the analysis of conceptual structures in terms of conceptual dimensions is discussed. Finally, the design principles are presented and explained using the ROLLOUT diagram as an example.

Conceptual Dimensions

The conceptual structure of a problem domain should be analyzed in terms of its constituent conceptual dimensions. A conceptual dimension is a subdivision of a given system of knowledge and comprises similar types of ideas or notions that are taken from the same perspective within the domain. A conceptual dimension may be considered, in general terms, as an ontology that defines the ways of describing associated facets of a domain. A conceptual dimension may be heterogeneous, possessing different levels or aspects to which its concepts may belong. The nature of these levels and aspects will be specific to the conceptual dimension concerned.

From the studies of bakery scheduling (Cheng et al., 2006) and previous work, seven conceptual dimensions have been identified as general perspectives that have been important in characterizing the nature of knowledge in the domains studied. Table 5.1 lists them and identifies the levels or aspects belonging to each. Each is considered in turn.

The entity-taxonomic conceptual dimension concerns basic objects, things, and types of things that exist in the domain. Under this dimension, two levels are distinguished in terms of particular instances of objects and classes of objects of the same kind. For example, in the bakery scheduling domain, some of the main classes of entities include the following: types of bakery (e.g., plant versus in-store), types of products (bread or loaves, buns or rolls, biscuits), types of processing stage (mixing, dividing, proving, baking, cooling), types of equipment (e.g., mixer, deck oven, rack oven), and types of dough (white, brown, wholemeal, granary). Each type of object may consist of subtypes, in the form of a taxonomic hierarchy: for instance, a bakery will have different dough recipes for each type of dough, which will be used for different sets of product types.

TABLE 5.1

Conceptual Dimensions

Conceptual Dimension	Levels–Aspects and Examples
Entity-taxonomic	Existing things: entities, objects Classifications: category, subcategory, group
Property	Measure: Nominal, ordinal, cardinal, interval, ratio Type: intrinsic property, extrinsic property
Temporal	Perspectives: point (specific times, deadlines, start, end); interval (duration, delays, lead and lags); relational (before, after, tomorrow)
Structural	Aspects: spatiality (position, orientation); angularity (obtuse, orthogonal, acute); divisions (component, partition, department, region); arrangement (containment, alignment, abutment, alignment, framework, chain); connection (intersection, overlap, link, bridge, crossing); association (group, pair, central, peripheral); paths (line, branch, network, lattice) Levels: granularity scales (local, global)
Functional	Aspects: Process (assemble, [de]compose, partitioning, group, maximize, control, target, tune, randomize, interact, supply, demand); change (transitions, development, evolution); motion (traverse, flow, navigate, follow); organizing (arrange, distribute, assign, allocate, align); sorting (prioritize, rank, order); repetition (cycle, loop, iterate, recursing, hyseresis); copy (reproduce, inherit, duplicate); cause and effect (drive, force, affect, outcome, result); rules (conditions and actions); differentiate (options, contingencies, alternatives); variability (fluctuate, constancy, noisy) Levels: generality (concrete, abstract)
Formal relational models	Aspects: set theory (disjunction, conjunction, conditionality); arithmetic (addition, subtraction, division, multiplication); algebra (distributive, associative, commutative); differential calculus (rate of change, integration); other mathematical (correlation, specific functions) Levels: abstraction with variables; concrete with actual values
Evaluative	Aspects: evaluation (cost, benefit, efficiency, importance, salience); purposes (goals, focus, rewards, violation avoidance); constraints (requirements, limits, minima, constancy)

The property conceptual dimension concerns the observable and measurable attributes or properties of things in a domain. Concepts within this dimension can be classified in terms of ideas about the nature of quantities. One attribute of a type of entity is the number of actual entities (e.g., the number of batches in a production run). The properties of entities can be distinguished in terms of the nature of the scale on which it may be measured: nominal, ordinal, interval, and ratio (e.g., Ellis, 1968). The difference between types of dough is nominal. The sequence of process stages is ordinal. The duration of the production steps are interval measures of time. The amount of product and capacity of equipment are ratio quantities. Another distinction that may be useful to make under this dimension is whether a property is extrinsic or intrinsic (directly measurable or derived); for example, the mass versus density, respectively, of a loaf of bread. For the purpose of bakery scheduling, the quantity percentage capacity of equipment is a useful derived measure, as this allows considerations of the use of equipment without the need to deal with the actual physical sizes of products and equipment.

The temporal conceptual dimension includes various perspectives or measures of time. Time can be specified as points, intervals, or as relations (Shahar, 1997). Start and end times of batches or process steps, and also deadlines, are examples of time points. Examples of time intervals include production durations, lead or lag times between process steps, and spare time or delays with respect to deadlines. Time relations include notions such as before and after, or binary temporal relations, such as "produce white bread before wholemeal."

The structural conceptual dimension is concerned with the static form, shape, or organization of things in a domain. Concepts in this dimension include spatial, geometrical, anatomical, architectural, and topological notions. Table 5.1 identifies a sample of different aspects of this dimension (with some examples of concepts). For a given domain, these concepts may be applicable at different levels of granularity, ranging from overarching ideas about the organization of a domain through to low level, local configurations of entities. In terms of bakery scheduling, one of the major structural concepts is the organization of the process of baking into distinct process stages, typically mixing, proving, dividing, final proof, baking, and cooling. Some of these stages have substages. The composition of orders is also a structural concept as the products to be made are components of an order. The same general notion also applies to configurations of equipment, such as the simple subdivision of shelves in deck ovens. The lowest level considered in this conceptual dimension is, perhaps, the arrangement of individual items of product on trays.

The functional conceptual dimension concerns activities and processes. Concepts considered under this dimension include physiological, operational, behavioral, and other ideas relating to dynamic processes. The concepts can be considered at different levels of generality. Bakery scheduling at the most general level is concerned with the abstract notions of satisfying demands using given resources. The demands are quantities of products to be produced to certain deadlines using particular processing stages, each with certain physical and spatial requirements. Resources are the capacity of equipment and its temporal availability. At a more specific level, there will be considerations of concepts such as the sequencing of processing stages, the flow and continuity of production, the decomposition of production orders into runs, and how manufactured product is aggregated to fulfill orders. At an even lower level, there will be functional consideration of the process of distribution or alignment of products in relation to the available equipment capacity.

The formal relations conceptual dimension has the role of modeling aspects of the domain using formal systems such as logic, set theory, arithmetic, algebra, and so forth. The aspects modeled under this dimension may be specific relations that pertain to one fragment of a domain. Alternatively, the concepts may be fundamental relations of the domain, its underpinning relations, universal invariants, conserved higher order quantities, symmetries, axioms, or laws. When such fundamental relations exist, they are particularly important for the design of representations of the domain. There are similarities between aspects of the structural dimension and the formal relations dimension. An aspect of a domain will belong to the formal relational models dimension when it is necessary to consider the aspect precisely and in depth. For example, when simple collections of things are being considered and there are no complex relations (e.g., exclusive-or), then the structural or functional dimension is more appropriate for the target concepts. However, the precise classification of concepts under particular dimensions is less critical to the approach than to successfully identify concepts relevant to the domain.

In bakery scheduling, there are no fundamental laws, but set theoretic and arithmetic relations have important roles. Orders may be considered as nonintersecting sets comprised of disjoint collections of product. Similar notions apply with the packing of batches of product into a piece of equipment, but arithmetic relations govern the quantities under consideration; for example, *free capacity = total capacity −* Σ *individual batch size*. In many domains, the more specific cases are such obvious relations that they are not explicitly considered, but for the purpose of designing an effective representation they are important to address. For any formal relation it is necessary to consider different levels of abstraction. On the one hand, there is the concrete level, in which particular values are assigned to variables for specific cases (e.g., in terms of the previous equation: free capacity, $22\% = 100\% - [33\% + 45\%]$). On the other hand, the abstract level concerns general relations expressed using variables, which are applicable to a wide range of pertinent cases.

Finally, the evaluative conceptual dimension encompasses concepts to do with the assessment or judgment of the domain in different ways, often in relation to particular purposes. Such evaluations may range from local assessment of particular parts of the problem domain to more global assessment of the domain as a whole. Local evaluations concern things such as proximity to limits or whether particular constraints have been violated. Combinations or more complex relations of local evaluation may constitute global evaluations, which assess the overall characteristics of a domain, using concepts such as efficiency or cost–benefit ratio. In terms of bakery scheduling, there are a multitude of local and global evaluative characteristics. Deadlines for specific orders, capacity limits of pieces of equipment, and no lags between process steps are just a few examples of evaluative concepts at a local level. At an intermediate level, evaluations may, for example, concern how efficiently a piece of equipment is used, or how easy production is with regard to the number of dough changes, or whether there are many severe peaks and toughs in staff work load. The overall performance of a bakery is typically considered in relation to how well production deadlines and quantities are satisfied.

These seven conceptual dimensions have been identified for the REEP approach. Not all of them will be applicable in every domain and their degree of relevance will depend on the particular knowledge system of a domain. No claim is made that this is an exclusive list, or that the dimensions are formally distinct categories of knowledge, such that every concept belongs uniquely to only one dimension. The notion of constraint is included under the evaluative dimension, but it may warrant being considered as a conceptual dimension in its own right. One might also argue that the temporal dimension is the application of the structural dimension to the domain of time, so it should be subsumed under the structural dimension. In the REEP approach, it is treated as a distinct dimension, because temporal concepts are often considered independently of other structural concepts and we have found the distinction to be useful in creating representations in our previous work. The purpose of conceptual dimensions is to provide a sound basis for the analysis of the conceptual structure of a domain, which the next subsection now considers.

Conceptual Structure

The key idea of the REEP approach is to preserve the conceptual structure of the problem-solving domain in the representational structures of the interface. It is assumed that detailed descriptions of the target domain have been obtained by normal knowledge acquisition methods such as interviews, problem walk-through, verbal protocol analysis, task analysis, and so forth. These methods will have been applied across the range of environments and tasks that define the target problem-solving domain.

The conceptual dimensions allow the conceptual structure to be derived from the descriptions of a domain in a systematic fashion at two levels. The first level concerns the structure of relations within each of the conceptual dimensions, which deal with aspects and levels specific to each conceptual dimension. The previous subsection discussed aspects and levels for each conceptual dimension. Table 5.1 may be used as a list of queries to identify those aspects and levels present in each conceptual dimension. The example from the bakery scheduling domain shows the richness of conceptual relations that may occur within each of the individual conceptual dimensions of the domain.

The second level of a conceptual structure is the interrelation between conceptual dimensions. Some combination of dimensions will be primary, because they are central to a domain; others will be more peripheral secondary dimensions. Primary conceptual dimensions will possess the greatest number, most complex, and pervasive concepts in the domain, and they will most often be considered simultaneously with many other conceptual dimensions. Secondary dimensions will involve concepts that are considered in a relatively narrow spectrum of cases and often in relative isolation from other conceptual dimensions. Alternative conceptual dimensions will be primary in different types of domains. In previous work on instruction domains for science and mathematics, the formal relational models and property dimensions were particularly important as those domains were focused on promoting an understanding of the underpinning theoretical principles or laws of the domain (Cheng, 2002, 2003; Cheng & Shipstone, 2003). In other work on event and personnel scheduling, the temporal, structural, and functional dimension were the primary dimensions (Barone & Cheng, 2004; Cheng at al., 2002).

Determining what are the most effective methods for distinguishing primary and secondary conceptual dimensions is the subject of current work. One approach is to select and analyze a representative sample of problem-solving protocols and analyze the frequency of occurrence of the aspects and levels of each dimension and the frequency of simultaneous consideration of particular combinations of conceptual dimensions. Another approach is to obtain a list of the most important domain concepts and examine which conceptual dimensions are implicated in the description of those concepts. The frequency of references to a concept in descriptions or protocols of problem solving, or the judgment of domain experts, can be used to assess the relative importance of the concepts.

Table 5.2 shows such an analysis for common bakery scheduling domain concepts. The entries in the cells of the table are the levels or aspects of the

TABLE 5.2

Analysis of Domain Concepts in Terms of Conceptual Dimensions

Domain Concept	Entity	Structural	Functional	Temporal	Property	Evaluative	Formal Relational
Product type	Thing, Types	Association	Organize		Nominal		
Process stage	Thing, Types	Path, Association					
Equipment	Thing, Types	Divisions, Arrangement			Nominal, Ratio	Constraint	
Order	Thing	Association		Point, Interval, Relations		Constraint, Evaluation	Set theory, Arithmetic
Dough	Thing, Types		Rule		Nominal		
Batch	Thing		Organize, Move	Point, Interval, Relations		Constraint, Evaluation	
Run	Thing	Association	Organize, Sort	Point, Interval, Relations			
Process step	Thing, Types	Division	Organize, Move	Point, Interval, Relations	Ratio, Nominal		Arithmetic
Bulk process	Thing		Change	Point, Interval			
Conveyor process	Thing	Divisions	Change, Sorting, Move	Point, Interval, Relations			

Conceptual Dimension

conceptual dimensions that are germane to the concept. Although the number of entries (in a column) for each conceptual dimension should not be taken too literally, it does indicate the importance of that dimension across the domain concepts. Similarly, the co-occurrence of entries (in a row) for each domain concept gives some indication of which conceptual dimensions often co-occur in considerations of the domain. Of the chosen domain concepts, all can be considered as distinct facets in the domain with many possessing subcategories.

For the bakery scheduling the entity-taxonomic, temporal, structural, and functional domains are the primary dimensions. Time provides a context for thinking about most of the concepts, with the majority being considered in terms of all three temporal perspectives. Product, process stage, and equipment are a-temporal concepts, because they are essentially invariant in time. The structural dimension is important, because scheduling must take into account the spatial, associative, and componential forms that permeate the baking process (stages), bakeries themselves (equipment), and orders. Not surprisingly, the functional dimension is a primary dimension as scheduling is an activity that involves notions of organizing and sorting products, batches, runs and process steps, in time and space. Further, the idea of a product moving through the bakery, or individual items through a conveyor process, gives additional weight to the relevance of functional dimension.

The property, formal relational, and evaluative dimensions are secondary dimensions as they have a minority role in common domain concepts. Given the importance of the evaluative dimension in the scheduling-related domains previously studied (Barone & Cheng, 2004; Cheng at al., 2002), it is perhaps unexpected that this dimension in not a primary one. There are two reasons for this. First, the bakery scheduling domain is more complex with respect to the greater range of things to be assigned and to which they can be assigned, so the relative importance of the role of evaluative dimension is reduced. Second, the number of different types of constraints and the entities to which they apply is less in the bakery scheduling domain, at least compared to examination timetabling. However, the clear implication is that the evaluative and other dimensions can take a subsidiary role in the design of a representation for the domain.

Principles of Representation Design

How can the knowledge of the conceptual dimension and conceptual structures of a domain be used to design an effective representation? In the REEP approach, the fundamental idea is to support the interrelation between meaningfully connected concepts while differentiating those that are unconnected. This must be done within and between the conceptual dimensions. Four principles are proposed for use as heuristics in the process of design to structure a representation so that it satisfies these requirements. The principles specify the manner in which a representation should be structured to preserve the conceptual structure; how representational schemes should be used to encode conceptual dimensions and their interrelations and intrarelations.

First, it is necessary to clarify the notion of representational schemes, or formats. These are particular techniques used to encode information by making a correspondence or mapping between a concept and some component or property of the representation. Engelhardt (2002), Bertin (1983), Zhang (1996), Burns and Hajdukiewicz (2004), Card et al. (1999), and others, provided common examples of how such mappings may be achieved using various representational techniques. These include the following: location in metric horizontal space (x-axis) or vertical space (y-axis); spatial properties of graphical objects, such as shape, size, and orientation; visual properties of objects, such as color, shading, or outlining; regions or subdivisions of space, such as embedded panels, separate windows, and layers; alphanumeric labeling; and relations among objects, such as spatial association, aligning in space, superposition, containment, or linking.

The four representational design principles are as follows:

1. Global interpretive framework—A global interpretive framework should be devised that coherently interrelates all of the primary conceptual dimensions of a domain at the highest level in the representation. The aim is to provide an overarching interpretative framework that can be used to interpret, contextualize, and interrelate concepts across any combination of the primary conceptual dimensions. The selection and organization of representational dimensions should be such that they encode the overarching interrelations among the primary conceptual dimensions. A global interpretive framework is achieved when single expressions in the representation can stand for complex concepts that involve all of the primary conceptual dimensions.

2. Differentiate primary conceptual dimensions—The global interpretive framework should clearly differentiate the primary conceptual dimensions, so that identifying and thinking about concepts from each dimension can be done in isolation as required. This is done by selecting different representational schemes (or unique combinations of schemes) for each of the primary conceptual dimensions. This principle is satisfied when an expression for a concept from a single conceptual dimension can be interpreted using only its interpretive scheme without reference to, or interference from, schemes from any other dimension.

3. Integrate secondary conceptual dimensions—The global representational framework should be augmented with representational schemes

for each secondary conceptual dimension in a manner that allows the relations with other relevant dimensions to be made. Expanding schemes for existing primary conceptual dimensions or adding new representational schemes that interlock with relevant schemes can be used to achieve this.

4. Coherent schemes for conceptual dimensions—For each conceptual dimension, a representational scheme should be provided that interrelates the different levels and aspects of that dimension but that also allows the levels and aspects to be clearly differentiated. The aim of this principle is to support the unambiguous interpretation and contextualization of concepts within a dimension. This is done by selecting a representational scheme (or a unique combination of schemes) whose structural characteristics match the structural characteristics of the conceptual dimension.

The four principles should all be applied together in the design of a representation. They were developed by generalizing over various representations that we have designed and successfully evaluated. They also echo previous theoretical claims about what constitutes an effective mapping between structures in the representing world and the represented world; in particular, claims about the importance of homomorphic and analogous representations (Barwise & Etchemendy, 1995; Kosslyn, 1989; Palmer, 1978; Sloman, 1985; Stenning & Oberlander, 1995; Zhang, 1996). One important difference is that the principles explicitly acknowledge the heterogeneity of conceptual systems and specify how conceptual structure within and between conceptual dimensions should be represented. Previous accounts may be interpreted as addressing relations within a single conceptual dimension.

Design of ROLLOUT

Figure 5.1 shows an example of the ROLLOUT for bakery scheduling. The design of ROLLOUT is described with reference to the four principles. The primary conceptual dimensions for the domain are the entity-taxonomic, temporal, structural, and functional dimensions. The individual representational schemes used for each are first presented before their roles in the global interpretive framework are discussed.

Figure 5.2 shows how different types of icons represent different classes of entities and how individual instances are identified using labels. Figure 5.2a shows a product and Figure 5.2b is an order that is comprised of a number of such products. Figure 5.2c represents a product allocated to the schedule, which we call a *batch*. Figures 5.2d and 5.2e are icons representing bulk and conveyor or piecewise processing steps. A staircase-like strip of

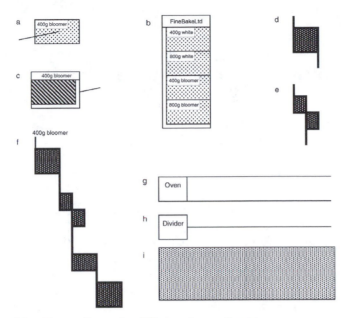

Figure 5.2.   Types of icons for different classes of entities.

icons represents the production of a batch consisting of a set of process steps (see Fig. 5.2f). Figures 5.2g and 5.2h represent the two types of equipment, bulk equipment or conveyor equipment, respectively. Figure 5.2i is the generic representation of a process stage that could be performed by alternative pieces of equipment. The use of labeled icons for most entities in the bakery domain, with distinct types of icons for different types of entity, satisfies principle D that concerns the use of a coherent interpretive scheme for a conceptual dimension. An exception to this is the representation of types of dough, or mix recipes, which are shown by the color of product and process step icons. This particular scheme is used because each type of dough can make several different products; a one-to-many correspondence that cannot be adequately captured using more types of icons.

The temporal dimension is encoded by horizontal space (the x-axis) in ROLLOUT, with a linear timeline for reference running from left to right. Points in time are given by the location of graphical objects, as shown in Figure 5.3. Durations are distances between graphical objects or their parts. General temporal relations are encoded by the horizontal ordering of objects, with later things toward the right. This provides a coherent representational scheme for this conceptual dimension (principle D), because the different perspectives of time are encoded using the one representational scheme, but each perspective is differentiated by the use of distinct graphical elements (points versus distance versus order).

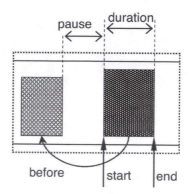

Figure 5.3. Aspects of the temporal conceptual dimension.

The structural conceptual dimension is encoded by the organization of graphical objects in vertical spatial dimension (y-axis). The representation of a group of products that makes up an order is achieved by arranging them together as a vertical stack, as shown in Figure 5.2b. Such groupings appear in the upper half of ROLLOUT (the planner diagram). The sequence of bakery processing stages is represented by the vertical sequence of process stage bars, their descending arrangement indicating their order in baking. The items of equipment that can be used for each process stage, which makes up the overall bakery configuration, are represented by equipment bars at the same level as the appropriate process stage bar. For example, Figure 5.4 shows the first two process stages in a bakery with one mixer and two dividers in the stages, respectively. These process stage and equipment configurations are placed in the bottom half of ROLLOUT (the scheduling diagram). The coherent interpretive scheme for each conceptual dimension principle (D) is satisfied by the use of positioning and grouping in vertical space, plus the differentiation of simple grouping (of products) and sequential configuration (of process stages and steps) into two separate panels (top and bottom).

The functional dimension concerns the dynamic activities of scheduling, which comprises three main aspects. First, there is the decomposition of orders and their collation into runs of the same type of product. This is achieved by associating together the icons for allocated batches, with lines connecting them to their respective orders, as shown in Figure 5.5. Second, the process of assigning a given process step to a particular piece of equipment is represented by the superposition of the process step icon on the bar for each piece of equipment. Figure 5.4 shows the result of assigning a batch to the mixer and then to the first of two available dividers. Third, a product moves through the bakery as it is being processed and this sense of transition is captured by the descending chain of process step icons linked to-

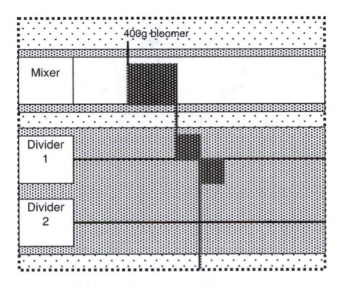

Figure 5.4. Structure of processing stages and assignment of processing steps.

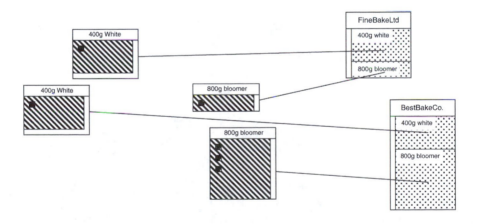

Figure 5.5. Decomposition of orders and assembly of runs: orders to the right and groupings of batches into run on the left.

gether by connecting lines, as shown in Figure 5.2f. The representational scheme for this conceptual dimension is that of relations among graphical objects and the use of different types of relations are used for the different aspects. Hence, principle D is satisfied for this dimension.

These are the pairings of conceptual dimensions and representational schemes: entity dimension to graphical object shape, temporal dimension to horizontal space, structural dimension to vertical space, function dimensions to relations among graphical objects. Hence, the design of the ROLLOUT diagram satisfies the principle B, which requires that each primary conceptual dimension be encoded using a different representational scheme. This means that changes in any one conceptual dimension are independent of the concepts in the other dimensions. For example, moving a process step icon to the right in ROLLOUT will give a delay to the start time, but its assignment to a process stage and a piece of equipment will remain the same (functional dimension), as will its processing order with respect to other steps (structural dimension). Similarly, functionally reassigning a process step from one piece of equipment to another within a process stage, for instance by moving the icon in Divider 1 to Divider 2 in Figure 5.4, does not change its timing or duration, or its structural relation to other process steps.

The ROLLOUT diagram satisfies principle A. The representational schemes work together to provide an integrated interpretive framework because they all share the same space. Figure 5.6 shows schematically how they are coordinated in the ROLLOUT diagram. Most domain concepts that span more than one conceptual dimension can usually be read as a sin-

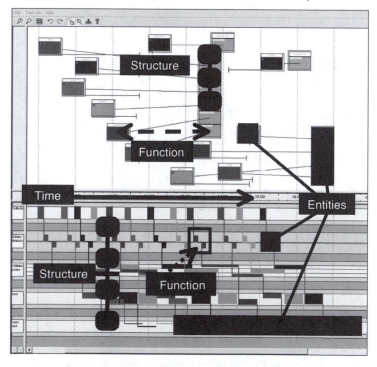

Figure 5.6.   ROLLOUT global interpretive framework.

gle expression. For any given entity, information from each dimension is co-located with the icon representing the entity: its class is represented by the type of icon, temporal information by the icon's position and width, structural information by vertical position, functional information by its links to other icons or overlaying other icons. Further, the temporal dimension does not just apply to particular entities but also to relations between entities, such as the distance between two process steps standing for a pause in production in a piece of equipment, as shown in Figure 5.3. More complex relations across the dimension are also expressed. Consider Figure 5.5, which has two pairs of runs for similar products, with 400 g white loaves to the left and bloomers in the middle of the diagram. Their deadlines are given by the horizontal positions of the right-hand edges of their order icons and the start times for the allocated batches are given by the left sides of their icons. Hence, it is clear that the order of production of the bloomers is temporally consistent with the order deadlines, but not so for the white loaves; but this may not matter as the white loaves are being made ahead of time compared to the bloomers.

ROLLOUT is divided into two halves, with the planner panel (top) and the scheduling panel (bottom), which reflect the particular structural and functional aspects of the domain. The planner panel possesses the representational scheme for structural concepts dealing with groups of orders and products, and hence the functional scheme for representing the decomposition of orders and the assembly of runs is naturally part of that top panel. The scheduling panel possesses the schemes for structural concepts that deal with the configuration of process stages and bakery equipment, and hence the functional scheme for the assignment of process steps to equipment is naturally part of the bottom panel.

An important distinction in the domain is the difference between bulk process stages and conveyor stages, which process dough in a piece-wise fashion. Bulk process stages are represented by simple rectangular icons, which combine the entity (rectangular icon), temporal (width), and property dimensions (height—discussed later). The representation of conveyor stages additionally requires the combination of structural, functional, and more complex temporal concepts. Figure 5.7 shows the various components of a conveyor processing stage, including the distinct sequencing of items, the operations on those items, and the timings associated with each part of this processing step. This shows how, at a finer scale, the interpretive framework supports the expression of concepts that combine components from multiple conceptual dimensions.

The secondary conceptual dimensions are the property, formal relational models, and evaluative conceptual dimensions. The overall interpretive framework is augmented to encode these secondary conceptual dimensions to satisfy principle C. The main aspect of the property dimen-

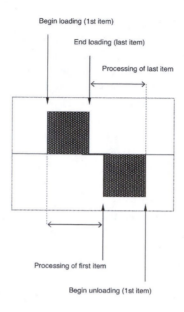

Figure 5.7.   Interpretation of conveyor processing stage.

sion concerns the capacity of equipment and sizes of batches relative to the capacity of a particular piece of equipment. These quantities are represented by the height of the bars for the equipment and the height of process step rectangles, respectively, as shown in Figure 5.8. This method of representing (interval) quantities means the arithmetic rules—formal relation models dimension—that are used to compute capacity consumption (or spare capacity) are graphically encoded as the total height of a stack of process steps (or the unfilled space in an equipment bar). In the planner diagram, the height of the product icons in order groupings and the corresponding batch allocation icons, may also be used to represent the absolute size of batches (ratio quantities).

There are two aspects to the evaluative conceptual dimension: the general evaluation of schedule quality and the identification of violations of particular constraints. Particular graphical expressions in ROLLOUT can be used to reason about overall quality and to find specific violations. For instance, how effectively a piece of equipment is used can be visually assessed by inspecting how densely its bar is packed within process step icons. At a higher level, the quality of a schedule can be assessed by considering factors such as the packing density or uniformity of batches, or the sequence of different types of dough (block of icons of the same color). Similarly, particular graphical relations show violations. A missed deadline is shown by the end of a production strip in the schedule diagram being located to the right of its product grouping. A process step icon flowing over the boundaries of an equipment bar shows that the capacity has been exceeded, as shown in Figure 5.9a. Similarly, overlapping process step icons show clashes of product in a piece of equipment (see Fig. 5.9b). As violations of the constraints in a schedule correspond physically to impossible states of affairs or the breaking of important limits, these graphical relations are highlighted, augmenting the overall framework for a particular aspect of a conceptual dimension (principle C). In Figures 5.9a and 5.9b, the overflow and overlap are highlighted in red (black in the figure). For batches that miss deadlines, the whole process is highlighted by outlining all the process step icons and the links between them in red. Figure 5.9c shows one highlighted process step.

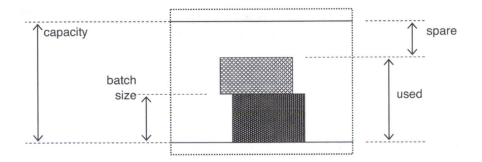

Figure 5.8.   Representing property and formal relations conceptual dimensions.

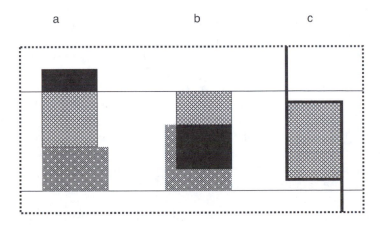

Figure 5.9.   Various violations of constraints.

This section has shown how the REEP approach can be used to design representations that preserved the conceptual structure of a domain using appropriate representational structures. Conceptual dimensions are identified and used to explicate the conceptual structure of the domain. The design principles are then used to create a representation with a global interpretive framework, consisting of distinct and coherent conceptual schemes for each conceptual dimension. Such design is effortful, but the representations created may confer substantial benefits for complex problem solving and learning. These benefits are discussed in the next section.

BENEFITS OF REPRESENTATIONS DESIGNED USING REEP

The REEP approach has been successfully used to design representations for instructional domains and complex problem-solving domains. The latest is the ROLLOUT diagram, which has been shown to effectively support bakery planning and scheduling. Generalizing over these successful cases, various beneficial characteristics appear to be shared by them all: semantic and syntactic traits that enhance cognitive support at a number of different levels in such REEP representations. These characteristics are presented in order of increasing cognitive sophistication, and how they address the generic issues of complex problem solving, identified earlier, is now discussed.

Comprehension and Mental Models

The REEP approach seems to produce designs that support the comprehension of the problem domain and that help users to maintain good mental models of the problem. This appears to work in three interrelated ways (Cheng, 2002). First, the concepts tend to be represented by easily remembered and recognized patterns of graphical objects. Such patterns as graphical expressions may stand as composite icons for those concepts. Second, the encoding of concepts within and between conceptual dimensions using particular representational schemes and a global interpretive framework has the desired consequence that meaningful interpretive contexts are naturally provided for all graphical expressions. Third, the differentiation of the aspects and levels within conceptual dimensions, and the differentiation of conceptual dimensions themselves, further supports comprehension by reducing the likelihood of confusion between graphical expressions. Problem states are readily perceptible, which aids users in their acquisition of mental models of the problem environment, and also means that the cognitive cost of maintaining an accurate and detail mental model is relatively low.

An additional way in which representations designed using the REEP approach manage to support comprehension is through meaningful graphical expressions that happen naturally to emerge from the structure of the representation, which would not otherwise have been deliberately represented in a conventional design. Figure 5.10 shows such an example from ROLLOUT. It is necessary to identify the processing steps belonging to a given production batch. This is done with lines linking the bottom right and top left corners of successive steps, as in Figure 5.10a. These links can then be read as icons representing the transfer of the product between different process stages. The orientation of the links is an emergent property that encodes the information about the nature of the transfer. In Figure 5.10a, the transfer is immediate, whereas in Figure 5.10c, the downward slope means there is a delay. In Figure 5.10b, the upward slope represents a scheduling error, with a process step being set backward in time. These status, or warning, signals emerged from ROLLOUT without having been deliberately designed into the representations of the relations between process steps. When the basic semantics of process steps has been understood, users readily and correctly spot and then interpret the meaning of the slopes for themselves.

The REEP approach embraces the informational and conceptual complexity of a domain. The principles specify how such complexity can be addressed by using alternative representation schemes for different conceptual dimensions, but integrate the representations so that concepts and relations spanning multiple conceptual dimensions can be readily accessed. ROLLOUT and other REEP representations tend to be visually complex, as they bring together information from many conceptual dimensions within a single representation. However, users of the representations do not find this to be a particular difficulty, because they are able to selectively attend to those parts of the representations that are relevant to the particular goal and task context they have in mind, while ignoring other aspects of the representation that are irrelevant at the time. This form of se-

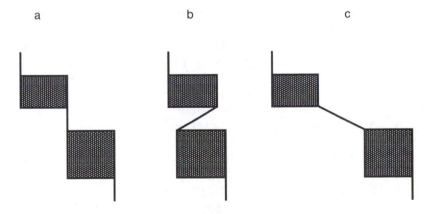

Figure 5.10. Transfer between process steps.

lective visual adaptation of the representation to current local problem requirements occurs easily without specific training and appears to be grounded in our natural ability to shift our focus of attention to different parts of complex environments depending upon task demands.

Supporting Problem Solving

REEP representations designed so far have all been diagrammatic. As such they accrue the well-understood benefits that most diagrams have when used for problem solving, such as reducing the effort needed for search and recognition (Larkin & Simon, 1987), and permitting the use of powerful schemas (Koedinger & Anderson, 1990). It also appears that REEP representations can address task and solution process complexities by providing more powerful problem operators and simpler solution procedures. A problem operator recognizes a problem state, or expression, and its action modifies that state in some way. The operators tend to be more powerful as more complex graphical expressions can be recognized and more complex transformations applied to them, because the expressions can encompass multiple aspects of a conceptual dimension or multiple conceptual dimensions. For example, to the bottom right in Figure 5.1, there is a cluster of three process steps that clash with each other. When attempting to resolve this, a user is not only aware of the clashes but also of the local spatial and temporal context, and also the broader context of the relations between the process steps upstream. The action to resolve the clash can be more sophisticated than just changing the start time of a process step, but can simultaneously involve moving a whole batch and an individual step within a piece of equipment. Problem-solving procedures are comprised of sequences of operator applications. REEP representations may improve these in various ways. The number of operators that are seen to be applicable to a problem state may be fewer and the selection of meaningful sequences of operators easier. For example, in ROLLOUT, all process steps can potentially be moved forward or backward in time, but the availability of the rich interpretive context means that operations that do not cause overcapacity clashes are readily apparent. An alternative way to describe these benefits is in terms of how accessible REEP representations make the many and varied constraints in a problem task. There are limitations or restrictions on the permissible relations under each conceptual dimension but these constraints, and how they interact, can often be read directly from the representation. More powerful operators, as mentioned earlier, may also mean a reduction in the number of operators needed in a procedure to achieve a goal. In other words, the branching factor and depth of problem state spaces given by REEP representations are likely to be smaller than for conventional representations (Cheng, 2002).

Problem-solving procedures are well supported by REEP representations, with users often adopting more sophisticated solution strategies than with conventional representations. One strategy involves looking ahead at the consequence of particular problem steps to plan sequences of actions that may temporarily make the problem state worse, but that subsequently result in much greater improvements. Such strategies are more effective than the trial and error incremental approaches found with conventional representations (Barone & Cheng, 2004; Cheng at al., 2002). For example, ROLLOUT users may move the start time of a batch to one that is better but simultaneously create predictable clashes with other batches, which are then immediately resolved.

Complexity due to ill-structured problems and problems requiring the coordination of multiple problem state spaces may be alleviated by REEP representations. The provision of a coherent interpretive framework may allow the user to more easily jump from an ill-structured problem space to an overarching problem space and to find constraints to resolve the ill-structured parts for the first space. Different problem spaces may be associated with alternative combinations of conceptual dimensions, but as all such combinations are integrated within a single interpretive framework the coordinated search of the spaces is supported. For example, bakery scheduling requires the coordinated search of at least two spaces, the decomposing of orders into suitable runs and the allocation of batches to meet deadlines. The switching between the two spaces is facilitated by ROLLOUT as the planning and scheduling components are closely coordinated by the complementarity of planning and scheduling diagrams.

Studies on ROLLOUT and other REEP representations show that they have a dual character, allowing users to solve problems in knowledge-lean and knowledge-rich fashions, that are suited to users who are novices or experts in bakery scheduling, respectively. As the constraints of a domain are directly encoded in the representation, at one extreme, it is possible to solve problems as purely abstract geometry puzzles, in which graphical objects are arranged into diagrammatic configurations that satisfy given graphical constraints (which capture the requirements of the goal). At the other extreme, problems can be solved by knowledgeable users who interpret patterns in the representation as meaningful states of the domain and reason at that level. More typically, users do a mixture of both forms of reasoning, with their preference depending on their knowledge of the domain. This inherent flexibility means the complexity of problem solving due to the individual differences of the knowledge of users is naturally addressed.

Enhancing Learning

Some of the ways that REEP representations can effectively support learning build directly on the problem-solving benefits. As problem solving is easier, more episodes of problem solution will be experienced for a given amount of practice time, and more of the solutions found will be correct (Cheng, 2002). Also, fewer classes of operators and shorter, less complex solution paths mean that learning problem-solving procedures will be easier.

The representations can better support the development of expertise because they, in effect, capture the knowledge of the domain at multiple levels, which are then readily accessible as and when the learner is ready for them. As a learner acquires an understanding of the meaning of patterns of graphical objects, which are perceptual chunks for particular concepts, relations among them will be considered at higher level and the learner will naturally begin to acquire more complex conceptual relations. A possible hypothesis is that REEP representations provide learners with a self-adapting Vygotskian Zone of Proximal Development (e.g., Wood, 1988), which constantly changes as the learners becomes more knowledgeable. This parallels, at a higher level, the manner in which users appear to selectively adapt the representation to their current task goals and context. Possessing large meaningful patterns for use in problem solving is one of the characteristics of expertise (Chi, Glaser, & Farr, 1988), the acquisition of which REEP representations may be able to bootstrap.

Supporting System Development

The development of ROLLOUT progressed through several cycles of prototyping, evaluation, and feedback from the users. Through the cycles, it was found that the underlying interpretive framework provided a rational basis for incorporating new developments. For example, bakery production was initially conceptualized as a sequence of bulk processes, but it became apparent that continuous, piece-by-piece processes, were just as important. Fortunately, the overall interpretive scheme provided appropriate constraints to devise a specific representation that incorporated the temporal, structural, and functional complexities of such conveyor processes. Figure 5.7 shows the representation, where the upper and lower rectangles represent the incremental loading and unloading of the equipment, respectively, and the offset between them represents the duration of the process.

Another way in which the REEP approach supports system development is through the emergence of useful novel concepts and relations, that were previously unavailable to the users. For example, in the ROLLOUT diagram, the horizontal distance between the points corresponding to the end of the production of a batch and the deadline of its order indicates the amount of spare time in production; something that was not readily available to the bakery schedulers. They considered this information to be so useful that they requested us to provide an even easier way of comprehending the spare time. This was achieved by adding an indicator bar to the icon for allocated batches in the planner window, as shown in Figure 5.11. The length of the line from the start to the bar (head of the rotated "T") gives the spare time. If the whole of the batch icon is to the right of the ideal start bar, then the batch will breach the deadline.

CONCLUSION

Designing representations for complex problems is important, because most real-world problems are complex. Research on the nature and design of representations has shied away from complex problems, because of the major challenges that complex problem pose. This chapter described some of these challenges and then presented an approach to the design of representations for such problems. The REEP approach contends that the conceptual structure of a domain and its underpinning system of knowledge should be preserved in the structure of the representation using an appropriate interpretive framework and representational schemes. The notion of conceptual dimensions was introduced as a basis for analyzing the conceptual structure of a domain. Seven such dimensions were described and applied to the bakery scheduling domain. The result was the ROLLOUT diagram, which effectively supports complex problem solving in that domain. This in turn adds further evidence to the claim that the REEP approach is an effective method for creating representations for complex problems.

ACKNOWLEDGMENTS

This research was support by the UK ESRC/EPSRC/DTI through the PACCIT research program (RES-328–25-001). Our thanks go to present

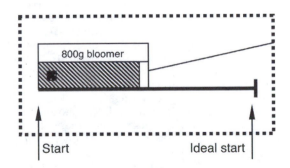

Figure 5.11. Allocated batch icon augmented with ideal start time bar.

and past members of the project team: Mark Auckland, John Wilson, Nikoleta Pappa, and Bill Dawson. We would also like to express our gratitude to the members of the ROLLOUT consortium for sharing their knowledge and insights into the fascinating world of the bakery industry and for their support of project, in particular Linda Young and Stan Cauvain of the CCFRA and BakeTran. Finally, we thank Jo Cheng for proof reading the manuscript.

REFERENCES

Barone, R., & Cheng, P. C.-H. (2004). Representations for problem solving: On the benefits of integrated structure. In E. Banissi, K. Börner, C. Chen, M. Dastbaz, G. Clapwortht, F. A., E. Izquierdo, C. Maple, J. Roberts, C. Moore, A. Ursyn, & J. J. Zhang (Eds.), *Proceedings of the 8th international conference on information visualisation* (pp. 575–580). Los Alamitos, CA: Institute of Electrical and Electronics Engineers.

Barwise, J., & Etchemendy, J. (1995). Heterogenous logic. In J. Glasgow, N. H. Narayanan, & B. Chandrasekaran (Eds.), *Diagrammatic reasoning: Cognitive and computational perspectives* (pp. 211–234). Menlo Park, CA: American Asssociation for Artificial Intelligence Press.

Bertin, J. (1983). *Seminology of graphics: Diagrams, networks, maps.* Madison: University of Wisconsin Press.

Burns, C. M., & Hajdukiewicz, J. R. (2004). *Ecological interface design.* Boca Raton, FL: CRC Press.

Card, S., MacKinlay, J., & Shneiderman, B. (Eds.). (1999). *Readings in information visualization: Using vision to think.* Mahwah, NJ: Lawrence Erlbaum Associates.

Cheng, P. C.-H. (1999). Interactive law encoding diagrams for learning and instruction. *Learning and Instruction, 9,* 309–326.

Cheng, P. C.-H. (2002). Electrifying diagrams for learning: Principles for effective representational systems. *Cognitive Science, 26,* 685–736.

Cheng, P. C. H. (2003). Diagrammatic re-codification of probability theory: A representational epistemological study. In R. Alterman & D. Kirsh (Eds.), *Proceedings of the twenty fifth annual conference of the cognitive science society* (pp. 234–239). Boston: Cognitive Science Society.

Cheng, P. C.-H. (2004). Why diagrams are (sometimes) six times easier than words: Benefits beyond locational indexing. In A. Blackwell, K. Marriot, & A. Shimojima (Eds.), *Diagrammatic representation and inference: Third international conference, diagrams 2004* (pp. 242–254). Berlin, Germany: Springer-Verlag.

Cheng, P. C.-H., Barone, R., Cowling, P. I., & Ahmadi, S. (2002). Opening the information bottleneck in complex scheduling problems with a novel representation: Stark diagrams. In M. Hegarty, B. Meyer, & N. H. Narayanan (Eds.), *Diagrammatic representations and inference: Second international conference, diagrams 2002* (pp. 264–278). Berlin, Germany: Springer-Verlag.

Cheng, P. C.-H., Barone, R., Pappa, N., Wilson, J. R., Cauvain, S. P., & Young, L. S. (2006). Understanding bakery scheduling: Diverse methods for convergent constraints in user-centred design. In P. D. Bust (Ed.), *Contemporary ergonomics* (pp. 45–49). London: Taylor & Francis.

Cheng, P. C.-H., & Shipstone, D. M. (2003). Supporting learning and promoting conceptual change with box and avow diagrams. Part 1: Representational design and instructional approaches. *International Journal of Science Education, 25,* 193–204.

Cheng, P. C.-H., & Simon, H. A. (1995). Scientific discovery and creative reasoning with diagrams. In S. Smith, T. Ward, & R. Finke (Eds.), *The creative cognition approach* (pp. 205–228). Cambridge, MA: MIT Press.

Chi, M. T. H., Glaser, R., & Farr, M. J. (Eds.). (1988). *The nature of expertise.* Hillsdale, NJ: Lawrence Erlbaum Associates.

Ellis, B. (1968). *Basic concepts of measurement.* Cambridge, England: Cambridge University Press.

Engelhardt, J. (2002). *The language of graphics.* Amsterdam: Institute for Logic, Language, and Computation, University of Amsterdam.

Evans, J. (1989). *Bias in human reasoning: Causes and consequences.* Hillsdale, NJ: Lawrence Erlbaum Associates.

Glasgow, J., Narayanan, N. H., & Chandrasekaran, B. (Eds.). (1995). *Diagrammatic reasoning: Cognitive and computational perspectives.* Menlo Park, CA: American Association for Artificial Intelligence Press.

Green, T. R. G. (1989). Cognitive dimensions of notations. In A. Sutcliffe & L. Maclaulay (Eds.), *People and computers 5.* Cambridge, England: Cambridge University Press.

Kaplan, C. A., & Simon, H. A. (1990). In search of insight. *Cognitive Psychology, 22,* 374–419.

Klahr, D., & Dunbar, K. (1988). Dual space search during scientific reasoning. *Cognitive Science, 12,* 1–48.

Koedinger, K. R., & Anderson, J. R. (1990). Abstract planning and perceptual chunks: Elements of expertise in geometry. *Cognitive Science, 14,* 511–550.

Kosslyn, S. M. (1989). Understanding charts and graphs. *Applied Cognitive Psychology, 3,* 185–226.

Kotovsky, K., Hayes, J. R., & Simon, H. A. (1985). Why are some problems hard? *Cognitive Psychology, 17,* 248–294.

Larkin, J. H., & Simon, H. A. (1987). Why a diagram is (sometimes) worth ten thousand words. *Cognitive Science, 11,* 65–99.

Newell, A., & Simon, H. A. (1972). *Human problem solving.* Englewood Cliffs, NJ: Prentice Hall.

Palmer, S. E. (1978). Fundamental aspects of cognitive representation. In E. Rosch & B. B. Lloyd (Eds.), *Cognition and categorization.* (pp. 259–303). Hillsdale, NJ: Lawrence Erlbaum Associates.

Pinker, S. (1990). A theory of graph comprehension. In R. Freedle (Ed.), *Artificial intelligence and the future of testing* (pp. 73–126). Hillsdale, NJ: Lawrence Erlbaum Associates.

Scaife, M., & Rogers, Y. (1996). External cognition: How do graphical representations work? *International Journal of Human–Computer Studies, 45,* 185–213.

Shahar, Y. (1997). A framework for knowledge-based temporal abstraction. *Artificial Intelligence, 90,* 79–133.

Sloman, A. (1985). Why we need many knowledge representation formalisms. In M. Bramer (Ed.), *Research and developments in expert systems* (pp. 163–183). Cambridge, England: Cambridge University Press.

Simon, H. A. (1973). The structure of ill-structured problems. *Artificial Intelligence, 4,* 181–201.

Simon, H. A., & Lea, G. (1974). Problem solving and rule induction: A unified view. In L. W. Gregg (Ed.), *Knowledge and cognition* (pp. 105–127). Hillsdale, NJ: Lawrence Erlbaum Associates.

Stenning, K., & Oberlander, J. (1995). A cognitive theory of graphical and linguistic reasoning: Logic and implementation. *Cognitive Science, 19*, 97–140.

Ware, C. (1999). *Information visualisation: Perception for design.* San Francisco: Kaufmann.

Wood, D. J. (1988). *How children think and learn.* Oxford, England: Blackwell.

VanLehn, K. (1989). Problem solving and cognitive skill acquisition. In M. Posner (Ed.), *Foundations of cognitive science* (pp. 527—580). Cambridge, MA.: Bradford/MIT Press.

Zhang, J. (1996). A representational analysis of relational information displays. *International Journal of Human–Computer Studies, 45*, 59–74.

Zhang, J. (1997). The nature of external representations in problem solving. *Cognitive Science, 21*, 179–217.

Zhang, J., & Norman, D. A. (1994). A representational analysis of numeration systems. *Cognition, 57*, 271–295.

Chapter 6

Of Memes and Teams: Exploring the Memetics of Team Problem Solving

Michael A. Rosen, Stephen M. Fiore, and Eduardo Salas
Institute for Simulation and Training, and University of Central Florida

Increasing attention has been paid to temporal and developmental aspects of teams with the growing complexity in the context surrounding modern work teams driving research in areas such as team evolution, maturation, and adaptation (e.g., Burke, Stagl, Salas, & Pierce, in press; Morgan, Salas, & Glickman, 2001). The rapid pace of change in work conditions and consequently the knowledge and skills developed to accomplish tasks in these ever changing environments compels researchers to develop an understanding of evolutionary processes that can be applied to the understanding, design, and evaluation of work teams. Much can be added to this discussion of team evolution and adaptation through a consideration of the evolutionary perspective of memetics— the application of evolutionary theory to the study of culture. Specifically, by applying the concept of memes—the evolutionary units of cultural transmission—to the domain of team problem solving, insights can be generated into the development of problem-solving skills in teams over time and how this development is responsive to environmental change.

Modern theories of evolution rest on five core ideas: (a) change occurs in the biological world, (b) evolution diverges in a branched tree pattern with organisms descending from ancestors, (c) new species of organisms arise when a population is physically separated and then diverges, (d) evolutionary change occurs gradually as few organisms that are radically different than their parents are likely to survive, and (e) natural selection drives the adaptive change process (Mayr, 1991; Sterelny, 1999). Therefore, any attempt to apply evolutionary theory to culture and problem solving in teams must address the fundamental challenge of how these propositions function metaphorically within the context of teams nested within cultural organizations. For this reason, the evolutionary nature of team problem solving is best viewed through a multilevel perspective—as individual, team, and organizational factors that interact to form the inheritance, mutation, and selection mechanisms of cultural evolution. We suggest that it is this process that drives the adaptation of key knowledge structures involved in team problem solving.

In this chapter, memetics is used as a framework to explore the processes by which both long-term knowledge (e.g., knowledge structures about taskwork and teamwork) and dynamic understanding (e.g., team situation and problem models) are developed and leveraged in team problem solving. This perspective contributes to the understanding of how expertise is built within teams and how that expertise is translated (e.g., mechanisms of mutation) through the sociocognitive processes (i.e., mechanisms of inheritance and transmission) into the knowledge structures (i.e., memes) needed for effective problem solving by explicating the nature of how culture is transmitted and how it adapts to meet changing environmental demands (i.e., mechanisms of selection). To that end, the following objectives are met: (a) there is a review of the memetics literature (in particular the cultural selectionism approach), including a discussion of the theoretical and empirical issues involved with the meme concept; (b) from the memetic literature, a coherent conceptual framework of sociocognitive processes currently believed to operate in the transmission and mutation of memes is developed; (c) this framework is then applied to the team problem solving and shared cognition literature to elucidate the role of cultural evolution in the development of team problem models; and (d) implications of the memetic perspective for team problem solving are then discussed within the context of the five core principles of evolutionary theory. Findings of this review and analysis show that team problem solving viewed through a memetic perspective is a multilevel phenomenon whereby memes determine the core knowledge structures involved in team problem model construction. These memes are transmitted between team members through sociocognitive processes that serve the dual roles of inheritance and mutation. Through interaction with the environment over time, a team selects successful memes that support more effective problem-solving behaviors.

THE FUNDAMENTALS OF CULTURAL EVOLUTION

The theory of memetics proposes that there are discrete and identifiable units of cultural replication called memes (Dawkins, 1976). These memes can represent a broad range of cultural information from musical tunes to religious beliefs to scientific theories and can be construed as the external influences that shape human thought (Pleh, 2003). Memes adhere to evolutionary principles in that they have an inherent tendency to replicate or to be transmitted from person to person. In the process of transmission, memes mutate and these mutations are subject to selection processes such that the memes that make people more culturally fit are adopted over competing memes. Memetics can be divided into two divergent lines based on the underlying metaphor chosen to represent the process of cultural transmission (Alvarez, 2004; Pleh, 2003). The first model is based on the meme as a germ metaphor and takes epidemiology as its guiding science— the view popularized by Gladwell (2002). It comprises the ideas of thought contagion (e.g., Sperber, 2000) and a virus of the mind (e.g., Lynch, 1996), both artifacts of Dawkins's (1982) revised definition of a meme—"a unit of information residing in the brain" (p. 109). This definition sparked ideas of a virus or host relation between memes and minds as well as the idea that memes jump from one person to the next in an infectious manner. The second model of memetics is rooted in Dawkins's (1976) original definition of a meme, "a unit of cultural transmission, or a unit of imitation" (p. 206). This definition seeded the original model of memetics, one based on evolutionary science (e.g., Wimsatt, 1999). This branch of research—the gene-oriented perspective—has the advantage of maintaining continuity between the metaphorical applications of memetics and the attempts to apply memetics in a literal sense. Marsden (1998) argued that these two perspectives are essentially equivalent and that each can be informed through mutual exploration; however, there are strong sentiments that the contagion metaphor is severely impeding progress in memetics from those engaged in research based on the genetic metaphor (Gatherer, 1998). And still yet other researchers argue for the position that adhering too closely to either metaphor produces deleterious results on the quality of memetics as a science by creating a forced ignorance to existing knowledge bases such as social learning (Gil-White, 2004).

Defining the Meme

As evident in the two definitions provided earlier, the meme generally can be thought of as the smallest unit of cultural information that is subject to the processes of selection. Beyond this point, there exists much confusion in the definitions due in part to the division in model sciences discussed earlier as well as the inherent difficulty of the task. In evolutionary genetics, the size of a unit of analysis is determined by the size of a unit that can be selected through interaction with the environment (Dawkins, 1982). This same logic has guided attempts to quantify or locate specific memes. However, the best definition of meme available is likely that provided by the Oxford English Dictionary as it makes no theoretical assumptions about the nature of transmission, mutation, or selection (Gil-White, 2004). This leaves room for divergent theoretical stances and thus facilitates the comparative testing of hypothesis across researchers employing any one of the varying theoretical frameworks of memetics. Therefore, for the purposes of creating an easily transportable and generalizable definition, the meme is taken to be "an element of culture that may be considered to be passed down by non-genetic means" (Oxford English Dictionary, as cited in Gil-White, 2004). See Aunger (2000) for an exhaustive discussion of views on defining the meme.

Outlining the Processes of Cultural Evolution

An evolutionary system must have three characteristics: (a) a mechanism of inheritance (e.g., a method for transmitting information to progeny), (b) the unit of information must exhibit mutation, and (c) a selection process for inhibiting unsuccessful mutations and perpetuating adaptive ones. Memetics must address each of these to be faithful to the evolutionary perspective. The meme represents the cultural knowledge that is enacted through interaction with the environment (the environment consisting of the physical and social worlds). This relation is moderated by mutation and selection processes. A meme mutatesevery instance it is enacted by an individual; however, this change is assumed to be only a slight deviation from howthat person generally enacts the meme. Each slightly mutated enactment of a meme is subject to the selection process, the feedback from the environment detailing the adaptive nature of the behavior. This interaction with the environment provides opportunities for others to observe the individual and to inherit memes (e.g., learn, imitate, etc.). The mutation process moderates this relation as well as variations in memes that are introduced in the observation and adoption of behaviors by those witnessing the enactment of the original meme. The mutation, selection, and inheritance mechanisms are discussed in more detail later.

Inheritance and Mechanisms of Transmission.   Intense debate surrounds the mechanisms of memetic transmission. One line of reasoning is that if Darwinian theories are to be applied to culture, then the meme must adhere to a strict interpretation of replication (e.g., Blackmore, 1999), specifically through the single pathway of direct imitation of the behaviors of others. A second major perspective advocates including processes under the umbrella of social learning into the realm of memetic transmission (e.g., Gil-White, 2004). From this broadened perspective, the vagaries of terms like *imitation* or *contagion* can be broken down into the specific cognitive processes that serve as the proving ground or environment for selection of memes. The inclusion of more complex cognitive mechanisms as a means for memetic transmission does not preclude the existence of a low level process analogous to genetic replication. It merely suggests that there are different cognitive processes at work involved in the interpretation of observed and enacted behavior as well as in the internal representations of this experience. A science of memetics informed by human cognition and social learning theories allows for more purposeful and directed transmission of memes. Succinctly put, it is by accepting superior behaviors and tools one has observed or which has been transmitted to them, that individuals are able to better adapt to their organizational environment.

Mutation.   The idea of mutation is contentious in memetics as well. The "hard-line" replication stance requires that memes have the ability to make copies of themselves with a high level of fidelity (e.g., the meme must not deviate too much from its original form when it is transmitted from one individual to another). However, this is not the case, as there are great differences in the ways that memes and genes mutate. Specifically, the rate and degree of mutation for memes is apparently much different than that of genes, a point that troubles some researchers. Sperber (2000) suggested that the mutation rate of memes is 1; that is, every time a meme is transmitted or enacted it is altered. This makes sense from both the imitation perspective (e.g., an attempt to imitate behavior does not produce a precise and accurate duplication) and from the broadened perspective of social learning. However, these variations are not necessarily large enough to alter the relation between the meme and the associated adaptation to the environment while consequently affording a more significant opportunity for selection (e.g., more variations in memes participating in the selection process). Additionally, mutation in genes is seen as random whereas mutation in memes can be purposeful and directed (Castelfranchi, 2001; Gil-White, 2004). Someone deliberately practicing a set of behaviors is much more likely to reach higher levels of competence through "better" memes. This is consistent with expertise research focused on practice and learning in that superior (e.g., more adaptive) performance is achieved via deliberate practice in increasingly challenging situations, a process in which people repeatedly engage in behaviors with the intent of improving performance (Ericsson & Smith, 1991). A memetic interpretation is that deliberate practice is a process in which memes are enacted with the intent of taking advantage of directional mutation. That is, each time a meme is enacted, it mutates; therefore, deliberate practice is a testing ground for memetic variations with environmental feedback driving the adoption of more successful memes.

Selection. As various mutations of a meme are enacted in the environment, each will meet with varying degrees of success. Some mutations will fit the environmental context better than others. These memes are then likely to be transmitted to other people observing the interaction between the meme holder and the environment, as they will want to imitate the success they have witnessed. As the mutation rate of memes is generally said to be 1 (i.e., the meme mutates with each enactment or transmission), the rate of selection must be equally high as well. For instance, Wilkins' (1998) definition of a meme, "the least unit of sociocultural information relative to a selection process that has favorable or unfavorable selection bias that exceeds its endogenous tendency to change" (p. 8), embodies the idea that the mutation rate cannot exceed the systems ability to discern the adaptive nature of the mutation. If this were not the case, then cumulative progress toward more adaptive states would not be possible as more variations would be produced than a selection mechanism could evaluate.

In summary, memes are the smallest units of cultural information subject to natural selection. This cultural information is enacted in human behavior, a process exhibiting mutation of memes in every instance. The enactment of memes is observable by other humans who subsequently internalize the cultural information when feedback from the environment suggests that it is beneficial to do so. The process of inheritance through observation exhibits mutation in memes as well. In the next section, we discuss characteristics of team problem solving as traditionally represented in the literature. Subsequently, we apply the aforementioned described perspective of cultural evolution to the process of team problem solving.

TEAM PROBLEM SOLVING

The first step in discussing team problem solving is to adequately define what is meant by a team. To do so, we adopt a widely accepted definition of a team. Specifically, a team is taken to be

> a distinguishable set of two or more people who interact dynamically, interdependently, and adaptively toward a common and valued goal/objective/mission, who have each been assigned specific roles or functions to perform, and who have a limited life span of membership. (Salas, Dickinson, Converse, & Tannenbaum, 1992, p. 4)

Increasingly, the work assigned to teams is of a cognitive nature such as is the case with problem-solving tasks and teams. In the general problem-solving literature, researchers have identified multiple stages that contribute to the overall process of problem solving such as searching through hypothesis generation and testing spaces (Klahr & Dunbar, 1988; Simon & Lea, 1974), as well as stages preceding formal generation of hypotheses or possible courses of action (e.g., Klein, 1993; Montgomery, Lipshitz, & Brehmer, 2005; Moreland & Levine, 1992). In this chapter, we focus on the problem identification and conceptualization stages of team problem solving for several reasons. First, problem representation is instrumental to the problem-solving process (Fiore & Schooler, 2004; Newell & Simon, 1972) such that expert problem solvers can be differentiated from novices by the amount of time they spend assessing the problem (Chi, Glaser, & Rees, 1982). Similarly, Orasanu and Connolly (1993) stated that in decision making, "experts are distinguished from novices mainly by their situation assessment abilities, not their general reasoning skills" (p. 20). Randel, Pugh, and Reed (1996) found that expert decision makers spent more time evaluating the situation whereas novices spent more time evaluating courses of action. The second reason for a focus on problem identification and conceptualization is that it is in these stages of problem solving that memetics can most be useful, as is illustrated in the following section. The remainder of this section is dedicated to a discussion of the problem identification and conceptualization stages of team problem solving as well as aspects of shared cognition crucial to effective team problem solving.

Problem Identification and Conceptualization

The first stage of team problem solving we include in our analysis is problem identification—the initial sensing or detection that a problem exists or will exist in the near future (e.g., Klein, 1993). At the team level, problem identification is triggered when an awareness of the problem spreads through the team members (Larson & Christensen, 1993; Moreland & Levine, 1992). Problem identification is a crucial step for team problem solving. Only after the existence of a problem has been recognized by the team can the next stage begin—problem conceptualization.

Problem conceptualization, or the development of a problem space, is the stage where the problem solver encodes the salient aspects of the problem at hand such as the characteristics of the environment, the goals of agents relevant to the problem, as well as rules for operating (Newell & Simon, 1972). Originating in human information processing theories, problem space theory has more recently been developed in the context of teams (e.g., Fiore & Schooler, 1999, 2004; Hinsz, Tindale, & Vollrath, 1997; Orasanu, 1994). A major addition to the problem conceptualization stage in team versus individual problem solving is the aspect of sharedness. That is, some level of overlap between team members' understanding of the essential problem characteristics is a mandatory factor that contributes to a team's ability to build representations that are effective in the generation of quality problem solutions. In its most simple form, a team must share an understanding of what the problem is before the problem can be addressed and the heterogeneity of knowledge and perspective within a team can be exploited (Fiore & Schooler, 2004). In the following section, the shared cognition mechanisms that underlie the team problem identification and conceptualization stages of problem solving are reviewed. It is through these mechanisms that teams begin the problem-solving process, and it is within these mechanisms that cultural evolution influences team problem solving.

Shared Cognition in Teams

Problem identification and conceptualization on the team level are driven by shared knowledge structures and shared cognition, a construct describing "how processes at the intraindividual level are dependent on and interact with processes at the interindividual level" (Fiore & Schooler, 2004, pp. 137–138). Three aspects of shared cognition are discussed in further detail due to their relevance to problem identification and conceptualization. These are shared mental models, team situation awareness, and team problem models. The relations between these aspects of shared cognition are illustrated in Figure 6.1 and described as follows.

Shared Mental Models. Mental models are knowledge structures involved in the integration of knowledge as a person works toward understanding the situational information he or she receives from the environment (Johnson-Laird, 1983). When mental models are shared within a team, the individual members are better able to interact with the environment and process incoming information in a similar or complimentary manner to that of their fellow team members. By virtue of sharing aspects of mental models, team members can form explanations for environmental conditions and expectations for tasks and team members that are congruent with those of their fellow

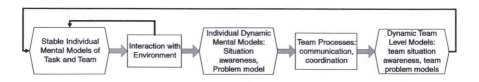

Figure 6.1.   Framework of knowledge structures in team problem solving.

team members (Cannon-Bowers, Salas, & Converse, 1993), abilities which promote higher levels of team performance and decision making (Mathieu, Heffner, Goodwin, Salas, & Cannon-Bowers, 2000; Stout, Cannon-Bowers, & Salas, 1996;). Therefore, research supports the idea that shared mental models among team members help to account for the implicit and fluid coordination that is characteristic of highly effective teams (Mohammed & Dummville, 2001). In terms of team problem solving, shared mental models must at a minimum contain information concerning the roles and skills of fellow team members as well as a representation of the problem structure (Fiore & Schooler, 2004). A specific type of mental model, a strategic mental model, is of significant importance in team problem solving (Salas, Stout, & Cannon-Bowers, 1994). The strategic mental model can be thought of as the combination of procedural and declarative knowledge, such that it comprises

> information that is the basis of problem solving, such as action plans to meet specific goals, knowledge of the context in which procedures should be implemented, actions to be taken if a proposed solution fails, and how to respond if necessary information is absent. (Converse & Kahler, 1992, p. 6)

It is the sharedness of this type of mental model that allows for accurate and coordinated problem identification in teams as well as problem conceptualization (e.g., Stout, Cannon-Bowers, Salas, & Milanovich, 1999). However, these relatively stable and long-term mental models must be applied to the environmental situations, often dynamic in nature, that form the context of problems. Team situational awareness is a vital result of this process for team problem solving.

Team Situational Awareness (TSA). TSA represents a much more dynamic knowledge structure than shared mental models and as such can be thought of as an ongoing process wherein any one point in time represents the team's current understanding of the environment. Individual situational awareness (SA) does not summate to produce TSA, that is, TSA is produced through an active coordination and communication between team members (Artman, 2000). It is important to recognize that TSA is "built on a combination of the degree of shared understanding within the team (i.e., shared mental models) and each individual member's SA (based on preexisting knowledge bases and cue/pattern assessments)" (Salas, Cannon-Bowers, Fiore, & Stout, 2001. p. 173). The importance of TSA is increased in complex and dynamic systems (Salas, Prince, Baker, & Shrestha, 1995). The distinction between shared mental models and TSA is analogous to the distinction between knowledge and cognition with team knowledge held in the sharedness of mental models which is then processed through team processes such as communication to produce dynamic understanding or

TSA (Cooke, Salas, Kiekel, & Bell, 2004). TSA is essential to team problem identification because it allows team members to compare their representations of normal or expected environmental states with actual environmental states, detect deviations between the two, and reason about causes, future states of the environment, and possible courses of action (Cannon-Bowers, Salas, & Converse, 1993; Orasanu & Salas, 1993; Salas, Prince, Baker, & Shrestha, 1995; Salas, Stout, & Cannon-Bowers, 1994).

Team Problem Model.   Accurate and complete situation awareness on the individual and team levels is necessary for effective team problem solving (Orasanu, 1990), but is insufficient by itself. Specifically, effective team problem solving requires that teams develop a team level problem model. This is defined as a

> shared understanding of the situation, the nature of the problem, the cause of the problem, the meaning of available cues, what is likely to happen in the future, with or without action by the team members, shared understanding of the goal or desired outcome, and a shared understanding of the solution strategy. (Orasanu, 1994, p. 259)

The team problem model therefore places specific constraints on TSA such that it must include all situation and task specific knowledge requirements listed earlier (Klimoski & Mohammed, 1994; Orasanu & Salas, 1993). The point that relatively stable mental models are essential to the development of dynamic situation awareness and problem models cannot be understated for the purposes of this analysis. Lipshitz and Ben Shaul (1997) stated that people use schemata to translate situational information into the dynamic understanding and representational models of the problem space necessary for decision making and problem solving. The transformation of shared mental models (i.e., team knowledge) into dynamic understanding (i.e., TSA and team problem models) through team behaviors (i.e., team level cognitive mechanisms) is critical to the team problem-solving process.

In summary, problem identification and problem conceptualization are the beginning stages of the team problem-solving process. Performance in both of these stages emerges first from the application of individual level knowledge structures to the environmental context surrounding a team. The long-term knowledge structures at the individual level are used to construct dynamic models of the current situation. In turn, these individual dynamic models are processed through team communication and coordination processes into a shared understanding of the problem within the team. Figure 6.1 illustrates the framework of knowledge structures involved in the team problem-solving process. In the following section, this process is analyzed from a memetic perspective.

INTEGRATING MEMETICS AND TEAM PROBLEM SOLVING

The aforementioned understanding of team problem identification and conceptualization through shared cognition can be augmented with an analysis of cultural evolutionary processes within the team and the organization that contains the team. Generally, relatively stable knowledge in the form of mental models can be thought of as memes or as comprising multiple memes in the case where different aspects of a particular mental model may change as the person interacts with the environment without changing the entire mental model. Mental models guide interaction and contain information about task behavior; therefore, mental models as cultural knowledge structures, in part or in whole, are likely subject to the evolutionary processes germane to memes. An individual's interaction with the environment will change the mental model in the direction of greater accuracy given appropriate feedback, a process also interpretable as the selection of more adaptive memes. Memetic processes of inheritance, mutation, and selection function within the framework of shared cognition and team problem solving. These relations are discussed later in relation to changes in teams as they develop over time in problem-solving processes. Table 6.1 summarizes the key memetic processes at work on the team level.

Team Problem Solving in the Context of Team Evolution and Maturation

Characteristics of the team such as individual expertise, and organizational structure, as well as the roles and responsibilities of team members, serve as inputs to the team problem-solving process (Warner, Letsky, & Cowen,

TABLE 6.1
Elements of Cultural Evolution in Teams

Characteristics of Evolutionary System	Process Within Teams
Inheritance	Memetic transmission and inheritance occurs through the sociocognitive mechanisms used to build team level dynamic knowledge
Mutation	Memetic mutation occurs in every instance of team members enacting their cultural knowledge; mutation can be both random or purposeful
Selection	Memetic selection occurs during team level interactions with the environment, wherein the goal-directed acceptance of more successful knowledge is made possible through feedback between team members and between the team and the environment

2005). These characteristics exhibit change over time. Morgan, Salas, and Glickman (1993) have advanced a model of team evolution that synthesizes what is known about team development over time. The Team Evolution and Maturation (TEAM) model (Morgan et al., 1993) is built on earlier developmental theories of teams (Tuckman, 1965) and comprises seven core stages (i.e., the first meeting [forming], initial exploration of the environment [storming], efforts toward the creation of roles [norming], patterns of occasional inefficient performance [performing-I], reevaluation and transition [reforming], refocusing of efforts toward more effective performance [performing-II], and completion of team assignments), which teams proceed through in a nonlinear manner. Within this process of development, two distinct tracks or lines of development are discernable—one defined as operational skills including experience with procedures, policies, tools, and other task related work, and the second defined as generic team skills that are focused on improving the processes of team work interactions such as interdependencies, team affect, relationships, cooperation, and coordination. Each of these lines of development are relevant to both the shared mental models that form the basis of team problem solving as well as the team processes that produce TSA and team problem models.

Inheritance and Transmission in Team Problem Solving. Memetic inheritance and transmission mechanisms function through the sociocognitive mechanisms used to process individual level knowledge (i.e., team knowledge—shared mental models) into team level dynamic representations such as problem models and TSA. By engaging in the communication and coordination behaviors necessary to manifest team level dynamic models, team members are afforded the opportunity to observe how their teammates process the available environmental cues as well as how they complete their individual task work. Following memetic theory, "individuals accept new behaviors, plans or tools as better solutions for their own problems, as good means for their goals; the groups diffuse and preserve (memorize) and transmit the best (discovered) solutions" (Castelfranchi, 2001, p.5); therefore, memetic inheritance is a learning process driven by the observation of other group members' goal relevant successes and failures at interacting with the environment. In relation to the two separate lines of development in the TEAM model, memes concerning operation skills and generic team skills are inherited during activities through all seven stages of team development. However, the forming stage is particularly important, as it is the first opportunity for team members to interact with each other and to share knowledge. The storming phase, consisting of the first exploration of the environment, allows team members to witness others enact memes in the operational context. The reforming stage allows team members to communicate the memes that have been most successful in the environment.

Mutation in Team Problem Solving.   Memetic mutation occurs in team problem solving through the interaction of team members exhibiting performance. Specifically, it is by interacting within a team and throughout an organization, that memes are mutated. Conceptually, teamwork can be a proving ground in that memetic variations are tested through environmental feedback. In this way, teamwork provides the context for the eventual adoption of memes demonstrated to be successful. Developmentally, within the performance-I stage of the TEAM model, where team members make the first unstable and relatively ineffective attempts at performance, memes are rapidly mutated in efforts to find adaptive patterns of interaction with the environment. Radically ineffective mutations are culled during this stage and subsequently the reforming stage where team members assess the effectiveness of their efforts. The performance-II stage of development represents the period where memes generally suited to the task are enacted and adaptive performance is witnessed. Memes are fine tuned in this period as slight variations, random and purposeful, and are produced and subjected to selection mechanisms continuously.

Selection in Team Problem Solving.   Team situational awareness contains information about actions and consequent changes in the environment. Hence, team situational awareness stores the information used to select variations of memes, and to judge the adaptive nature of each meme. Additionally, team situation awareness contains goals that can aid in purpose-driven mutation of memes. As with mutation then, it is through interaction on a team level that provides the environmental context in which the selection process occurs. In the TEAM model, selection is most readily witnessed in the forming stage of development where team members originally meet and the norming stage where aspects of team culture such as roles, responsibilities, and goals are formalized and hence stored in individual team members' shared mental models of the team members.

To summarize, team development over time can be viewed as a process of cultural evolution wherein a team develops the operational and generic team skills and knowledge necessary for high levels of problem-solving performance. Up to this point we have primarily considered the individual and team levels of cultural evolution in team problem solving. In the next section, we discuss some of the organizational influences at work in problem solving teams nested within cultural organizations.

ORGANIZATIONAL LEVEL MEMETIC INFLUENCES ON TEAM PROBLEM SOLVING

A number of organizational researchers have adopted the notion that the modern organization is too complex to effectively manage in a completely top-down fashion; that is, there is no optimal solution for organizational structure and no architecture that can be imposed that will create maximally effective performance. Instead, organizations are seen in part as self-organizing systems with massively interconnected processes and subprocesses that cannot be fully mapped. Researchers have been inspired by simulations of organizational evolution that suggest processes similar to those of biological evolution that represent an archetypal process of change that increases the effectiveness of complex systems without top-down control (e.g., Carley, 1997; Edmonds, 1998; Hines & House, 1998; Holland, 1995). Investigations by artificial life researchers into the emergence of intelligence in a mind and attempts to develop quantitative models of the relation between biological and cultural evolution (Bedau, 2003) are examples of the type of research contributing to a well-developed evolutionary perspective on organizations.

A brief review of the macrolevel perspectives on organizations is useful to highlight the role that an evolutionary perspective can play in modern organizational studies and the influence that memetic processes on the organizational level have on team problem solving. The most long-standing view of organizations is based in transaction cost economics (Coase, 1937; Williamson, 1985). Essentially, this perspective views organizations as a way to reduce the cost of doing business; material transactions are at the heart of the organization. Recent years have given birth to the idea of the knowledge-based economy and consequently to an understanding of organizations as a knowledge-based entity (e.g., Grant, 1996). In many ways, the knowledge-based view of organizations can be seen as an addendum or extension to the transaction-based view of organizations in that the knowledge-based view recognizes types of transactions other than material (e.g., cognitive or knowledge based). The evolutionary perspective has triumphed as a means to continue this expansion in that an evolutionary theory of organizations (i.e., a memetic theory of organizations) will include a view of the organization as a cultural entity. The knowledge-based view extends the transactional view in that the organization is now seen as a system that provides an identity to its constituents, an identity instantiated in shared language, beliefs, morals, values, and so forth. This sharing of culture is what enables lower costs for knowledge-based transactions; however, knowledge-based theories of organizations leave the underlying assumption of organizations as cultural entities explicitly unaddressed (Weeks & Gallunic, 2003). This is the lacuna sought to be filled by memetic analyses of organizations. The cultural aspects of organizations exert influence on team problem solving through memetic processes. The remainder of this section explores several areas of research which highlight organizational level memetic processes that affect team problem solving, specifically, organizational learning and adaptation, norms and policy, and transactive memory. Table 6.2 summarizes the key memetic processes at the organizational level.

Organizational Learning and Adaptation

Although the business world identifies with the phrase "survival of the fittest," recognition of organizations as evolutionary systems does not frequently progress past vague metaphors. However, research in organizational learning and adaptation is replete with evolutionary thinking. Although there is no shortage of interest in the topic, presently no theory of organizational learning enjoys widespread acceptance (Crossan, Lane, & White, 1999, Fiol & Lyles, 1985). However, there is consensus on a broad meaning for the term—a pattern of behaviors that allows the organization to adapt to environmental change (Senge, 1990). The literature on organizational learning is often conflated with work on organizational adaptation (Fiol & Lyles, 1985). Organizational adaptation has been defined as "change in a significant organizational attribute, such as basic business strategy or organizational structure in response to environmental change" (Levinthal, 1994, p. 171). These definitions of organizational learning and adaptation dovetail such that organizational learning can be seen as the process of responding to the environment and organizational adaptation is the outcome (e.g., the change in the organization that aligns it with external forces). A recent and popular framework of organizational learning, the 4I framework (Crossan et al., 1999), conceptualizes the process as one driven by strategic renewal—the need of the organization to balance consistency and adaptation, past knowledge and policies with new approaches. Organizational learning is the process by which mismatches between current organizational configurations (knowledge or material) and the environment are perceived, acted on, and ultimately codified into the organizational knowl-

TABLE 6.2
Elements of Cultural Evolution in Organizations

Characteristics of Evolutionary System	Process Within Organizations
Inheritance	Memes are distributed throughout the organization by the codification of cultural knowledge into formal policy and informal norms
Mutation	Memetic mutation at the organizational level is a product of purposeful alterations in organizational knowledge or material configurations in response to environmental change

edge. The 4I framework is defined as comprising four learning processes: intuiting, interpreting, integrating, and institutionalizing. Intuiting occurs on the individual level, where a person senses patterns in the environment; interpreting is the process of explaining this pattern through words and occurs on either the individual (e.g., in the case of explaining to oneself) or the group level (e.g., in the case of explaining to others). Taken together, the intuiting and interpreting phases of the 4I model map onto the problem identification stage of team problem solving discussed earlier. Integrating is the process of reaching shared understanding of the situation and coordinated action on the group level and can be equated with the problem conceptualization stage of team problem solving. The interpreting and integrating phases are where individuals witness variations of behavior and inherit the adaptive variants. The final phase of the 4I model, institutionalizing, involves the process of codifying decision choices to ensure that the organization responds to the environment in a routinized manner. Essentially, the institutionalizing phase is an attempt to propagate the most successful memes available throughout the organization for the benefit of those individuals that did not have access to the original problem-solving episode, individuals that did not witness the original successful enactment of memes. The phase of institutionalizing leads to the topic of memes as policy and norms.

Memes as Norms and Policy

There is a trend to associate memes with organizational policies (e.g., Giroux, Taylor, & Cooren, 1998; Hines & House, 1998; Speel, 1997). That is, the meme of the organizational organism is a policy; the policy is the smallest unit of cultural information subject to selection processes at the organizational level. In terms of the 4I framework, the policy is the institutionalized knowledge product obtained by engaging in the process of organizational learning. The idea of memes as policy is an artifact of exploring memetics in a metaphorical sense. Policy affects team problem solving by altering aspects of memes—content in the shared mental models of team members relating to roles, goals, and general rules of the problem space. In a literal interpretation of memetics, a policy is an external thing that does not necessarily map directly onto the culture of that organization's members; therefore, the memes involved represent the aspects of the policy that are held by the individual and not the externalized, codified policy.

In parallel to the idea of memes as policy is the idea of memes as a cultural norm. Norms as cultural rules of engagement exist outside of codified policy yet they serve a similar purpose—to bound and direct the actions and interactions of units within the organization. In opposition to external and formalized nature of policy, norms reside within the individuals of the organization.

Castelfranchi (2001) proposed that norms are a type of metameme, a knowledge structure that guides the process of social interaction—the mechanism of memetic inheritance. Therefore, norms, and to an extent policies, impact team problem solving by influencing both the content of the relatively stable and long-term knowledge structures, the methods of interaction used by individuals and teams to update those stable shared mental models, and the processes used to construct shared dynamic understanding.

Transactive Memory

Transactive memory is a type of shared cognition, but it differs from those previously discussed in that it can extend past the immediate members of a team. Transactive memory is a knowledge structure detailing what members of the team and organization posses, what knowledge is individual expertise, and what knowledge is shared. Essentially it is knowledge about who in the organization knows what information. This knowledge is advantageous in that transactive memory allows members of the organization to have access to a greater amount of knowledge than any one person could remember as an individual (Austin, 2003). The ability of a transactive memory system to improve team performance increases as the complexity of the task grows and as individual contributions of knowledge from individual team members is required (Faraj & Sproull, 2000; Lewis, 2000). Reduced cognitive load for individuals, access to an extended pool of specialized knowledge and skill, and a reduction in the redundancy of efforts are all advantages to developing transactive memory systems (Hollingshead, 1998a, 1998b). It is recognized that cultural evolutionary processes can be purpose driven and guided by the intentionality of agents. It is in this way that transactive memory assists in cumulative cultural evolution—by serving an important role in identifying desirable memes. A transactive memory system essentially provides a map of which individuals have the highest degree of aptitude for certain tasks, who has the most adaptive memes. This can speed the transmission of memes and ensure that the most adaptive memes are disseminated broadly.

In summary, the aspects of organizational learning and adaptation, policies and norms, and transactive memory systems represent organizational level influences on team problem solving that are subject to cultural evolutionary mechanisms. The organization can be seen both as a cultural entity—a logical extension of the knowledge-based view of organizations—as well as a cultural ecosystem where memes that ultimately form the building blocks of the shared representations necessary for effective team problem solving are inherited, mutated, and selected for their relative adaptive qualities. The next section will further examine these effects at work.

THE FIVE PILLARS OF EVOLUTIONARY THEORY IN TEAM PROBLEM SOLVING

Modern evolutionary theory is rooted in five core principles. Each of these principles is discussed below in the context of teams—comprising individuals nested in cultural organizations—solving problems. The purpose of such an exercise is theoretical triangulation. By viewing a phenomenon of interest from multiple theoretical vantage points, new insights can be generated and prevailing understandings can be further evaluated.

Change Occurs in the Biological World

This is a fundamental and simple assertion of evolutionary science that has a basic analog in the context of memetics in team problem solving. Change is a prerequisite to evolution and adaptation. If the environment a team experiences can be viewed as a steady state, then adaptation is not necessary or even possible. Accepting the proposition that teams encounter dynamic changing contexts and that they must develop new ways of meeting the challenges that solving problems in this environment places on them satisfies the first condition of evolutionary theory. More specifically, a cybernetic view of decision making involves the assertion that "the organism adapts to its environment not only by changing itself, but also by changing the environment" (Brehmer, 1996, p. 225). Therefore, causality in a system is reciprocal between the organism (team or individual) and the environment (operational context) and problem-solving and decision-making activities involve acting in a system characterized by perturbations with the aim of controlling that system while working toward a goal. In terms of problem-solving teams, knowledge about how the environment changes and reacts to various aspects of problem solutions is critical. Teams must represent this knowledge at the individual level to build an accurate and complete shared understanding—a team problem model.

Evolution Diverges in a Branched Tree Pattern With Organisms Descending From Ancestors

Memeticists believe that cultural evolution can be documented in a manner akin to a lineage (e.g., Lord & Price, 2001; Speel, 1997); however, there is no direct evidence to support this from within the field due to measurement issues with memes (Edmonds, 2002). Within the domain of expertise research, it has been found that there are definite ceilings to performance increases realized through iterative practice and that these ceilings are very different depending on the initial representations of the task that people hold when they first begin practicing (Ericsson & Smith, 1991). In certain training situations where trainees have learned incorrect forms of basic skills, trainers are forced to return to instruction on the remedial skills before the trainee can progress to higher levels of performance. Taken together, this suggests that one "species" of meme or mental representation can only become a better or more adapted version of the original, but for radical change, an entirely new representation is needed. Parallels to this can be witnessed in teams solving problems within the context of large organizations viewed as cultural entities. Dougherty (1992) reported on the difficulties encountered by project teams attempting to span organizational divides. She classified one of the main obstacles as one of different "interpretive schemes" (mental models and memes in the language of this chapter) within different organizational components fostering different aspects of adaptation. This created distinct "thought worlds," which can be thought of as memetic lineages. Additionally, Edmondson, Bohmer, and Pisano (2001) reported on medical organizations adopting new technology that radically changed the standard operating procedures in place. One of the hallmarks of the organizations that made successful transfers of routines was the promotion of shared understanding through early episodes of reflective practice. These practice sessions can be thought of as a replacement of the old organizational memes pertaining to process and procedures with new memes relating to the technology shift that, once put into the actual operational context, are capable of evolving into adaptive knowledge structures.

NEW SPECIES OF ORGANISMS ARISE WHEN A POPULATION IS PHYSICALLY SEPARATED AND THEN DIVERGES

The memetic parallel to the idea of physical separation being crucial to the development of new species of organisms in biological systems can be used to reframe some findings from the shared cognition literature. Levesque, Wilson, and Wholey (2001) found that the mental models of team members diverge over time when the team members' roles become increasingly specialized. Whereas this is an anomalous finding that is inconsistent with most thinking on mental model development (i.e., as a team works together, its mental models should converge over time and not diverge; e.g., Boldstad & Endsley, 1999), Levesque et al.'s findings are consistent with the memetic perspective particularly in terms of separation leading to differentiation. Each individual team member pursued unique aspects of the team task and therefore team members were essentially isolated from the rest of the team in regard to the cultural knowledge the task required them to enact. This isolation, as in biological evolution, favored divergence as the distinct environmental contexts of the team members selected different variations of memes. Other work shows that the amount of interaction a team member has with another is more predictive of mental model congruency (i.e., memetic similarity) than physical proximity (e.g., Graham, Schneider, Bauer, Bessiere, & Gonzalez, 2004). Therefore, the isolation that fosters divergence in memetics is a sociocognitive separation and not a physical one as in biological systems. Team members that do not engage in the communication behaviors necessary for updating knowledge structures, or who do not interact in a manner conducive to other types of memetic transfer (e.g., opportunities to witness the enactment of memes), will naturally develop memes and knowledge structures that are specialized to the separate sociocognitive and cultural environmental contexts of their operation.

When team members' memes diverge, several possible impacts on problem-solving abilities are possible. First, the divergence only involves individual task-related knowledge that does not affect the ability of the team to construct accurate and complete TSA and problem models and therefore does not produce deleterious effects on problem identification or conceptualization. Second, the divergence occurs in the knowledge structures governing team interaction, an outcome that affects the processes by which team members update long-term knowledge structures and construct TSA and problem models. A third outcome based on the adaptive nature of the patterns of divergence involves the evolutionary principle of punctuated equilibrium (Eldredge & Gould, 1972). That is, separation of particular units of an organization (e.g., individuals from teams, teams or units from organizations) creates the opportunity for the development of innovation (Price, 1995). The adaptive divergence occurring in a team isolated from the broader organization or a team member from the team can be reintegrated into the larger team or organization at which time the adaptive memes can be inherited through interaction with team members or broader organizational dissemination (e.g., formal policies and organic norms).

Evolutionary Change Occurs Gradually as Few Organisms That Are Radically Different Than Their Parents Are Likely to Survive

Although there is a general understanding of the emergence of organizations through communication, there is a much weaker understanding of what causes organizational features to persist (e.g., Giroux, Taylor, & Cooren, 1998; Nardi, 1996). However, despite instances of rapid organizational innovation and change through punctuated equilibrium, adaptations accumulate through the process of many small changes—success approximations of memes leading to superior performance. Most readily, this principle of evolution interacts with team problem solving from the organizational level and manifests in the codification of memes into policy and the subsequent effects of policy and norms on memes.

Natural Selection Drives the Adaptive Change Process

This tenet is perhaps the reason why evolution is an intuitively attractive perspective to apply in many domains. Understanding the processes by which adaptive knowledge and culture is distinguished from less adaptive knowledge and culture can drive organizational design that fosters adaptation. Levine and Choi (2004) have shown that teams that experience unsuccessful performance episodes were more likely than more successful teams to engage in higher frequencies of strategy-relevant communication after the performance episode. This indicates that teams enacting unsuccessful memes are more likely to engage in the team communication processes necessary to revise their shared understanding of the task or situation or to reinforce the underlying "sharedness" of the requisite knowledge about task and teamwork (i.e., certain members may detect that others are not operating as if they possessed the appropriate meme).

CONCLUDING REMARKS

Memetics provides a useful perspective by which to view a conceptual issue and more specifically to reinterpret the current understanding of team problem solving. By viewing teams as cultural entities nested within larger organizational cultural entities, an expanded and developmental picture of team problem solving can be created. The context of teams is increasingly complex and adaptation increasingly essential. Cultural knowledge influences how teams solve problems and the memetic processes of inheritance, mutation, and selection can be used to generate new insight into team evolution and adaptation.

REFERENCES

Alvarez, A. (2004). Memetics: An evolutionary theory of cultural transmission. *SORITES: Electronic Magazine of Analytical Philosophy, 15,* 24–28.

Artman, H. (2000). Team situation assessment and information distribution. *Ergonomics, 43*(8), 1111–1128.

Aunger, R. (Ed.). (2000). *Darwinizing culture: The status of memetics as a science.* Oxford, England: Oxford University Press.

Austin, J. R. (2003). Transactive memory in organizational groups: The effects of content, consensus, specialization, and accuracy on group performance. *Journal of Applied Psychology, 88,* 866–878.

Bedau, M. A. (2003). Artificial life: Organization, adaptation and complexity from the bottom up. *TRENDS in Cognitive Science, 7,* 506–512.

Blackmore, S. (1999). *The meme machine.* Oxford, England: Oxford University Press.

Bolstad, C. A., & Endsley, M. R. (1999, September). *Shared mental models and shared displays: An empirical evaluation of team performance.* Paper presented at the 43rd annual meeting of the Human Factors and Ergonomics Society, Houston, TX.

Brehmer, B. (1996). Man as a stabiliser of systems: From static snapshots of judgement processes to dynamic decision making. *Thinking and Reasoning, 2*, 225–238.

Burke, C. S., Stagl, K.C., Salas, E., Pierce, L., & Kendall, D. (in press). Understanding team adaptation: A conceptual analysis & model. *Journal of Applied Psychology.*

Cannon-Bowers, J. A., Salas, E., & Converse, S. (1993). Shared mental models in expert team decision making. In N. J. Castellan, Jr. (Ed.), *Individual and group decision making* (pp. 221–246). Hillsdale, NJ: Lawrence Erlbaum Associates.

Carley, K. M. (1997). Organizational adaptation. *Annals of Operations Research, 75*, 25–47.

Castelfranchi, C. (2001). Towards a cognitive memetics: Socio-cognitive mechanisms for memes selection and spreading. *Journal of Memetics—Evolutionary Models of Information Transmission, 5.* Retrieved March 10, 2006, from http://cfpm.org/jom-emit/2001/vol5/castelfranchi_c.html

Chi, M. T. H., Glaser, R., & Rees, E. (1982). Expertise in problem solving. In R. J. Sternberg (Ed.), *Advances in the psychology of human intelligence* (pp. 7–75). Hillsdale, NJ: Lawrence Erlbaum Associates.

Coase, R. H. (1937). The nature of the firm. *Economica, 4*, 386–405.

Converse, S. A., & Kahler, S.E. (1992). *Knowledge acquisition and the measurement of shared mental models.* Unpublished manuscript, Orlando, FL, Naval Training Systems Center.

Cooke, N. J., Salas, E., Kiekel, P. A., & Bell, B. (2004). Advances in measuring team cognition. In E. Salas & S. M. Fiore (Eds.), *Team cognition: Understanding the factors that drive process and performance* (pp. 83–106). Washington, DC: American Psychological Association.

Crossan, M. W., Lane, H. W., & White, R. E. (1999). An organizational learning framework: From intuition to institution. *Academy of Management Review, 24*, 522–537.

Dawkins, R. (1976). *The selfish gene.* Oxford, England: Oxford University Press.

Dawkins, R. (1982). *The extended phenotype.* Oxford, England: Oxford University Press.

Dougherty, D. (1992). Interpretive barriers to successful product innovation in large firms. *Organization Science, 3*, 179–202.

Edmonds, B. (1998). On modelling in memetics. *Journal of Memetics—Evolutionary Models of Information Transmission.* Retrieved March 9, 2006, from http://cfpm.org/jom-emit/1998/vol2/edmonds_b.html

Edmonds, B. (2002). Three challenges for the survival of memetics. *Journal of Memetics—Evolutionary Models of Information Transmission, 6.* Retrieved March 10, 2006, from http://cfpm.org/jom-emit/2002/vol6/edmonds_b.html

Edmondson, A. C., Bohmer, R. M., & Pissano, G. P. (2001). Disrupted routines: Team learning and new technology implementation in hospitals. *Administrative Science Quarterly, 46*, 685–716.

Eldredge, N., & Gould, S. J. (1972). Punctuated equilibrium: An alternative to phyletic gradualism. In T. J. M. Schopf (Ed.), *Models in paleobiology* (pp. 82–115). San Francisco: Freeman.

Ericsson, K. A., & Smith, J. (1991). Prospects and limits of the empirical study of expertise: An introduction. In K. A. Ericcson & J. Smith (Eds.), *Toward a general theory of expertise: Prospects and limits* (pp. 1–38). Cambridge, England: Cambridge University Press.

Faraj, S. A., & Sproull, L. (2000). Coordinating expertise in software development teams. *Management Science, 46*, 1554–1568.

Fiol, C. M., & Lyles, M. A. (1985). Organizational learning. *Academy of Management Review, 10*, 803–813.

Fiore, S. M. & Schooler, J. W. (1999, July). Problem space and group problem solving. In S. M. Fiore (Chair), *Cognition and the small group: Inter- and intra-individual cognitive processes in group problem solving and decision making*. Symposium conducted at the third biennial meeting of The Society for Applied Research in Memory and Cognition, Boulder, CO.

Fiore, S. M., & Schooler, J. W. (2004). Process mapping and shared cognition: Teamwork and the development of shared problem models. In E. Salas & S. M. Fiore (Eds.), *Team cognition: Understanding the factors that drive process and performance* (pp. 133–152). Washington, DC: American Psychological Association.

Gatherer, D. (1998). Why the 'thought contagion' metaphor is retarding the progress of memetics. *Journal of Memetics—Evolutionary Models of Information Transmission, 2*. Retrieved March 10, 2006, from http://cfpm.org/jom-emit/2002/vol6/edmonds_b_letter.html

Gil-White, F. J. (2004). Common misunderstandings of memes (and genes): The promise and the limits of the genetic analogy to cultural transmission processes. In S. Hurley & N. Chater (Eds.), *Perspectives on imitation: From mirror neurons to memes* (pp. 317–338). Cambridge, MA: MIT Press.

Giroux, H., Taylor, J. R., & Cooren, F. (1998, August). *Memes and the persistence of organizational structures*. Paper presented at the Symposium on Memetics: Evolutionary Models of Information Transmission, 15th International Conference on Cybernetics, Namur, Belgium.

Gladwell, M. (2002). *The tipping point: How little things can make a big difference*. New York: Little, Brown.

Graham, J., Schneider, M., Bauer, A., Bessiere, K., & Gonzalez, C. (2004, September). *Shared mental models in military command and control organizations: Effect of social network distance*. Paper presented at the 48th annual meeting of Human Factors and Ergonomics Society, New Orleans, LA.

Grant, R. M. (1996). Toward a knowledge-based theory of the firm. *Strategic Management Journal, 17*, 109–122.

Hines, J., & House, J. (1998, October). *Harnessing evolution for organizational management*. Paper presented at the International Conference on Complex Systems, Nashua, New Hampshire.

Hinz, V. B., Tindale, R. S., & Vollrath, D. A. (1997). The emerging conceptualization of groups as information processors. *Psychological Bulletin, 121*, 43–64.

Holland, J. H. (1995). *Hidden order: How adaptation builds complexity*. Reading, MA: Addison-Wesley.

Hollingshead, A. B. (1998a). Communication, learning, and retrieval in transactive memory systems. *Journal of Experimental Social Psychology, 34*, 423–442.

Hollingshead, A. B. (1998b). Retrieval processes in transactive memory systems. *Journal of Personality and Social Psychology, 74*, 659–671.

Johnson-Laird, P. N. (1983). *Mental models*. Cambridge, MA: Harvard University Press.

Klimoski, R., & Mohammed, S. (1994). Team mental model: Construct or metaphor? *Journal of Management, 20*(2), 403–437.

Klahr, D., & Dunbar, K. (1988). Dual space search during scientific reasoning. *Cognitive Science, 12*, 1–48.

Klein, G. (1993). A recognition primed decision (RPD) model of rapid decision making. In G. Klein, J. Orasanu, R. Calderwood, & C. E. Zsambok (Eds.), *Decision making in action* (pp. 138–147). Norwood, NJ: Ablex.

Larson, J. R., & Christensen, C. (1993). Groups as problem_solving units: Toward a new meaning of social cognition. *British Journal Social Psychology, 32*, 5–30.

Levesque, L. L., Wilson, J. M., & Wholey, D. R. (2001). Cognitive divergence and shared mental models in software development project teams. *Journal of Organizational Behavior, 22,* 135–144.

Levine, J. M., & Choi, H. (2004). Impact of personnel turnover on team performance and cognition. In E. Salas & S. M. Fiore (Eds.), *Team cognition: Understanding the factors that drive process and performance* (pp. 153–176). Washington, DC: American Psychological Association.

Levinthal, D. (1994). Surviving schumpeterian environments: An evolutionary perspective. In J. A. C. Baum & J. V. Singh (Eds.), *Evolutionary dynamics of organizations* (pp. 167–178). New York: Oxford University Press.

Lewis, K. (2000, August). *Transactive memory and performance of management consulting teams: Examining construct and predictive validity of a new scale.* Paper presented at the annual meeting of the Academy of Management, Toronto, Canada.

Lipshitz, R., & Ben Shaul, O. (1997). Schemata and mental models in recognition-primed decision making. In C. E. Zsambok & G. Klein (Eds.), *Naturalistic decision making* (pp. 293–303). Mahwah, NJ: Lawrence Erlbaum Associates.

Lord, A., & Price, I. (2001). Reconstruction of organizational phylogeny from memetic similarity analysis: Proof of feasibility. *Journal of Memetics - Evolutionary Models of Information Transmission, 5.* Retrieved March 10th, 2006, from http://cfpm.org/jom-emit/2001/vol5/lord_a&price_i.html

Lynch, A. (1996). *Thought contagion: How belief spreads through society.* New York: Basic Books.

Marsden, P. (1998). Memetics and social contagion: Two sides of the same coin? *Journal of Memetics—Evolutionary Models of Information Transmission, 2.* Retrieved March 9th, 2006, from http://cfpm.org/jom_emit/1998/vol2/marsden_p.html

Mathieu, J. E., Heffner, T. S., Goodwin, G. F., Salas, E., & Cannon-Bowers, J. (2000). The influence of shared mental models on team process and performance. *Journal of Applied Psychology, 85,* 273–283.

Mayr, E. (1991). *One long argument: Charles Darwin and the genesis of modern evolutionary thought.* London: Penguin.

Mohammed, S., & Dumville, B.C. (2001). Team mental models in a team knowledge framework: Expanding theory and measure across disciplinary boundaries. Journal of Organizational Behavior, 22(2), 89-103.

Montgomery, H., Lipshitz, R., & Brehmer, B. (Eds.). (2005). *How professionals make decisions: Expertise, research and applications.* Mahwah, NJ: Lawrence Erlbaum Associates.

Moreland, R. L., & Levine, J. M. (1992). Problem identification by groups. In S. W. Worchel, W. Wood, & J. A. Simpson (Eds.), *Group processes and productivity* (pp. 17–47). Newbury Park, CA: Sage.

Morgan, B. B. Jr., Salas, E., & Glickman, A. S. (1993). An analysis of team evolution and maturation. *The Journal of General Psychology, 120,* 277–291.

Nardi, B. A. (1996). Studying context: A comparison of activity theory, situated action models, and distributed cognition. In B. A. Nardi (Ed.), *Context and consciousness: Activity theory and human–computer interaction* (pp. 35–52). Cambridge, MA: MIT press.

Newell, A., & Simon, H.A. (1972). *Human problem solving.* Englewood Cliffs, NJ: Prentice-Hall.

Orasanu, J. (1990). *Shared mental models and crew decision making* (No. 46). Princeton, NJ: Princeton University, Cognitive Science Laboratory.

Orasanu, J. (1994). Shared problem models and flight crew performance. In N. Johnston, N. McDonald, & R. Fuller (Eds.), *Aviation psychology in practice* (pp. 255–285). Brookfield, VT: Ashgate.

Orasanu, J., & Connolly, T. (1993). The reinvention of decision making. In G. Klein, J. Orasanu, R. Calderwood, & C. E. Zsambok (Eds.), *Decision making in action: Models and methods* (pp. 3–20). Norwood, NJ: Ablex.

Orasanu, J., & Salas, E. (1993). Team decision making in complex environments. In G. Klein, J. Orasanu, R. Calderwood, & C. E. Zsambok (Eds.), *Decision making in action: Models and methods* (pp. 327–345). Norwood, NJ: Ablex.

Pleh, C. (2003). Thoughts on the distribution of thoughts: Memes or epidemies. *Journal of Cultural and Evolutionary Psychology, 1,* 21–51.

Price, I. (1995). Organizational memetics?: Organizational learning as a selection process. *Management Learning, 26,* 299–318.

Randel, J. M., Pugh, H. L., & Reed, S. K. (1996). Differences in expert and novice situation awareness in naturalistic decision making. *International Journal of Human–Computer Studies, 45,* 579–597.

Salas, E., Cannon-Bowers, J. A., Fiore, S. M., & Stout, R. J. (2001). Cue-recognition training to enhance team situation awareness. In M. McNeese, E. Salas, & M. Endsley (Eds.), *New trends in collaborative activities: Understanding system dynamics in complex environments* (pp. 169–190). Santa Monica, CA: Human Factors and Ergonomics Society.

Salas, E., Dickinson, T. L., Converse, S., & Tannenbaum, S. I. (1992). Toward an understanding of team performance and training. In R. W. Sweezy & E. Salas (Eds.), *Teams: Their training and performance* (pp. 3–29). Norwood, NJ: Ablex.

Salas, E., Prince, C., Baker, D. P., & Shrestha, L. (1995). Situation awareness in team performance: Implications for measurement and training. *Human Factors, 37,* 123–136.

Salas, E., Stout, R. J., & Cannon-Bowers, J. A. (1994). The role of shared mental models in developing shared situational awareness. In R. D. Gilson, D. J. Garland, & J. M. Koonce (Eds.), *Situational awareness in complex systems* (pp. 297–304). Daytona Beach, FL: Embry-Riddle Aeronautical University Press.

Senge, P. (1990). *The fifth discipline: The art and practice of the learning organization.* New York: Doubleday.

Simon, H. A., & Lea, G. (1974). Problem solving and rule induction: A unified view. In L. Gregg (Ed.), *Knowledge and cognition* (pp. 105–128). Hillsdale, NJ: Lawrence Erlbaum Associates.

Speel, H. (1997). A memetic analysis of policy making. *Journal of Memetics—Evolutionary Models of Information Transmission, 1.* Retrieved March 10th, 2006, from http://cfpm.org/jom-emit/1997/vol1/speel_h-c.html

Sperber, H. (2000). An objection to the memetic approach to culture. In R. Aunger (Ed.), *Darwinizing culture: The status of memetics as a science* (pp. 163–173). New York: Oxford University Press.

Sterelny, K. (1999). Evolution. In R. A. Wilson & F. C. Keil (Ed.), *The MIT encyclopedia of the cognitive sciences* (pp. 290–292). Cambridge, MA: MIT Press.

Stout, R. J., Cannon-Bowers, J. A., & Salas, E. (1996). The role of shared mental models in developing team situational awareness: Implications for training. *Training Research Journal, 2,* 85–116.

Stout, R. J., Cannon-Bowers, J. A., Salas, E., & Milanovich, D. M. (1999). Planning, shared mental models, and coordinated performance: An empirical link is established. *Human Factors, 41,* 61–71.

Tuckman, B. (1965). Developmental sequence in small groups. *Psychological Bulletin, 63*, 384–399.

Warner, N., Letsky, M., & Cowen, M. (2005, September). *Cognitive model of team collaboration: Macro-cognitive focus.* Paper presented at the 49th Annual Meeting of the Human Factors and Ergonomics Society, Orlando, FL.

Weeks, J., & Galunic, C. (2003). A theory of the cultural evolution of the firm: The intra-organizational ecology of memes. *Organization Studies, 24*, 1309–1352.

Wilkins, J. S. (1998). What's in a meme? Reflections from the perspective of the history and philosophy of evolutionary biology. *Journal of Memetics—Evolutionary Models of Information Transmission, 2.* Retrieved March 10th, 2006, from http://cfpm.org/jom-emit/1998/vol2/wilkins_js.html

Williamson, O. E. (1985). *Markets and hierarchies: Analysis and antitrust implications.* New York: Free Press.

Wimsatt, W. C. (1999). Genes, memes and cultural heredity. *Biology and Philosophy, 14*, 279–310.

Part II

SCIENTIFIC VIEWS
OF PROBLEM SOLVING

Chapter 7

Moving Students From Simple to Complex Problem Solving

Craig A. Ogilvie
Iowa State University

Picture a university physics classroom where two groups of engineering students are working on the same problem. They've been asked to estimate how high the starting gate in a new ski jump should be so that the ski jumpers land safely and without injury. One group has rewritten the given values and variables from the problem-statement onto its sheet (values such as the coefficient of friction of the snow, mass of the skier, etc.), and group members are searching through their notes and textbook trying to find either a similar worked-example or equations that they could use. The other group is discussing what it means by a "safe landing," coming to a consensus that it places a limit on how fast the skier hits the ground, and then outlines a plan of combining that constraint with the free-fall of gravity to calculate the maximum speed the skier should have at takeoff. This then determines the height of the starting gate.

Why did one group of students manage to identify the main issue in the problem, and then attack that idea by bringing in the necessary qualitative analysis, concepts, and eventually quantitative work, whereas the other group used a series of poor strategies that might have succeeded for simpler problems, but are almost guaranteed to fail as the complexity of the problem increases? A rhetorical question follows: which group of students is more likely to excel in their future careers as they face an ever-changing multitude of broad, open-ended problems?

The challenge of developing strong problem-solving skills in our students is in its early stages and no consensus has emerged on which pedagogical methods work best. It is, however, clear that this is a vital challenge for us to solve. The main innovation described in this chapter uses multifaceted problems that act as a bridge between well-structured and ill-defined, open-ended problems. However just adding in multifaceted problems to a course is unlikely to improve students' problem-solving skills. Hence we also discuss complementary course components that have been shown to help students develop base problem-solving skills, and how these can be used in conjunction with multifaceted problems. Because teaching general problem-solving skills independent of a domain, for example, general heuristics, has been shown to produce no improvement in problem-solving performance (Taconis, Ferguson-Hessler, & Broekkomp, 2001), we focus on pedagogies that are anchored within the science domains of physics, mathematics, chemistry, and biology.

The chapter is organized as follows: First I outline the big picture, that is, how multifaceted problems work in conjunction with other components of instruction. I then review how conceptual understanding and working simple problems can be used to develop students' schema. Implementing multifaceted problems in a classroom is described in detail, and I finish the chapter with methods to develop students' metacognitive problem-solving skills and to improve their beliefs about problem solving.

MULTIFACETED PROBLEMS WITHIN COURSES

In kindergarten through 12th-grade and university education, students work on a variety of problem-solving tasks (Jonassen, 2000), ranging from well-structured exercises that require applying a set algorithm to produce a unique answer, for example, geometrically bisect an angle, to ill-structured problems, for example, develop a plan to increase energy savings in your school. In ill-structured problems, there are multiple approaches to the task, and the criteria for choosing between proposals may not be completely specified (King & Kitchener, 1994). Students, who are used to working on algorithmic problems, struggle when confronted with the multiple challenges of ill-structured tasks. Typically they either approach the problem by searching for an algorithm that might work, or freeze completely and ask immediately for direct help, or flounder by doing a large amount of busy-work with no real planning or direction.

Although there has been considerable research on the effectiveness of instruction in helping students solve well-structured problems (Gabel, 1993; Taconis et al., 2001), there is currently no consensus on how to best develop students' ability to solve more complex, ill-structured problems. It is, however, feasible that successful pedagogy will include elements that are known to help students solve well-structured problems and then add methods to help students plan, monitor, and justify their solutions (Shin, Jonassen, & McGee, 2003).

We outline in this chapter four components of pedagogy that the author and others are currently prototyping and assessing. There are several options and methods available to instructors within each of the categories: until the research is done comparing these, the choice may be more determined by instructor preference, student population, or institutional constraints. Nevertheless, it is likely that any successful approach will include components from each of these areas:

1. Develop conceptual knowledge—Lack of conceptual understanding is rife throughout science students, as demonstrated in physics (Hake, 1998) and chemistry (Schmidt, 1990). Yet students can often solve straightforward problems through algorithmic approaches, despite having major conceptual misunderstandings (Gabel, 1993; Mazur, 1997; Sawrey, 1990). This algorithmic approach is, however, limiting, and faced with complex tasks, novices, without a solid understanding of the concepts, flounder and make little progress toward a solution. In contrast, domain experts have been shown to use deep and structured conceptual knowledge when solving complex problems (Bransford, Brown, & Cocking, 2000). Hence improving problem-solving *first* requires improving student conceptual understanding. For the many pedagogical methods available to help students understand concepts, the reader is referred to the excellent summaries of Angelo and Cross (1993) and Bransford et al. (2000).

2. Build strong structured knowledge that strengthens links between conceptual and procedural knowledge as well as between different concepts—Experts first analyze problems at a conceptual level and then draw from long-term memory the procedural knowledge that is associated with these concepts. This efficient and flexible approach not only requires strong structured conceptual knowledge with links between concepts, but also robust links between concepts and procedures. Methods to improve these linkages and schemata have been developed in the past three decades in many science domains, and we review some of the best practices in this chapter.

3. Strengthen metacognitive skills via explicit instruction and guided practice via, for example, multifaceted problems—Metacognitive problem-solving skills such as analysis, planning, monitoring, and justification skills come strongly to the fore when experts solve ill-structured problems. Students can practice these skills in complex, multifaceted problems (Heller, Keith, & Anderson, 1992) that bridge the gap between well-structured and ill-structured problems. Like ill-structured problems, multifaceted problems may have incomplete information, incompletely defined objectives,

and often cannot be resolved with a high degree of certainty. Yet they are smaller in scope and typically only require students to bring two or three concepts together to forge a solution. They serve as vehicles to explicitly teach, and for students to practice, metacognitive problem-solving skills. The extent to which this practice helps students apply these skills to larger ill-structured problems is an open research question. In university sophomore physics courses that I run, students end their semester with a large, ill-structured, open-ended modeling project where they apply the planning and argumentative skills (Shin et al., 2003) that they have worked during a series of multifaceted problems throughout the semester.

4. Improve student epistemology, that is, student beliefs about what is problem solving, and why it is important—Without improving students' interest in improving their problem-solving skills, any gains achieved during a course will be short-lived and unlikely to transfer to future courses or careers. Because MacGregor (1993) reported success in improving students' attitudes toward learning by having them intentionally reflect on their learning experiences, we discuss in this chapter ways students can reflect on their problem-solving tasks and skills.

These four components of instruction are linked via an overall strategy of "Progressive Problem Solving" (PPS), namely, that before students work on ill-structured problems in a domain, they first develop their conceptual understanding and domain schema by working on conceptual tasks and well-structured problems. PPS is different than Problem Based Learning (PBL; Duch, Groh, & Allen, 2001), where students start out with ill-structured problems and use these challenges to research topics and build their conceptual understanding. Both approaches (PPS and PBL) are promising, and as they are further developed, their effectiveness in improving problem-solving skills should be compared.

BACKGROUND ON PROGRESSIVE PROBLEM SOLVING

The idea that people learn by being challenged by tasks that are just beyond their current capabilities has a rich history in psychology. Vygotsky (1978) introduced the concept in terms of what he called the *Zone of Proximal Development*. Vygotsky described it as "the distance between the actual development level as determined by independent problem solving and the level of potential development as determined through problem solving under adult guidance or in collaboration with more capable peers" (p. 86). The implication is that learning is an iterative process, where students are challenged to work on complex tasks that are more difficult than the ones they currently solve, that this work is done with the support of peers or scaffolding from the teacher, and by successfully accomplishing these tasks, the students learn and are able to solve by themselves more complex tasks. This places them in a stronger position to be able to work on tasks that are even more complex, that is, the process is iterative or cumulative.

Anderson (1982) refined the idea of skill development by proposing different stages of skill: (a) a declarative stage where the learner encounters the ideas and concepts of a domain, (b) a knowledge compilation stage where the learner forms the links between the concepts and the procedures that are used to solve problems, and (c) a procedural stage where the learner strengthens the links between declarative and procedural knowledge.

Bereiter and Scardamalia (1993) moved beyond the ideas of Vygotsky and Anderson by incorporating the motivation of the learner. They discussed learning as a "growing-edge of expertise" (p. xi), that is, working on tasks that are just at the edge of one's current skill. However, for this to be a growing edge depends critically on your response to these tasks. As a learner, you either incorporate into your understanding the knowledge that was needed to solve the complex problem, or you react by restricting future challenges so you are less likely to work on problems just beyond your ability. If you follow the constructive path, then the cycle produces an "ever-deepening knowledge that grows out of problem-solving and keeps feeding back into it" (Bereiter & Scardamalia, 1993, p. 16).

Bereiter and Scardamalia (1993) provided examples of this process in a range of careers (e.g., repair work, architects, social policy). People who relish new challenges that broaden their knowledge become "experts," to be contrasted with others who become experienced nonexperts:

> The career of the expert is one of progressively advancing on the problems constituting a field of work, whereas the career of the non-expert is one of gradually constricting the field of work so that it more closely conforms to the routines the non-expert is prepared to execute. (p. 11)

The key difference is whether the person is motivated to learn from the tasks at hand.

In applying these ideas to developing problem-solving skills in our students, our charge is twofold: (a) to develop significant challenges that are just beyond a student's ability, and (b) to motivate the students so that they embrace these challenges, reflect on what they have learned after solving the problem, and incorporate that knowledge into their growing understanding and greater ability to solve more complex problems.

Motivating students may be the more difficult of the two tasks. Multifaceted problems fit nicely within the ARCS (Attention, Relevance, Confidence, and Success) framework proposed by Keller (1987). Placing students in the center of the problems, for example, "you have a summer internship," helps grab students' attention. Students gain confidence by solving challenging problems in their group. However, for students to gain the

most benefit they need to buy into the goal of improving their problem-solving skills, that is, to see the relevance of the tasks. The main approach suggested here is for students to reflect on their experience and
problem-solving growth (MacGregor, 1993), but it is also possible to judi-
ciously tap into students' career ambitions. Early on in the course that I run
(taken by many engineering students), I match students' career goals to the
goal of improving their problem-solving skills by reminding them that simple engineering problems can be solved by either computer programs or
via outsourcing. If they want a good job, then they will need to develop
strong problem-solving skills and this course will help them get started.

STRONGER SCHEMA

Simple problems can help develop strong links between conceptual knowledge and procedures that students can then apply in both complex and
ill-structured problems. However, many instructors know that students can
often solve simple quantitative problems while having a poor or flawed conceptual understanding of the topic. Because this phenomenon has been
documented in genetics (Stewart, 1983), chemistry (Gabel & Bunce, 1991),
and physics (Mazur, 1997), it is likely to pervade all fields of science and
technical education. Bypassing understanding, students learn instead how
to execute an algorithm: they analyze the problem-statement in front of
them, match quantities in the problem to a list of possible equations, and
plug in numbers. This approach has been termed the *Rolodex* method of
problem solving (Bunce, Gabel, & Samuel, 1991). Although this is by no
means a trivial task, it is a weak strategy that cannot be extended to more realistic, complex challenges that require both a stronger conceptual understanding and stronger problem-solving skills such as qualitative analysis,
planning, and justification skills.

   Because simple problems can often be solved without a strong conceptual understanding, their use has been implicitly deprecated in the education literature. Yet a few approaches (Bunce & Heikkinen, 1986; Cooper &
Sweller, 1987; Jonassen, 2004; Sweller & Cooper, 1985; Van Heuvelen,
1991) have shown that simple problems can develop stronger links between
conceptual and procedural knowledge, which students can then use in
more complex problems.

   The collection of links between declarative knowledge (concepts and
facts) and procedural knowledge (methods and algorithms) is commonly
termed *schema*. Chi, Feltovich, and Glaser (1981) observed that experts approached problems by analyzing the deep structure of the task, looking for
concepts and underlying principles. Once the principles were identified,
the procedures (equations and algorithms) for working with those concepts
were retrieved from long-term memory. Novices on the other hand focused

on the surface features of the problem and wrote equations that matched the variables without regard of whether those equations were applicable. It is thought that schema help experts solve problems by efficiently using their working cognitive memory. By first analyzing the problem in terms of principles, then in terms of the details associated with the chosen principles, experts are using an efficient hierarchical memory organization. In contrast, by attacking problems first at the level of equations, variables, or surface features, novices can very quickly overload their working memory which will very likely cause their problem-solving attempt to fail (Niaz, 1988).

The pedagogical challenge is to develop and strengthen student schema, that is, the links between conceptual and procedural knowledge, without the instruction degenerating into students merely applying specific algorithms to problems without understanding the concepts. We describe here several methods that meet this challenge.

Multistep Strategies

One suggested pedagogy is to provide a procedure of several steps that makes the linkages between concepts and procedures explicit. Many examples exist in the literature that encourage students to follow several steps as they solve a problem. These steps subtly change from domain to domain:

1. In mathematics, Polya (1957) not only outlined general mathematic heuristics to be used to solve a variety of problems, he also emphasized a general problem-solving approach of understanding the problem, devising a plan, and carrying out the plan.
2. In chemistry, Bunce and Heikkinen (1986) developed the Explicit Method of Problem Solving (EMPS): Given, Asked for, Recall, Overall Plan, Mathematics, and Review.
3. In physics, there have been many multistep approaches explicitly taught to students. Perhaps the first reported in the literature was from Reif, Larkin, and Brackett (1976), where the method was summarized as Description, Planning, Implementation, and Checking. This was extended by Halloun and Hestenes (1986), who showed that student solving performance improved with guided practice on explicit problem-solving strategies.
4. In biology, Hurst and Milkent (1996) explicitly taught students the importance of predicting the effect of one variable on another in solving biology problems.
5. In genetics, Hackling and Lawrence (1988) analyzed the steps followed by experts (as summarized by Stewart & Hafner, 1993): (a) peruse pedigree to identify key features that indicate the most likely mode of in-

heritance, (b) generate the most plausible hypothesis and then test it by assigning genotypes to all the individuals in the pedigree, (c) test some alternative hypotheses in an attempt to disprove them and confirm the initial hypothesis, and (d) search for any evidence that could be used to determine which of the two hypotheses was most probable.

Listing such domain strategies is now common in textbooks. Perhaps the critical step in developing links between concepts and procedures is exemplified by "Recall" in the EMPS strategy, where students write down key principles or concepts that are cued for in the problem statement or the "given" or "asked for" variables. The idea is that writing the principles before students work on the subsequent procedures helps strengthen students' schema.

External Prompts or Structure

This pedagogy is taken a step further when a tangible space is provided for students to follow the explicit multistep procedure. For example Active Learning Problem Sheets (ALPS) devised by Van Heuvelen (1991) contain separate, identified, sections where students must represent the problem graphically and develop a qualitative analysis before working on the mathematical representation. There are also sections on evaluation, on units, and magnitude of the answers.

This approach has been transformed to a computer environment, Hierarchical Analysis Tool (HAT), in which students are constrained to first choose the principles involved in the problem from a pull-down menu, followed by associated concepts, then finally the equations they might be able to use (Dufresne, Gerace, Hardiman, & Mestre, 1992; Leonard, Dufresne, & Mestre, 1996). This tool has been shown to help students both categorize problems as well as improve their problem-solving performance.

A similar environment is provided by the Story Problem-Solving Environment (SPSE; Jonassen, 2004). A story problem is presented to students who must then follow a series of tasks, ranging from identifying the principles involved, to qualitatively analyzing the problem, to building a quantitative representation of the problem.

Worked Examples

Worked examples can be found in almost any textbook. However, many students use these worked examples merely as a resource to copy. When a student is asked to solve a simple problem, he or she searches the textbook for a similar worked example to duplicate. Stronger uses of worked examples have been suggested that engage the student to analyze the worked problem. See the following, for example:

1. Paired problems have been used by Ward and Sweller (1990), where the first is a worked example, the second a very similar task that the student must solve. Such close pairings have been shown to improve students' ability to solve transfer problems. The students are presumed to use the worked example as a direct guide as they solve the matched task. The structure of the worked example also seems to be critical: worked examples that split students' attention between multiple modes, for example, graphics, equations, texts, are ineffective, whereas integrating this information into a single-mode presentation seems to be more effective (Ward & Sweller, 1990).

2. Dissecting worked examples—In this approach, students assess how well the worked example has been solved, for example, did the solver draw a productive diagram, did the qualitative analysis identify the main stages of the problem, and were the checks of the solution adequate (Taconis & Van Hout-Walters, 1999)?

Knowledge Organization

When solving complex problems, experts readily identify which concepts were involved, how the concepts are related, and how they could be combined to build a solution (Chi, Feltovich, & Glaser, 1981). Students tend to have isolated "islands of knowledge" with weak links between different concepts, so they cannot be effectively combined when a complex task calls for more than one idea.

If we can improve the relations between areas of knowledge that students have, we should be able to improve their ability to solve complex problems. There have been at least three instructional methods developed to improve how knowledge is organized:

1. Problem categorization—Students are asked to categorize problems according to the concepts or principles involved (Bunce et al., 1991). Noteworthy in this study is that the categorization task was attempted after the students had worked on the problem. The guided discussion focused on identifying relevant cues and eliminating irrelevant information. Students were encouraged to broaden the names of categories and how to use categorization at the start of a problem. This treatment led to a slight improvement in solving multiple-concept problems.

2. Explicit emphasis on relations—Steiner and Stoecklin (1997) had students solve a straightforward problem (in fractions), then changed the problem in some small way. The students must describe the transformation, anticipate its consequences, and then verify the anticipated effect by solving the transformed problem. The whole cycle is repeated with a new change to the revised problem. By emphasizing how problems are related to each other, students were able to better solve fraction problems that re-

quired conceptual thinking in addition to pure algorithmic procedures (Steiner & Stoecklin, 1997). Similarly, VanderStoep and Seifert (1993) taught their students when, and under what conditions, to apply similar principles for problems in probability courses. This improved students' ability to recognize the appropriate principle in a complex task, but unfortunately did not lead to stronger performance in completion of the task.

3. Concept maps are graphical representations of a set of concepts and how they are related to each other (Novak & Gowin, 1984). A well-organized map is hierarchical with a general concept at the top and successive layers containing more specific ideas. The concepts are linked with each other using propositions such as "is an example of," or "made of," or "determined by." Maps created by novices tend to be disorganized with no structure, whereas expert maps have a high degree of structure and multiple cross-links within each level. Constructing concept maps has the potential to help students learn relations between concepts. Novak, Gowin, and Johansen (1983) found that middle-school students who constructed maps performed better on problem-solving tasks. This has been confirmed by Pankratius (1990) in high-school physics and Okebukola (1990) in biology. Recently, Lee and Nelson (2005) also showed that students who constructed concept maps performed better on well-structured problems compared to students who studied concept maps that were supplied to them. However, there was interestingly little difference between these two groups on more ill-structured tasks. The authors speculated that there may have been other factors involved in influencing performance on the ill-structured tasks, including students' beliefs and attitudes on problem solving. Later in this chapter we discuss improving students' beliefs about problem solving.

MULTIFACETED PROBLEMS

The anchor to progressive problem solving (PPS) is the use of multifaceted problems that require students to incorporate several concepts in building a solution. Typically these problems are context-rich, that is, they place the student in the middle of a challenge, for example, "You are a design engineer for a company that has been asked to build a ski ramp." However, the main characteristic is that students cannot solve these problems with a direct algorithmic approach (plug and chug), instead the students must first identify the goal, qualitatively analyze the problem, recognize missing or redundant information, possibly break the problem into subtasks, and from there build a solution. Multifaceted problems have been advocated by several groups across many disciplines for both school and university use, for example, the physics education research groups at University of Minnesota (Heller, Keith, & Anderson, 1992) and Ohio State University (Van

Heuvelen, 1991), in chemistry (Reid & Yang, 2002), industrial engineering (Olafsson et al., 2003; Olafsson et al., 2004; Ryan, Jackman, Peters, Olafsson, & Huba, 2004), and across several disciplines by the Cognition and Technology Group at Vanderbilt (1992), and the IMMEX project at University of California, Los Angeles (UCLA; Stevens & Palacio-Cayetano, 2003; Stevens, Soller, Cooper, & Sprang, 2004).

There are also databases of problems available for instructors to use, especially in physics. At Iowa State Univerity (ISU), we have written and used approximately 40 context-rich problems, primarily in areas of thermal physics, electricity and magnetism, and optics. These problems and their solutions are available to all physics instructors at http://owl.physics.iastate.edu. The Minnesota database has many problems that focus primarily on kinematics and dynamics (http://groups.physics.umn.edu/physed/Research/CRP/on-lineArchive/ola.html). Other sources of physics problems can be found in recent textbooks, for example, *Six Ideas That Shaped Physics* (Moore, 2003).

To gain some impression for the complexity of these tasks, consider the following problem in introductory physics:

> You are in charge of keeping drinks cold at a picnic that will start at 3 p.m. and need to place ice inside a cooler at 6 a.m., when the temperature outside is 10°C. The day is forecast to warm up steadily to reach 30°C by 3 p.m. Estimate how much ice you will need.

This problem involves at least two concepts: heat transfer through a wall, and the amount of heat required to melt ice. It is also moderately ill-structured, in that the problem statement does not specify how thick are the walls of the cooler, or of what they are made. Students need to provide reasonable estimates for these quantities. Although the problem is not mathematically complex, it does require the students in a group to discuss the problem, identify the main concepts that are involved, qualitatively analyze the problem, and from there build a solution.

At ISU, multifaceted problems are assigned once every 2 weeks during a regularly scheduled recitation class (50 min) in a course taken mainly by sophomore physics, chemistry, math, and engineering students. The problems come after the concepts involved have been worked on and wrestled with by the students during lectures that use peer instruction (Mazur, 1997), homework, and lab. In a sense, these are capstone challenges for a section of the course. During the problem-solving sessions, students form groups of two to three and they work the problem on a 2 foot by 2 foot whiteboard where each student has a different color dry-erase pen. The whiteboard serves as the focal point for the group. If regular sheets of paper are used, students tend to work individually on the problem. The board also helps the teaching assistant (TA) as he or she is wandering around the class: the work is clearly visible and the different color pens help the TA identify who is writing which section.

The photographs in Figure 7.1 show three groups of students working on a multifaceted problem.

Instructor Training

The person running these sessions plays a vital role. In our course teaching assistants (TAs) staff these recitations. Extensive training is critical both before the course and in weekly meetings of course instructors. In these meetings, we discuss how students solve problems, research on problem solving, as well as more immediate issues about next week's multifaceted problem and what opportunities it presents. We also discuss classroom management techniques, such as waiting for 5 min or so after handing out the problem before discussing the problem with any group to allow students time to engage with the task, and how to manage several groups working simultaneously in the room.

The TAs are trained to use leading prompts in all their discussions with students. At the start of the semester, this is a challenge for the TAs because their inclination is to provide more direct help to the students, for example, to make a suggestion of an approach or to identify the key constraint in a problem. We train the TAs how to scaffold: to ask "prompts" that support the

Figure 7.1.   Three groups of students working on a multifaceted problem. Note the use of a whiteboard as the common working space for the group's solution.

students in the early stages of the semester, but as students increase their problem-solving abilities, these questions become owned by the students. The goal of the TA is to get students to ask these questions themselves as they solve a problem. Table 7.1 shows the prompts used for different stages of problem solving that was developed by Xun and Land (2004).

Problem-Solving Groups

Multifaceted problems have been designed to be very difficult for a single person, but manageable for a group of three. The role of peers in increasing learning has been extensively documented (Angelo & Cross, 1993): in working together on complex problems, students not only bring multiple knowledge resources, but there is also considerable discussion within the group about how to solve the problem, what to do, and debate about why they should attempt a particular strategy. Many private problem-solving strategies are made public and explicit.

Heller et al. (1992) argued that effective groups contain students with a range of abilities, and that roles be assigned to each student for that session: manager, skeptic, and recorder. At ISU, we typically let students self-select their groups, but periodically ask for new groups to form every few weeks or so to bring in new perspectives. TAs are trained to monitor group dynamics and use assigned roles if there is a need to improve a group's behavior, for example, if a student is dominating a group, then he or she may be taken to one side after class, praised for his or her strong contribution, and asked to help develop the strengths of the other group members, perhaps by playing the role of recorder for the next week.

TABLE 7.1
List of Prompts for Problem Solving

Situation	Suggested Prompts
Problem representation	What information is missing? How are ... interrelated to each other? What do you think are the primary factors of this problem? Why is it ...? Please explain. What does ... mean?
Generating or selecting solutions	Explain how your proposed system works. How is this approach compared with the other one? Can you explain why you took that approach? What is your chain of reasoning for selecting that solution?
Making justifications	Do you have evidence to support your solution? How do you justify your decision? What are the pros and cons of the solution?
Monitoring and evaluating	Have I thought about alternative solutions? Have I identified all the constraints? Am I on the right track? What could have been done differently?

For many sophomore science students, these complex, multifaceted problems are a surprise and the format of recitation is different than what they expect. The typical mode of instruction in university science recitations is the TA working through simpler, mono-topic problems that can be found at the end of chapters in textbooks. The students' initial reaction is quite often negative and even hostile, with many complaints posted on the course bulletin board. My strategy for dealing with these complaints is to communicate often to students the goal of improving their problem-solving skills for their later careers. However, as students experience success with the multifaceted problems, the concerns diminish and end-of-semester evaluations have been largely positive.

At the start of the semester, I provide students with a sheet that contains problem-solving guidelines, such as understand the problem, qualitatively analyze the situation, plan a solution, and monitor the solution as it progresses (more details on these guidelines are discussed later in this chapter). However, we have found that students at the university level have seen similar guidelines before and they tend to ignore them. The students are not convinced they will need to abandon their plug and chug strategies and hence at this stage, explicit problem-solving instruction is not very well received. Therefore, at the start of the semester, we make the instruction low key and let students encounter the complexity of these problems.

After students understand the challenge of multifaceted problems, then the TAs re-introduce the guidelines. The goal is for students to realize the benefits based on their own struggles in the previous few weeks. Our current approach is to emphasize one part of the strategy at a time. For example, if the week's focus is how to rerepresent the problem (discussed later in this chapter), then during that week's problem, the students will be asked to debate and document how they rerepresent the task. At the end of class, the TA leads a class discussion on the benefits of problem rerepresentation, calling for suggestions on what the students did. This guided instruction is repeated for the other key parts of the strategy, one per week, for example, qualitative analysis, ongoing monitoring, and cross-checking strategies at the end of a problem.

Assessment

The 0th law of education is that students will note what the instructor gives grades for and put effort into those tasks. Hence grade allocation should match what is stated as important, in our case the use of strong problem-solving processes while solving complex problems. At ISU, we hold two group exams each semester. For the exam, each group works on a multifaceted problem (this time on a large piece of paper instead of the whiteboard), the exam is open-book, and each group in the room has a different problem to cut down on overhearing other groups' discussions. Before the exam, students are provided with a rubric (discussed later) on how we will assess their solution. Grading is predominantly on the processes the group uses in working on the problem, that is, we assess students on how they approach the task, rather than only on getting a correct answer (Henderson, Yershalmi, Kuo, Heller, & Heller, 2004). The rubric also acts as an external guideline for students to use during the rest of the semester: a role for rubrics that was highlighted in a metastudy of problem-solving research (Taconis et al., 2001).

The rubric that is Tables 7.2 and 7.3 is divided into two sections: "Mileposts" and "Process." These two sections are not independent of each other: the main role of Mileposts is to provide a reasonable minimum score for the problem, that is, any viable solution should contain the elements in the baseline and hence get greater than 50% for a total score. The Process section emphasizes problem-solving strategies and provides most of the discrimination for the assessment.

METACOGNITIVE STRATEGIES

We use multifaceted problems as the vehicle for students to improve their problem-solving skills and potentially strength their schema. These problems are complex enough to provide many "teachable moments" or "learning moments," such as how to qualitatively analyze a problem, the benefits of planning, and what to look for as you check your solution. These strategies are taught within the context of a particular domain, but they also can be considered general strategies that are common across many domains.

There is extensive debate in the literature about the role of general strategies in problem-solving instruction, partially due to different meanings implied by the phrase "general problem solving strategies." We restrict ourselves to "common skills" that are in use across a broad range of scientific domains, and we are not suggesting that a person who excels in these skills can be generally expert in multiple domains. In our list of common skills, we restrict the scope to three metacognitive strategies: representation, planning, and monitoring. These strategies are briefly described here followed by more details on how different pedagogies can be used to develop these skills:

1. Representation—*redescribing* or *representing* (we use both terms synonymously) the problem in different formats. In complex problems, experts often redescribe the problem in different ways, drawing diagrams, changing how the task is represented, sorting out key parts, discarding irrelevant information, and realizing that some key parts are missing. These processes help the expert brainstorm and identify the key princi-

TABLE 7.2

Mileposts

Criteria	Excellent (4)	Good (3)	Marginal (1)	Unacceptable (0)
Diagram	A diagram or series of diagrams is given which clearly illustrate the workings of the problem.	A diagram, or series of diagrams, is given which clearly captures most of the workings of the problem.	A diagram is given which has limited useful content or is confusing.	No diagram is given.
Physical principles	The relevant physical principles are cited in a concise form.	Most of the key physical principles are given but either some are left out or confusing or irrelevant information is included.	Crucial physical principles are omitted.	No relevant physics principles are cited.
Basic equations	The basic equations clearly follow from the physics principles and provide the required formalism to proceed with the problem.	Basic equations are given but contain some errors or are mixed with irrelevant equations.	An incomplete set of basic equations is given or equations do not follow from given physics principles.	Basic equations are not to be found.
Algebra	Basic equations are correctly manipulated to final expressions which are relevant to the solution of the problem. The final expressions are general in the sense that the specific numbers are not substituted into them.	Basic equations are manipulated to final expressions which are relevant to the solution of the problem but either (a) there is either some minor algebraic error along the way, or (b) there is a major algebraic error which is caught by the checks but not corrected, or (c) the final expressions are not as general as they could be due to the specific numbers from the problem being plugged in.	Basic equations are manipulated incorrectly to a final form which is not a credible solution to the problem and is left unchallenged or unchecked.	Algebraic manipulation from the basic equations to a useful form is not carried out to any meaningful degree.
Conclusions	The physical principles and equations developed are applied to solve the given problem, specific numerical values are correctly substituted into the equations, and a well-justified answer to the problem is clearly stated.	The physical principles and equations developed are applied to solve the given problem, specific numerical values are substituted into the equations and the relevance to the problem is clearly stated but either (a) some calculation errors are made at this stage, or (b) the connection to the original question is not clearly and explicitly stated.	Some conclusions are given but (a) they are not supported by previous work, or (b) they are largely disconnected from the problem.	No meaningful conclusions for the problem are reached.

TABLE 7.3

Process

Criteria	Excellent (4)	Good (3)	Marginal (1)	Unacceptable (0)
Focus the problem	Key issues are identified from problem description. The main goal is specified and the problem is recast into governing physical principles. Exploration is initially qualitative and various paths to the solution are considered by group members.	Key issues are identified from problem description. In particular, the main goal is specified. Exploratory work, however, appears perfunctory or not well focused on the problem at hand.	Some key issues are identified from the problem description. Students launch into details before assessing the goals. Little meaningful exploratory work takes place.	Students launch into details before assessing the goals.
Qualitative representation	The task is analyzed qualitatively, for example, if a water-filled pan is on a stove, you predict the pan will warm up, which will warm the water. Then the water will start to boil and the pan might eventually become empty. To make predictions, you need not know the exact values of the variables involved. The qualitative analysis identifies key moments or locations in the problem, for example, the time when all the water is boiled.	Task is analyzed qualitatively but not all key moments or locations or other key elements are identified.	Qualitative analysis is inadequate or not focused on the problem.	No qualitative analysis is done.
Planning	An explicit plan is developed giving an outline of likely steps to the solution. As work develops, revisions of the plan are noted.	Once a feasible path is identified, an explicit plan is developed outlining the first few steps in the solution.	Planning is perfunctory and shows little anticipation of what will develop. The plan is described in such general terms that it appears rote and has a weak connection to the problem at hand.	Solution is not planned.
Quantitative representation	Plan is recast into mathematical form, coordinate system is established, and variables are defined. Constraints and initial conditions are determined. Diagrams should be redrawn in an abstract form, for example, a free-body diagram that shows only key details.	Plan is recast into mathematical form, but one or two items are missing.	The plan is recast into a mathematical form, but either the mathematical model is wrong or it is very difficult to see how the algebraic variables relate to the physics of the problem.	No meaningful mathematical representation of the plan is derived.

(continued)

TABLE 7.3 (*continued*)

Criteria	Excellent (4)	Good (3)	Marginal (1)	Unacceptable (0)
Ongoing review	Periodic, explicit checks are made that solution is progressing toward end-goal, and that the algebra is making sense. For example, if the solution is becoming unwieldy an explicit stop is made, followed by a period of new exploration.	Periodic explicit checks are made that the solution is progressing toward end-goal, and that the algebra is making sense. However, the action after review is not the best. For example, if the solution is becoming unwieldy, an explicit stop is made, but this is not followed by a period of new exploration.	Some checking is indicated but appears perfunctory.	No checking is done to see if the solution is progressing well. Students continue to unquestioningly slog through unwieldy algebra.
Verification	Solution is cross-checked as applicable in terms of units, that the magnitude makes sense, that the answer is compatible with all known initial conditions, and that the assumptions made are valid.	Some cross-checks of the solution are performed but there are additional checks that could easily be performed.	Some cross-checking is done, but it is clearly inadequate.	No checks of the solution are attempted.

ples in the problem as well as set the stage for more detailed subsequent analysis of the problem. This level of performance requires both strong domain knowledge and also the strategic knowledge that working through this redescription step will help lay out possible paths to a solution.

2. Planning—Experts spend considerable amounts of time planning alternative approaches to problems, realizing that it is more efficient to make these sketches at the start, rather than wasting time developing a detailed solution down a path that eventually reaches a dead end. In contrast, novices spend very little time planning their strategies and often begin work immediately without analyzing whether their detailed work has any bearing on the task at hand.

3. Monitoring—Schoenfeld (1985) was one of the first to identify the difference between novices and experts in ongoing monitoring of their work. He analyzed many tape recordings of students and faculty solving mathematics problems. Experts would periodically stop, check if the solution was making good progress, whether it was consistent with the original plan, or whether the algebra was getting too messy. Novices, on the other hand, would plow on regardless of how the solution was progressing.

It is an important research question to establish the extent that these metacognitive strategies have far-transfer, that is, if a student develops good monitoring habits while working on chemistry or physics problems, does he or she also apply these monitoring skills in an engineering design class? As a start toward answering this question, Chinnappan and Lawson (1996) have shown that explicit teaching and guided practice of three metacognitive strategies (rereading, planning, and checking) while students work on geometry problems improves students' ability to solve both similar and near-transfer problems (although still within the domain of geometry).

More research is described next identifying how each of these metacognitive skills differ between novices and experts and whether attempts to teach these skills have been successful for near-transfer, that is, on similar problems.

Rerepresentation Skills

Experts represent problems in multiple ways compared to novices (Chi et al., 1981; Lee, 1985). Exploring multiple views for complex problems that do not lend themselves to an immediate solution path can lead the problem solver toward building a solution. Novices rarely make these explorations. Some rerepresentations are applicable over a wide range of subjects: drawing a schematic diagram, or noting specific stages and key moments in a problem and using these to anchor a qualitative analysis. Other rerepresentations are more domain-specific, for example, changing the view on mechanics problems in physics from a view where forces are applied, to a view where energy is transformed from kinetic to potential energy.

During instruction, emphasis can be placed on recasting the problem into alternative modes rather than just having students solve the problem. Sutherland (2002) assessed her students on how well they had produced a coherent problem representation. The instructor models the process of rerepresentation, provides structured support to students, and allows time to practice on several problems. Sutherland (2002) also found that stronger performance on problems was achieved when the instructor either embedded strategy prompts or reminders in the practice questions or had students write reflective evaluations on how they had analyzed the question.

Savelsbergh, Jong, and Ferguson-Hessler (2002) suggested that students redescribe the problem after the problem has been solved instead of before. The idea is that students may achieve more success in using different representations after the problem has been solved. More research is needed to establish whether this encourages redescriptions at the start of problems when a student is stuck.

The key role that diagrams play in rerepresentations of the problem and as a gateway to finding a solution has been documented in several fields; for example, genetics (Kindfield, 1991) and physics (Van Heuvelen, 1991).

Planning

Getting students to plan solutions to complex problems seems to be very difficult. For example, in geometry, Schoenfeld (1985) observed many students embark on complicated construction procedures that were undirected by any goal toward a solution. Pairs of students busily worked for a considerable amount of time, and even when asked at the end of the problem-solving session, they could not answer why they had chosen to follow that path.

Changing this habit in students seems very hard. Reid and Yang (2002) described explicit training and guided practice in how to outline a plan for a range of ill-structured, complex, and multifaceted problems in chemistry. Yet students "set off with what was familiar and hoped the way forward would emerge" (p. 1326). It is possible that students have had success without planning in simple problems and because this is often the dominant type of problems they encounter in an academic setting, a lack of planning has become habitual.

One suggestion is to have students write a "plan" after a problem has been solved (K. VanLehn, personal communication, 2005). The "plan" would be an outline of a solution that the student has already obtained. Students would experience success in sketching these plans at a stage when there is no other cognitive load from other tasks. It is an open research question whether this would help students to plan possible solutions at the early stages of a complex problem.

Monitoring

Once started on a feasible solution, novices often keep on going down that path, performing a tremendous amount of calculations, algebra, or graphs, irregardless of whether they are making progress toward a solution (Schoenfeld, 1985). Experts, on the other hand, continually monitor their solution and if the work is getting messy, they stop and check for internal inconsistencies, examining whether the solution is still consistent with the problem goal. If not, they often revisit their initial qualitative analysis and explore if another solution path is viable (Schoenfeld, 1985).

In contrast to these observations, most problem-solving strategies highlight the need for students to check their solution at the end (e.g., Polya, 1957). In physics problems, this often takes the form of checks for units, or placing extreme conditions on particular variables; for example, what happens if the mass goes to zero or infinity, does the solution make physical sense? It is important for these strategies to be practiced while the student is in the middle of his or her solution.

Beyond explicitly discussing the role of monitoring, and having it as part of the assessment (see aforementioned rubric), one way of developing this skill as students solve multifaceted problems may be to assign one student in a group to explicitly play the role of "monitor" while the group solves the problem. The job description of the monitor is to question the reasons why a particular approach is being used, to watch the solution progress, check that the work is still consistent with the early qualitative analysis, and raise a red flag if the work is getting messy or complicated. The role of monitor should be rotated through the different members of the group as the semester progresses.

STUDENT EPISTEMOLOGY

Epistemology is the study of student beliefs about what constitutes knowledge in a domain and how, as a student, one develops that knowledge (Hammer, 1994). Without changing student beliefs about problem solving, any gains in problem-solving skill are likely to be short-lived. Hammer (1994) summarized how students approach learning into three categories and arranged the beliefs in each of these areas from "weak" to "strong," where the adjective reflects the usefulness of the belief for student learning:

1. Beliefs about the structure of a domain: from "pieces" to "coherence."
2. Beliefs about the content a student needs to master: from "formulas" to "concepts."
3. Beliefs about how a student should learn: from "By authority" to "Independent."

These beliefs affect how novices approach problem solving in particular and science courses in general. Schoenfeld (1985) was one of the first to document student beliefs about mathematics problem solving. One common view was that if a problem can't be solved in 10 minutes or less it is an impossible problem. Such an approach precludes any productive approach to multiple-faceted, ill-defined problems. Larkin, McDermott, Simon, and Simon (1980) documented a theme mentioned already in this chapter that physics students expect to solve problems by searching for an equation that matches with variables in the problem.

In genetics education (Stewart & Hafner 1993), more successful novices recognize that they need to develop a solution that is both internally consistent and externally valid with respect to the rest of their domain knowledge. These students also take a knowledge development approach to the solution in that they try to relate the solution to other parts of their knowledge, and hence they construct stronger understanding.

How to Change Beliefs of Students

One of the more alarming results in recent years has been that some courses that are based on cognitive-conflict improve student understanding, yet damage student's beliefs and attitudes toward learning (Redish, Jeffery, Saul, & Steinberg, 1998). In response, Elby (2001) suggested suffusing epistemology throughout the course: asking students to explicitly relink and reconcile their new and old thinking just after being challenged conceptually. Students are asked to reflect, and write, after a cognitive-conflict session about how the new idea informs and refines their common sense. This has also been advocated by May and Etkina (2002), who asked students to write weekly reports reflecting on what and how they learned. Such intentional self-reflection improved students' conceptual understanding (May & Etkina, 2002).

This idea can be extended to having students reflect on their problem-solving tasks and skill growth, that is, to have students intentionally reflect on what happened as they solve problems. Via reflection, they can integrate the concepts or procedures that were used in the problem into their existing knowledge.

Reflection possibilities range from informal discussions between members of the group about what happened during the problem-solving session: what went right, where the breakthrough in the problem occurred, or where the group struggled and spun their wheels. It requires a strong session leader to insist on this reflective effort at the end of the problem-solving session when students are keen to move on (and possibly to their next class). The strongest argument is to convince the students that intentional reflection produces a payoff in better problem-solving performance.

An alternative is for individual students to keep a log of their problem-solving experience, that is, what happened when they were stuck, how did they get unstuck, and how they could use that during a problem-planning stage, or what unforced errors did they make, and what types of monitoring might have caught error. This reflective journal can be private or submitted to the instructor. One intriguing technical option that may appeal to students is to have this learning journal in the format of a blog (Hernández-Ramos, 2004; Williams & Jacobs, 2004).

A potentially powerful opportunity is for students to reflect on their problem-solving skills at more spaced intervals, for example, monthly or two to three times a semester (MacGregor, 1993). Students have little experience examining their academic work in any systematic way, and because students often perceive their role as receiving knowledge, they may be uncomfortable at first in describing their role in developing problem-solving skills. The benefits documented in courses and institutions where self-reflections are pervasive range from students becoming more involved in the course, beginning to integrate material across courses, attaching more meaning and relevance to course goals and topics, and developing more self-directedness (Kusnic & Finley, 1993).

For problem-solving skills, it is not yet clear what format or frequency is optimal for self-reflection and it may depend on the local environment and student population.

OPEN RESEARCH QUESTIONS

We do not know the best way to develop skills in students that help them solve ill-structured, open-ended problems. We have described in this chapter PPS, that has students work on conceptual challenges, followed by schema development using simple problems, followed by multifaceted problems as a vehicle to develop qualitative analysis, planning, and monitoring skills. At ISU, students cycle through these three types of tasks several times a semester before attacking a large, ill-structured modeling task. Several other groups are using similar instructional methods: University of Minnesota PER group (Heller et al., 1992), Ohio State University (Van Heuvelen, 1991), Vanderbilt (Cognition and Technology Group at Vanderbilt, 1992), the IMMEX project at UCLA (Stevens et al., 2003, 2004), ISU (Olafsson et al., 2003, 2004; Ryan et al., 2004), and Reid and Yang (2002).

The range of research questions about the effectiveness of these pedagogies is vast, but can be perhaps separated into two types of questions:

1. Short-range, where the queries concern the impact multifaceted problems have on skills or cognitive processes known to be used by experts; for example, the extent to which multifaceted problem solving leads to more organized knowledge and stronger production schema, which would enable students to solve even more complex, ill-defined, and open-ended problems. Do these benefits differ between stronger and weaker students? Do they depend on implementation details?

2. Long-range, where the queries concern the far-transfer of these skills, for example, the extent to which planning and monitoring skills transfer to later courses or careers. We also need to understand more about student epistemology and what factors affect students' beliefs about problem solving.

In parallel to PPS, the PBL approach has been developed (Duch et al., 2001) where students predominantly work on large, ill-structured problems. As both methods are further refined and examined, it would be interesting (but very difficult) to compare the outcomes of the two pedagogies.

It is a vital challenge for us as educators and researchers to help build strong problem-solving skills in our students. The methods and issues raised in this chapter are in their early stages of development, and yet this is an important task: our students will need strong problem-solving skills as they face the broad, open-ended challenges in their future careers.

REFERENCES

Anderson, J. R. (1982). Acquisition of cognitive skill. *Psychological Review, 89,* 369–406.

Angelo, T. A., & Cross, K. P. (1993). *Classroom assessment techniques, a handbook for college teachers* (2nd ed.). San Francisco: Jossey-Bass.

Bereiter, C., & Scardamalia, M. (1993). *Surpassing ourselves: An inquiry into the nature and implications of expertise.* Chicago: Open Court Publishing.

Bransford, J. D., Brown, A. L., & Cocking, R. R. (Eds.). (2000). How people learn: Brain, mind, experience. Washington, DC: Commission on Behavioral and Social Sciences and Education of the National Research Council, National Academy Press.

Bunce, D. M., Gabel, D. L., & Samuel, J. V. (1991). Enhancing chemistry problem-solving achievement using problem categorization. *Journal of Research in Science Teaching, 28,* 505–521.

Bunce, D. M., & Heikkinen, H. (1986) The effects of an explicit problem-solving approach on mathematical chemistry achievement. *Journal of Research in Science Teaching, 23*(1), 11–20.

Chi, M. T. H., Feltovich, P. J., & Glaser, R. (1981). Categorization and representation of physics problems by experts and novices. *Cognitive Science 5,* 121–152.

Chinnappan, M., & Lawson, M. J. (1996). The effects of training in the use of executive strategies in geometry problem solving. *Learning and Instruction, 6,* 1–17.

Cognition and Technology Group at Vanderbilt. (1992). The Jasper experiment: An exploration of issues in learning and instructional design. *Educational Technology Research and Development, 40,* 65.

Cooper, G., & Sweller, J. (1987). "Effects of schema acquisition and rule automation on mathematical problem solving. *Journal of Educational Psychology, 79,* 347.

Duch, B. J., Groh, S. E., & Allen, D. E. (2001). *The power of problem-based learning: A practical "how to" for teaching undergraduate courses in any discipline.* Sterling, VA: Stylus Publishing.

Dufresne, R. J., Gerace, W. J., Hardiman, P. T., & Mestre, J. P. (1992). Constraining novices to perform expertlike problem analyses: Effects on schema acquisition. *Journal of the Learning Sciences, 2,* 307.

Elby, A. (2001). Helping physics students learn how to learn. *Physics Education Research, American Jpournal of Physics* (Suppl. 69), S54.

Gabel, D. L. (1993). Research on problem solving. In D. Gabel (Ed.), *Handbook of research on science teaching and learning* (pp. 301–326). New York: Macmillan.

Hackling, M., & Lawrence, J. (1988). Expert and novice solutions of genetic pedigree problems. *Journal of Research in Science Teaching, 25,* 531–546.

Hake, R. R. (1998). Interactive-engagement vs traditional methods: A six-thousand-student survey of mechanics test data for introductory physics courses. *American Journal of Physics, 66,* 64–74.

Halloun, I. A., & Hestenes, D. (1987). Modelling instruction in mechanics. *American Journal of Physics, 55,* 455–462.

Hammer, D. (1994). Epistemological Beliefs in Introductory Physics. *Cognition and Instruction, 12,* 152.

Heller, P., Keith, R., & Anderson, S. (1992). Teaching problem solving through cooperative grouping. Part 1: Group versus individual problem solving. *American Journal of Physics, 60,* 627–636.

Henderson, C., Yershalmi, E., Kuo, V. H., Heller, P., & Heller, K. (2004). Grading student problem-solving: The challenge of sending a consistent message. *American Journal of Physics, 72,* 164–169.

Hernández-Ramos, P. (2004). Web logs and online discussions as tools to promote reflective practice. *Journal of Online Interactive Learning, 3.* Retrieved January 15, 2007, from http://www.ncolr.org/jiol/issues/showissue.cfm?volID=3&IssueID=10

Hurst, R. W., & Milkent, M. M. (1996). Facilitating successful prediction problem solving in biology through application of skill theory. *Journal of Research in Science Teaching, 33,* 541–552.

Jonassen, D. H. (2004). Learning to solve problems: An instructional design guide. San Francisco: Pfeiffer Publishing.

Keller, J. M. (1987). Strategies for stimulating the motivation to learn. *Performance and Instruction, 26*(8), 1–7.

Kindfield, A. C. H. (1991). Confusing chromosome number and structure: A common student error. *Journal of Biological Education, 25,* 193–200.

King, P. M., & Kitchener, K. S. (1994). *Developing reflective judgment: Understanding and promoting intellectual growth and critical thinking in adolescents and adults.* San Francisco: Jossey-Bass.

Kusnic, E., & Finley, M. L. (1993) Student self-evaluation: An introduction and rationale. *New Directions for Teaching and Learning 56,* 5–14.

Larkin, J., McDermott, J., Simon, D. P., & Simon, H. A. (1980). Expert and novice performance in solving physics problems. *Science, 208,* 1335.

Lee, K. W. (1985). Cognitive variables in problem solving in chemistry. *Research in Science Education, 15,* 43–50.

Lee, Y., & Nelson, D. M. (2005). Viewing or visualizing: Which concept map strategy works best on problem-solving performance. *British Journal of Educational Technology, 36,* 193–203.

Leonard, W. J., Dufresne, R. J., & Mestre, J. P. (1996). Using qualitative problem-solving strategies to highlight the role of conceptual knowledge in solving problems. *American Journal of Physics, 64,* 1495.

MacGregor, J. (Ed.). (1993). Student self-evaluation: Fostering reflective learning. New Directions for Teaching and Learning 56. San Francisco: Jossey-Bass.

May, D. B., & Etkina, E. (2002). College physics student's epistemological self-reflection and its relationship to conceptual learning. *American Journal of Physics, 70,* 1249.

Mazur, E. (1997). *Peer instruction: A user's manual. Series in educational innovation.* Upper Saddle River, NJ: Prentice Hall.

Moore, T. A. (2003). *Six ideas that shaped physics.* New York: McGraw-Hill.

Niaz, M. (1988). The information-processing demand of chemistry problems and its relation to Pascual-Leone's functional M-capacity. *International Journal of Science Education, 10,* 231.

Novak, J. D., & Gowin. D. B. (1984). *Learning how to learn.* Cambridge, England: Cambridge University Press.

Novak, J. D., Gowin, D. B., & Johansen, G. T. (1983). The use of concept mapping and knowledge Vee mapping with junior high school science students. *Science Education, 67,* 625–645.

Okebukola, P. A. (1990). Attaining meaningful learning of concepts in genetics and ecology: An examination of the potency of the concept mapping technique. *Journal of Research in Science Teaching, 27,* 493–504.

Olafsson, S., Huba, M., Jackman, J., Peters, F., & Ryan, S. (2003). Information technology based active learning: A pilot study for engineering economy. *Proceedings of the 2003 ASEE Annual Conference.* Retrieved January 15, 2007, from http://www.asee.org/acPapers/2003–1605_Final.pd

Olafsson, S., Saunders, K., Jackman, J., Peters, F., Ryan, S., Dark, V., et al. (2004). Implementation and assessment of industrial engineering curriculum reform. *Proceedings of the 2004 ASEE Annual Conference.* Retrieved January 15, 2007, from http://www.asee.org/acPapers/2004-398_Final.pdf

Pankratius, W. J. (1990). Building an organized knowledge base: concept mapping and achievement in secondary school physics. *Journal of Research in Science Teaching, 27,* 315–333.

Polya, G. (1957). *How to solve it* (2nd ed.). Princeton, NJ: Princeton University Press.

Redish, E. F., Jeffery, M., Saul, R., & Steinberg, M. (1998). Student expectations in introductory physics. *American Journal of Physics, 66,* 211.

Reid, N., & Yang, M.-J. (2002). Open-ended problem-solving in school chemistry: A preliminary investigation. *International Journal of Science Education, 24,* 1313–1332.

Reif, F., Larkin, J. H., & Brackett, G. C. (1976). Teaching general learning and problem-solving skills. *American Journal of Physics, 44,* 212–217.

Ryan, S., Jackman, J., Peters, F., Olafsson, S., & Huba, M. (2004). The engineering learning portal for problem solving: Experience in a large engineering economy class. *The Engineering Economist, 49,* 1–20.

Savelsbergh, E., Jong, T. de, & Ferguson-Hessler, M. G. M. (2002). "Situational knowledge in physics: The case of electrodynamics. *Journal of Research in Science Teaching, 39,* 928.

Sawrey, B. A. (1990). Concept learning versus problem solving: Revisited. *Journal of Chemical Education, 67,* 459.

Schmidt, H. (1990). Secondary school students' strategies in stoichiometry. *International Journal of Science Education, 12,* 457.

Schoenfeld, A. (1985). *Mathematical problem solving.* London: Academic.

Shin, N., Jonassen, D. H., & McGee, S. (2003). Predictors of well-structured and ill-structured problem-solving in an astronomy simulation. *Journal of Research in Science Teaching, 40,* 6.

Steiner, G. F., & Stoecklin, M. (1997). Fraction calculation — A didactic approach to constructing mathematical networks. *Learning and Instruction, 7,* 211–233.

Stevens, R., & Palacio-Cayetano, J. (2003). Design and performance frameworks for constructing problem-solving simulations. *Cell Biology Education, 2,* 162–179.

Stevens, R., Soller, A., Cooper, M., & Sprang, M. (2004). *Modeling the development of problem solving skills in chemistry with a web-based tutor. Computer science editorial III.* Heidelberg, Germany: Springer-Verlag.

Stewart, J. (1983). Student problem solving in high school genetics. *Science Education, 67,* 523–540.

Stewart, J., & Hafner, R. (1993). Research on problem solving: Genetics. In D. Gabel (Ed.), *Handbook of research on science teaching and learning* (pp. 284–300). New York: Macmillan.

Sutherland, L. (2002). Developing problem solving expertise: The impact of instruction in a question analysis strategy. *Learning and Instruction, 12,* 155.

Sweller, J., & Cooper, G. A. (1985). The use of worked examples as a substitute for problem solving in learning algebra. *Cognition and Instruction, 2,* 59.

Taconis, R., Ferguson-Hessler, M. G. M., & Broekkamp, H. (2001). Teaching science problem solving: An overview of experimental work. *Journal of Research in Science Teaching, 38,* 442.

Taconis, R., & Van Hout-Wolters, B. (1999). Systematic comparison of solved problems as a cooperative learning task. *Research in Science Education, 29,* 313.

VanderStoep, S. W., & Seifert, C. M. (1993). Learning "how" versus learning "when": Improving transfer of problem-solving principles. *The Journal of the Learning Sciences, 3*(1), 93–111.

Van Heuvelen, A. (1991). Overview, case study physics. *American Journal of Physics, 59,* 898.

Vygotsky, L. S. (1978). *Mind and society: The development of higher mental processes.* Cambridge, MA: Harvard University Press.

Ward, M., & Sweller, J. (1990). Structuring effective worked examples. *Cognition and Instruction, 7,* 1–39.

Williams, J. B., & Jacobs, J. Exploring the use of blogs as learning spaces in the higher education sector. *Australasian Journal of Educational Technology, 20,* 232.

Xun, G. E., & Land, S. M. (2004). A conceptual framework for scaffolding ill-structured problem-solving processes using question prompts and peer Interactions. *Educational Technology Research and Development, 52,* 5.

Chapter 8

Use of Information in Collaborative Problem Solving

Sarah Ryan, John Jackman, Piyamart Kumsaikaew,
Veronica A. Dark, and Sigurdur Olafsson
Iowa State University

Everyday and workplace problem solving occurs in information-rich environments. In corporate settings, the growth of the Internet, widespread adoption of enterprise-wide information systems, and proliferation of distributed sensors and tags such as radio-frequency identification are creating an enormous and growing stream of real-time electronic information. Informal information systems, also aided by mobile information and communication technologies, increase the immediacy and volume of information available. Both the formal and the informal information systems in these environments can be overwhelming to individual or team problem solvers. The sheer volume of information is intimidating. In addition, information elements that a problem solver perceives as necessary may be unavailable, inaccessible, inaccurate, or involve uncertainty. But how does a problem solver know what information is needed? Problems that are ill-structured can have too little information (partial or missing information that is relevant) or too much (irrelevant information). Moreover, a problem may be cognitively ill-structured if relevant information is effectively unavailable to the problem solver. This may occur if the problem solver fails to recognize relevant information, interprets it incorrectly, or does not know how to use it effectively.

This chapter examines the role of information in problem solving from a problem space perspective. Problem Space Theory (Newell & Simon, 1972) is considered to be a major school of thought in problem solving along with other approaches such as Gestalt Theory, Analogies, Mental Models, and so forth. A problem space is defined by a set of problem states that describe the problem solution at a point in time. Transition operators are used by a problem solver to move between states. A problem is solved by moving (navigating) from an initial state to intermediate states and then finally a goal state. In Polya's "problems of finding," the initial and goal states correspond to the data given and the unknowns, respectively (Polya, 1985). Learning problem solving from this perspective is focused on the cognitive skills necessary to recognize what problem space is appropriate for a problem, set up the initial state, perform transitions, and recognize when the goal state is reached. Performing transitions involves processing information that corresponds to the problem space. Therefore, it is critical that problem solvers have the ability to identify, collect, evaluate, and analyze information relevant to the problem space.

Following an outline of the research to date on information use and its relation to external and internal problem representations, we describe our experience with a problem-solving learning environment designed to mimic authentic information environments faced by engineers in the workplace. The chapter concludes with research issues related to developing pedagogy that will prepare engineering students for their lifelong roles as problem solvers in information-rich environments.

RESEARCH ON INFORMATION PROCESSING IN PROBLEM SOLVING

Cognitive psychologists have examined information use in cognitive tasks for the past half century. More recently, investigators have explored the relation between information environments and problem representations. However, the design of information environments for problem-solving pedagogy has not been investigated systematically.

Using Information

Information in cognitive tasks such as problem solving is structured as a set of chunks (Miller, 1956). A chunk is considered to be a meaningful and identifiable unit of information that could contain multiple items. Knowledge is grouped into chunks, with experts having larger size chunks than novices. Miller (1956) suggested that humans can work with up to seven chunks at a time during cognitive tasks. Chunks are processed as the problem solver moves through the problem space to form new chunks or expressions. Newell and Rosenbloom (1981) referred to this as "The Chunking Hypothesis." Support for the existence of chunks can be found in the work of Chase and Simon (1973). Subsequent work suggested that the number of chunks used during a task may be on the order of two to four (Broadbent, 1975; Coltheart, 1972; Gobet & Clarkson, 2004).

Chunks move between working memory and long-term memory depending on the nature of the cognitive task (Atkinson & Shiffrin, 1968). Looking for chunks of information in the information infrastructure involves multiple iterative stages and strategies (Marchionini, 1995). Macpherson (2003) proposed a two-stage model for information seeking. In the first stage, a problem solver's need for information is mapped to concepts the solver understands in terms of declarative knowledge. The second stage involves search strategies and evaluation of the information.

At some stage in the problem-solving process, chunks must be recognized as being relevant to a problem. A chunk is relevant if it can be connected to one or more concepts in the problem space. This implies that a problem solver has already learned the problem space in terms of the set of concepts (i.e., chunks) involved and the relations between the concepts. Novak (2002) stated that knowledge in long-term memory is a network of concepts that has been described as a concept tree. For novices, the concept tree may be incomplete or inaccurate, leading to difficulty in the problem-solving process. This can be attributed to the inability of a novice to recognize relevant chunks of information in a problem.

Learning is a process of constructing and modifying the concept trees in long-term memory. For well-structured problems, problem solvers must learn the related declarative and procedural knowledge before they can begin to address a problem scenario. Ill-structured problems pose greater challenges because the problem space is unknown and evolves over time. Therefore, the information is revisited periodically to determine its relevance to the current problem space.

Limited Human Information Processing Capacity

From an information processing perspective, the brain is considered to be a single processor unit that performs operations on chunks in working memory. Long-term memory provides archival storage of chunks that can be retrieved as needed by the processor. Multitasking becomes difficult due to limitations in processing capacity and working memory (Baddeley & Hitch, 1974; Shiffrin & Schneider, 1977; Simon, 1973). Ramsey, Jansma, Jager, Van Raalten, and Kahn (2004) found that with practice, the demand on working memory was reduced for multitasking situations.

Simon (1997) has pointed out that the scarce resource in organizational decision making is not information but rather human time and attention. Therefore, "irrelevant information is not simply useless; it is positively harmful because it wastes users' time and distracts their attention" (Simon, 1997, p. 4). The significance of time wasted by irrelevant information has increased recently as time-based competition requires firms to bring new products to market quickly, deliver items to customers with minimum delays, and respond promptly to changing conditions.

Problem Representations

Information is used throughout the problem-solving process and appears in various forms. Problem representations are descriptions of the problem at different stages in the process. The descriptions may consist of oral communication, written text, graphics, figures, tables, mathematical expressions, or some combination thereof. Internal representations are descriptions stored in the brain of a problem solver; they describe the internalized knowledge of a problem. External representations are the information structures found in the problem-solving environment. The information in these descriptions can be characterized by some level of accuracy, ambiguity, redundancy, and conflict. Most studies have focused on external representations due to the difficulty of measuring or identifying internal representations.

Zhang (1997) studied the nature of external representations in a simple problem-solving scenario. He suggested that the external representations have a major effect on cognitive tasks and can provide memory aids and guidance for problem solving. Zhang stated that this type of information is not just a set of stimuli, but affects the way in which a problem is solved.

For those scenarios where we as educators have control over the representation, our understanding of the impact of representations can be used to improve the representations such as computer displays, textbook problems, or problem-solving pedagogy. For ill-structured environments where there is little or no control over the representations, this is problematic. Barone and Cheng (2004) studied external representations from a decision support perspective. They showed that certain representations helped participants in their problem-solving strategies. Cheng (2002) studied the effects of Law Encoding Diagrams on learning problem solving in the domain of electricity. The study compared the use of standard mathematical representations to a diagram approach as participants proceeded through the problem space. Participants using the diagrams exhibited better problem-solving performance. Cheng suggested that the diagrams helped students construct perceptual chunks in their long-term memory (i.e., internal representations).

Irrelevant, Redundant, or Conflicting Information

When ample information is available, the problem solver must select which information to use. In some cases, the task-relevant information may be available from multiple sources and may appear in multiple representations. For example, consider the redundant information in Figure 8.1 and Table 8.1 for a set of data points. Both representations contain the same information showing the demand for a product as the price increases. In the context of a problem, a participant may select the table over the figure if some additional analysis needs to be performed. This is because the numeric values are available directly. In this case, Table 8.1 is considered to be task relevant and Figure 8.1 is redundant. The graph in Figure 8.1 might be selected if the goal is to perform a simple comparison, summary of the data, or identification of trends.

TABLE 8.1

Demand As a Function of Price

Price	Demand
10	459
20	324
40	229
80	162
160	115
320	81
640	57
1280	41

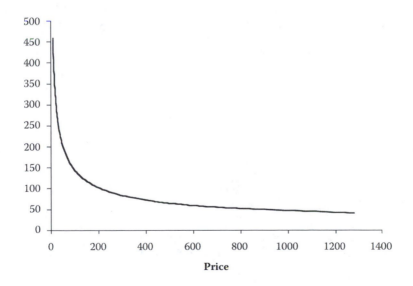

Figure 8.1.   Demand as a function of price.

When redundancies occur, a problem solver must make a decision about which source is most relevant to the problem space. Green and Wright (2003) investigated the selection of task relevant information in the context of multiple sources. Green found that when some of the redundant information is unreliable, then participants will switch to another source.

In many real-world problems, different sources of information are in conflict. In some cases, the information can be in conflict because a source is invalid, inaccurate, or unreliable. In other cases, the conflict may be due to unknown phenomena that affect the information and therefore, the information should be considered as valid. When a conflict occurs, a problem solver makes decisions in an attempt to resolve the conflict. Consider the conflict between Table 8.1 and Figure 8.2. Both sources indicate that as the price increases, the demand is decreasing. However, the linear nature of that relation in Figure 8.2 is in conflict with the data provided in Table 8.1. To resolve this conflict, the sources can be checked to assess their validity or additional data could be collected.

Research on Information Use

Studies by Egner and Hirsch (2005) found that participants resolved conflicting information by increasing their focus and attention on task-relevant information (which they termed as *attentional target-feature amplification*). In a modified Stroop test, they collected and analyzed data on the ability of participants to select targets on a computer display. In a standard Stroop test, participants are supposed to identify the color of a word and ignore the content of the word. The cognitive challenge of the test is that the words are

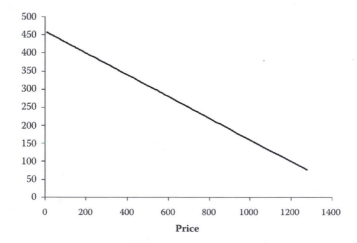

Figure 8.2.   Conflicting information example.

color words (e.g., red, green, blue, etc.), which causes confusion for participants. Brain scans were obtained during the task to identify the regions of the brain that were active. A previous study by Banich et al.(2000), also using brain scans and a Stroop test, indicated that there were two modes in which the brain processes the information. In the first mode, prefrontal regions focused attention on task-relevant information. For the other mode, posterior regions focused attention on task-irrelevant information, perhaps indicating that some processing time is spent trying to prevent further use of irrelevant information. This suggests that the identification of task-relevant and irrelevant information involves some marking or tagging of information during the cognitive task.

Haider and Frensch (1996) found that with practice, participants were able to reduce the amount of information that was used in a cognitive task and therefore, reduce task time. They suggested that this can be attributed to a participant acquiring a skill of focusing on primarily task-relevant information. The tasks in their studies involved identifying correct and incorrect sequences of alphanumeric strings based on a set of predefined rules.

Lee and Anderson (2001) used eye tracking for the Kanfer-Ackerman Air-Traffic Controller Task (Ackerman, 1988) to collect data on the time spent looking at task-relevant and task-irrelevant information for a series of trials. The time spent on both types of information decreased as a function of the number of trials. The time spent on irrelevant information was consistently longer than on relevant information until the number of trials reached 15. At this point, the time spent on both types of information was equivalent.

ROLE OF INFORMATION IN PROBLEM-SOLVING PEDAGOGY

The types of information used in teaching problem solving include declarative knowledge, procedural knowledge, and problem representations. For a given domain, students must acquire the declarative and procedural knowledge necessary to navigate the related problem spaces. This information is communicated through media such as lectures, textbooks, tutorials, and reference material. Formal problems are introduced to help students learn how to use their knowledge in some limited context. Problems are also used to assess a student's knowledge of a domain. The amount of task-relevant information in a problem as well as the information density can affect the difficulty of the problem-solving tasks. Information density is a measure of the percentage of task-relevant information in a problem.

A Collaborative Problem-Solving Learning Portal

A Web-based portal for collaborative problem solving of ill-structured problems has been developed and studied by Olafsson et al. (2004). The

Problem Solving Learning Portal (PSLP) supports the development and use of modules containing real-world problems. It provides an active learning environment where students (working in teams) formulate and solve difficult problems using the tools and domain-specific knowledge learned in class.

For each module, students must independently define goal states, formulate problems, and develop solution strategies while mastering the declarative and procedural knowledge. This environment is thus a fundamental shift from the existing emphasis on the traditional lecture format to active learning. This is also an ideal tool to encourage cooperation and communication with other students through collaborative learning. The PSLP contains the necessary content and structure used to (a) provide scenario-specific information based on student-initiated requests, (b) structure the problem-solving process, (c) collect information on cognitive processes, (d) collect work in multiple formats from each student team, and (e) provide feedback to teams on their progress. After connecting to the PSLP, students have access to a large set of information resources for a scenario. This information can take the form of reports, spreadsheets, design specifications, drawings, pictures, or streaming video. The problem-solving process is structured by the PSLP in stages. A typical set of stages includes the following:

- Objective—Students formulate and describe a goal state in terms of the problem space. This occurs before they attempt to solve the problem. They may also define measures that will be used to assess their results in the goal state. A justification of the objective is also required.
- Plan—Students define a set of actions that will be performed to solve the problem. These actions involve some application of declarative and procedural knowledge. Justification must be given for each action in the plan. Where information is missing or incomplete, assumptions must be stated and defended.
- Solution—After completing their plan, students describe their solution, which should be consistent with their goal state described in the Objective stage. A justification of the solution must be provided in order to submit the solution.
- Performance—A scenario-specific Monte Carlo simulation model presents results for the scenario based on the solution submitted by the students. Students can reflect on the "goodness" of their solutions based on their goal state.

An example of a PSLP document for a problem in the engineering economy field is shown in Figure 8.3. The statement at the top of the document is a short description of the problem statement and appears on every docu-

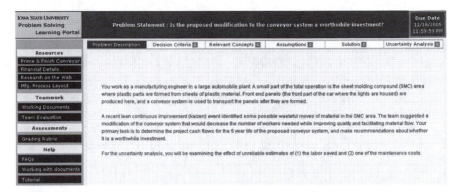

Figure 8.3. Information in the Problem Solving Learning Portal.

ment. Immediately below this statement is the set of stages for this problem beginning on the left side and proceeding to the right. Each stage has a set of information specific to the stage and some interaction with the system.

Problems in the PSLP are designed to be ill-structured as in real-world scenarios. Therefore, information is not provided to students in well-defined packages as in traditional textbook or case study problems. Students can select items under Resources on the left side of the screen that can contain task-relevant or irrelevant information. Higher order cognitive skills (Bloom, 1956), such as application, analysis, synthesis or evaluation, must be used to determine which information is necessary for the problem space. Some of the information can be used directly, whereas other information must be used to produce information that can be used in the problem space.

Student Use of Information in Problem Solving

Because the PSLP is Web-based, large amounts of data on student interaction with the system are available. The following sections summarize our observations of student behavior as well as their reactions to the system obtained from focus groups and surveys. The PSLP has been used continuously with regular modifications since fall 2002, beginning with the engineering economic analysis course (Ryan, Jackman, Peters, Olafsson, & Huba, 2004), and with subsequent modules added for manufacturing systems, production systems, and optimization courses. Hundreds of engineering students have used it to solve a variety of realistic problems, developed in consultation with industry partners. Notably, U.S. students have worked in teams with their counterparts in Scotland, Mexico, and Taiwan to design a global supply chain (Min et al., 2005). In 2006, it was used for administering shorter multifaceted problems in physics (see chap. 7 by Ogilvie in this volume).

Data Mining of Student Behavior

To obtain insights about student behaviors in the PSLP for the engineering economy domain, we tracked their actions by recording the documents accessed and the actions performed in those documents. Data mining of this tracking data was performed to identify clusters of student behaviors. The attributes used in data mining included the documents accessed and the actions performed by a team as they worked on the problem. A cluster is defined by a set of teams in the PSLP that exhibits similar actions. Clustering analysis was performed using the Waikato Environment for Knowledge Analysis system and the X-means algorithm (Pelleg & Moore, 2000). After clustering, we examined the actions within each cluster to characterize the nature of the student behavior. The clustering results shown in Table 8.2 indicate that the first three clusters involve the use of information for the problem scenario. The behaviors indicate different modes in which students are using information. Cluster 1 indicates an exploratory mode in which students appear to be assessing the scope of the information. There may also be some initial assessment of task-relevant information. In Cluster 2, students are looking for specific items indicating that they have identified the information needs for the problem and are looking for only

TABLE 8.2

Types of Behaviors for an Engineering Economy Problem

Cluster	Type	Behaviors	Percentage of Total Sessions
1	Exploration	Students view all information resources and download all documents and templates.	25.41
2	Hunting for details	Students revisit all documents and look for details in each information resource but perform relatively few downloads.	11.88
3	Problem formulation	Students visit each stage but do not look at the information resources. The number of submissions in each stage is small. They appear to want to see the overall problem.	3.31
4	Arrival at the goal state	Students complete each stage of a problem.	45.58
5	Work in process	Some sections are completed.	9.39
6	Other	Other	4.70

task-relevant information. The mode of Cluster 3 suggests that students are in the process of formulating the problem space so that they will arrive at the goal state. They are focusing on information related to the problem-solving stages.

Focus Groups

Focus groups were conducted to obtain additional insights into how students perceived and used the information. Two students explained that they did not like the PSLP because they found it confusing. They stated that when they asked the instructor for clarification about the problem, they did not get direct answers. For example, when asked where to start, the instructor responded by saying that the students could start in various places. Two students also explained that there was a great amount of information. When they clicked on the information resources, they were unsure what to do with the amount and type of information provided. The students explained that they are more accustomed to problems that have one solution. In the class, the instructor explained that multiple solutions are possible. They also heard a statement regarding the fact that there is one solution that is preferable. These students were anxious about grading due to the uncertainty of finding the preferred solution. The students explained that they are used to going to the professor to find out if they are solving the problem correctly.

One team said that they were initially overwhelmed by the amount of data and information. The team thought that the information would be in one data sheet, but commented that the PSLP is more realistic.

When asked about examples of things that helped them learn, students said that the problem corresponded to information covered in the lectures. The problem pulled together the information and helped students learn how to connect the concepts. One student explained that they are typically given only the information they need for a problem. The PSLP forced the students to seek and acquire the task-relevant information.

In describing problem-solving strategies, one student team placed all of the information they selected as task relevant into one spreadsheet to compile the data in one place. A different team performed each action in small parts. Members of a third group stated that they found their own order of problem-solving stages. One student commented that it was tedious going through all of the information resources. Another stated that there was a lot of extra information.

When asked what they learned, one student explained that it was not "what" they learned, but their ability to learn "how" to use the information. This student explained that it was more important to use what they had already learned to solve the problem. Students explained that it was nice to have a lot of information to explore, but it was hard to find some task-relevant information, which students found to be more realistic. There was some con-flicting information. One student explained that some energy costs were not given and so the student went to the Internet to find the information.

When asked to describe their problem-solving process, group members described various processes:

- One group initially removed extraneous options and data.
- One team described working backward by finding out trends and per-centage of growth.
- One team delegated various parts of the project.
- Another team worked as a group and "bounced ideas off one another."

Some students said that the format "bothered" them, whereas others de-scribed an "initial shock" to the format. The students explained that the for-mat was different from what they are used to and it required them to find information for themselves. Students also explained that in the workplace, they would be more familiar with the context and that considerable time was needed in the PSLP to find information. Some students explained that it was difficult to remember where they saw information initially.

Survey Findings

In the fall semester of 2005, engineering economy students worked in teams of three or four to solve two case studies. The first was a personal fi-nance problem of selecting between an adjustable or fixed rate mortgage in view of interest rate uncertainty. Information sources included simulated consultations with a banker, realtor, and tax specialist; recent testimony by Federal Reserve Chairman Alan Greenspan; interest rate and housing price histories; and sample calculations related to both types of mortgages. The second case study was the industry capital investment problem illus-trated in Figure 8.3. Besides cost estimates and financial details, descrip-tions of the current and proposed conveyor systems were supplied in text and diagrams along with detailed descriptions of thermoset composites and the sheet molding process. A survey was administered after each case study.

For case study 1, students were asked to rate the helpfulness of the infor-mation resources ($1 = $ *unhelpful,* $5 = $ *helpful*). The mean response was 2.96. When asked to evaluate the resources in the second case study on a scale where $1 = $ *confusing* and $5 = $ *helpful,* the mean response was 3.6, indicating an increase in the perceived helpfulness of the information resources from the first case study to the second. Other responses revealed that students felt the number of different resources available in the second case study was neither too few nor too many. In the second survey, students' responses to the open-ended question, "Please comment on any changes that would make these case studies a more effective learning experience," revealed more about their opinions of the amounts of information available and the pedagogical value of the information-rich case studies. Actual student comments are copied in italics in the following list.

- Students were uncomfortable with extraneous information and may have suspected the instructor of deliberately trying to confuse them, with no apparent pedagogical purpose.

  - *Case Study 2 was much more clear on what was required and did not have as much irrelevant information.*
  - *I felt the information provided was much more effective unlike Case Study 1 which had a lot of irrelevant information.*
  - *I realize in economy problems there are many things (criteria) that can factor into a problem, but I think only the information that we should use be given to us. You should eliminate any other unnecessary information, to prevent confusion of the students.*
  - *Expectations need to be explained more clearly and the extra info added to confuse us should be eliminated.*

- On the other hand, having too little or conflicting information requires students to make assumptions. Students recognized that the problem then lacks the degree of structuredness to which they have become accustomed in class assignments.

  - *To be more effective, don't have so much information available to us as well as having us make so many assumptions. This allows for the whole project to be varied in many, many different directions.*
  - *I think students are generally nervous when given freedom to make assumptions; they are used to following instructions exactly in every class.*
  - *Some of the wording of the documents can lead to a different set of assumptions. This was the only problem our group had in this case study.*
  - *Assumptions should not be part of a case study. You either have something or you don't. Making the wrong assumption can cost a company millions of dollars, so telling students that they can just make assumptions does not prepare them very well for real situations. In short, assumptions are not good when you are working with other people's money and careers.*

- Although some students doubted the realism of exercises in which they must search for and sift the information provided while filling in gaps, others did recognize their value in preparing them for real-world problem-solving experiences. To help prepare students for ill-structured problem-solving exercises, instructors may need to explain the critical role of information skills.

> ◦ *I know we have to search for the information in real life, but the time spent on this takes away much needed time for people, especially seniors, with more in depth and useful capstone type projects. These case studies have many good things that can be learned, so they are useful projects to have.*
> ◦ *This method of case studies is one of the best things to come out of [the course], because it spurs creativity and a break away from plug and chug formulas.*
> ◦ *Make student aware that knowing where to find right information is part of problem solving.*

RESEARCH ISSUES

Given the modes of student behavior in solving problems and their perceptions of working in an information-rich environment, a number of research issues become apparent.

Information Environment in the Engineering Workplace

Given that students need better preparation for the workplace, a better understanding of the nature of the information environment in the workplace is needed. In addition, the context and the type of problem being solved are related to the information environment. In the typology of Jonassen (2000), design problems are presented as the most ill-structured type. The design of a standard component may be a well-defined problem because of preexisting designs or experience with this type of design. This information includes a library of designs and expert knowledge that is internal to the designers. In contrast, many of the problems that workplace engineers solve are more similar to diagnosis-solution problems. For example, a manufacturing engineer may need to find and fix the cause(s) of missed deadlines for the delivery of products to customers. The possible causes are numerous and varied, whereas the information necessary to identify them may be difficult to locate, unreliable, and mingled with a large quantity of irrelevant information. The messy information environment is a key contributor to the nature of this ill-structured problem. Typically, a manufacturing engineer will identify a small number of possible causes and will then face a decision-making problem of determining where to devote the available resources to investigate them. This problem is relatively well-structured, but only because the requisite work of processing relevant information and narrowing the decision space has already been done.

Navigating the Workplace Information Environment

In the process of becoming experts, engineers must learn to distinguish task-relevant from irrelevant information. They must develop strategies for storing and retrieving information as well as processing it in manageable chunks to operate within the constraints of their cognitive processing ability. Finally, in view of the always-limited time available for solving problems, they must avoid wasting time and effort on collecting and analyzing information that is less relevant. This distinction may be related to identifying which problem-solving paths are more promising to pursue (Bereiter & Scardamalia, 1993).

Learning to Use Information in Problem Solving

What pedagogies can help novices become more like experts in how they use information in problem solving? It seems evident that to create authentic learning and assessment tasks, we must reproduce the engineering workplace information environment to some extent. Furthermore, we must devise new ways to observe, measure, and describe the information a novice or expert problem solver uses and how it is being used. Our preliminary studies varied the information density and used different distributions of relevant information in engineering problem descriptions. Novice and expert engineering students were asked to identify task-relevant information in these descriptions without solving the problems. The results were analyzed using signal detection theory and clustering analysis. It was clear that students with more expertise were more successful in identifying task-relevant information. Other results suggested that the structure of problem descriptions can affect student performance.

REFERENCES

Ackerman, P. L. (1988). Determinants of individual differences during skill acquisition: Cognitive abilities and information processing. *Journal of Experimental Psychology: General, 117*, 288–318.

Atkinson, R. L., & Shiffrin, R. M. (1968). Human memory: A proposed system and its control processes. In K. W. Spence & J. T. Spence (Eds.), *The psychology of learning and motivation: Advances in research and theory* (Vol. 2, pp. 89–195). New York: Academic.

Baddeley, A. D., & Hitch, G. H. (1974). Working memory. In G. H. Bower (Ed.), *The psychology of learning and motivation: Advances in research and theory* (Vol. 8, pp. 47–89). New York: Academic.

Banich, M. T., Milham, M. P., Atchley, R., Cohen,, N. J., Webb, A., Wszalek, T., et al. (2000). fMRIstudies of Stroop tasks reveal unique roles of anterior and posterior brain systems in attentional selection. *Journal of Cognitive Neuroscience, 12*, 988–1000.

Barone, R., & Cheng, P. C.-H. (2004). Representations for problem solving: On the benefits of integrated structure. In E. Banissi, K. Börner, C. Chen, M. Dastbaz, G. Clapworthy, A. Faiola, et al. (Eds.), *Proceedings of the 8th International Conference on Information Visualisation* (pp. 575–580). Los Alamitos, CA: Institute of Electrical and Electronics Engineers.

Bereiter, C., & Scardamalia, M. (1993). *Surpassing ourselves: An inquiry into the nature and implications of expertise.* Chicago: Open Court Press.

Bloom B. S. (1956). *Taxonomy of educational objectives, handbook I: The cognitive domain.* New York: McKay.

Broadbent, D. E. (1975). The magic number seven after fifteen years. In A. Kennedy & A. Wilkes (Eds.), *Studies in long-term memory* (pp. 3–18). London: Wiley.

Chase, W. G., & Simon, H. A. (1973). Perception in chess. *Cognitive Psychology, 4,* 55–81.

Cheng, P. C.-H. (2002). Electrifying diagrams for learning: Principles for effective representational systems. *Cognitive Science, 26,* 685–736.

Coltheart, M. (1972). Visual information-processing. In P. C. Dodwell (Ed.), New horizons in psychology, II (pp. 62–85). Harmondsworth, England: Penguin.

Egner, T. & Hirsch, J. (2005). Cognitive control mechanisms resolve conflict through cortical amplification of task-relevant information. *Nature Neuroscience, 8,* 1784–1790.

Gobet, F., & Clarkson, G. (2004). Chunks in expert memory: Evidence for the magical number four … or is it two? *Memory, 12,* 732–747.

Green, A. J. K., & Wright, M. J. (2003). Reduction of task-relevant information in skill acquisition. *European Journal of Cognitive Psychology, 15,* 267–290.

Haider, H., & Frensch, P. (1996). The role of information reduction in skill acquisition. *Cognitive Psychology, 30,* 304–337.

Jonassen, D. H. (2000). Toward a design theory of problem solving. *Educational Technology Research and Development, 48,* 63–85.

Lee, F. J. & Anderson, J. R. (2001). Does learning a complex task have to be complex?: A study in learning decomposition. *Cognitive Psychology, 42,* 267–316.

Macpherson, K. (2003). An information processing model of undergraduate electronic database information retrieval. *Journal of the American Society for Information Science and Technology, 55,* 333–347.

Marchionini, G. (1995). *Information seeking in electronic environments.* New York: Cambridge University Press.

Miller, G. A. (1956). The magical number seven, plus or minus two: Some limits on our capacity for processing information. *Psychological Review, 63,* 81–97.

Min, K. J., Jackman, J., Patterson, P., Kumsaikaew, P., Li, J., & Vuthipadadon, S. (2005). Global enterprise perspective initiative in a production systems course. In *Proceedings of the 2005 American Society for Engineering Education Annual Conference* [CD-ROM]. Washington, DC: American Society for Engineering Education.

Newell, A., & Rosenbloom, P. S. (1981). Mechanisms of skill acquisition and the law of practice. In J. R. Anderson (Ed.), *Cognitive skills and their acquisition* (pp. 1–51). Hillsdale, NJ: Lawrence Erlbaum Associates.

Newell, A., & Simon, H. A. (1972). *Human problem solving.* Englewood Cliffs, NJ: Prentice Hall.

Novak, J. D. (2002) Meaningful learning: The essential factor for conceptual change in limited or inappropriate propositional hierarchies leading to empowerment of learners. *Science Education, 86,* 548–571.

Olafsson, S., Saunders, K., Jackman, J., Peters, F., Ryan, S., Dark, V., et al. (2004). Implementation and assessment of industrial engineering curriculum reform. *Pro-*

ceedings of the 2004 American Society for Engineering Education Annual Conference
[CD-ROM]. Washington, DC: American Society for Engineering Education.
Pelleg, D., & Moore, A. (2000). X-means: Extending K-means with efficient estima-
tion of the number of clusters. *Proceedings of the 17th International Conference on
Machine Learning, 727–734.*
Polya, G. (1985). *How to solve it.* Princeton, NJ: Princeton Science Library.
Ramsey, N. F., Jansma, J. M., Jager, G,. Van Raalten, T., & Kahn, R. S. (2004).
Neurophysiological factors in human information processing capacity. *Brain,
127,* 517–525.
Ryan, S., Jackman, J., Peters, F., Olafsson, S., & Huba, M. (2004). The engineering
learning portal for problem solving: Experience in a large engineering economy
class. *The Engineering Economist, 49,* 1–20.
Shiffrin, R. M., & Schneider, W. (1977). Controlled and automatic human information processing: II. Perceptual learning, automatic attending and a general theory. *Psychology Review, 84,* 127–190.
Simon, H. A. (1973). The structure of ill-structured problems. *Artificial Intelligence, 4,*
181–202.
Simon, H. A. (1997). The future of information systems. *Annals of Operations Research, 71,* 3–14.
Zhang, J. (1997). The nature of external representations in problem solving. *Cognitive Science, 21,* 179–217.

Chapter 9

Toward a New Approach to Teaching Problem Solving in Dynamics

Gary L. Gray
Francesco Costanzo
The Pennsylvania State University

Introductory Dynamics is one of the first engineering courses taken by most engineering students. As such, it is important that Dynamics instill in students not only a sense of what engineering is, but it should also begin to develop those skills that the student will need throughout his or her academic and postacademic career. For Dynamics, this means the ability to apply a few principles to model and analyze simple mechanical systems. This is all done in the context of solving problems, which is really what engineers do—they solve problems.

Dynamics is the science of motion. As such, the students are expected to develop the ability to analyze engineering problems concerning the motion of objects and the system of forces acting on them. The solution of these problems requires the use of very few basic principles. In particular, the students are expected to learn to apply some elementary ideas from geometry and calculus to describe the geometry of motion (which is called *kinematics*). In addition, they apply the laws of motion due to Newton and Euler (and derived principles, such as the work-energy principle and the impulse-momentum principle) to develop the remaining equations required to solve a problem. It is hoped that students realize that Dynamics is not a sequence of independent methods for solving problems, but is a coherent class of techniques all based on Newton's laws.

To be a little more specific, in Dynamics students are presented with what might commonly be called "word problems," and they are expected to distill these problems down to their essential elements, model them via free-body diagrams,[1] and then apply the appropriate principles to their model to generate the mathematical equations that govern the system they are analyzing. Once these equations have been generated, they are expected to be able to use concepts and ideas from algebra, trigonometry, calculus, and to a lesser extent, differential equations, to solve these equations for some aspect or aspects of the motion. It has been our experience[2] and that of many other instructors (see, e.g., Kremer, 2001) that this sequence of problem-solving steps proves to be very difficult for most students. We believe there are several reasons for this difficulty: (a) Dynamics is the first "synthesis" course, that is, it requires students to take ideas from several previous courses and bring them to bear on each problem they need to solve, and (b) it is the first time that students need to start thinking like "engineers," that is, the first time they need to take a real system, decide on a model of that system, write the governing equations based on that model, and then solve those equations to infer the needed information about the behavior of the original system.[3]

In addition to the fact that it is a foundation course for other many courses in engineering curricula, another reason to "get Dynamics right" and use it as a vehicle to improve the teaching of problem solving is that so many students take Dynamics. At the main campus of The Pennsylvania State University (Penn State), students studying mechanical, aerospace, industrial, civil, bio, architectural, environmental systems, petroleum and natural gas, and mining engineering all are required to take Dynamics. At Penn State (whose total enrollment is over 40,000), almost 70% of all engineering students take Dynamics, which amounts to more than 800 students per year.

As we have already stated, the vast majority of students find Dynamics to be a very difficult class. Students know this coming into the class because information like this spreads quickly within the student "grapevine." In addition, Dynamics is taught using textbooks whose first editions were written in the 1950s and 1960s. With few exceptions, these textbooks continue to use homework problems and examples that, apart from a few classics, have become a bit overused and disconnected from current applications. That is, the problems consist of balls on inclined planes, abstract points moving along mathematically defined curves, and

---

[1]A free-body diagram is a simple sketch of a mechanical system, or portion of a system, that is separated or made "free" from its environment and/or other portions of the system, and that shows all forces and/or moments that act on the system.

[2]The authors have a combined 27 years of experience teaching Dynamics.

[3]Statics, which is the prerequisite course for Dynamics, also does this, but in a much more limited way. That is, the original systems are generally simpler and the choices to make for the model are substantially fewer. In fact, most students who find Dynamics to be very difficult found Statics to be very straightforward.

many other systems to which the students have difficulty relating. In addition, most problems are solved at specific moments in time or positions in space (e.g., if a pendulum is released from rest at an angle with respect to the vertical of 30°, determine its speed when the angle is 0°), so students never solve problems the way engineers have to solve them—over ranges of time or positions so that results can be used as inputs for design. All of these issues combine to make the course not only difficult for students, but also very dull. We had been teaching Dynamics in this mode for a number of years when we decided that we would try and improve student performance (as measured by their ability to solve problems on exams and homework) by increasing their interest and active participation in the course (see also Bransford, Brown, & Cocking, 2000). This led to our 2-year experiment teaching a "studio" version of the course we called *Interactive Dynamics*[4] (Costanzo & Gray, 2000; Gray & Costanzo, 1999).

INTERACTIVE DYNAMICS

Traditional Dynamics is taught in the "chalk and talk" mode, wherein an instructor presents three weekly, 1-hr lectures and there is frequently little interaction with the students. In this type of learning environment, students may not experience the following:

- Computers as tools for solving engineering problems.
- Working in teams.
- Writing a technical report.
- A hands-on or laboratory experience.
- Real-world engineering Dynamics problems.

As with a traditional Dynamics class, Interactive Dynamics used traditional "chalk and talk" lectures 50% to 60% of the time. It is the other 40% to 50% of the class that profoundly differentiated Interactive Dynamics from traditional Dynamics. On days in which we were not doing standard lectures, the Interactive Dynamics class typically began with a 15- to 45-min introductory lecture in which the goal of the day's activity was presented. This introduction was intended to point out any particularly important things the students should look for during that day's activity and to put that activity into a proper engineering context. After the introductory lecture, the activity began.

An activity was, in essence, a project that required the solution of a difficult problem. The level of complexity of these problems was such that teamwork was absolutely essential to complete the activity in the allocated time. In fact, activities were substantial enough such that they could not usually be completed in one class period (when we taught it, the course met two times per week for 1 hr

---

[4]Interactive Dynamics is largely based on the so-called "studio" concept developed at Rensselaer Polytechnic Institute (Wilson, 1992a, b, 1994, 1996).

and 55 min each time) and their completion almost always required students to meet outside of class. In addition to teamwork, computer tools and an understanding of how to present technical information were essential elements of any activity (these elements were all taught in the class). Students were not "taken by the hand" as they worked their way through each activity. In fact, we tried to make the process of completing each activity to be as "real-world" as we could make it. In this sense, the students were the active element in their education and the instructor played the role of listener, mentor, and advisor.

Within each activity, the notion that Dynamics is about modeling mechanical systems to develop mathematical equations that can predict their behavior (largely for the purpose of design) was strongly emphasized. In addition, each activity required the students to work in teams and to either take on or assign roles for each of the team members. This required communication, leadership, and management skills that are typically not required of students in the first Dynamics course. Finally, Interactive Dynamics introduced students to an abundance of concepts and ideas that students in a traditional Dynamics course never see. Again, all of these elements were intended to make the Interactive Dynamics classroom an environment which was as close as possible to the workplace that the students would experience when they leave school.

In addition to the aforementioned goals, it was also our intent to address some of the Accreditation Board for Enginnering and Technology (ABET)[5] goals for programs in engineering (see ABET Engineering Accreditation Commission, 2005) as well as some of the well-publicized issues with engineering education that have been raised in recent years (see, e.g., Advisory Committee to the National Science Foundation, 1996). Although these goals were lofty, we discovered a number of things that made teaching Interactive Dynamics prohibitive:

- For a class of 20 to 30 students, at least two faculty members were needed to mingle among the students to keep them on track and moving forward.
- Students needed training and guidance on how to effectively work as a team and we needed to make sure teams functioned harmoniously.
- Students needed training in the mathematical software that was used as a tool in most activities (e.g., Mathematica or Matlab).
- Because most sophomores have not had a technical writing class, they needed some guidance in how to report their findings from an activity.

These issues conspired to make the course substantially more work for faculty, and unfortunately, less fun for most students. Although we found that

---

[5]ABET, Inc. is the generally recognized body for accrediting college and university programs in applied science, computing, engineering, and technology. ABET currently accredits more than 2,700 programs at over 550 colleges and universities across the United States.

most students found the course to be more interesting when taught in the studio format, most students also found that they were also spending much more time on the course than were their peers who were taking nonstudio sections. In addition, we also found that all of the extra material that needed to be covered (writing, mathematical software, etc.) meant that we had difficulty covering all of the topics that most mechanics educators deem essential in the course. For these reasons, we no longer teach Interactive Dynamics, although students did show a measurable improvement in their ability to solve problems as posed on exams. On the other hand, because of the close contact we had with hundreds of students, the experiment yielded valuable insights into two things: the way students approach problem solving, and students' conceptual understanding of the material. These insights lead us down two different, but very complementary, paths with regard to engineering mechanics education: we began writing introductory mechanics textbooks in Statics and Dynamics and we developed a Dynamics Concept Inventory (DCI).

THE NEXT GENERATION OF INTRODUCTORY MECHANICS TEXTS

Engineering courses in mechanics differ from their companion courses offered by physics departments in that, in engineering, there is a strong emphasis on engineering standards and design, on the one hand, and on the acquisition of effective problem-solving techniques, on the other. Although there exists a wide literature on problem solving in engineering and the National Science Foundation (NSF) has spent significant sums on funding research in the improvement of engineering problem solving, we do not feel that this specialized work has significantly impacted the way engineering mechanics courses are taught, at least in the United States. With this said, there are two main sources of problem-solving instruction in undergraduate mechanics courses: (a) the textbook adopted in class, and (b) the instructor teaching the course. With the right approach, a textbook can have a profound impact on both sources of instruction because it can inform both the student *and* the instructor. We are writing introductory mechanics textbooks (Plesha, Gray, & Costanzo, 2006; Gray, Costanzo, & Plesha, 2006; Costanzo, Plesha, & Gray, 2006) that will promote structured problem solving as a means of helping the student avoid a trial and error approach to a problem's solution and will promote the teaching and learning of concepts as a means of building the necessary foundation for the modeling and solution of engineering problems.

Structured Problem Solving

Historically, problem solving in introductory mechanics courses has involved a "high priest" (the instructor) going before the class and invoking a mysterious "bag of tricks" to solve problems. Although this may make the instructor look like a genius to the students, it doesn't really help them become expert problem solvers in mechanics. This impression is also born out by feedback we have received from colleagues and from the approximately 50 expert reviewers of the Statics and Dynamics books that the we are currently writing (Costanzo et al., 2006; Gray et al., 2006; Plesha et al., 2006). Interestingly, it appears that the teaching of problem solving has changed little in the more than 40 years since the publication of the first editions of Meriam (1952), Shames (1959), and Beer and Johnston (1962) changed the way engineering mechanics was taught. Furthermore, it appears that indeed most books, although making an effort to develop problem-solving skills, do not focus enough on the development of a problem-solving framework that can be applied to all problems in mechanics.

The textbooks we are developing include features that cannot be found in any other introductory mechanics texts, namely the following:

1. A problem-centered presentation of material:
   - Each new topic begins with an opening problem whose framing and solution require new concepts and skills or the substantial refinement of previously acquired concepts and skills.
   - Section opening, example, and homework problems engage the students in a discussion of what assumptions are needed to make the problem tractable; in addition, all of these problems are interesting, relevant, and current and show students the real-life connections between the course material and applications.

2. Emphasis on modeling and a *structured approach* to problem solving:
   - A presentation of modeling as the process of transforming a real-world system into mathematical equations that are able to predict the system's behavior—this is the foundation of problem solving.
   - An emphasis on the close relation between modeling and problem solving by the creation of a structured solution paradigm based on the fact that *any* model of motion (at least within the confines of classical mechanics) is constructed using three basic elements: (a) the Newton-Euler equations and/or balance laws; (b) the kinematic equations; and (c) material or constitutive equations. This solution paradigm is widely used by practicing mechanicians.

3. Homework problems with a modern context. This shows students that mechanics is as relevant today as it was 100 years ago by showing its application to bioengineering, nanotechnology, and other fields at the forefront of engineering research.

4. Use of computer tools to help solve problems once they have been formulated. Although the emphasis is still on modeling and problem formulation, computers allow the students to solve more realistic problems, especially in Dynamics.

5. Pedagogy of Concepts—As an integral part of the textbooks, we have developed a feature called "Concept Alert" designed to strongly reinforce new concepts that are introduced in the main narrative. Along with this feature we have developed an extensive library of "Concept Problems." These are homework problems that do not require calculations for their solutions but only the application of the concepts emphasized in the textbooks. As discussed in the next section, this component of the textbooks can be assessed by the use of the DCI test that we have developed.

We believe that this approach "stands on the shoulders of giants" in the sense that it builds on the foundation laid by the most recent generations of Statics and Dynamics textbooks that began appearing about 50 years ago. We believe that our approach discourages the attitude developed by students according to which all problems in Statics, and especially Dynamics, are solved using a bag of tricks that appear to be different for every problem.

Integration of Conceptual Knowledge

We have found (and the literature has also demonstrated; see, e.g., Bagno & Eylon, 1997; Heyworth, 1999; Niemi, 1996; Zimmerman, 2000) that students who do not have a strong conceptual foundation are unable to formulate the proper models so that they can even begin the problem-solving process. This is especially true in mechanics, a discipline for which fundamental conceptual knowledge is everything (Leonard, Dufresne, & Mestre, 1996). We believe that our highly structured approach to problem solving will help students build a strong foundation for becoming expert problem solvers by removing the perception that engineering problems can only be solved by experts who are familiar with a special "bag of tricks." In addition, through the explicit teaching of concepts and the assessment of their understanding via the DCI and a library of concept questions, we believe that we can begin to build the strong conceptual foundation that is required of expert problem solvers. With this in mind, we have introduced several features into our textbooks that will help the student gain a fundamental conceptual understanding of mechanics and will help the instructor facilitate the students' path to conceptual understanding. We have integrated a "pedagogy of concepts" into our textbooks weaving "asides" called *concept alerts* and *common pitfalls* throughout the books and by posing purely conceptual questions in the exercises found at the end of each section.

Concept alerts are marginal materials that are a different take on, and a reinforcement of, concepts that have been introduced and discussed within the main flow of the text. These concept alerts don't generally point out misconceptions, but they do try and give a different perspective on a concept that has already been covered.

Common pitfalls are also marginal materials, but unlike concept alerts, they point out misconceptions commonly held by the students. This provides an opportunity to point out many of the misconceptions we have discovered during our many years of teaching and during the development of the DCI. When common pitfalls are presented the right way, they can give the students a real "forehead slapping" moment in which they permanently remove a misconception from their knowledge base.

Concept questions, several of which are presented at the end of each section, provide an opportunity to probe the students' understanding of the conceptual ideas presented in that section. These questions never require any computation and can always be answered with a simple qualitative plot and/or a sentence or two of narrative.

With this in mind, we end this section by posing two questions that we have only partially begun to answer:

1. What impact does teaching concepts have on the ability to solve problems and on the student's transition from novice to expert problem solver?
2. What impact does our structured approach to problem solving have on the students' ability to solve problems and does it accelerate the student's transition from novice to expert problem solver?

To measure the impact of conceptual instruction and understanding, it is, of course, essential that we have a tool and a metric for doing so. The metric we are using is the DCI, which was briefly described earlier. In the sections that follow, we describe the DCI we have developed and give some quantitative results we have obtained during its first few semesters of use. We close with our final thoughts on the issues we have raised as well as with some suggestions we have for finding the answers to the questions posed earlier.

CONCEPTUAL INSTRUCTION AND ASSESSMENT IN DYNAMICS

Introduction

Roughly speaking, all engineering courses offer students two types of knowledge: concepts and problem-solving skills. The claim that a course is delivering this knowledge should be supported by objective measures of concept retention and problem-solving skill gains.

In our experience, there are few engineering courses for which metrics exist to measure conceptual learning. Furthermore, the existence of a metric for a particular course may not be accompanied by a testing instrument that can be easily used by the average instructor.

A few years ago, we embarked on an effort to create a test capable of reliably measuring the gains in conceptual understanding of undergraduate students in sophomore-level Dynamics courses. Throughout the development of this test, we worked under the assumption that an improved conceptual understanding is a key to improving the students' problem-solving skills. However, to date we have not developed a corresponding testing instrument for the assessment of gains in problem-solving skills, although we hope to make progress in this direction in the coming years.

In the remainder of this section, we summarize the history of the test we have contributed to and describe how this work has influenced the way we deliver our instruction in the sophomore-level Dynamics course we teach.

History of the Dynamics Concept Inventory

The impetus to create a DCI began at a miniconference on Undergraduate Education in Dynamics, Vibrations and Strength of Materials in San Antonio, TX, in September 2002. The purpose of the meeting was to discuss instructional innovations in these subjects, assessment instruments over and above the Force Concept Inventory (FCI; Hestenes, Wells, & Swackhamer, 1992), found in the physics community, that would be beneficial to these subjects, and the extent to which these subjects might be brought closer together in delivery. Among other things, it was generally agreed that if we are to discuss the efficacy of innovations in mechanics education, we need a tool with which we can quantitatively assess each innovation. Based on the success of the FCI at assessing innovation in physics instruction, it was agreed that a DCI might provide the same sort of impetus for change and innovation in Dynamics instruction. With all of this in mind, it was decided that a DCI team would be formed (for more of the history of the DCI, see Gray, Evans, Cornwell, Costanzo, & Self, 2003).

To identify Dynamics concepts that students find difficult, we utilized a modified Delphi process (Clayton, 1997) in which 25 veteran instructors of Dynamics were asked to "describe the concepts in 2D rigid body Dynamics that your students find difficult to understand."[6] They then provided a "brief description of common misunderstandings your students have about

---

[6]We limited our focus to two-dimensional rigid body Dynamics because (a) everyone covers planar Dynamics of rigid bodies, but a minority of schools cover three-dimensional Dynamics of rigid bodies; and (b) we felt that the physics Force Concept Inventory (FCI) adequately covers planar particle Dynamics and the physics FCI has undergone substantial testing and refinement.

the concept." After the responses were collated and similar themes combined by the DCI team, the experts were asked to examine 24 different concepts. They rated each concept on (a) how important it is, and (b) whether their students understand the concept.

The 24 resulting concepts were then ranked according to importance and difficulty. As the goal was to design a 30-question test (similar to the FCI), 10 concepts were selected so that each concept could be tested more than once. One of the top 11 most important concepts, "Work and energy are scalar quantities," was discarded because the DCI team felt that this concept was addressed in other concepts. This allowed us to include an additional concept for testing. Progress to this point was reported at the 2003 American Society for Engineering Education (ASEE) conference in Nashville, TN (Gray et al., 2003).

Each DCI team member was then tasked to develop multiple-choice questions for two of the concepts or misconceptions. The questions were critiqued by other members of the team and discussed until a consensus was reached. One of the concepts, "Dynamics are governed by 2nd order differential equations and have time dependent behavior," was ranked as the fourth most important by the Delphi process. Unfortunately, the team found that this concept was nearly impossible to assess using a multiple-choice question, so the concept was dropped from the inventory. An additional reason for dropping this concept is that it is not taught directly or indirectly in the vast majority of curricula because it requires the coverage of ordinary differential equations, which is generally not a prerequisite for most sophomore-level Dynamics courses. At this stage, the questions were ready to be tested on students.

Focus groups were held at three of the universities with which DCI team members are affiliated (two large public universities, Arizona State and Penn State, and a small private university, Rose-Hulman). Although the original questions developed by the team members included distractors, in the first focus group, students were given questions without corresponding multiple-choice answers so as to elicit distractors from the students. There is no better way to develop distractors than to use answers given by students themselves. In subsequent focus groups, students were divided into two groups, some of whom were administered questions with multiple-choice answers and some of whom were asked to provide the answers as was done in the first focus groups. After the questions were answered by the students, the students were interviewed to determine their logic during the solution process. The DCI team also discovered whether the students found wording to be tricky or confusing; this resulted in rewording several different problems. Many of the student answers were then included as distractors in the multiple-choice version of the DCI.

Finally, several beta tests were given at different universities across the nation. The scores from testing at three different institutions were presented at an ASEE sectional meeting (Self et al., 2004) and the 2004 ASEE annual conference (Gray, Evans, Costanzo, Cornwell, & Self, 2004). Based on audience feedback at these two meetings and discussions with some of our colleagues, we decided to add "Coriolis acceleration" as one of the concepts or miconceptions in our inventory. This concept did appear in our original Delphi process and it was the second least understood concept rated by instructors, although the overall importance was low (17th most important out of 24 concepts). In the end, the DCI team decided that Coriolis acceleration must be addressed in the DCI for it to be a true test of Dynamics conceptual knowledge. To "work the bugs out" of these new questions, we gave them to students at Rose-Hulman Institute of Technology and we also conducted a focus group at Penn State. We conducted the focus group in much the same format as those ran earlier in our development of the DCI. That is, we gave some of the students the questions with the multiple-choice answers we created and we gave some of the students the questions (without answers) and we asked the students to supply the answers. This allowed us to not only "debug" the questions and our answers, but it also allowed us to confirm distractors and to discover new ones.

We should also add that the presence of friction in relation to rolling without slipping was also included as an important concept, although it did not explicitly appear in the feedback we received from the Delphi process (although there were other concepts related to this one). In consultation with colleagues, the DCI team decided to include this concept because our experience (89 years combined experience teaching Dynamics) has shown that students have substantial difficulty with rolling bodies in the presence of friction. In particular, it has been our experience that students have difficulty knowing the direction of the friction force between a rolling body and the surface on which it is rolling, both in the case of slipping and in the case of rolling without slip.

With all of the aforementioned in mind, the final 11 concepts or misconceptions we chose to include on the DCI are listed as follows:

1. Different points on a rigid body have different velocities and accelerations, which vary continuously.
2. If the net external force on a body is not zero, then the mass center must have an acceleration and it must be in the same direction as the force.
3. Angular velocities and angular accelerations are properties of the body as a whole and can vary with time.
4. Rigid bodies have both translational and rotational kinetic energy.
5. The angular momentum of a rigid body involves translational and rotational components and requires using some point as a reference.
6. Points on an object that is rolling without slip have velocities and acceleration that depend on the rolling without slip condition.

7. In general, the total mechanical energy is not conserved during an impact.
8. An object can have (a) nonzero acceleration and zero velocity or (b) nonzero velocity and no acceleration.
9. The inertia of a body affects its acceleration.
10. The direction of the friction force on a rolling rigid body is not related in a fixed way to the direction of rolling.
11. A particle has acceleration when it is moving with a relative velocity on a rotating object.

We note that there are four questions from the FCI on the DCI; these concepts are not given in the aforementioned list. In addition, some of the concepts listed earlier were tested using particle Dynamics problems. The DCI Web site can be found at http://www.esm.psu.edu/dci/ and the DCI, along with some guidelines for its use, are available there.

Dynamics Concept Inventory Results From Two Very Different Schools

Version 0.96[7] of the DCI was administered during the fall 2003 semester to 166 students as a posttest at a very selective, small, private university (SPU) and to 147 students as a posttest at a large public university (LPU).[8] In addition, it was administered during the spring 2004 semester to four sections of a Dynamics class at a large public university (441 students as a pretest and 310 posttest).

With regard to the fall 2003 administration of the test at the large public university, it should be noted that the course was taught in a traditional lecture format with two sections, each of which had a class size of roughly 110 students. By contrast, at the small private university, there were six sections of the course, each one containing between 25 and 30 students. At the small private university, instructors of these courses frequently give short quizzes at the beginning of class that often include concept-type questions. Contrary to how the course was managed in the fall 2003 semester, during the spring 2004 semester, the instructors at the large public university used the eInstruction Classroom Performance System (CPS)[9] throughout the semester to quiz the students on concepts. That is, about once every week and a

---

[7]The only major changes between version 0.96 and the current version 1.0 are the addition of the two questions involving the Coriolis component of acceleration and the removal of two FCI questions.

[8]The DCI was administered at the start of the semester as a "pretest" and at the end of the semester as a "posttest." There are no pretest results for the small private university because the DCI was not given at the start of the term there.

[9]For further information, see http://www.einstruction.com/

half, the instructors would ask the students three to four concept questions with multiple-choice answers and the students would respond using the CPS. Therefore, although the students were not directly asked the concept questions from the DCI, they were asked different questions on the same concepts addressed in the DCI. After the questions were answered, they were discussed with the students so that their misconceptions could be addressed. All of the results should be interpreted in light of this information.

A statistical analysis of the results from both universities is presented in the next section.

A STATISTICAL ANALYSIS OF TEST RESULTS

The DCI data for both the large public university and the small private university were statistically analyzed and the overall results are shown in Table 9.1. There is no pretest data for either of the fall 2003 administrations of the DCI.

The results in Table 9.1 show the sample size N for each administration of the test, the mean, median, standard deviation, and Cronbach's alpha, which is a measure of the reliability or internal consistency of a test. The most important numbers in this table for the purpose of validating the DCI are the Cronbach's alpha values.

Two issues of primary importance in any testing situation are test content validity and test reliability. Content validity addresses how well a test covers the content of the subject matter that the test is designed to assess. That is, does the test cover the correct knowledge? Test reliability addresses whether the test will always elicit consistent and reliable responses even if questions are replaced with other similar questions or if the test is repeated using the same students.

The design team believes that the DCI questions that have now undergone testing cover the concepts important in rigid body Dynamics. However, this question will not be completely settled until the test is more widely

TABLE 9.1

Overall Results for the Tests Administered at the LPU and SPU.
N Is the Size of the Sample

Test	N	Mean (%)	Median (%)	SD (%)	Cronbach α
LPU 2003 Post	147	32.1	31.8	15.0	0.640
LPU 2004 Pre	441	30.6	26.7	14.2	0.719
LPU 2004 Post	310	55.7	56.7	19.3	0.837
SPU 2003 Pre	172	34.9	—	—	—
SPU 2003 Post	166	63.9	63.6	16.8	0.730

used by instructors (people still debate the validity of many of the questions on the FCI). The Delphi development process used to reach instructor- or expert-based consensus on the concepts to be examined should have, if followed up appropriately, led to validity of the beta DCI content. The many focus groups used to validate the authenticity of the developed questions and associated answer sets also should have contributed to the validity of the beta DCI test items. The beta testing at the five participating institutions did uncover some minor areas that needed to be addressed—some were uncovered by students who wrote comments on their test packets, a few were noted by instructors who passed on some specific suggestions for minor changes, and a few others were noted by the DCI design team as they surveyed the distribution of student answers.

To assess reliability, the DCI team analyzed the scores of the 754 participating students at the LPU and SPU described earlier. As shown in Tables 9.1 and 9.2, the mean score, median score, standard deviation, Cronbach's alpha, and quartile scores were computed for the exams and each question on the exams.[10] There was considerable variability in the average student scores among the three participating groups from two institutions, but the variability was consistent with that found in multiple instructor FCI data (Hake, 1998).

The most frequently used internal consistency measurements are the Kuder-Richardson 20 (K-R20) and Cronbach's alpha, and either measure provides a conservative estimate of the reliability of a set of test results (Cortina, 1993; Cronbach, 1951; Miller, 1995; Nunnaly, 1978). Cronbach's alpha has the advantage of applying to weighted or nondichotomous data. Cronbach's alpha estimates the proportion of variance in test scores that can be attributed to true score variance. In other words, Cronbach's alpha is used to estimate the proportion of variance that is systematic or consistent in a set of test scores. Cronbach's alpha can range from 0.0 (if none of the variance is consistent) to 1.0 (if all the variance is consistent). So, for example, if the Cronbach's alpha for a set of scores turns out to be 0.90, one generally interprets that as meaning that the test is 90% reliable. Nunnaly (1978) indicated that a Cronbach of 0.7 or greater indicates a test with acceptable reliability.

With this in mind and referring to Table 9.1, we make the following observations:

- The DCI passes Nunnaly's tests for reliability. In fact, as one can see in Table 9.2, each individual question exhibits strong reliability.
- Although not immediately relevant to the DCI, the change in the mean (or median) posttest scores from 2003 (32.1%) to 2004 (55.7%) at

---

[10]We only report these data for a representative selection of the questions on the exam.

TABLE 9.2

Quartile and Cronbach α Results for Some of the Questions on the Dynamics
Concept Inventory

Test	Problem	Quartile (%)				Cronbach α
		1	2	3	4	
LPU 2003 Post	9	3.57	14.3	22.0	41.7	0.617
	10	28.6	45.2	48.8	50.0	0.643
	13	17.9	26.2	29.3	61.1	0.622
	21	0.00	16.7	12.2	41.7	0.607
	22	35.7	50.0	68.3	77.8	0.623
	26	3.57	4.76	9.76	11.4	0.638
LPU 2004 Pre	9	5.04	13.0	13.9	34.5	0.710
	10	31.6	40.8	42.1	34.9	0.734
	13	2.54	4.00	3.70	8.18	0.719
	21	5.93	5.05	15.9	22.0	0.716
	22	5.13	9.09	15.9	37.6	0.708
	26	11.4	9.38	10.8	13.9	0.722
LPU 2004 Post	9	15.7	11.9	30.4	61.8	0.834
	10	66.3	91.0	93.5	88.2	0.837
	13	33.7	53.7	54.3	86.8	0.833
	21	31.3	47.8	68.5	83.8	0.832
	22	54.2	76.1	87.0	86.8	0.836
	26	4.82	5.97	8.70	16.2	0.838
SPU 2003 Post	9	19.0	25.5	60.0	68.1	0.710
	10	47.6	70.2	76.7	95.7	0.711
	13	16.7	36.2	26.7	59.6	0.720
	21	45.2	68.1	76.7	95.7	0.707
	22	42.9	76.6	86.7	97.9	0.700
	26	0.00	14.9	13.3	40.4	0.709

Note.   LPU = large public university; SPU = small private university.

the LPU seems to indicate that even a minimal teaching of concepts
might make a dramatic difference in conceptual knowledge. Of course,
we don't have the pretest data for the LPU 2003 pretest, so we don't know
what gains were achieved for that class. On the other hand, the population of students is such that the pretest scores for LPU 2003 are likely the
same as the pretest scores for LPU 2004. As you can see, the pretest mean

for the LPU 2004 pretest is essentially the same as the *posttest* mean for the LPU 2003. Analysis of the posttests compared not only the differences in the overall means between groups at the LPU, but also the means within the 11 content areas (subscales or concepts) contained on the inventory. Results indicated that the mean score of the spring 2004 students was significantly higher ($t = -10.345$, $p < 0.001$) than the fall 2003 students.[11] Further analysis of the mean scores within each subscale indicated that the spring 2004 students outperformed the fall 2003 students in all of the content areas, with the means being significantly higher in 10 of the 11 content areas (see Table 9.3).

SUMMARY

Based on the results reported earlier, we are convinced that concepts need to be taught and tested separately from problem solving and we have found that the use of technology such as the CPS is extremely beneficial for this

TABLE 9.3

Postinventory Subscales at a Large Public University
(Fall 2003 versus Spring 2004)

Subscale (Concept)	t-test	Significance (p)
A realistic impact entails loss of mechanical energy	−3.141	0.002
Angular momentum of a rigid body	−3.426	0.001
Balance of work and energy for a rigid body	−1.502	0.134[a]
$F = m^a$ for rigid bodies	−5.231	< 0.001
Free-body diagram of a rolling rigid body with friction	−10.172	< 0.001
Kinetic energy of a rigid body	−8.902	< 0.001
Relation between friction and velocity	−2.131	0.034
Relation between inertia and acceleration	−3.277	0.001
Rigid body kinematics	−6.470	< 0.001
Vectorial nature of acceleration	−4.227	< 0.001
Vectorial nature of velocity	−6.608	< 0.001

[a]This is the only significance greater that 0.05, indicating the only subscale that does not show significant difference between means. That is, although the spring 2004 students had a higher mean in this subscale, it was not significantly higher.

---

[11]The *t*-test is a statistical test used to determine if there is any significant difference between the means of different samples of data. The "*p* value" is the probability that the observed value of the test statistic is equal to or greater than the actual computed value "*t*." The smaller the *p* value, the more significant the result. See Freedman, Pisani, and Purves (1997).

purpose. In fact, we have dramatically altered the way we teach the course—concept quizzes are now given regularly in class and we ask concept questions on all exams.

Some Final Thoughts

We have presented our thoughts and ideas regarding the improvement of the transition from novice to expert problem solver. Namely, it is our belief that this transition can be aided by two separate, although complementary, things: (a) the teaching of concepts as a critical foundation to the ability to model engineering problems, and (b) the teaching of a structured approach to solving problems. Unfortunately, at this time, we have no data (other than anecdotal evidence) that backs up our theses. It is our goal in the coming years to continue to explore these ideas and determine whether these two things really do aid the transition from novice to expert problem solver.

REFERENCES

ABET Engineering Accreditation Commission. (2005). *Criteria for accrediting engineering programs.* Retrieved December 26, 2006, from http://www.abet.org/forms.shtml

Advisory Committee to the National Science Foundation. (1996). Shaping the future: New expectations for undergraduate education in science, mathematics, engineering, and technology. *National Science Foundation Directorate for Education and Human Resources, NSF,* 96–139.

Bagno, E., & Eylon, B. S. (1997). From problem solving to a knowledge structure: An example from the domain of electromagnetism. *American Journal of Physics, 65*(8), 726–736.

Beer, F. P., & Johnston, E. R. J. (1962). *Mechanics for engineers: Statics and dynamics* (2nd ed.). New York: McGraw-Hill.

Bransford, J. D., Brown, A. L., & Cocking, R. R. (Eds.). (2000). *How people learn: Brain, mind, experience, and school* (Expanded ed.). Washington, DC: National Academy. Committee on Developments in the Science of Learning, Commission on Behavioral and Social Sciences and Education, National Research Council.

Clayton, M. (1997). Delphi: A technique to harness expert opinion for critical decision-making tasks in education. *Educational Psychology, 17,* 373–386.

Cortina, J. M. (1993) What is coefficient alpha? An examination of theory and applications. *Journal of Applied Psychology, 78,* 98–104.

Costanzo, F., & Gray, G. L. (2000). On the implementation of interactive dynamics. *International Journal of Engineering Education, 16*(5), 385–393.

Costanzo, F., Plesha, M. E., & Gray, G. L. (2006). *Mechanics of materials.* Manuscript in preparation.

Cronbach, L. J. (1951). Coefficient alpha and the internal structure of tests. *Psychometrika, 16,* 297–334.

Freedman, D., Pisani, R., & Purves, R. (1997). *Statistics* (3rd ed.). New York: Norton.

Gray, G. L., & Costanzo, F. (1999). The interactive classroom and its integration into the mechanics curriculum. *International Journal of Engineering Education, 15*(1), 41–50.

Gray, G. L., Costanzo, F., & Plesha, M. E. (2006). *Engineering mechanics: Dynamics.* Manuscript in preparation.

Gray, G. L., Evans, D., Cornwell, P., Costanzo, F., & Self, B. (2003). Toward a nation-wide dynamics concept inventory assessment test. In *Proceedings of the 2003 American Society for Engineering Education Annual Conference, 1168* [CD-ROM]. Washington, DC: American Society for Engineering Education.

Gray, G. L., Evans, D., Costanzo, F., Cornwell, P., & Self, B. (2004, June). *Progress on the dynamics concept inventory.* Paper presented at the meeting of the American Society for Engineering Education Annual Conference, Salt Lake City, UT.

Hake, R. R. (1998). Interactive-Engagement versus traditional methods: A six-thousand-student survey of mechanics test data for introductory physics courses. *American Journal of Physics, 66*(1), 64–74.

Hestenes, D., Wells, M., & Swackhamer, G. (1992). Force concept inventory. *The Physics Teacher, 30,* 141–158.

Heyworth, R. M. (1999). Procedural and conceptual knowledge of expert and novice students for the solving of a basic problem in chemistry. *International Journal of Science Education, 21*(2), 195–211.

Kremer, G. G. (2001). *Teaching a rigorous problem-solving framework in entry-level mechanical engineering courses—Theory and practice.* Paper presented at the Proceedings of the 2001 American Society for Engineering Education Annual Conference & Exposition. Retrieved November 6, 2006, from http://www.asee.org/acpapers/00975_2001.pdf

Leonard, W. J., Dufresne, R. J., & Mestre J. P. (1996). Using qualitative problem-solving strategies to highlight the role of conceptual knowledge in solving problems. *American Journal of Physics, 64,* 1495–1503.

Meriam, J. L. (1952). *Mechanics.* New York: Wiley.

Miller, M. B. (1995). Coefficient alpha: A basic introduction from the perspectives of classical test theory and structural equation modeling. *Structural Equation Modeling, 2,* 255–273.

Niemi, D. (1996). Assessing conceptual understanding in mathematics: Representations, problem solutions, justifications, and explanations. *Journal of Educational Research, 89,* 351–363.

Nunnaly, J. C. (1978). *Psychometric theory* (2nd ed.). New York: McGraw-Hill.

Plesha, M. E., Gray, G. L., & Costanzo, F. (2006). *Engineering mechanics: Statics.* Manuscript in preparation.

Self, B. P., Gray, G. L., Evans, D., Cornwell, P., Costanzo, F., & Ruina, A. (2004, April). Progress on the Dynamics Concept Inventory. Paper presented at the Rocky Mountain Section Meeting of the American Society for Engineering Education, Laramie, WY.

Shames, I. H. (1959). *Engineering mechanics.* Englewood Cliffs, NJ: Prentice Hall.

Wilson, J. M. (1992a). The comprehensive unified physics learning environment: Part 1. Background and system operation. *Computers in Physics, 6*(2), 202–209.

Wilson, J. M. (1992b). The comprehensive unified physics learning environment: Part 2. Materials. *Computers in Physics, 6*(3), 282–286.

Wilson, J. M. (1994). The cuple physics studio. *Physics Teacher, 32,* 518.

Wilson, J. M. (1996). A multimedia model for undergraduate education. *Technology in Society, 18,* 387.

Zimmerman, C. (2000). The development of scientific reasoning skills. *Developmental Review, 20,* 99–149.

Chapter 10

Transfer of Learning in Problem Solving in the Context of Mathematics and Physics

N. Sanjay Rebello, Lili Cui, Andrew G. Bennett, Dean A. Zollman, and Darryl J. Ozimek
Kansas State University

Transfer of learning, which has sometimes been considered to be the ultimate goal of education (McKeough, Lupart, & Marini, 1995), is often described as the ability to apply what one has learned in one situation to a different situation (Reed, 1993; Singley & Anderson, 1989). Problem solving involves transfer in several ways. Problem solving in semi-structured and unstructured domains often involves the transfer of knowledge and skills from a structured (classroom) domain to the semistructured or unstructured domain. Furthermore, even within a structured domain, a standard heuristic for developing a strategy is to ask if a similar problem has been encountered in the past and to see if a similar technique will work for the new problem (Pólya, 1957). Until recently, several researchers who have studied transfer of learning in the context of sequestered problem solving have often found that transfer is rare (Duncker, 1945; Gick & Holyoak, 1980; Reed, Ernst, & Banerji, 1974). Most students are unable to recognize similarities between the learning context and the transfer context, whether within a structured domain or moving from a structured to a semistructured or unstructured domain, and are therefore unable to successfully solve problems in the latter context, although they may have been trained to do so in the original learning context. Researchers have often explained the lack of such transfer in terms of students' inabilities to construct a coherent schema in the learning domain to begin with (Reed, 1993). Lack of a robust schema in the initial domain impedes students' abilities to apply their knowledge in new domains.

CONTEMPORARY VIEWS OF TRANSFER

Recently researchers (Bransford & Schwartz, 1999; Greeno, Moore, & Smith, 1993; Lobato, 1996) have begun to expand their notions of transfer and how to assess them. Rather than examine students' abilities to successfully solve a problem in the new domain, researchers have been examining students' abilities to learn how to solve problems in the new domain (Bransford & Schwartz, 1999).

In addition to the cognitive aspects affecting transfer, researchers have also been paying attention to the mediating factors such as students' epistemologies and expectations (diSessa, 1993; Hammer & Elby, 2002). Also, rather than focus on robust schemas to describe transfer, researchers have been focusing on activation of pieces of knowledge (diSessa, 1988) or cognitive resources (Hammer, 2000) in the new domain and the dynamic construction of similarities between the learning and transfer context (Lobato, 1996). Our research (Rebello et al., 2005) has combined these contemporary perspectives of transfer to construct a model that explains the dynamic transfer of learning which occurs as we conduct a "think-aloud" interview involving a problem-solving task. The model enables us to gain insights into students' thinking processes as they solve problems in unfamiliar domains.

Our model of transfer, described in detail in a recent publication (Rebello et al., 2005), encapsulates several of the contemporary views of transfer described earlier. As per this model, transfer is the dynamic creation of associations between a learner's prior knowledge and information that is "read out" by the learner from a new situation. Read out of information as well as activation of prior knowledge is controlled by a learner's epistemic mode, motivation, and other mediating factors. This model of transfer does not make distinctions between productive and unproductive associations that a learner might make in a given situation, rather it examines all possible associations that a learner might make in a given situation. Therefore, the model describes the dynamics of the process of knowledge construction in a new situation. In this chapter, we apply our model of transfer to the process of problem solving. We discuss two qualitatively different types of transfer processes that we believe learners use when solving problems.

RESEARCH CONTEXTS

This chapter focuses specifically on transfer of learning from mathematics to physics contexts. Although all of the problem contexts that we examine are associated with classroom learning, the physics contexts are more closely connected with real-world unstructured problems than typical mathematics problems. Therefore, by examining students' transfer of learning from mathematics to physics, we can gain insights into the types of barriers students might face if they attempt to transfer their learning to even more unstructured domains such as authentic real-world problems. In other words, if students are unable to transfer what they have learned from mathematics to physics, they are extremely unlikely to transfer successfully what they have learned to authentic real-world situations.

The studies discussed later in this chapter focus on transfer from mathematics to physics courses. The first investigates transfer of learning from a calculus course to a calculus-based physics course taken primarily by engineering and physics majors. The second study focuses on transfer of learning from a trigonometry course to an algebra and trigonometry-based physics course taken primarily by life science majors. We use a combination of qualitative and quantitative methods to examine transfer and problem solving. The qualitative studies utilize data collected through individual clinical interviews as well as teaching interviews (Engelhardt, Corpuz, Ozimek, & Rebello, 2003; Steffe & Thompson, 2000). Although the former aim to examine students' states of knowledge and the ideas that they spontaneously transfer to a new problem situation, the latter shed light on how students assemble their knowledge elements to construct problem solutions and new knowledge in previously unfamiliar situations. In addition to clinical and teaching interviews, we also examine students' transfer of learning through quantitative analysis of correlations between online homework and exam scores in mathematics and physics and engineering classes (Ozimek, 2004). A significant correlation between scores on two temporally separated components of evaluation might indicate an underlying factor that is common to both contexts and therefore might point to hidden associations that students have activated in the new context based on their familiarity with the previous context.

CHAPTER OVERVIEW

We utilize transfer of learning as a lens through which we examine students' problem solving in previously unfamiliar domains. In the first section, we begin with a review of the multiple perspectives that have been used to study transfer as well as the factors that affect it. In the second section, we identify the particular perspectives of transfer that shape our research and describe a theoretical framework that serves as a lens with which to analyze our research results. In the last two sections, we examine students' problem solving and transfer from a relatively more structured domain—an undergraduate mathematics course to a somewhat less structured domain—an undergraduate physics course. Through a combination of quantitative and qualitative methods, we gain insights into the factors that mediate students' transfer of learning and problem solving in physics. We interpret these insights from the perspective of our theoretical framework on transfer.

MULTIPLE PERSPECTIVES ON TRANSFER

Traditionally, transfer of learning is often (Reed, 1993; Singley & Anderson, 1989) defined as applying what one has learned in one situation to another situation. Due to the lack of evidence of transfer in many studies based on traditional models, recent views of transfer have shifted to look at transfer from other perspectives.

Traditional models (Adams et al., 1988; Bassok, 1990; Brown & Kane, 1988; Chen & Daehler, 1989; Nisbett, Fong, Lehmann, & Cheng, 1987; Novick, 1988; Reed, 1993; Singley & Anderson, 1989; Thorndike & Woodworth, 1901; Wertheimer, 1959) are based on a researcher's predefined concept that they hope students will transfer. These models also view transfer as a static passive process. The traditional models of transfer have tended to focus on the cognitive aspects of transfer. Thorndike's theory of identical elements asserts that training in one kind of activity transfers to another only if the activities share common elements, which are generally taken to mean identical at the level of the surface features of the stimulus environment (Thorndike & Woodworth, 1901). According to Judd's (1908) theory of deep structure transfer, it depends on the extent to which the learner notices underlying shared causal principles between two problems. More recently, as per the information processing perspective, transfer is mediated by abstract, symbolic mental representations (Singley & Anderson, 1989). The learner constructs an abstract mental representation or schema through experiences in the learning situation and deploys the schemas in the transfer situation.

Contemporary models of transfer have gone beyond focusing solely on the cognitive aspects of transfer. Rather they have included several other mediating factors that affect transfer. The sociocultural perspective asserts that the social and cultural environment affects transfer through language, cultural tools, and more knowledgeable individuals such as parents, teachers, or other domain experts. Transfer in terms of affordances and constraints of activity focus on the extent to which participating in an activity while being attuned to the affordances and constraints in one situation influences the learner's ability to participate in a different situation (Greeno et al., 1993). The actor-oriented perspective conceives transfer as the personal construction of similarities between activities where the "actors," that is, learners, see situations as being similar (Lobato, 1996). Preparation for future learning focuses on whether students can learn to solve problems in transfer situations in a similar way in which they initially learned the content, that is, using available resources (Bransford & Schwartz, 1999). Contemporary models of transfer (Bransford & Schwartz, 1999; Greeno et al., 1993; Lobato, 2003) account for aspects the traditional models neglect. They take into account the sociocultural factors that mediate transfer and view transfer from the students' points of view rather than the researcher's point of view. A common feature of all of these perspectives is that they consider transfer as an active dynamic process. In the next section, we briefly describe a model of transfer that is consistent with these contemporary perspectives. Based on the model, we construct a theoretical framework that distinguishes between different kinds of transfer processes relevant to problem solving.

THEORETICAL FRAMEWORK

Two Kinds of Associations

Our model of transfer, which is based on a framework presented by Redish (2004) and earlier cognitive psychologists, views transfer as the dynamic creation of associations by the learner in a new problem situation. This model provides a useful lens in examining transfer from the contemporary perspectives discussed earlier. We believe that there are two kinds of associations that a learner can create in a problem-solving scenario.

The first kind of association involves assigning information read out from a problem to an element of the learner's prior knowledge. An example is reading out a numerical value from the problem statement and assigning it to a particular physical quantity. For instance, if a problem states that a car is moving at 20 m per sec, the learner recognizes that the 20 m per sec is the car's "velocity" and more specifically that "$v = 20$ m/s" must be plugged into a particular equation. The equation in this case is a part of the learner's internal schema to solve the problem. These kinds of associations—between new information gleaned from the problem and elements of the learner's internal knowledge structure—are usually firmly established in the learner's mind and easily articulated by the learner. A second kind of association occurs between a knowledge element read out from the problem with an element of the learner's internal knowledge structure, which in turn is based on their prior knowledge. This association is usually more abstract and tenuous and often the learner may not be able to clearly articulate it. For instance, a student who is shown an animation of a moving car, without even being told that velocity has anything to do with the problem, begins to think about the car's velocity as an important feature of the problem. This learner is making an implicit association between two ideas—motion (shown in the problem animation) and velocity (knowledge of which is deemed necessary to describe the motion).

Two Kinds of Transfer

We believe that it is important to distinguish between these two flavors of associations that a learner might make in a problem scenario because they are tied to two different kinds of transfer processes. In the first kind of transfer—"horizontal" transfer—the learner reads out explicitly provided information from a problem scenario that activates a precreated knowledge structure[1] that is aligned with the new information read out from the problem. This alignment between the provided information and the learner's knowledge structure determines whether the learner can solve the problem. If such alignment or assignment does not naturally occur, that is, if the external problem representation does not match the learner's knowledge structure or internal problem representation, the learner is unable to solve the problem. A typical example of horizontal transfer occurs when learners solve "plug-and-chug" problems at the end of chapters in some science and mathematics textbooks. The learner reads the problem statement, which explicitly provides information in terms of the required variables, for example, the initial velocity, acceleration, and time of a moving vehicle, and clearly states the goal of the problem such as finding the displacement of the vehicle. On reading out this information from the problem, the learner activates a particular equation of motion from their memory. In this case, this equation is the learner's internal schema or mental model for solving this problem. The learner plugs the variables from the problem into this equation to solve the problem. Neither does the learner need to consider the underlying assumptions of the equation that determines the situation in which the equation is applicable nor does the learner have to choose between several different equations to decide which is used in this problem situation. Several end-of-chapter problems in textbooks fall under this category. The problem statement often explicitly provides all of the required information and no more. The equation or representation that is applicable to the problem scenario can often be found in the text by matching the information provided in the problem to a limited set of equations and finding one that matches—often a pattern matching task. The learner

---

[1]The term *internal knowledge structure* refers to a precreated set of tightly associated knowledge elements. Other terminology that is often used in literature includes *schema*, *internal representation*, *mental model*, or *coordination class*.

is never called on to critically examine the situation or the assumptions underlying the model (i.e., equation) that he or she uses to solve it.

In the second kind of transfer—"vertical" transfer—a learner recognizes features of the situation that intuitively activate elements of his or her prior knowledge. In this type of transfer, the learner typically does not have a preconceived knowledge structure that aligns with the problem information. Rather, the learner constructs a mental model *in situ* through successive constructions and deconstructions of associations between knowledge elements. For instance, rather than being told the initial velocity and acceleration of the vehicle, the learner is shown a video clip or animation of the vehicle and asked to find out how much farther the vehicle may have traveled after going off the edge of the video clip. Nowhere is the learner told the initial velocity or acceleration or even that these variables are relevant to the situation. In this case, the learner first must recognize that the vehicle was accelerating and may even confront the assumption that this acceleration may not be uniform. Nowhere is any hint provided about the equation that must be used or even that an equation may be applicable. So the learner cannot activate a clearly identifiable preconceived knowledge structure or internal representation that neatly aligns with the situation. At the very least, the learner must choose between competing internal representations or construct a new one for this situation. Choosing the most productive internal representation from several representations depending on the problem situation is a key feature of "vertical" transfer. Few, if any, problems in most science or mathematics textbooks require vertical transfer. Most real-world problems require "vertical" transfer. Often the problems are too complex to solve without neglecting some confounding features or variables. Solving real-world problems requires learners to decide which variables can be neglected and also decide what schema or model is applicable under those assumptions or create one specifically for the situation. Real-world problem solving also requires students to know the limitations of the model that they have decided to use and under what hypothetical conditions the model would no longer be applicable.

Figure 10.1 shows the difference between "horizontal" and "vertical" transfer. We find that that the graphical metaphor with a horizontal and vertical axis to represent the two kinds of transfer is a useful pictorial representation to highlight the distinctiveness of the two kinds of transfer processes. It also is useful in representing the notion that a given process can have components of both "horizontal" and "vertical" transfer and that these two processes are not mutually exclusive in any way.

Similar Views From Others

The notions of "horizontal" and "vertical" transfer described earlier are not new. Indeed there is a vast body of literature on knowledge and conceptual

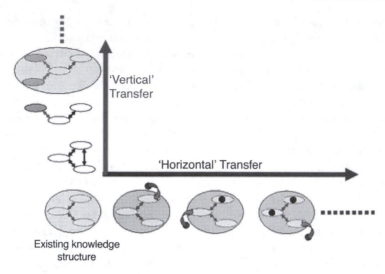

Figure 10.1.   "Horizontal" transfer involves activation and mapping of new information onto an existing knowledge structure. "Vertical" transfer involves creating
a new knowledge structure to make sense of new information.

change that expresses ideas along these lines. Several decades ago Piaget
(1964) proposed two mechanisms of conceptual change—"assimilation," in
which new information was incorporated into a learner's internal knowledge structure without modification, and "accommodation," in which new
information led to a modification of the learner's internal knowledge structure. Although Piaget's ideas focused on conceptual change and not on
transfer per se, we believe that the mechanisms of assimilation and accommodation align closely with "horizontal" and "vertical" transfer, respectively. Similar ideas are also expressed by Broudy (1977), who identified at
least two kinds of knowing—"knowing what" or "applicative" knowing versus "knowing with" or "interpretive" knowing. The former includes clearly
articulated procedures or schema that a learner uses in a given situation.
The latter, which is much more subtle and intangible, refers to a sense of intuition or "gut instinct" that a learner brings to bear as he or she makes
sense of a new situation and frames the problem. We believe that Broudy's
notions of applicative and interpretive knowing align closely with our ideas
of "horizontal" and "vertical" transfer, respectively. Much more recently,
diSessa and Wagner (2005) have discussed transfer in light of their coordination class theory of conceptual change. diSessa (1998) had previously described the theory of a "coordination class"—a class or concept that allows
the learner to read out and process information from the real world. In
their more recent article, diSessa and Wagner (2005) applied their coordination class theory to elucidate their perspective on transfer of learning.

They distinguished between what they called "Class A" and "Class C" transfer. Class A transfer, which we believe is analogous to horizontal transfer, occurs when a learner applies "well-prepared" knowledge such as a coordination class to a new situation. Class C transfer, which we believe is analogous to vertical transfer, occurs when "relatively unprepared" learners use prior knowledge to construct new knowledge. In a sense, Class C transfer is indistinguishable from learning. There is at least one point of caution in making the comparisons between our classification and the one used by diSessa and Wagner. diSessa and Wagner's assertion that Class C transfer happens all the time whereas Class A transfer is relatively rare might appear to contradict our earlier comparisons between horizontal and vertical transfer. On closer examination, however, we believe that there is in fact no contradiction. Although learners continuously process new information and construct knowledge (Class C transfer), it is relatively difficult for learners to construct knowledge that is useful, well-prepared, or easily applicable later (Class A transfer). So, the reason Class A transfer is rare is because the learner does not possess well-prepared knowledge. Class C transfer must precede Class A transfer and although the former may occur all the time, it does not necessarily yield well-prepared knowledge that is required for Class A transfer.

Our notion of horizontal and vertical transfer is also similar to classifications by other transfer researchers. Salomon and Perkins (1989) distinguished between "low road" and "high road" transfer. Low road, or more typically, "near" transfer, occurs when the scenario in which original learning had occurred is similar to the new problem scenario so that the learner can successfully apply preconceived problem-solving processes. High road, or more typically, "far" transfer, is much more challenging in that it requires the learner to abstract the new situation and engage in reflection and metacognition to help construct a way to solve the problem. The distinction between low road and high road transfer is akin to the distinction between horizontal and vertical transfer, respectively. A similar distinction was made by Bransford and Schwartz (1999) when they compared two measures of transfer—"sequestered problem solving" (SPS) and "preparation for future learning" (PFL). Although the former measure focuses on whether students can directly apply their learning to a new situation "cold," that is, without any scaffolding or support, the latter measure focuses on whether their learning has prepared them to learn in the future. To measure transfer as per the PFL perspective, we must observe whether a learner can bring to bear his or her earlier experiences and learn to construct a solution to his or her new problem. Bransford and Schwartz pointed out that most traditional transfer measures focus on SPS rather than PFL and consequently fail to find evidence of transfer. More recently, Schwartz, Bransford, and Sears (2005) have contrasted the notions of "efficiency" and "innovation" in transfer. Efficiency refers to a learner's ability to rapidly recall and apply his or her knowledge in a new situation whereas innovation is the learner's ability to restructure his or her thinking or reorganize the problem scenario so that it becomes more tractable than before. We believe that developing efficiency in problem solving is analogous to engaging in horizontal transfer whereas innovation is analogous to vertical transfer.

Finally, the notion of horizontal and vertical transfer has often been used by researchers in problem solving who distinguish between "well-structured" and "ill-structured" problems (Jonassen, 2000, 2003). Well-structured problems have clearly defined information and goals. Therefore, they are akin to problems that require mainly, if not only, horizontal transfer. Unstructured problems, on the other hand, have multiple solutions, may require the learner to choose between several competing internal representations, and may require the learner to question several underlying assumptions about what model or representation is applicable in the given situation. These problems are those that typically require significant vertical transfer.

One of the commonly used problem-solving strategies is case-reuse. Jonassen (2003) described two kinds of case-reuse strategies often used by learners. The first strategy involves recalling the most similar case from memory and applying it with little or no modification to solve a new problem. This strategy is analogous to what we call "horizontal" transfer. The second strategy involves using inductive reasoning to construct an internal representation by looking across various cases and later using this representation to solve a new problem. This strategy is analogous to what we call "vertical" transfer.

Some Caveats

When we distinguish between horizontal and vertical transfer, there are at least a few caveats that we must bear in mind. First, the two transfer processes, although distinct, and in our opinion fundamentally different from each other, are not mutually exclusive in any way. A given problem scenario when examined closely might require a learner to engage in both kinds of transfer processes. Indeed, Schwartz et al. (2005) argued that we must prepare learners to engage in both kinds of transfer rather than one at the expense of the other. They pointed out that there is indeed value in developing efficiency or horizontal transfer because it frees up the mental resources that allow the mind to focus on other efforts such as being more innovative in other ways. Similarly, diSessa and Wagner (2005) pointed out that most traditional assessments focus on Class A rather than Class C transfer using "few minute, little-or-no-learning" (p. 124) transfer texts. However, they did not devalue the use of these tests and stated that indeed, in some situations, such tests can be useful. As researchers, however, it is useful to focus on various types of transfer processes—Class A through Class C. Therefore, transfer researchers appear to converge on the consensus that it is important to value both kinds of transfer processes.

Second, we believe that there is often no unique definition one can apply to identify whether a particular process involves horizontal or vertical transfer. If a learner already possesses a well developed knowledge structure such as a well prepared coordination class (diSessa & Wagner, 2005), then from that learner's perspective a particular task might require only horizontal transfer, that is, applying this well prepared knowledge structure in the present scenario. However, a different learner who does not possess this mental model or internal representation may need to construct one "on the fly" to solve the particular problem. Therefore, this learner has to engage in vertical transfer to solve the same problem. This criterion essentially distinguishes between experts and novices. A particular task that might be perceived as horizontal transfer by an expert might in fact be perceived as vertical transfer from a novice's perspective. Therefore, any distinction that we attempt to make between the two kinds of transfer must be tied to a particular perspective. In keeping with the learner-centered perspective, we believe it is most useful to view transfer processes from the perspective of the learners who engage in them rather than from a researcher's perspective.

Finally, it is important to recognize that the distinction between horizontal and vertical transfer depends on features of the overall learning context. These contextual features may include but are not limited to learners' or teachers' expectations and culture of a given situation. For instance, in a mathematics course that focuses on learning how to solve quadratic equations, any problem that has a real-world connection may be perceived as requiring vertical transfer. The same problem, however, in a physics course that routinely expects its students to solve "word" problems, might be seen as a regular plug-and-chug problem that requires only horizontal transfer.

The distinction between horizontal and vertical transfer, as we shall see later in this chapter, has provided us with a useful theoretical framework to analyze our results, identify problems, and hypothesize possible remedies. However, it is important to point out that for all of the aforementioned reasons, the framework is not rigid. The distinctions between whether a particular process is categorized as horizontal or vertical transfer often depends on the perspective of the learner and researcher and several other contextual factors of the problem scenario.

RESEARCH STUDIES: TRANSFER FROM MATHEMATICS TO PHYSICS

Prior research on transfer from algebra to physics (Bassok & Holyoak, 1989) found transfer asymmetry between these two domain areas. Most students who learned algebra could apply their knowledge to an isomorphic physics problem; however, very few of the students who learned physics could apply their knowledge to the isomorphic algebra problem. The study appears to highlight the effect of contextual factors in transfer of learning. Learning to apply mathematics in a physics context did not prepare students to solve a more abstract mathematics problem in which the physics context was "stripped away." We can interpret the results to imply that the physics course did not adequately prepare students to construct new problem-solving mental models or schema in contexts other than the physics. The students were unable to engage in vertical transfer. Although the Bassok and Holyoak (1989) study showed positive transfer from algebra to physics, most physics problems use more than algebra skills. Therefore, we sought to investigate transfer from two other areas of mathematics: calculus and trigonometry.

Transfer From Calculus to Physics

In most U.S. universities, calculus and physics are taught as two separate subjects in their respective departments. Students are usually required to take at least one calculus course prior to taking physics. Integrated curricula have been developed and were found useful in teaching calculus and physics (Dunn & Barbanel, 2000). Yeats and Hundhausen (1992), who used their own experiences in talking about the difficulties—"notation and symbolism," "the distraction factor," and "compartmentalization of knowledge"—that students have when transferring their knowledge between calculus and physics, also provided some recommendations. However, unlike the integrated curriculum developed by Dunn and Barbanel (2000), calculus and physics are taught as separate subjects in most universities.

This study focused on how students retained and transferred the knowledge from their calculus course when solving problems in their physics course. We conducted semistructured one-on-one think-aloud interviews to assess how students transfer their calculus knowledge in a physics context. Horizontal transfer was explored through interviews in which students were asked to solve physics problems that were similar to their homework or exam problems and required use of simple integration or differentiation. We deemed these problems to involve horizontal transfer because from our (i.e., the researchers') perspective, the problems did not require students to construct or to even choose between competing schemas or mental models to solve the problem. Interviewees were asked to solve four sets containing two problems each. Each set consisted of a physics problem and an isomorphic calculus problem that utilized the same calculus concept. The goal was to identify the extent to which students would connect the two problems. The problems also provided a context within which to discuss the overall connections between physics and calculus as seen from the students' perspectives.

Vertical transfer was assessed using think-aloud interviews in which students were asked two kinds of problems—"compare and contrast" problems and jeopardy problems. The compare and contrast problem presented situations in which interviewees would use "integration" instead of "summation." The jeopardy problems presented interviewees with an intermediate step in the form of a mathematical integration and asked students to come up with a physical scenario relevant to the integral provided. Both of these problems were nontraditional and required students to engage in vertical transfer in several ways. Unlike end-of-chapter problems, the students could not apply a preconstructed schema or mental model to solve these problems. Because these problems were unfamiliar to students, they had to construct a schema or mental model on the spot to solve these problems. Thus, these problems provided a useful context in which to examine vertical transfer by the students.

In the compare and contrast problem, students were provided with two problem situations such as the ones shown in Figure 10.2.

They were first asked which of the situations would require the use of integration and why. The goal of this type of problem was to examine whether students could transition between two internal representations that are typically used to solve these kinds of problems. One internal representation involves point-wise summation or superposition. The other internal representation involves integration. Learners who productively engage in vertical transfer are typically able to transition between different internal representations depending on the external representation of the problem.

In jeopardy problems, students were provided with a mathematical expression that included integration as well as some other symbols. An example follows.

$$\frac{\mu_0 \int_0^R J(r) \bullet (2\pi r dr)}{2\pi R} \tag{10.1}$$

Students were asked to describe the physical problem situation in which they would encounter the expression shown. The goal of this problem was

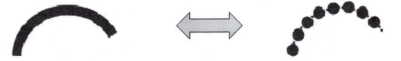

Figure 10.2. Contrasting two situations. Students are asked to compare the way in which one would find the electric field due to each of the charge distributions shown. The one on the left can be solved using integration whereas the one on the right requires point-wise summation.

to examine the process by which students deconstruct the external representation provided and reconstruct it in the form of a physical situation. Jeopardy problems have been used by others. Van Heuvelen and Maloney (1999) pointed out that jeopardy problems help students prevent the use of typical plug-and-chug methods because they help require students to "give meaning to symbols in an equation" and to "translate between representations in a more robust manner" (p. 255). Learners who productively engage in vertical transfer are typically able to deconstruct an external representation and reconstruct it in a form that matches their internal representation, which in this case is the physical situation corresponding to the problem. Both the compare and contrast tasks as well as jeopardy problems are, by any standards, difficult problems. The focus here was not on learner performance but on the process. Examining how learners approached these problems provided us insights into vertical transfer process.

Our results from examining horizontal transfer while solving end-of-chapter problems indicate that students typically do have an adequate calculus knowledge and skills required for solving end-of-chapter physics problems. Most student difficulties focused around setting up calculus-based physics problems. These difficulties included deciding the appropriate variable and limits of integration. Students often tended to use oversimplified algebraic relations to avoid using calculus because they do not understand the underlying assumptions of the relations. It is worth pointing out that when presenting students with end-of-chapter problems, we had assumed that the problems would involve horizontal transfer and therefore be perceived as relatively straightforward by the students. It appears, however, that this was not the case with most students. This observation underscores the caveat that we had mentioned earlier: Whether a given task involves horizontal or vertical transfer depends on the perspective of the actor or student. What may be perceived as horizontal transfer by the expert may in fact involve vertical transfer from a researcher's point of view.

Finally, when asked what would help them in solving physics problems, most students said they would prefer more application-oriented problems in their calculus course and better scaffolding to solve physics problems. Students also seem to believe that a focus on conceptual understanding and concurrent teaching of calculus and physics would facilitate their application of calculus in physics.

Transfer From Trigonometry to Physics

The second study that we describe here concerns transfer from trigonometry to physics. We measured conceptual understanding in trigonometry in terms of students' abilities to use multiple models or representations of trigonometric relations. The three models generally used in trigonometry to define trigonometric relations are in terms of "right triangles," the "unit circle," or as abstract "functions."

At the first (right triangle) level, the use of trigonometric relations is limited to solving for various features of a right triangle. Students thinking at this level define the basic trigonometric entities in terms of ratios of sides of a right triangle. Students thinking at the geometric level are also able to think abstractly and solve triangles to obtain sides and angles that are labeled with variables. At the second (unit circle) level, trigonometric relations are defined in terms of points on a circle. Student thinking at this level is still geometric in nature, but it is different from the first (right triangle) level because it involves the use of circles and horizontal and vertical projections of a point moving along a circle rather than a triangle. Finally, at the third (function) level, trigonometric relations are defined in terms of abstract mathematical function. Thinking at this level is in our view substantially different from the first two levels. At the function level, students must be able to think of trigonometric relations as divorced from their geometric underpinnings. Thinking at the function level involves extracting physical variables from a given graph or mathematical expression that contains either concrete numbers or variables.

Trigonometric concepts can be understood and applied using different models by the same students depending on the problem context. Although the right triangle model seems to be the easiest and most common for students to learn, our interviews have found that different students can learn the different models in different orders (even within the same class) and that even students who understand multiple models have a great deal of difficulty moving between models but tend to use just one model for each single problem (Ozimek, 2004; Verbych, 2005).

Students in this study were enrolled in an algebra-based physics course. We focused on those students who had previously taken a trigonometry course at Kansas State University rather than elsewhere. We used two assessments to measure transfer of learning. First, student learning in trigonometry was assessed using online trigonometry homework assignments. Performance was measured by the score divided by the number of attempts taken to achieve that score. Second, transfer to physics was assessed using a multiple choice inventory which contained 18 items that were organized into three groups—one for each model. Each group contained abstract questions that tested trigonometry concepts devoid of a physics context paired with contextual questions that required students to apply trigonometry concepts in a physics context. The inventory was administered twice to the students: on the first day of class and again after students had completed the relevant material in class.

These assessments allowed us to analyze transfer from trigonometry to physics from both the traditional perspective as well as a couple of contemporary perspectives. A different metric was used to assess transfer of learning from each perspective. In our quantitative study, we decided that an appropriate metric for the possible existence of transfer was correlation of performance on task T_1 and a subsequent task T_2. Although correlation does not imply causality or transfer, it at least indicates the possibility of the existence of transfer. In other words, although a statistically significant correlation does not imply transfer, the lack of a statistically significant correlation between performance on one task T_1 and a performance on a subsequent task T_2 does indicate the lack of transfer.

In one perspective that we call the "traditional" perspective, transfer is measured as the ability to apply knowledge learned in a prior situation to a new situation. Researchers seek evidence that the students have been able to transfer the predefined concept from a context in which the concept was initially learned to a different context. From this perspective, transfer is a static or passive process. Either a student can transfer or a student cannot.

It is important to note that by labeling this perspective as traditional, we do not intend to imply that it is somehow incorrect or irrelevant in any way. We simply imply that it is incomplete. There are many instances, such as when we want students to learn a simple procedure or skill, when this perspective of measuring transfer can be worthwhile, that is, either a student has acquired a transferable skill or he or she has not. However, we believe that if we intend to gain insights into complex cognitive processes such as ill-structured problem solving, this perspective may yield incomplete information. Therefore, the traditional perspective, although useful in some cases, may not be productive in other cases.

How does the traditional perspective map onto our theoretical framework of horizontal versus vertical transfer discussed earlier? We believe that adopting a traditional perspective to examine transfer is equivalent to seeking application of well-prepared knowledge in new situations. In other words, the traditional perspective subsumes that the learner possesses a well-prepared knowledge structure, which he or she should easily be able to activate in a new context. We believe that adopting a traditional perspective is in many ways equivalent to examining horizontal transfer.

As per this perspective, transfer can be measured by comparing performance in the new situation (physics) with performance in the situation in which the knowledge was learned (trigonometry). In our study, we assessed transfer in terms of correlations between students' online trigonometry scores with their scores on the contextual physics problems on the pre-instruction and postinstruction surveys for the same model. The rationale was that the physics questions provided a new problem context within which to examine transfer of the trigonometry mathematical concepts learned in the previous course.

In addition to the traditional perspective of transfer described earlier, two other perspectives were also employed to assess transfer. Taken together we label these the "contemporary" perspectives. Clearly, other researchers (Beach, 1999; Greeno et al., 1993) have also articulated other contemporary perspectives that we do not utilize in our study. Rather we focus on two perspectives—one by Bransford and Schwartz (1999) and another by Lobato (2003).

Bransford and Schwartz (1999) provided a contemporary perspective of transfer called "preparation for future learning" (PFL). The focus is on whether the initial learning helps students learn to solve problems in the new situations with the opportunity to utilize resources (i.e., texts, colleagues, feedback) they may have had available during the initial learning situation. In this study, we examined whether students' learning in a trigonometry course prepared them to learn physics. Because students taking our surveys were not permitted to use resources, a way to measure transfer from the PFL perspective is by looking at each student's gain in scores on the physics (contextual) survey questions. These gains serve as a measure of learning that occurs during the physics course. The gain on the contextual questions was correlated with the online trigonometry homework assignments and the pre-instruction survey mathematics (abstract) question scores. The rationale for using gains is that they are a measure of learning in the physics context. Thus, using gains to measure transfer is consistent with the PFL perspective, which views transfer as the ability to learn in the new context. To obtain a deeper insight into transfer of learning from the PFL perspective, the online trigonometry homework assignments and the pre-instruction survey mathematics (abstract) questions were also categorized into the respective models.

Lobato (1996) conceived transfer as the personal construction of similarities between activities. She examined transfer by looking at the nature of situations and the similarities people construct across situations. Evidence for transfer is gathered by scrutinizing a given activity for any indication of influence from previous activities. In Lobato's "Actor-Oriented Transfer" (AOT) perspective, evidence of transfer is found when students create "relations of similarity" between two situations, that is, when they notice that two situations are similar in some way (Lobato, 2003). Therefore, to examine transfer of learning from the actor-oriented perspective, we examined correlations between scores on the abstract (mathematics) and isomorphic contextual (physics) questions using the same model on the same (pre-instruction and postinstruction) survey. The rationale for using correlations between abstract and contextual questions is that the degree of correlation between the scores on an abstract (mathematics) problem and an isomorphic contextual (physics) problem is a measure of the similarities perceived by students between these two problems. The fact that students' performance on two questions is significantly correlated implies that these questions have something similar about them from the students' perspectives. This student-centered notion of perceived similarity is considered sufficient evidence of transfer.

How do the aforementioned contemporary perspectives (PFL and AOT) of transfer map onto our theoretical framework of horizontal versus vertical transfer discussed earlier? Both the PFL and AOT perspectives focus on the dynamics of the transfer process rather than the outcome alone. They do not subsume the existence of a knowledge structure in the learner's mind; rather they focus on the process by which learners construct such a structure in a new situation. Therefore, we believe that adopting either of these contemporary perspectives is in many ways equivalent to examining vertical transfer.

Table 10.1 summarizes the various perspectives that provided a lens for analyzing our data and understanding the extent to which students transferred their knowledge and conceptual understanding gained in trigonometry to problem solving in physics.

We now discuss the results of our quantitative study from all three perspectives described earlier. As per the traditional perspective, we calculated correlations between average scores on online trigonometry assignments and scores on the contextual physics questions (pre-instruction and postinstruction survey) for each model. No statistically significant correlations were found for any of the models for either the pre-instruction or postinstruction survey. Thus, no evidence of transfer was found from the traditional perspective.

As per the PFL perspective, we calculated correlations between the gains (postinstruction—preinstruction) on the physics survey for each model with the scores on online trigonometry assignments for the same model. A statistically significant ($p < 0.05$) correlation was found only for the first model (right triangles). Thus, as per the PFL perspective, it appeared that stu-

TABLE 10.1

Transfer From Multiple Perspectives, Their Alignment With Our
Theoretical Framework and How They Are Assessed in This Study

Perspective	Alignment With Framework	Criteria for Transfer	Measure of Transfer in This Study
Traditional	Horizontal	Apply knowledge learned in a prior context to solve a problem in a new context.	Correlation between online trig score per attempt and "contextual" physics score in presurvey or postsurvey.
Contemporary Preparation for Future Learning	Vertical	Apply knowledge learned in a prior context to learn to solve problems in a new context.	Correlation between online trig score per attempt and gains in "contextual" physics questions.
Contemporary Actor-Oriented Transfer	Vertical	Recognize relations of similarity between the two contexts.	Correlations between "abstract" and "contextual" scores on the same survey.

dents successfully transferred their learning at the geometric level of triangles but not at the unit circle level or the functional level.

As per Lobato's (2003) AOT perspective, we calculated correlations between abstract (mathematics) and contextual (physics) questions on the same survey for both the pre-instruction and post-instruction surveys. Statistically significant correlations were found for the right triangle and functional models on both the pre-instruction and post-instruction surveys. Thus, as per the AOT perspective, it appeared that students were able to dynamically transfer their knowledge from the abstract (mathematics) to the contextual physics questions for right triangles and functions but not for the unit circle.

As expected, the perspective of transfer that we adopted directly influenced whether we found evidence of transfer. We did not find any evidence of transfer from trigonometry to physics as per the traditional perspective. However, when we broadened our perspective, we found evidence of transfer as per the contemporary PFL and AOT perspectives. We believe that this observation is not a weakness of our study; rather it underscores the importance of examining transfer from a variety of different perspectives. Transfer was also found to be nonuniform across models. Stronger evidence of transfer was detected for right triangle concepts than for function concepts and none was detected for unit circle concepts. This may not be unrelated to the fact that trigonometry students are generally more comfortable with right triangle concepts.

Table 10.2 summarizes our results. Each checkmark indicates evidence of transfer from the corresponding perspective and model. These results appear to converge on two conclusions. First, students have most difficulty in transferring the unit circle model to solving problems in physics. This fact may indicate that the learners do not view the unit circle model as being useful or do not have an adequately developed model that they can use in a new situation. Second, vertical transfer appeared to have occurred more often than horizontal transfer for all but the unit circle model.

TABLE 10.2

Multiple Perspectives of Transfer and Their Assessment Used in This Study

Perspective	Type of Transfer	Model		
		Right Triangle	Unit Circle	Function
Traditional	Horizontal			
Contemporary Preparation for Future Learning	Vertical	✓		
Contemporary Actor-Oriented Transfer	Vertical	✓		✓

At first glance, this result may appear to be contrary to our expectations—after all, isn't vertical transfer more challenging than horizontal transfer? If so, why do we not see more evidence of horizontal transfer than vertical transfer? We believe that there is in fact no contradiction. In presenting our theoretical framework, we stated that horizontal transfer involved activating a knowledge structure in a given situation and associating the variables of the problem situation with elements in the knowledge structure. This description of horizontal transfer subsumes that the learner already possesses a knowledge structure that he or she can appropriately activate whenever necessary. diSessa and Wagner (2005) called this type of transfer Class A transfer. They pointed out that Class A transfer is in fact rather rare because most students do not possess what they called a "well-prepared" coordination class that they can activate appropriately in a wide range of scenarios. They contrasted this kind of transfer with Class C transfer in which "relatively unprepared" learners reuse prior knowledge in a new scenario. Class C transfer is in fact indistinguishable from learning. Therefore, horizontal (or Class A) transfer is indeed rare because it requires learners to have first developed an internal knowledge structure that they can activate in a variety of different situations. The inherent difficulty that learners experience as they construct an internal knowledge structure is what makes horizontal transfer rare as observed in this study.

CONCLUSIONS

We have presented a theoretical framework that describes transfer of learning in problem solving. This framework builds on our earlier model of transfer (Rebello et al., 2005), in which transfer is the dynamic creation of associations between information read out by the learner in a new situation and a learner's prior knowledge. Our framework distinguishes between two kinds of transfer processes that we believe, although not mutually exclusive, are fundamentally different from each other. Horizontal transfer involves associations between a learner's well-developed internal knowledge structure and new information gathered by the learner. Vertical transfer involves associations between various knowledge elements that result in the creation of a new knowledge structure that is productive in the new situation.

The studies described in this chapter have several implications for educators and educational researchers who are interested in transfer of learning to aid problem solving in semistructured or unstructured domains. Our results demonstrate that transfer of learning from structured domains such as mathematics to relatively semistructured or unstructured domains such as physics or engineering must be examined from multiple perspectives of transfer. When viewed from a traditional perspective that focuses primarily on horizontal transfer of a well-developed internal knowledge structure, students often appear to fail to transfer what they have learned in one context to solve problems in another context. However, on expanding our perspective to focus on students' abilities to learn how to solve problems in the new context by building new knowledge structures as in vertical transfer, we are more likely to find evidence of transfer.

Educators have sometimes speculated whether providing students with a structured problem followed by a semistructured isomorphic problem could increase performance on the latter. Results from our studies indicate that students may recognize that the problems are similar in some ways. However, these constructions of similarity by the students do not necessarily translate into improved performance by the students on problems in the unstructured domain. We found no evidence that providing students with the structured problem will necessarily help them solve the isomorphic semistructured problem that follows on the same exam.

Many physics and engineering educators often lament that their students do not enter their class with the adequate mathematics preparation. Our results appear to indicate that the main difficulty that students appear to have does not lie in their lack of understanding of mathematics per se, rather it lies in their inability to see how mathematics is appropriately applied to physics problems. Students often do not understand the underlying assumptions and approximations that they might need to make in a physics problem before they apply a particular mathematical strategy. It appears that students do not possess adequately well-prepared internal knowledge structures pertaining to solving quantitative physics problems that require the use of mathematics. Their structures are inadequate in that students are often unable to align their internal knowledge structures with the problem information (horizontal transfer). They are also equally unable to modify or choose between knowledge structures (vertical transfer). Therefore, they apply mathematical strategies that are inconsistent with the particular situation, for instance, using discrete summation rather than continuous integration in a given problem.

Our research also provides some insights into strategies that students believe might be helpful to them as they transition from mathematics to physics or engineering classes where they apply their mathematics knowledge in relatively semistructured problems. To adequately prepare them for these classes, mathematics classes that often focus on developing students' mathematical skills should also provide opportunities for helping students solve contextualized and semistructured word problems. In studying transfer from one mathematics problem to another, Schoenfeld (1985) found that explicit instruction in recognizing similarities improved students' abilities to transfer ideas in solving novel problems. The students' requests for increased word problems in calculus may be related to their need for seeing such explicit instruction in recognizing similarities across contexts. Physics courses should facilitate students' development of their problem-solving skills by helping them learn how to set up semistructured problems. Both mathematics and physics courses should focus on helping students understand the concepts that underpin the mathematical strategies and equations that they use rather than merely the strategies themselves. Finally, the mathematics and physics courses should be taught in an integrated format, or at least concurrently so that students can be provided adequate opportunities to transfer internal knowledge structures that they have constructed in their mathematics course to solving problems in relatively semistructured domains such as physics.

ACKNOWLEDGMENTS

This work is supported in part by the U.S. National Science Foundation Grants DUE-0206943 and REC-0133621. Opinions expressed in this article are of the authors and not necessarily those of the Foundation.

REFERENCES

Adams, L., Kasserman, J., Yearwood, A., Perfetto, G. A., Bransford, J. D., & Franks, J. J. (1988). The effects of facts versus problem-oriented acquisition. *Memory and Cognition, 16,* 167–175.

Bassok, M. (1990). Transfer of domain-specific problem-solving procedures. *Journal of Experimental Psychology: Learning, Memory, and Cognition, 15,* 522–533.

Bassok, M., & Holyoak, K. (1989). Interdomain transfer between isomorphic topics in algebra and physics. *Journal of Experimental Psychology: Learning, Memory, and Cognition, 15,* 153–166.

Beach, K. (1999). Consequential transitions: A sociocultural expedition beyond transfer in education. *Review of Research in Education, 24,* 101–140.

Bransford, J. D., & Schwartz, D. (1999). Rethinking transfer: A simple proposal with multiple implications. *Review of Research in Education, 24,* 61–100.

Broudy, H. S. (1977). Types of knowledge and purposes of education. In R. C. Anderson, R. J. Spiro, & W. E. Montague (Eds.), *Schooling and the acquisition of knowledge* (pp. 1–17). Hillsdale, NJ: Lawrence Erlbaum Associates.

Brown, A. L., & Kane, M. J. (1988). Preschool children can learn to transfer: Learning to learn and learning from example. *Cognitive Psychology, 20,* 493–523.

Chen, Z., & Daehler, M. W. (1989). Positive and negative transfer in analogical problem solving. *Cognitive Development, 4,* 327–344.

diSessa, A. (1988). Knowledge in pieces. In G. Forman & P. B. Pufall (Eds.), *Constructivism in the computer age* (pp. 49–70). Hillsdale, NJ: Lawrence Erlbaum Associates.

diSessa, A. (1993). Towards an epistemology of physics. *Cognition and Instruction, 10,* 105–225.

diSessa, A. (1998). What changes in conceptual change? *International Journal of Science Education, 20,* 1155–1191.

diSessa, A., & Wagner, J. (2005). What coordination has to say about transfer. In J. P. Mestre (Ed.), *Transfer of learning from a modern multidisciplinary perspective* (pp. 121–154). Greenwich, CT: Information Age Publishing Inc.

Duncker, K. (1945). On problem solving. *Psychological Monographs, 58,* 1–110.

Dunn, J. W., & Barbanel, J. (2000). One model for an integrated math/physics course focusing on electricity and magnetism and related calculus topics. *American Journal of Physics, 68,* 749.

Engelhardt, P. V., Corpuz, E. G., Ozimek, D. J., & Rebello, N. S. (2003). The teaching experiment—What it is and what it isn't. *Proceedings of the Physics Education Research Conference, 270,* 157–160.

Gick, M. L., & Holyoak, K. J. (1980). Analogical problem solving. *Cognitive Psychology, 12,* 306–355.

Greeno, J. G., Moore, J. L., & Smith, D. R. (1993). Transfer of situated learning. In D. K. Detterman & R. J. Sternberg (Eds.), *Transfer on trial: Intelligence, cognition and instruction* (pp. 99–167). Norwood, NJ: Ablex.

Hammer, D. (2000). Student resources for learning introductory physics. *American Journal of Physics—Physics Education Research Supplement, 68,* S52–S59.

Hammer, D., & Elby, A. (2002). On the form of a personal epistemology. In P. R. Pintrich & B. K. Hofer (Eds.), *Personal epistemology: The psychology of beliefs about knowledge and knowing* (pp. 169–190). Mahwah, NJ: Lawrence Erlbaum Associates.

Jonassen, D. H. (2000). Toward a design theory of problem solving. *Educational Technology: Research & Development, 48*(4), 63.

Jonassen, D. H. (2003). Using cognitive tools to represent problems. *Journal of Research in Technology in Education, 35,* 362–381.

Judd, C. H. (1908). The relation of special training to general intelligence. *Educational Review, 36,* 28–42.

Lobato, J. E. (1996). *Transfer reconceived: How "sameness" is produced in mathematical activity, Ph.D. Dissertation.* Unpublished doctoral dissertation, University of California, Berkeley.

Lobato, J. E. (2003). How design experiments can inform a rethinking of transfer and vice versa. *Educational Researcher, 32*(1), 17–20.

McKeough, R. E., Lupart, J., & Marini, A. (1995). *Teaching for transfer: Fostering generalization in learning.* Mahwah, NJ: Lawrence Erlbaum Associates.

Nisbett, R. E., Fong, G. T., Lehmann, D. R., & Cheng, P. W. (1987). Teaching reasoning. *Science, 238,* 625–630.

Novick, L. (1988). Analogical transfer, problem similarity, and expertise. *Journal of Experimental Psychology: Learning, Memory & Cognition, 14,* 510–520.

Ozimek, D. J. (2004). *Student learning, retention and transfer from trigonometry to physics.* Unpublished master's thesis, Kansas State University, Manhattan, KS.

Piaget, J. (1964). Development and learning. *Journal of Research in Science Teaching, 2,* 176–186.

Pólya, G. (1957). *How to solve it* (2nd ed.). New York: Doubleday.

Rebello, N. S., Zollman, D. A., Allbaugh, A. R., Engelhardt, P. V., Gray, K. E., Hrepic, Z., et al. (2005). Dynamic transfer: A perspective from physics education research. In J. P. Mestre (Ed.), *Transfer of learning from a modern multidisciplinary perspective* (pp. 217–250). Greenwich, CT: Information Age Publishing Inc.

Redish, E. F. (2004, July). *A theoretical framework for physics education research: Modeling student thinking.* Paper presented at the International School of Physics, "Enrico Fermi," Course CLVI, Varenna, Italy.

Reed, S. K. (1993). A schema-based theory of transfer. In D. K. Detterman & R. J. Sternberg (Eds.), *Transfer on trial: Intelligence, cognition and instruction* (pp. 39–67). Norwood, NJ: Ablex.

Reed, S. K., Ernst, G. W., & Banerji, R. (1974). The role of analogy in transfer between similar problem states. *Cognitive Psychology, 6,* 436–450.

Salomon, G., & Perkins, D. N. (1989). Rocky roads to transfer: Rethinking mechanisms of a neglected phenomenon. *Educational Psychologist, 24,* 113–142.

Schoenfeld, A. (1985). *Mathematical problem solving.* Orlando, FL: Academic.

Schwartz, D., Bransford, J. D., & Sears, D. (2005). Efficiency and innovation in transfer. In J. P. Mestre (Ed.), *Transfer of learning from a modern multidisciplinary perspective* (pp. 1–51). Greenwich, CT: Information Age Publishing Inc.

Singley, K., & Anderson, J. R. (1989). *The transfer of cognitive skill.* Cambridge, MA: Harvard University Press.

Steffe, L. P., & Thompson, P. W. (2000). Teaching experiment methodology: Underlying principles and essential elements. In R. Lesh & A. E. Kelly (Eds.), *Research design in mathematics and science education* (pp. 267–307). Mahwah, NJ: Lawrence Erlbaum Associates.

Thorndike, E. L., & Woodworth, R. S. (1901). The influence of improvement in one mental function upon the efficacy of other functions. *Psychological Review, 8,* 247–261.

Van Heuvelen, A., & Maloney, D. P. (1999). Playing physics jeopardy. *American Journal of Physics, 67,* 252–256.

Verbych, E. (2005). *Student work and success using online homework in a trigonometry class.* Unpublished master's thesis, Kansas State University, Manhattan, KS.

Wertheimer, M. (1959). *Productive thinking.* New York: Harper & Row.

Yeatts, F. R., & Hundhausen, J. R. (1992). Calculus and physics: Challenges at the interface. *American Journal of Physics, 60,* 716.

Chapter 11

Metaproblem Spaces and Problem Structure

John Jackman, Sarah Ryan, Sigurdur Olafsson, and Veronica J. Dark
Iowa State University

The conceptualization of problem solving as a sequential process has a long history. Using a puzzle box to study animal problem-solving behavior, Thorndike (1898) defined a problem as a situation in which a goal must be achieved that requires more than just a simple action. The implication is that a set of actions is necessary to reach the goal. Although there are many approaches to problem solving (e.g., Gestalt Theory, Analogies, Mental Models), the focus in this chapter is on Problem Space Theory (Newell & Simon, 1972). A problem space is defined by a set of problem states that describe progress toward a solution at a point in time. A problem solver uses transition operators to move from the initial state and proceed toward the goal state. Problem spaces are based on an information processing view of cognitive behavior in which chunks of information are processed based on internal declarative and procedural knowledge. A problem is solved by moving (navigating) from an initial state to intermediate states and then finally reaching a goal state. Learning "problem solving" from this perspective consists of acquiring the cognitive skills necessary to recognize what problem space is appropriate for a problem, set up the initial state, perform transitions, and recognize when the goal state is reached.

TYPES OF PROBLEMS: WELL-STRUCTURED AND ILL-STRUCTURED

Problems can be characterized by the level of difficulty. Of course, difficulty is in the eye of the beholder. From a problem space perspective, the level of difficulty will be inversely related to a person's understanding of the problem space (in terms of states and transition operators) and the person's ability to match that problem space with the problem description. More generally, problems have been categorized as well-structured and ill-structured based on the problem description. According to Jonassen (1997), well-structured problems

- Present all elements of the problem to the solver.
- Require the application of a limited number of regular and well-structured rules and principles.
- Have knowable, comprehensible solutions where the relationship between decision choices and all problem states is known or probabilistic.

The typical end-of-chapter textbook problems, quiz questions, and exam problems used to assess a student's recall and comprehension of principles and methods are well-structured problems. For these types of problems, learning is focused on the constituent elements of the corresponding problem spaces.

Ill-structured problems, which are more commonly encountered in the real world, lack predictable or convergent solutions and typically require the integration of multiple knowledge domains. Additional characteristics of these problems include the following characteristics:

- Some problem elements are unknown or not known with any degree of confidence (Wood, 1983).
- Multiple solutions or solution paths are possible (Kitchener, 1983).
- Multiple criteria are used for evaluating solutions (Jonassen, 2000).

Hong, Jonassen, and McGee (2003) found that solving ill-structured problems required different skills than solving well-structured problems, including argumentation and metacognition. A key cognitive skill in ill-structured problem solving is the ability to formulate or structure a problem in such a way that content knowledge can be applied. Students must learn to structure problems before they can take advantage of knowledge previously acquired.

Simon (1973) suggested that "... there are no well-structured problems, only ill-structured problems that have been formalized for problem solvers" (p. 186). This formalization process produces a new problem space that can be used by problem solvers. Once a problem space is well-defined (i.e., well-structured), a new set of knowledge has been created that describes the problem space and the preferred paths of navigation through the space.

Problem Representations for Well-Structured and Ill-Structured Problems

Learning in the science, technology, engineering, and mathematics (STEM) domains is typically focused on methods and skills that address well-structured problems. A student acquires the declarative and procedural knowledge necessary to navigate a well-defined problem space. Successful students know how to solve these problems by selecting the appropriate problem space for a problem scenario. Problem descriptions are constructed so that students can recognize the initial state and goal states. For those problems that have a unique path from the initial state to the goal state, the remaining states and operations are provided by a student's long-term memory. If they are missing from long-term memory, then the problem appears to be ill-structured to the student. If multiple problem spaces exist (i.e., multiple solution paths), a decision must be made to select a problem space based on some criterion. One criterion could be the cardinality of the problem space, resulting in the selection of the problem space with the smallest set of steps. Another criterion might be the perceived cumulative level of effort necessary to perform the operation sequence. In this case, a student might select a problem space with a larger set of states but requiring less total effort (i.e., minimizing the time spent on the solution).

Assessment of student learning in many STEM educational settings is limited to an evaluation of whether a student has reached the correct goal state, and, in some cases, verifying major steps in the solution process. If a student has reached the goal state, then it seems reasonable to infer that the student has an understanding of the problem space. Of course it is possible to guess the goal state, but the likelihood of this is usually quite small. If a student can successfully achieve the same outcome when presented with variations of the problem description, then some degree of mastery of the problem space and the underlying concepts has been achieved. The cognitive skills for these types of problems (i.e., well-structured problems) would correspond to the knowledge, comprehension, analysis, and application skills in Bloom's (1956) Taxonomy with an emphasis on analysis and application. The more difficult cognitive tasks in the taxonomy, namely, synthesis and evaluation, would not be emphasized with well-structured problems but they are important in ill-structured problems.

It has been recognized that ill-structured problems require a different set of cognitive skills. Learning to solve ill-structured problems should be focused on the cognitive skills necessary to create problem spaces when they are unknown, which implies a need for synthesis and evaluation skills. The space of problem spaces can be referred to as a *meta-problem space* (MPS) because it represents the problem of constructing a new, well-defined problem space. Heylighen (1988) described the MPS as a metarepresentation and recommended further research to understand the nature of the MPS.

Ill-structured problem solving cannot be understood without focusing on the MPS, or the cognitive processes necessary to create unknown problem spaces (Newell & Simon, 1972). Goel and Pirolli (1992) performed protocol studies of expert designers solving simple design problems that were considered to be ill-structured. Data from the preliminary design phase indicated that rough sketches or fragments were important representations used for these types of problems. These representations were part of an exploration phase of the problem-solving process. The magnitude of ambiguity was relatively high in this phase as the problem space was not well defined. These representations were characterized by syntactical, semantic, and transformation properties (Goel, 1995). The syntactical and semantic properties are based on the work of Goodman (1976) in language symbols. An actual representation consists of a set of tokens (i.e., actual instances of symbols). For example, these could be characters, words, or geometric entities. Symbols are considered to be a standard set of representations that are agreed on a priori. Table 11.1 shows a comparison of the properties from Goel (1995) for well-structured versus ill-structured problems.

TABLE 11.1

Properties for Problem Representations

Property Type	Property	Meaning	Well-Structured	Ill-Structured
Syntactic	Invariance	Extent to which a token is repeatable	Disjoint	Overlap
	Uniqueness	Ability to map a token to a unique symbol	Differentiated	Undifferentiated
Semantic	Unambiguity	One unique symbol to represent a concept (i.e., only one meaning)	Unambiguous	High ambiguity
	Invariance	Symbol always represents the same class of objects	Disjoint	Overlap
	Uniqueness	Ability to map a symbol to a class of objects	Differentiated	Undifferentiated
Transformation operators	Unambiguity of rules	The extent to which rules are well defined	Unambiguous	High ambiguity
	Persistence of valid moves	A measure of the invariant nature of the rules and properties with respect to time	Static	Dynamic

Problem representations or schemas play a central role in problem solving. Representations are used to describe a problem and to structure the problem-solving process. Results from Goel and Grafman (2000) suggested that well-structured representations are more associated with activation in the left hemisphere of the brain and ill-structured representations are more associated with activation in the right hemisphere, supporting the premise that a different set of cognitive skills are needed to address ill-structured problems. These studies provided insights into the types of representations used to solve design problems, but did not address the representations used in the metaproblem space.

IDENTIFICATION OF PATTERNS AND DEVELOPMENT OF EXPERTISE

Problem solving begins with a problem description that must be analyzed, evaluated, and understood by a problem solver. These higher order cognitive activities are essential skills that must be learned to develop expertise in problem solving. When interpreting problem descriptions, experts have an ability to recognize important problem features and patterns in the information (Bransford, Brown, & Cocking, 1999). Novices may be able to identify some of these features but have difficulty with the patterns. Berlyne (1965) suggested that stimulus patterns lead to abstractions, which are a form of information reduction. Schoenfeld and Herman (1982) studied the perceptions of novices when they were presented with problems in mathematics. Participants were asked to categorize problems based on similarities between problems. They found that students initially perceived the problems based on elements (i.e., the features) in the problem descriptions. After taking a problem-solving course, the novices demonstrated a greater knowledge of the underlying principles and solution methods (i.e., the patterns).

At some stage in the problem-solving process, a transition must be made between the external representation and internal representations. Voss and Post (1988) found that students have difficulties in developing mental representations for ill-structured problems. Chi, Feltovich, and Glaser (1981) studied the behavior of experts and novices who solved physics problems. They suggested that experts are able to identify internal schemas (i.e., patterns) based on recognizing fragments in the problem descriptions. This was followed by an evaluation of the match between the pattern and the problem. The initial pattern matching can be followed by a more limited search for a solution based on alternative patterns. The novices appeared to select relevant information, but had difficulty with abstraction, resulting in only a set of unrelated items.

Understanding differences between novices and experts helps researchers and educators identify cognitive skills that are associated with problem-solving expertise. Polson and Jeffries (1982) referred to the understanding of a novice as being fragmentary. That is, novices appear to possess a fragmented set of knowledge that creates obstacles during problem solving due to the inability to connect fragments. This limited understanding is evidenced by increased search activities such as trial and error or means-ends analysis during the problem-solving process. The theoretical framework Polson used to model behavior of novices includes a set of evaluation and memory processes. The evaluation processes focus on the determination of the next step and are based on information from long-term memory coupled with evaluation heuristics. Donald (2004) suggested that the transition from novice to expert involves an analysis stage in which a novice begins to acquire the internal representations (i.e., patterns) that experts use. After sufficient learning, these patterns become well-defined. Experts have the ability to map these internal patterns to the problem description and use the pattern(s) to solve the problem.

Problem Space Strategies

A heuristic is informally defined as a problem-solving strategy. In cognitive psychology, a heuristic is a simple, efficient rule of thumb that people follow to reduce the complexity of a task. In computer science and mathematical optimization, a heuristic is a search method that does not necessarily identify the best solution but generally finds a good solution in a reasonable amount of time. This section describes heuristics for constructing a problem space. The next section describes additional heuristics for searching through a defined space.

General Search Heuristic (Newell & Simon, 1972)

The general heuristic begins with an examination of a problem description to determine the principal components. Once they have been identified, operators are selected to move to the next state. The operations are performed and a set of results is produced. The results are evaluated and a decision is made whether to accept the new state or reject it and start over.

Means-End Heuristic

The well-known means-end heuristic has been used to describe the process used to move through the problem space (Newell & Simon, 1972). The difference between the current state and the goal state (i.e., end) is determined by the problem solver. An operation that will reduce the difference (means) is chosen. If an operation cannot be determined, the current state or goal state is modified to produce a subgoal. The process is repeated until the goal state is reached. MacGregor, Ormerod, and Chronicle (2001) investigated planning in the context of the nine-dot insight problem. This is a geometry problem starting with an initial state represented by nine dots as shown in Figure 11.1.

The goal state is to connect the dots by drawing four contiguous line segments without retracing a segment. It is considered an insight problem because most participants attempt to solve the problem by drawing line segments within the convex polygon of the nine dots. MacGregor et al. (2001) concluded that the primary strategy was the means-end heuristic where insight could occur with certain moves that were deemed promising by the problem solver based on some criterion. As shown in Figure 11.1, the construction of the problem space can be viewed as a two-stage process. Initial attempts in Stage 1 using the means-end heuristic show progress toward the goal state by staying within the convex polygon, but finally result in a dead end state. At this point the problem solver becomes aware that this approach to building the problem space will not be successful. When insight occurs (i.e., segments can extend outside the convex polygon), the problem solver enters Stage 2. In this stage the means-end heuristic can be used to reach the goal state through multiple paths as shown in Figure 11.1.

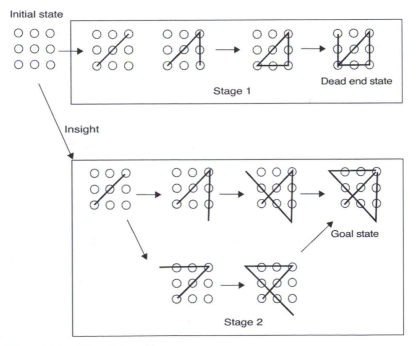

Figure 11.1.   Nine-dot problem.

Forward Navigation

A problem solver starts in an initial state and selects an operation that makes a transition to the next state (whether valid or invalid). Through a sequence of forward moves, the goal state is achieved. Experts in well-structured problems tend to follow this strategy.

Backward Navigation

A problem solver starts in the goal state and identifies the operation that preceded this state (i.e., what operations will produce the goal state?). The operation is performed in reverse, and the previous state is generated.

Planning

In this approach, a problem solver performs an abstraction of the problem description and creates an abstract problem space. The problem is solved in the abstract space or the solution may already be known (i.e., learned). The solution is then transformed into the actual problem space by identifying the corresponding elements in the problem description with the abstract problem space. The abstraction process is a critical step in this method, because the fidelity of the abstract problem space can affect the solution. Multiple iterations may occur when the abstract solution cannot be resolved with the original problem space.

Jeffries, Polson, Razran, and Tinsley (1977) studied how people used plans to solve word puzzles (such as the Missionaries and Cannibals problem). Some of the participants in the study were able to formulate plans prior to solving the problem. The plan is considered to be the set of moves that will be followed from the initial state to the goal state. In some cases it appeared that plans were formed during the problem-solving process as new understanding of the problem was acquired. Jeffries et al. suggested that the ability to form a plan depends on a problem solver's understanding of the problem structure.

Ormerod (2005) suggested that planning is critical in ill-structured problem solving. Planning occurs in terms of domain knowledge (declarative and procedural) and search strategies. This planning approach describes the plan in terms of monitoring search results and evaluating progress toward the goal state. The plan represents an exploration plan for the problem space.

General Search Strategies

Once the problem space has been defined, it is possible to define and follow more sophisticated strategies for navigating among the states. The search for the goal state can be seen as an optimization problem. In this context, a heuristic may consist of finding an optimal solution to a simplified version of the problem, or it may follow a procedure that would find the optimal solution if allowed to continue indefinitely, but stop once an acceptable solution is found.

Polson and Jeffries (1982) described the problem-solving process for puzzles as a mixture of understanding of domain specific knowledge and search strategies. When there is sufficient information in the problem descriptions and understanding of the underlying concepts, a problem solver can use known solution procedures and search techniques are unnecessary. Their model of problem solving with puzzles included a set of evaluation processes, memory processes, and move selection processes. The evaluation process is used to assess the characteristics of a potential move. The memory processes involve short-term memory for processing information at the current point in the problem-solving process and long-term memory for the history of the process (i.e., previous results). The move-selection processes use the results of the evaluation process to make a decision about the next move. The results of their studies using word puzzles (such as the Missionaries and Cannibals problem) were in agreement with the model.

Breadth-First Versus Depth-First

The objective of a search is to increase the problem solver's understanding of the problem, which will eventually lead to the goal state. After a transition from the current problem state to the next state, additional information is acquired from the cognitive activity performed during the transition. A search that allows the problem solver to obtain the necessary information in the fewest moves can be considered the best search strategy. Starting in a given state, two possible strategies are breadth-first and depth-first. In a breadth-first search strategy, all possible transitions from a state are explored. Suppose that at time t there are $K(t)$ possible transitions from the current state, $X(t)$, to a new problem state, $X^k(t)$, $k = 1, \ldots, K(t)$. A breadth-first strategy sequentially makes each of those transitions, so that the next sequence of states becomes $X(t+1) = X^1(t)$, $X(t+2) = X^2(t)$, $\ldots$, $X(t+K) = X^{K(t)}(t)$. The information gained from each of these steps can then be used to determine how to proceed. Because all transitions have been tried, a perceived best transition k^* can now be selected, that is $X[t+K(t)+1] = X^{k^*}(t)$. In the next step, the breadth-first search considers all possible transitions from state $X[t+K(t)+1]$ and the process continues until the goal state is finally reached.

A depth-first search takes the opposite point of view and pursues one path in an attempt to reach the goal state with no backtracking until no further progress can be made. Thus, from a current state $X(t)$, one of the $K(t)$

possible transitions is selected, say the $k(t)$-th transition to state $X^{k(t)}(t)$. From the new state $X(t+1) = X^{k(t)}(t)$, there are $K(t+1)$ possible transitions and one of those is selected. This creates a sequence of state $X(t), X(t+1), \ldots, X(t+T)$ that terminates after T steps when there are no possible transitions from state $X(t+T)$. If $X(t+T)$ is the goal state, the search terminates, otherwise the process can be repeated, starting again from $X(t)$, until the goal state is achieved. Note that it is also possible to combine breadth-first and depth-first strategies, and the best search strategy depends on the specific problem structure.

Hill Climbing

The search strategies described earlier use only information about the current state $X(t)$ to guide the search, and the effect of a transition from $X(t)$ to a possible state $X^k(t)$ is therefore unknown until the transition is actually made. When available, other search strategies take advantage of information about the effect of the change from one state to the next (e.g., second-order information or gradient information). Thus, there is an assumption that the impact of moving from one state to the next, $\Delta f(X(t), X^k(t))$, based on some objective function f is known at state $X(t)$. The simplest such search strategy is hill climbing, which always selects the transition that results in the largest improvement in the selected objective function, that is, the value for $X^k(t)$ that maximizes $\Delta f(X(t), X^k(t))$. This can be written as

$$X(t+1) = \arg \max_{\pi^k(t)} \Delta f(X(t), X^k(t)). \qquad (11.1)$$

This process is repeated until a state $X(t+T)$ is reached where all transitions result in deterioration of the objective function, which can be interpreted as having found the top of the hill. Hill climbing is also known as greedy search because the locally best move is always selected without consideration for future moves. Due to this myopic perspective, it is not guaranteed that the goal state is reached at the end of the search and it may need to be restarted from different initial states.

Probabilistic Search

The selection of the next state depends on the available information and understanding of the student or problem solver. This can be viewed in a probabilistic framework. When there is complete lack of problem understanding, each possible transition becomes equally likely and a student selects the next move using a discrete uniform distribution (e.g., a coin toss). This reduces a search to guessing and as a result becomes a time-consuming process, because the likelihood of reaching the goal state quickly is small. As a pure random search continues, additional information and understanding is obtained and the search can progressively become more focused. If there is some additional information indicating that one move has a greater likelihood of success than another (i.e., it will have a positive effect on the objective function), then the distribution is no longer uniform and a student will tend toward a move having the greatest likelihood of success. The primary difference between probabilistic search and hill climbing is that in hill climbing, the locally best transition is selected with a probability of one.

Any of the described search strategies may lead to dead ends or incorrect solutions, forcing the student to backtrack and move in another direction. These types of searches therefore fall into the category of classical trial and error moves. A trial consists of performing the selected transformation operation and recording the result. After a trial, an evaluation is made based on some criterion as to whether the move produced the desired result and is leading to a goal state. If it was unsatisfactory, then backtracking occurs and the process is repeated.

Well-Structured Problem Spaces

We suggest that the problem-solving process in a well-structured problem space can be depicted as shown in Figure 11.2. Given a problem descrip-

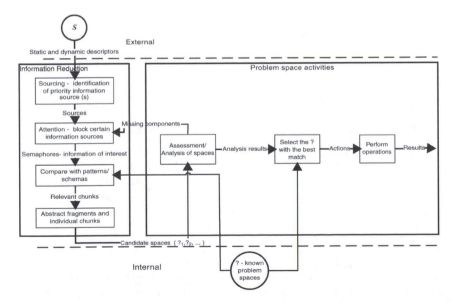

Figure 11.2.   Representation of problem solving in a well-structured problem space.

tion, S, there is some process of information reduction in which the student identifies potential patterns that can be mapped to problem spaces $\pi \in \Pi$ of which the student has knowledge from previous learning. Each π contains the related principal components such as concepts, initial state, operators, and goal state. Some of these components also may be part of other problem spaces. Next, there is some analysis of the appropriateness of the pattern or a decision must be made given multiple possible patterns. In the next phase, the transformation operations for the selected pattern are easily applied because the characteristics of the representation are as described under "Well-Structured" in Table 11.1. Difficulties occur when students have fragmented or incomplete patterns, lack information reduction capability, or do not have the cognitive skills to analyze candidate patterns. These difficulties may suggest some possibilities for formative assessment in providing feedback to students as they solve well-structured problems. Without feedback, students will proceed in a different mode as if this were an ill-structured problem having characteristics as shown under "Ill-Structured" in Table 11.1.

Well-Structured Problem Example

The knapsack problem is one example of a well-structured problem in optimization. A textbook example is provided by Winston (2004, p. 478):

> Stockco is considering four investments. Investment 1 will yield a net present value (NPV) of $16,000; investment 2, an NPV of $22,000; investment 3, an NPV of $12,000; and investment 4, an NPV of $8,000. Each investment requires a certain cash outflow at the present time: investment 1, $5,000; investment 2, $7,000; investment 3, $4,000; and investment 4, $3,000. Currently, $14,000 is available for investment. How should Stockco select from among investments 1 – 4 to maximize the total NPV?

This is a well-structured problem because all task relevant information is readily available, there is a single criterion for evaluating solutions, and there is a single best answer according to that criterion. Success in finding that solution, and the amount of time and effort required to do so, will depend on one's ability to structure and navigate the problem space. Some possible alternative problem spaces are as follows.

Greedy. A heuristic approach to this problem would consider each investment's "bang for the buck." Dividing NPV by the initial cash outlay yields ratios 3.2, 3.14, 3.0, and 2.66, respectively, for the four alternatives, encouraging the problem solver to select investment 1 along with one or two other investments. However, this would be wrong because the largest total NPV actually is achieved by foregoing the first investment and selecting the other three.

Combinatorial. The problem solver could think in terms of sets of possible investments. Preliminary explorations would reveal that any one or two investments are feasible because their total cash outlay would not exceed the $14,000 available. The combination of investments (1, 3, 4), with a total initial outlay of $12,000, is also feasible, but selecting 1 and 2 precludes also selecting either 3 or 4. There are $2^4 = 16$ possible subsets of investments, and solving the problem according to this approach means evaluating all possibilities in some more or less efficient manner.

Integer Program. A problem solver with a background in operations research might structure the problem as a mathematical program consisting of an objective function with a single constraint and binary decision variables as follows:

$$\begin{aligned}
\max \quad & 16x_1 \quad +22x_2 \quad +12x_3 \quad +8x_4 \\
\text{subject to} \quad & 5x_1 \quad +7x \quad +4x_3 \quad +3x_4 \quad \leq 14 \\
& x_1 \quad x_2 \quad x_{3,} \quad x_4 \quad \in \{0,1\}
\end{aligned} \qquad (11.2)$$

The objective function represents the total NPV whereas the constraint represents the initial cash outlay, both in thousands of dollars. This formulation would then open up possibilities for efficiently searching the combinatorial solution space using an established algorithm such as branch-and-bound.

Decision Network. A background in computer science or a more visual and graphical orientation might lead one to formulate the problem as finding the longest path from the node on the left to any node on the right in Figure 11.3. Here, the investments are considered sequentially, moving from left to right. The numbers in the nodes represent the remaining available cash, whereas those above the arcs represent the NPV added by including the investment under consideration. Each path represents a feasible set of investments and its length (sum of the arc lengths) is the combined NPV. Efficient methods are available for identifying the longest path with a total length of 42 (as shown by the bold arcs), which corresponds to selecting investments 2, 3, and 4.

Reasoning by analogy may help the problem solver to recognize the underlying structure in the problem. The characterization of this problem as a knapsack problem recognizes the analogy with the situation of a traveler who has a knapsack of limited capacity (either weight or volume) and a set of

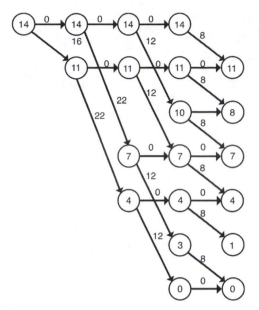

Figure 11.3.   Longest path network for well-structured example.

items to consider packing in it, each of which would provide some value on the journey. In this example, NPV is the value and initial cash outlay is the capacity resource consumed. Problem solvers who are familiar with the knapsack problem and have seen other analogous examples would be more likely to select the integer program or decision network representation and probably more successful at solving it efficiently. For those familiar with it, the knapsack problem is a known problem space from the set of known P in Figure 11.2 that matches the given problem perfectly. Therefore, the problem solver can perform operations within that space to locate an optimal solution efficiently.

Metaproblem Spaces

For an ill-structured problem space, there is an added element of search depending on the extent to which the problem is ill-structured. Given that a problem space does not exist in P for an ill-structured problem, a new problem space, $\pi_i(t)$, is created by the student, where t is time. Note that $\pi_i(t)$ changes as time increments because the student explores the problem space and gains new insights and understanding. From a set theory perspective (as shown in Figure 11.4), $\pi_i(t)$ may contain principal components from known problem spaces. These are the elements that a student may recognize in the problem description and represent problem space fragments.

The degree to which there are gaps (i.e., fragmentation) in $\pi_i(t)$ indicates the level of difficulty for the ill-structured problem. These gaps are represented by the region with the darker shading.

If the metaproblem space activities are successful, they will produce a sequence of problem spaces that somehow converges to the goal problem space, that is, a problem space for a well-structured problem that can then be searched using a combination of known methods. To understand these activities and their outcomes, measure progress toward structuring the problem, and grasp the relation between an ill-structured problem and its well-structured components, it may be useful to apply mathematical concepts of set distance and convergence. In topological set theory, the Hausdorff distance metric quantifies how much two sets overlap. If the two sets are the same, the Hausdorff distance between them is zero; otherwise, its positive value becomes larger with increasing disparity between them. Convergence of a sequence of sets can be measured in terms of decreasing distance from a limiting set, which implies decreasing distance between successive sets in the sequence.

The definition of the Hausdorff metric depends on the definition of a measure of distance between elements of the sets. In the problem space context, these set elements constitute elements of schema, that is, pieces of the declarative and procedural knowledge that constitute the schema. That is, if p and q are two elements of problem spaces, we must define a function $d(p, q)$ that satisfies the non-negativity, transitivity, and triangle inequality requirements for a distance metric (Munkres, 1975):

1. $d(p, q) \geq 0$ for all p, q; equality holds if and only if $p = q$.
2. $d(p, q) = d(p, q)$ for all p, q.
3. $d(p, r) + d(r, q) \geq d(q, p)$ for all p, q, r.

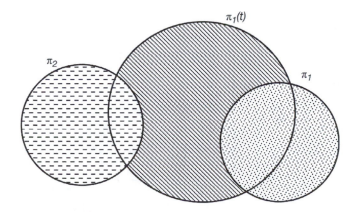

Figure 11.4.   Set representation of a new problem space.

The distance metric allows a notion of compactness. Then, having defined the metric for elements of problem spaces, if π_1 and π_2 are two compact problem spaces, the Hausdorff metric is defined as minimal number s such that closed s-neighborhood of π_1 contains π_2 and closed s-neighborhood of π_2 contains π_1 (Wikipedia, 2006). That is

$$d_H(\pi_1, \pi_2) = \max\left\{\sup_{p \in \pi_1} \inf_{q \in \pi_2} d(p,q), \sup_{p \in \pi_2} \inf_{q \in \pi_1} d(p,q)\right\} \qquad (11.3)$$

Ryan, Bean, and Smith (1992) previously applied this concept to analyzing sequential decision problems. To precisely define problem spaces and their elements in a way that a distance measure can be formulated poses a daunting challenge. However, we believe that attempting these definitions would greatly aid research into understanding the process of solving ill-structured problems.

The problem-solving mode to fill these gaps can be represented by the steps shown in Figure 11.5. It is an iterative search of the region that produces one realization of π_i from π_i (t) at some t when a determination is

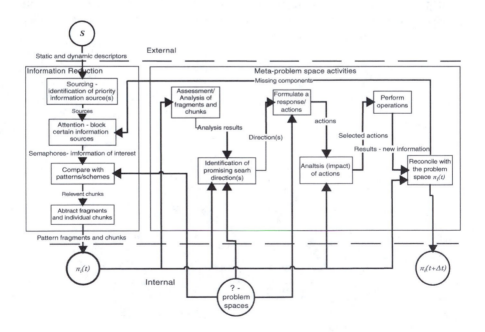

Figure 11.5.   Representation of problem solving in a metaproblem space.

made that the goal state has been reached. The ability to find π_i for small values of t is tied to a student's ability to navigate in a metaproblem space.

Based on the metaproblem space activities completed during the interval Δt, the problem space is updated to $\pi_i(t + \Delta t)$. Note that in this mode, students must rely heavily on their higher order skills of synthesis and evaluation. The problem space is instantiated over time as the student explores potential states. One potential measure of the degree to which a problem is ill-structured may be the number of fragments present. The search techniques are used to identify the connections that need to be made among the fragments. The number of connections that are made (i.e., new problem space states) may also prove to be a measure of ill-structuredness.

Ill-Structured Problem Example

An example of an ill-structured problem follows:

You have $14,000 to invest. What should you do?

Initially there is no perceptible structure for the problem space. Therefore, a metaproblem space is needed to guide the formation of the problem space. Based on Figure 11.5, the problem solver would begin by assessing fragments. These fragments could represent known methods for investing capital such as a stock portfolio, bonds, and so forth. One form of a metaproblem space is to structure the problem based on following a "rational economic decision making process," described by the following steps (Park, 2004, p. 6):

1. Recognize a decision problem. In this case, the problem is to decide how to invest the available cash. The goal state consists of the form of the investment.
2. Define the goals or objectives. During the process, a problem solver may search and evaluate a number of different goals to assess each goal's appropriateness in finding the solution. A typical individual or firm wishes to maximize wealth while controlling the level of risk.
3. Collect all the relevant information. This activity is described by the left side of Figure 11.5. Given the limited set of fragments available in this problem description, extensive information gathering and reduction would be performed. This step would involve researching the different investments available, collecting yield information, and estimating risks. The prevailing inflation rate and the risk-free interest rate would also be relevant information.
4. Identify a set of feasible decision alternatives. This step corresponds to identifying promising search directions in Figure 11.5 based on some assessment of the relevant information. This step might consist of reduc-

ing the possibilities to the best available option in each of a number of categories. For example, investment 1 in the well-structured example shown earlier could represent a stock mutual fund that has a minimum initial investment of $5,000. Investment 2 could represent a limited partnership that requires $7,000 to participate. Investment 3 might represent a bond selling for $4,000, and Investment 4 a certificate of deposit that requires a minimum deposit of $3,000 to earn the highest possible yield.

5. Select the decision criterion to use. This would correspond to formulating actions in Figure 11.5. In engineering economic analysis, students learn to consider the time value of money and inflation to estimate discounted cash flows. By adjusting the risk-free interest rate for inflation and the level of risk present in each alternative, the decision maker could compute the net present values given earlier for each investment.

6. Select the best alternative. This would correspond to "Perform operations" in Figure 11.5. At this point, the problem is well-structured, and can be described succinctly as in the textbook example. However, the possibility of choosing more than one alternative simultaneously under the budget constraint makes the problem more complex than simply selecting a single alternative.

Multiple iterations of this search may occur until the problem solver converges on the goal state.

Examples of Metaproblem Space Contexts

The design of a new concept has been recognized to be an ill-structured problem that relies heavily on synthesis and evaluation skills. The initial state is a known set of requirements (which may change over time). The goal state is a description of a concept that satisfies those requirements based on some form of testing and evaluation. These descriptions are intended to be an unambiguous representation of the concept and may include information such as drawings, text, or diagrams. Typically a design problem consists of multiple stages in which the level of detail in the design descriptions increases, conflicts are resolved, and changes are made. In this context, the evolving problem space, $\pi_i(t)$, is alternatively expanding and contracting based on the operations performed. Contraction occurs when the resolution of a conflict imposes one or more constraints, eliminating potential principal components in $\pi_i(t)$. Expansion occurs when multiple alternatives are discovered in the gap region.

In the field of industrial engineering, problems often fall into the category of ill-structured problems due to the scope and complexity of the problem scenarios. For example, in designing a manufacturing system to produce a product, an engineer must consider a large set of requirements, constraints, and evaluation criteria that may be ambiguous or in conflict with one another. Requirements can often be satisfied with alternative design elements. At the same time, the engineer must consider social, environmental, and economic impact.

An Ill-Structured Problem in Engineering Economics

A collaborative, Web-based, problem-solving environment has been developed for ill-structured problems (Olafsson et al., 2004). The Problem Solving Learning Portal (PSLP) is a learning management system that includes a set of problem scenarios, multiple problem scenario information resources that can be requested by students, a multistage structure for the problem-solving process, mechanisms for collecting information on cognitive activities, a repository that supports collaborative work in multiple formats for each student team, and feedback to teams on their progress.

For the engineering economics problem scenario, there are four stages in the problem-solving process. Students proceed in fixed sequence from one stage to the next with the ability to backtrack to previous stages. In the first stage ("Objective"), students formulate an objective based on the problem description and determine measures that they will use in subsequent decision-making processes. During the "Plan" stage, students determine the set of activities that they will perform to arrive at the goal state. This includes gathering information and performing various types of computations and analyses relevant to the knowledge domain. The "Solution" phase represents arrival at the goal state. Students specify their solution along with supporting documentation. In all these phases, justification must be provided in terms of a set of statements that support the chosen actions and decisions.

The Engineering Economy scenario was designed for our junior-level Engineering Economic Analysis course (which can be found at most engineering colleges). It has a large enrollment of approximately 200 students from multiple engineering majors (e.g., industrial, electrical, mechanical, and chemical engineering) each semester. The PSLP has been used three terms per year for 3 years as a project worth 15% to 20% of the final grade (Ryan, Jackman, Peters, Olafsson, & Huba, 2004). The ill-structured problem scenario, developed in consultation with a local manufacturer, centers on developing a 5-year manufacturing strategy.

Problem Description. Paragon International is a worldwide leader in the manufacture of professional concession equipment, including popcorn poppers, "sno-cone" machines, and cotton candy machines. Most of the company's operations occur at its headquarters in Nevada, IA. Products are manufactured mainly from sheet metal parts. These parts are cut from sheet steel and then formed into the desired shape. Batches of sheets are shipped to a subcontractor for painting, after which they are returned for final assembly. Glass parts are purchased from a supplier with any graphics preprinted. Electrical components are assembled from purchased components and wired during the assembly processes. The company also performs some other manufacturing processes. Additional parts are purchased from suppliers.

Besides the assembly operations, the other major manufacturing operation at the Nevada plant is the production of the sheet metal components. Because of aggressive product development and a strong sales and marketing network, demand has grown considerably throughout the 2 years this plant has been in operation. Production cannot satisfy current demand, and many potential orders are lost because of the 6-month waiting list. Depending on the product mix and other factors, the bottleneck in the operation is constantly changing. However, the company has identified the punch press as a potential bottleneck of the production process. Management has determined three feasible alternatives for expanding production capacity:

1. Add a second shift for the punching operations.
2. Outsource some of the punching operations.
3. Purchase an additional punch press to operate during the single shift.

The company needs a 5-year strategic plan for manufacturing. The plant manager is willing to implement at most one of the three alternatives at a time in each of the next 5 years (2005–2009). In addition to the material cost, variable costs for the punching operation using the current machine consist of maintenance and energy costs per hour of operation.

Fragments. By design, this problem was formulated to be ill-structured. Students who performed well in textbook problems in the engineering economy course learned problem spaces that would cover fragments of this problem. Other fragments come from the manufacturing domain. Figure 11.6 shows some of the principal components from one fragment in the form of a concept map for the net income associated with the problem. In Figure 11.7, a related fragment from manufacturing is shown. A significant gap exists between these two fragments. The difficulty for students is that they are not accustomed to integrating these fragments, although that is what they must do in a real-world problem. Therefore, the problem space is unknown and students must adjust to the search mode described in Figure 11.5. As indicated from feedback we received from students, this causes a high degree of discomfort and uncertainty for the students.

RESEARCH ISSUES

In this chapter, we have reviewed problem-solving literature, particularly as it relates to solving ill-structured problems. Our focus has been on the role of metaproblem spaces. As STEM educators, we have particular interest in obtaining better understanding of the cognitive processes in metaproblem spaces. Increased understanding of these processes should lead to better in-

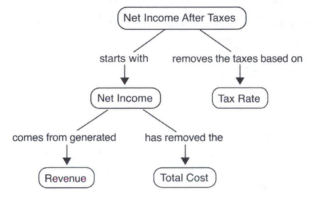

Figure 11.6.   Pattern fragment for determining net income after tax.

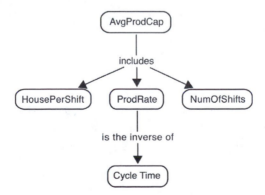

Figure 11.7.   Pattern fragment for manufacturing that shows how average production capacity is related to work shifts and the production rate within a shift.

structional methods that foster enhanced learning among STEM students. Research is needed in the following areas.

Search Techniques in Metaproblem Spaces

The effectiveness of different search techniques needs to be evaluated for metaproblem spaces in different contexts. This evaluation would require formal methods for structuring the problem descriptions, performance measures for search results, and methods for collecting data from students.

Measures for Problem Space Fragments

Multiple measures of problem space fragments are needed to estimate gaps between fragments, boundaries of fragments, and the cardinality or magnitude of fragments. Techniques from set theory show promise if the necessary data can be collected.

Methods for Teaching Metaproblem Spaces

Our experiences with using ill-structured problems indicate that a phased approach may be warranted in which students are gradually introduced to the metaproblem spaces by increasing the gap between problem space fragments.

Assessment of Student Learning in Metaproblem Spaces

Formal methods for formative and summative assessments are needed to determine if students are learning these processes. Real-time formative assessment methods could help guide novices as they are learning to deal with metaproblem spaces.

Metacognition in Metaproblem Spaces

Reflecting and monitoring progress during the navigation of the metaproblem space is certainly a critical step in evaluating the success of the search. Methods are needed to help students improve their metacognition and also to assess the type and level of metacognition that is occurring during the problem-solving process.

REFERENCES

Berlyne, D. E. (1965). *Structure and direction in thinking*. New York: Wiley.

Bloom B. S. (1956). *Taxonomy of educational objectives, handbook I: The cognitive domain.* New York: McKay.

Bransford, J. D., Brown, A. L., & Cocking, R. R. (1999). *How people learn: Brain, mind, experience, and school part II: Chapter 2 learners and learning.* Washington, DC: National Research Council.

Chi, M. T., Feltovich, P. J., & Glaser, R. (1981). Categorization and representation of physics problems by experts and novices. *Cognitive Science, 5,* 121–152.

Donald, J. G. (2004). Disciplinary differences in learning and thinking processes and in instructional strategies. *Proceedings of the Second National Conference: Integrating Research Into Undergraduate Education: The Value Added.* Retrieved December 15, 2006, from http://www.stonybrook.edu/reinventioncenter/Conference_04/proceedings.htm

Goel, V., Grafman, J. (2000). The role of the right prefrontal cortex in ill-structured planning. *Cognitive Neuropsychology, 17,* 415–436.

Goel, V., & Pirolli, P. (1992). The structure of design problem spaces. *Cognitive Science, 16,* 395–429.

Goel, V. (1995). *Sketches of thought.* Cambridge, MA: MIT Press.

Goodman, N. (1976). *Languages of art: An approach to a theory of symbols* (2nd ed.), Indianapolis, IN: Hackett.

Heylighen F. (1988): Formulating the problem of problem-formulation. In R. Trappl (Ed.), *Cybernetics and systems '88* (pp. 949–957). Dordrecht, The Netherlands: Kluwer.

Hong, N.S., Jonassen, D. H., & McGee, S. (2003) Predictors of well-structured and ill-structured problem solving in an astronomy simulation. *Journal of Research in Science Teaching, 40,* 6–33.

Jeffries, R., Polson, P., Razran, L., & Tinsley, M. (1977). *Detecting plans from data* (Institute for the Study of Intellectual Behavior, Program on Cognitive Factors in Human Learning and Memory Report No. 76). Boulder: University of Colorado.

Jonassen, D. (2000). Toward a design theory of problem solving. *Educational Technology: Research and Development, 48,* 63–85.

Jonassen, D. H. (1997). Instructional design model for well-structured and ill-structured problem-solving learning outcomes. *Educational Technology: Research and Development, 45,* 65–95.

Kitchener, K. S. (1983). Cognition, metacognition, and epistemic cognition: A three-level model of cognitive processing. *Human Development, 26,* 222–232.

MacGregor, J. N., Ormerod, T. C., & Chronicle, E. P. (2001). Information processing and insight: A process model of performance on the nine-dot and related problems. *Journal of Experimental Psychology: Learning, Memory, and Cognition, 27,* 176–201.

Munkres, J. R. (1975). *Topology: A first course.* Englewood Cliffs, NJ: Prentice Hall.

Newell, A., & Simon, H. A. (1972). *Human problem solving.* Englewood Cliffs, NJ: Prentice Hall.

Olafsson, S., Saunders, K., Jackman, J., Peters, F., Ryan, S., Dark, V. J., et al. (2004). Implementation and assessment of industrial engineering curriculum reform. *Proceedings of the 2004 ASEE Annual Conference.* Retrieved December 15, 2006, from http://www.asee.org/acPapers/2004-398_Final.pd

Ormerod, T. C. (2005). Planning and ill-defined problems. In R. Morris & G. Ward (Eds.), *The cognitive psychology of planning* (pp. 53–70). East Sussex; NY: Psychology Press.

Park, C. (2004). *Fundamentals of engineering economics.* Upper Saddle River, NJ: Prentice Hall.

Polson, P., & Jeffries, R. (1982). Expertise in problem solving. In R. Sternberg (Ed.), *Advances in the psychology of human intelligence* (pp. 367–411). Hillsdale, NJ: Lawrence Erlbaum Associates.

Ryan, S., Jackman, J., Peters, F., Olafsson, S., & Huba, M. (2004). The engineering learning portal for problem solving: Experience in a large engineering economy class. *The Engineering Economist, 49,* 1–20.

Ryan, S. M., Bean, J. C., & Smith, R. L. (1992). A tie-breaking rule for discrete infinite horizon optimization. *Operations Research, 40,* S117–S126.

Schoenfeld, A. H., & Herrmann, D. J. (1982) Problem perception and knowledge structure in expert and novice mathematical problem solvers. *Journal of Experimental Psychology: Learning, Memory and Cognition, 8,* 484–494.

Simon, H. A. (1973). The structure of ill-structured problems. *Artificial Intelligence, 4,* 181–202.

Thorndike, E. L. (1898). Animal intelligence. An experimental study of the associative process in animals. *The Psychological Review, Series of Monograph Supplements, 2*(8), 551–553.

Voss, J. F., & Post, T. A. (1988). On the solving of ill-structured problems. In M. T. H. Chi, R. Glaser, & M. J. Farr (Eds.), *The nature of expertise* (pp. 261–285). Hillsdale, NJ: Lawrence Erlbaum Associates.

Wikipedia. (2006). *Hausdorff distance*. Retrieved February 6, 2006, from http://en.wikipedia.org/wiki/Hausdorff_distance

Winston, W. (2004). *Operations research: Applications and algorithms* (4th ed.). Belmont, CA: Brooks/Cole.

Wood, P. K. (1983) Inquiring systems and problem structures: Implications for cognitive development. *Human Development, 26,* 249–265.

Chapter 12

Educating for Complex Problem Solving Using Theory of Inventive Problem Solving (TRIZ)

Madara Ogot and Gül E. Okudan
The Pennsylvania State University

The design process is a complex, information-intensive activity requiring the designer to coordinate and integrate a large amount of information from different sources, formats, media, and locations to arrive at a solution for a given design problem. With increasing globalization of products and services, engineering design firms have been forced to improve the productivity of their practices. To date, although advances in technology have been used in support of increasing productivity in latter stages of design (e.g., increased computing power in computer-aided design and engineering [CAD and CAE]), the efforts focusing on the initial stages have been limited (Sim & Duffy, 2004). Among the primary reasons are the following: (a) a lack of understanding of how design is done, and (b) an inadequate consideration of cognitive burdens due to the information-rich design environment.

Although there is consensus on a prescriptive definition of the design process, empirical studies of design have shown departures from the prescriptive process (Günther & Ehrlenspiel, 1999). Further, currently available design systems have various drawbacks as they are developed without an understanding of the design process and are therefore limited in their effectiveness (Sim & Duffy, 2004). In addition, the designers of technological systems to support design activities do not adequately address the cognitive and human factors of their systems (Lang, Dickinson, & Buchal, 2002). One of the important concerns regarding cognitive and human factors is the diversity of design information generated and utilized during the design process, which imposes a considerable burden on the designer (Baya, 1996).

Complicating this situation is the shorter product life cycles and the trend toward mass customization, which are placing increasing demands on design practitioners. In addition, competitive pressures lead to less time spent by designers in traditional mentorship and apprenticeship methods of practice. Therefore, less experienced designers are being given more responsibility for a larger number of design tasks (Okudan & Medeiros, 2005). Yet these designers are typically not well prepared to undertake these responsibilities. Accordingly, the demands from industry regarding this issue influenced one of the Accreditation Board for Engineering and Technology (ABET) 2000 criteria for accreditation that states, "engineering programs must demonstrate that their graduates have: ...an ability to design a system, component, or process to meet desired needs" (ABET, 2002).

This chapter focuses on a potential remedy for this situation: adoption of the Theory of Inventive Problem Solving (TRIZ), a systematic problem-solving methodology that provides a structured process during the initial stages of design and supports the problem-solving process by providing design information that novice designers may not possess. This is especially poignant for undergraduate students whose exposure to design and whose engineering knowledge is still very limited.

ENGINEERING DESIGN AS AN INFORMATION PROCESS: A REVIEW

Engineering design (ED) can be defined as a search for a satisfying solution to a problem that is facilitated through a conversion of customer requirements to design descriptions. For example, Kannapan and Marshek (1991) defined ED as an activity for converting specification descriptions to design descriptions which include manufacturing and product life-cycle related information. Likewise, Maher and Tang (2003) modeled the ED process as a co-evolutionary one, where the problem and solution spaces are iteratively searched using the other space as the fitness function when evaluating the alternatives. They indicated that ED can be formalized as the following: (a) a search when the goals of design are well documented before beginning, (b) exploration when the solution space expands during the course of the design, and (c) a co-evolutionary process when both the problem and solution space change through mutual interaction. Some researchers emphasized the information during this search and conversion process. For example, Huang and Kusiak (1998) define ED simply as the "process of conversion of information" (p. 66). Similarly, Bouchard and Aoussat (2003) viewed the ED process as an information process, where the design problem space is gradually transformed into a solution space.

The emphasis on information during design requires a deeper look into information forms, resources, and so forth. Data is usually described as numerical information or values obtained from scientific experimentation. Data by itself holds no meaning; it becomes information when dealt within a context or when it is interpreted by some data processing system. Knowledge, on the other hand, is information interpreted by the human mind. Likewise, Court (1995) described data as information in numerical form, and information as data within a context (in Ahmed, Blessing, & Wallace, 1999). However, the distinction between the terms is fuzzy and they are often used interchangeably. For example, Ahmed et al. (1999) analyzed the relations among data, information, and knowledge based on an observational study of novice and experienced designers. They concluded that these concepts are relative terms, and the distinction depends on the potential user of the data, information, or knowledge. According to them, awareness separates data and information whereas interpretation separates information and knowledge.

The ED process necessarily involves and is based on various information processing activities (Kryssanov, Tamaki, & Kitamura, 2001). Majumder (1994) defined the ED process as a controlled information evolution process), and emphasized the importance of capturing and managing the information generated to ensure traceability and establish design rationale. The diversity of design information generated and utilized during the ED process imposes considerable burden of information management on the designer (Baya, 1996).

Within an enterprise, information is a valuable resource, one that can be difficult to manage, and the value of which can grow if properly managed (Court, Culley, & McMahon, 1994). Moreover, the quick turnout of products forces efficient management of engineering knowledge so that it can be reused in new product design or redesign (Noel & Brissaud, 2003). As product information continually updates throughout the design process, and also as engineering knowledge available increases every day, effective sharing of design information also gains importance. For example, the exchange of data between the designer and manufacturer is important for effective concurrent engineering. This is especially true when firms concentrate on their core competency and delegate the manufacture and design of other components to outside suppliers. Effective utilization and management of information is important for a design team; they are described as a hub of information flow—receiving information from specialists, suppliers, and standards organizations and passing data to manufacturing engineers and the customer (Court et al., 1994).

In addition, most new product and process designs are variants of previous designs, therefore effective data storage and accessibility is also important. Some advantages of archiving and making available design information and design rationale include the following (Salzberg & Watkins, 1990; Yen, Fruchter, & Leifer, 1999):

- Effective sharing of knowledge between team members and clients.
- Reduction in the time taken by a new member to get acquainted with the context and evolution of the product.
- Improved accessibility to the company's and competitors' product data during the design of new products.
- Knowledge of the firm's manufacturing capabilities to help the designer design products which are easier to manufacture, and so forth.

Understanding the retrieval, transfer, storage, and flow of information during the design process can make it easier to develop design support tools and improve the interaction between designers and design information. Indeed, a number of computer-based tools exist to support the designer during the design process. However, most engineering design tools are applicable only in the later stages of the design process, when a conceptual solution has been generated and the tools are used in the refinement of its form (CAD tools), its performance (simulation tools), or its production (computer-aided manufacturing [CAM] tools). Some of the tools supporting engineering tasks include the following (Noel & Brissaud, 2003):

- Generalist CAD software for geometric modeling of the design—Mostly, engineers are not involved in the design until the model is complete, and these tools promote an understanding of the form, but knowledge of the product is quite poor.
- Knowledge-based engineering applications—for specific and expert tasks. These are limited by restricted application domains.
- Configurable software (such as spreadsheets) to automate routine tasks with simple rules.
- Project management tools to manage, organize, and coordinate the design process.
- Product data management systems to store and manage access to technical data.
- Synchronous collaboration tools to manage distributed collaboration.

After studying the design and software practices of Navy contractors, Sim and Duffy (2004) indicated that the best practices (use of computerized design tools and appropriate physical science analyses) primarily address the later stages of detailed design. They attribute this to the unavailability of design tools for the initial stages of the product development process, specifically "intelligent design assistant" systems.

Traditional ideation methods to solve engineering design problems, such as collaborative sketch (C-sketch) and method 6 to 3 to 5, call on the designer to look inward for inspiration on creative solutions, by drawing on past experiences and knowledge. This can be a daunting task that may or may not be fruitful. This is especially true for undergraduate students whose past engineering knowledge and experiences are still quite limited. Wood, Jensen, Bedzek, and Otto (2001) noted the following:

> Some students do not adapt well to having extremely open-ended problems as the first assignments they encounter. This may not necessarily be because they have trouble with open-ended problems (intellectual maturity), but because they lack the engineering elements to use to fill the blank sheet design. (p. 366)

The design information inherent in TRIZ may make it easier for undergraduate students to tackle open-ended engineering design problems.

SYSTEMATIC CREATIVITY WITH TRIZ

TRIZ is a systematic approach for generating innovative designs to seemingly intractable problems (Altshuller, 2002). It was first developed in Russia by Genrich Altshuller in the early 1960s and 1970s and has been used for many years in Europe and Asia. It is based on the analysis of thousands of patents. These original analyses articulated numerous solution patterns from diverse disciplines. The patterns and the tools are continually being updated by researchers worldwide (see., e.g., Dewulf, Mann, Zlotin, & Zusman, 2003).

TRIZ has been recognized as a concept generation process that can develop clever solutions to complex problems by using the condensed knowledge of thousands of past inventors. It provides steps that allow design teams to explore nontraditional solutions and not restrict themselves to common, comfortable ones. There are several methods in the TRIZ toolset. These include effects, the 76 standard solutions, the 4 principles to resolve physical contradictions, the 40 principles for the solution of technical contradictions, and the patterns and lines for the solutions of technical contradictions. Details of these methods can be found in Altshuller (1988), Savaransky, (2000), Terninko, Zusman, and Zlotin, (1998), Rantanen and Domb (2002), Orloff (2003), and Ogot and Kremer (2004).

Most TRIZ tools employ a four-step process similar to that in Figure 12.1. A design team using TRIZ converts their specific design problem

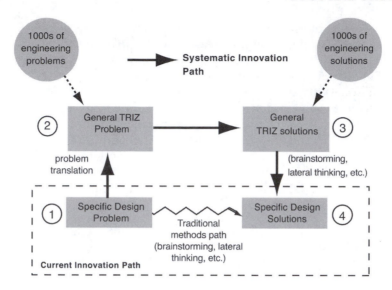

Figure 12.1.   Generation of design solutions using Theory of Inventive Problem Solving (Ogot & Kremer, 2004).

(step 1) to a general TRIZ one (step 2). The latter is based on the analysis and classification of a very large number of problems in diverse engineering fields. The general TRIZ design problem points to corresponding general TRIZ design solutions (step 3) from which the design team can derive solutions for their specific design problem (step 4). Step 4 employs traditional ideation methods, restricted, however, to the proposed general TRIZ solutions from step 3. The power of TRIZ, therefore, is its inherent ability to bring solutions from diverse and seemingly unrelated fields (embedded knowledge) to bear on a particular design problem.

Despite its strength and potential, several barriers exist, however, to the wider adoption of TRIZ in the undergraduate engineering curriculum. These include the following: (a) terminology and modeling methods unique to TRIZ and different from those found in engineering design (Smith, 2003); (b) the method is absent from nearly all introductory and capstone engineering design textbooks and where present, it is only mentioned in passing (e.g., Otto & Wood 2001; Ullman, 2003); (c) most engineering design faculty are unfamiliar with the method; and (d) the undergraduate engineering curriculum is already overcrowded. The latter problem can be addressed by introducing a small subset of the TRIZ toolset as part of existing design courses. Based on our experiences at The Pennsylvania State University, a reduced yet powerful toolset consisted of (a) problem clarification using the system operator and energy-material-signal (EMS) models, and (b) the 40 principles for the solution of technical contradictions. The concepts in the reduced toolset are relatively easy to grasp and can be applied with limited or advanced engineering knowledge, making them ideal for use at any undergraduate or graduate level.

To address the issue of terminology, a narrative was generated where a few unique TRIZ modeling methods were incorporated into methods commonly used in engineering design. For example, ideas from substance-field modeling (unique to TRIZ) were incorporated into black-box modeling already taught in engineering design courses, yielding EMS models (Ogot, 2005). Students therefore do not need to learn radically new modeling methods. The initial results of these efforts have been incorporated into an introductory design text, *Engineering Design: A Practical Guide* (Ogot & Kremer, 2004).

THE REDUCED TRIZ TOOLSET FOR INCORPORATION INTO EXISTING COURSES

As mentioned previously, the reduced toolset consists of problem clarification and the 40 design principles. To use both tools effectively, the steps illustrated in Figure 12.2 should be followed. Despite being only a subset of TRIZ, the steps provide a powerful algorithm for solving ED problems. With reference to Figure 12.2, the steps are as follows:

1. Problem clarification to ensure that the problem is well understood and a solution sought for the right problem. This step ends by determining if the problem can be defined by a *technical contradiction(s)*.

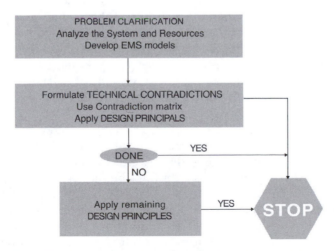

Figure 12.2.   Flow diagram of a simplified algorithm for use of three common Theory of Inventive Problem Solving tools.

2. If a *technical contradiction(s)* can be defined, it is formulated in terms of the *generalized engineering parameters*. Once complete, the *contradiction matrices* are used to determine the most probable *design principles* to solve the problem.
3. If none of the recommended design principles provide a suitable solution or if a technical contradiction cannot be defined, each of the other principles should be investigated in search of a solution.

Each of the TRIZ terms shown earlier in italics are defined and discussed in the following sections.

Problem Clarification—EMS Models and the System Operator

EMS Models.   EMS models are based on black-box modeling commonly used for problem decomposition in engineering design. They are used to analyze the design problem and available resources prior to concept generation, thereby, giving design teams a good understanding of the problem. This includes the relevant materials, systems, signals, and sources of energy, and their interaction with each other. It is only with a clear understanding of the design problem that good solutions can be found. Analysis of engineering systems reveals that they essentially channel or convert energy, material, or signals to achieve a desired outcome. Energy is manifested in various forms, including optical, nuclear, mechanical, electrical, and so forth. Materials represent matter. Signals represent the physical form in which information is channeled. For example, data stored on a hard drive (information) would be conveyed to the computer's processor via an electrical signal. An engineering system can therefore be initially modeled as a black box (Fig. 12.3) with energy, material, and signal inputs and outputs. In black-box modeling, energy is represented by a thin line, material flows by a thick line, and signals by dotted lines as shown. The engineering system, therefore, provides the functional relation between the inputs and the outputs (Pahl & Beitz, 1996).

Problem clarification involves forming a clear understanding of the problem. The overall problem represented by the black box can be broken down into smaller, simpler, subproblems that are easier to solve. Design teams can then focus on those subproblems critical to the success of the project first, deferring others. Subproblems are then mapped to subfunctions for which a design is created. Combining all the designs that achieve each of the subfunctions results in the desired system solution that achieves the overall desired function. Note that the functional decompositions and the resulting black-box diagrams are generic and do not commit the design team to any particular technological working principle. Black-box modeling of existing

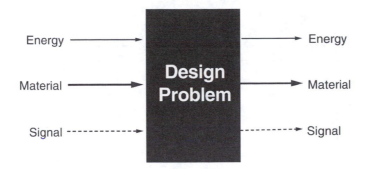

Figure 12.3.   Energy, material, and signal flows through a generic "black-box" design.

systems that are to be redesigned, on the other hand, decomposes the existing system into subsystems, as opposed to subproblems. The subsystems are then translated to subfunctions from where the redesign proceeds.

Example 1—Black-Box Model for Computer Hard Drive.   Consider the computer hard drive shown in Figure 12.4 with the cover removed. Within the hard drive, data is stored on a rotating magnetic disk from which data is read using a read–write head. The head, situated at the end of a moveable actuator arm, can magnetize (write) or sense the magnetic field (read) on the disk. The head floats on the airflow generated by the disk rotation, which maintains a very small gap between the two, preventing contact that may result in data loss. A black-box model of the hard drive in operation is shown in Figure 12.5.

The EMS model extends the black-box model by incorporating symbols that indicate harmful and insufficient energy, material and signal flows within the system. In addition, symbols are also included to allow the modeling of multiple scenarios and discrete time-separated events. Table 12.1 lists the additional symbols found in EMS models with a corresponding description. Detailed examples of EMS models are presented in the following section.

The System Operator.   The System Operator (SO) or multiscreen approach constitutes one of the main TRIZ tools. It provides a view of the current system (design problem) in the context of the supersystem and subsystems, all in the past, present, and future. This minimum view of the SO, therefore, consists of "nine windows" as illustrated in Figure 12.6. The SO allows designers to take a wider view beyond the system or subsystem currently under consideration, to see how they are all interrelated. It can combine different yet mutually complementary approaches: component approach to study the design composition (subsystems, systems, supersystems), structural approach that provides the arrangements of the com-

TABLE 12.1

EMS Model Symbols and Description

Symbol	Description
S	The original system
S^c	A copy of the original system
S^i	A modification of the original system
A	An additive can be material, energy, voids, systems, sub-systems or super-systems
E	The immediate system environment
---▶	Signal flow
▬▶	Material flow
▶	Energy flow
[I]	When placed next to an energy, material or signal flow signifies that flow as being *Insufficient* to perform its desired task adequately.
⌃⌃	A wavy line representing any of the three flows (energy, material, signal) indicates that flow to be harmful to the system receiving it
↓	Placed above a flow indicates a decrease in the flow level from the original problem
↑	Placed above a flow indicates an increase the flow level from the original problem
⊟⊟	Discrete sequential events
⊟	Each slot represents a different scenario and its effects on the EMS model
\$\$	Expensive, too costly
⊘	Not available

Shown are energy-material signal model symbols and description. The system could mean an assembly, subassembly, function, user, and so on.

Figure 12.4.   Image of hard drive with cover removed to reveal magnetic disk, actuator arm, and read–write head.

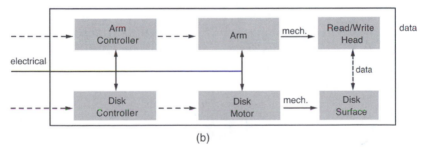

Figure 12.5.   Black-box model of a computer hard drive.

	PAST	PRESENT	FUTURE
SUPER-SYSTEM			
SYSTEM		Current Design Problem	
SUB-SYSTEM			

Figure 12.6.   Nine-window view of the world.

ponent in relation to each other in space and time, and functional coverage such as primary functions, useful functions, and so forth. The SO allows the designer to see the current state of the design and understand how it evolves from the past to the future (Savaransky, 2000).

The time line (past–present–future) in the SO model can be used to model two distinct scenarios: (a) different phases of design operation, and (b) design evolution of the system from the past (what it was before) to the present (its current state) to the future (potential solutions). EMS models can readily be incorporated within the SO framework (Ogot, 2005). With reference to Figure 12.7, EMS models can provide a systematic view of the interconnections between the supersystem, systems, and subsystems for the current design problem.

Example 2—Modeling Design Evolution on the System Operator Time line. The hard drive problem initially presented in Example 1 is extended to illustrate modeling of design evolution on the SO time line as a prelude to redesign. An area of concern arises when a computer that is turned off receives a hard external knock. Without the hard drive disk spinning, the head can be knocked off its rest position making contact with and causing damage to the disk surface. In the rest position, the head is typically held in place by a magnetic latch. When the computer is turned on, the airflow from the disk motion raises the head, and a permanent magnet or electro-magnet system situated at the arm's axes of rotation (the pin) generates enough force to release the arm from the magnetic latch and move the head to wherever data needs to be written or read (Royzen, 1999). In Figure 12.8, this design is modeled in the past time frame.

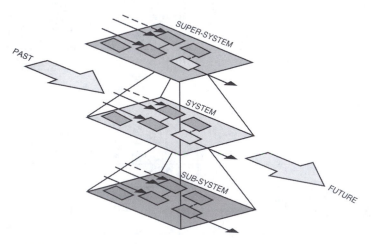

Figure 12.7. Multitiered energy-material-signal model in system operator framework.

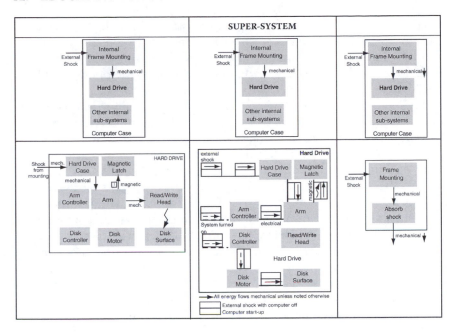

Figure 12.8.   System operator model for hard drive design problem.

The computer is modeled in the system window with the relevant inter-actions of subsystems from the external shock shown. As the damage occurs in the hard drive, it is modeled at the subsystem level. With reference to the EMS symbol definitions listed in Table 12.1, the EMS models track the se-quence of events (the flow) from when the computer chassis receives a hard knock (past-system window) to the point where there is damage (harmful ef-fect shown with a wavy energy line) to the disk surface by the read–write head (past-subsystem window). In the past-subsystem EMS model, the mag-netic field is revealed to be insufficient, and therefore illustrates the defi-ciency in the current design. The figure also includes other available resources that might be useful in a possible redesign. A main advantage af-forded by the use of EMS models over traditional black-box models is their ability to visualize the interactions of all relevant subsystems in the system diagram, and the interaction of all relevant subsubsystems in the subsystems diagram.

A possible solution suggested by Royzen (1999) may be to use a stronger magnetic latch. If this represents the current state of the design's evolution, it is modeled in the present time frame. The hard drive EMS model in the present-subsystem window reveals a new problem generated by this design: By increasing the magnetic strength of the latch, a desirable effect is achieved in response to reduction of damage from external knocks, but it also produces an undesirable effect during system start-up by making it difficult for the arm to be released (in TRIZ terminology, a technical contradiction). Accurately formulating the problem for this design required modeling of both distinct events that are essential to the operation of the hard drive.

Resolution of the initial problem creates a new one at different phases during the normal use of the hard drives. EMS models readily capture multiple operational scenarios in a single diagram, as shown in the present-subsystem window of the SO (Fig. 12.8). The top slot in the multiple scenario symbols represents the computer turned off and receiving a hard knock scenario, whereas the lower slot models the computer start-up. A possible avenue for finding a solution is modeled in the future windows. The future-system model now highlights the internal frame mounting subsystem as a source for a possible solution. The model in the future-subsystem window illustrates an additional feature of the EMS models. Here a subsystem whose function is to "Absorb Shock" is sought. The EMS models allow the inclusion of components that are known (such as the mounting frame) and those that are unknown but whose desired functions are known, in the same model. The six completed SO windows already give a comprehensive view of the initial problem (past), remedies initiated, and current deficiencies (present) as well as avenues to explore for improved designs (future). Similarly, super system models could be included to reveal other redesign possibilities.

Example 3—Modeling Design Operation Phases on the System Operator Time Line.   With reference to Figure 12.9, an automatic clothes washing machine has three main operational phases: loading of clothes and detergent, the wash and rinse cycle, and discharge of dirty water. Common customer complaints on a typical machine include noise, insufficient washing quality, insufficient rinse quality, and damage to clothes (Yashima, Ito, & Kawada, 2002). The model in the loading-system window shows the interaction between the main subsystems during this operational phase. As can be seen, there are no problems associated with this phase. The washing-rinse operational phase has models in the supersystem, system, and subsystem windows. Each model reveals problems that would not be apparent from the others alone. Specifically, in the supersystem model, the washing machine's vibration results in mechanical interactions with the floor (undesired action) that results in noise (undesired effect). This model can be used to trigger intervention solutions at the supersystem level, such as placing the machine on a shock absorbing rubber mat. The model in the system window reveals the source of the mechanical undesired vibration and additional sources of noise. Finally, the subsystem window models the interactions between the agitator, the clothes, and the water-detergent mix. Customer complaints related to washing quality, rinse quality, and clothes damage are revealed by this model. Washing quality and

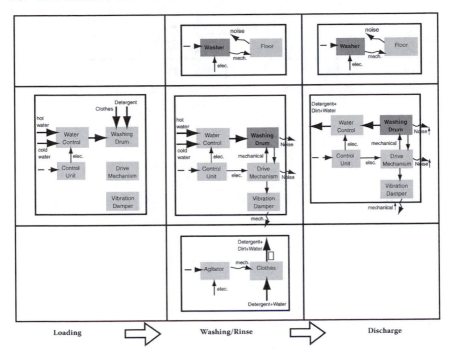

Figure 12.9.   System operator model for washing machine design problem.

clothes damage are related to the interaction of the agitator with the clothes
and the water-detergent mix. The stronger the interaction (increase in mechanical energy), the better the washing quality (good), but this also results in
an increase in damage to the clothes (bad). This forms a technical contradiction from which TRIZ solutions can be sought. Finally, in the discharge-system
window, increased noise and vibration levels are revealed.

Technical Contradictions and the 40 Design Principles

Characteristics of engineering systems can be described by a number of parameters that quantify or measure certain aspects of the design (metrics).
Based on his analysis of patents, Altshuller (2002) developed a list of 39
such parameters shown in Table 12.2. He then reformulated the problems
described by the patents in terms of these general parameters and noted
their solutions. What began to emerge was that nearly all the solutions could
be condensed into 40 general design principles summarized in Table 12.3.
Altshuller postulated that if most design solutions to thousands of design
problems could be condensed to 40 design principles, the reverse should be
true: For a current design problem, the 40 principles could be used to find a
solution.

TABLE 12.2
General Parameters Used to Describe Engineering Systems

1	Weight of moving object	21	Power
2	Weight of stationary object	22	Energy loss
3	Length of moving object	23	Substance loss
4	Length of stationary object	24	Information loss
5	Area of moving object	25	Waste of time
6	Area of stationary object	26	Quantity of a substance
7	Volume of moving object	27	Reliability
8	Volume of stationary object	28	Accuracy of measurement
9	Velocity	29	Manufacturing precision
10	Force	30	Harmful action affecting the design
11	Stress or pressure	31	Harmful actions generated by the design project
12	Shape	32	Manufacturability
13	Stability of object's composition	33	User friendliness
14	Strength	34	Repairability
15	Duration of action generalized by moving object	35	Flexibility
16	Duration of action generalized by stationary object	36	Complexity of design object
17	Temperature	37	Difficulty
18	Brightness	38	Level of automation
19	Energy consumed by moving object	39	Productivity
20	Energy consumed by stationary object		

The general parameters used to describe system metrics can be used to formulate the technical contradictions within a system. Technical contradictions refer to the standard engineering trade-offs (i.e., changing one parameter to make an aspect of the system better makes another aspect of the system worse). Elimination of the technical contradiction may yield the desired final design. How can one eliminate the technical contradiction easily? Do certain contradictions lend themselves to a particular solution irrespective of the actual problem at hand? These are the questions Altshuller (2002) set out to answer. In his patent analysis, Altshuller reformulated the problems in terms of the general parameters listed in Table 12.2 and noted their solutions. He soon realized that certain technical contradictions were associated more frequently with particular design

TABLE 12.3

Theory of Inventive Problem Solving (TRIZ) 40 Design Principles

1	Segmentation	21	Rushing through
2	Removal	22	Turning harm into good
3	Local quality	23	Feedback
4	Asymmetry	24	Go between
5	Joining	25	Self-service
6	Universality	26	Copying principle
7	Nesting	27	Inexpensive short life
8	Counterweight	28	Replacement of a mechanical pattern
9	Preliminary counteraction	29	Hydraulic or pneumatic solution
10	Preliminary action	30	Flexible or fine membranes
11	Protection in advance	31	Use of porous materials
12	Equipotentiality	32	Use color
13	Opposite solution	33	Homogeneity
14	Spheroidality	34	Discarding and regenerating parts
15	Dynamism	35	Altering an objects aggregate state
16	Partial or excessive action	36	Use of phase changes
17	Moving to a new dimension	37	Application of thermal expansion
18	Use of mechanical vibrations	38	Using strong oxidation agents
19	Periodic actions	39	Using an inert atmosphere
20	Uninterrupted useful action	40	Using composite materials

principles than others. He tabulated these observations to create the contradiction matrices.

The contradiction matrices list the most probable design principles for the solution of a particular technical contradiction. A portion of the matrix is shown in Table 12.4. Note that the column headings represent the worsening general parameter in the contradiction and the row headings the improving one. The recommended design principles are listed at the intersection of a particular row and column. For example, if the technical contradiction was defined with parameter 2 (weight of a moving object) as the improving feature and parameter 10 (force) as the worsening feature, the contradiction matrix recommends design principles 8 (counterweight), 10 (preliminary action), 19 (periodic actions), and 35 (altering an object's aggregate state). Then, using the recommended design principles, a design team could employ traditional concept generation techniques (for example, brainstorming) to solve the ED problem. Teams must remain disciplined and restrict them-

TABLE 12.4

Contradiction Matrix Fragment: Parameters 1 to 2 Versus Parameters 1 to 11

| | *Deteriorating Generalized Performance Parameters* | | | | | | | | | | |
	1	*2*	*3*	*4*	*5*	*6*	*7*	*8*	*9*	*10*	*11*
1		15 8			29 17		29 2		2 8	8 10	10 36
		29 34			38 34		40 28		15 38	18 37	37 40
2				10 1		35 30		5 35		8 10	13 29
				29 35		13 7		14 2		19 35	10 18

Note. The columns are the generalized performance parameters that deteriorate as the generalized parameters in the corresponding rows are improved.

selves only to ideas that fall within the current design principle under consideration. In the event that a solution cannot be found from the recommended design principles (recall that these are simply the most probable), the design team should consider all remaining design principles in search of a solution. The principles should be applied in the order of frequency of use as listed in Table 12.5 (Altshuller, 2002). Detail descriptions for each of the design principles and the complete contradiction matrices are in Altshuller (1988), Savaransky, (2000), Terninko et al. (1998), Rantanen and Domb (2002), Orloff (2003), and Ogot and Kremer (2004).

Example 4: Use of the 40 Design Principles and the Contradiction Matrices. A common reversible fastening method is the use of a nut and bolt arrangement. Standard nuts come in a variety of sizes, but generally have a hexagonal shape when viewed along their axis of rotation. Some tools, such as an adjustable wrench or pair of pliers, can accommodate a large range of nut sizes, but may slip and damage the nut being rotated, cause injury to the user, or both. As a result, fixed-size wrenches or sockets are often preferred. Socket sizes are not adjustable, and therefore sockets are usually maintained as a set of varying sizes. The entire set is often carried around from job to job. This is cumbersome and quite often one or more of the sockets are misplaced.

Several solutions have been attempted to overcome these problems. For example, some wrenches are dual-ended, each end being of a different size, which cuts in half the number of separate tools needed. Some automobile lug wrenches are designed in the shape of a cross and thus are able to accommodate four differently-sized sockets. The main shortcomings of these solutions, however, are that only a small number of sizes can be accommodated before the tool becomes too cumbersome to use, or the configuration of the tool makes it difficult to use in tight working spaces.

TABLE 12.5

Descending Order for Frequency of Design Principle Use As Revealed
Through Patent Analysis (Altshuller, 2002)

Descending Order ⇒
35, 10, 1, 28, 2, 15, 19, 18, 32, 13, 26, 3, 27, 29, 34, 16, 40, 24, 17, 6, 14, 22, 39, 4, 30, 7, 36, 25, 11, 31, 38, 8, 5, 7, 21, 23, 12, 33, 9, 20

Based on the general engineering parameters (Table 12.2), one can formulate the following technical contradiction: To improve the wrench's 35 (flexibility), 33 (user friendliness) worsens as the tools become too cumbersome. The contradiction matrices suggest that the most likely applicable design principles are as follows: 15 (dynamism), 16 (partial or excessive action), 1 (segmentation), 7 (nesting), and 34 (discarding and regenerating parts). A solution proposed by Layaou (2004) uses three of the suggested design principles: 7, 15, and 1. With reference to Figures 12.10 and 12.11, a multiple-size nut driver comprises a handle (7) and a socket portion (11). The socket portion is composed of nested hexagonal sockets (11) that can slide relative to each other along the driver's longitudinal axis. Each of the sockets can slide forward to an operative position and backward to a retracted position. The handle includes a socket selector (15) that holds a selected socket in the forward operative position while allowing unselected sockets to retract. The selected socket is then placed over a nut, loosening or tightening the nut when the socket is rotated by the handle.

The technical contradiction could have been stated in other ways. For example, to improve the 33 (user friendliness) of the wrenches, 7 (volume of a moving object) worsens as the tools become larger and cumbersome. The contradiction matrices suggest that the most likely applicable design principles are as follows: 1 (segmentation), 16 (partial or excessive action), 35 (altering an object's aggregate state), and 15 (dynamism). Notice the significant overlap between these principles and those previously suggested.

EXPLOITING ONE'S CREATIVE POTENTIAL TO SOLVE ENGINEERING DESIGN PROBLEMS: AN UNDERGRADUATE PERSPECTIVE

Over the past 20 years, engineering design has been viewed to involve more "science" and less "art." Although engineering design requires creativity and inventiveness ("the art"), engineering design is a process that can be taught, learned, and successfully implemented to solve engineering problems ("the science") (Dym, 1999; Ogot & Kremer, 2004). What is a person's creative po-

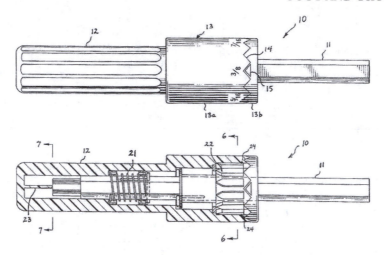

Figure 12.10.   Side view of multisized nut driver (Layaou, 2004).

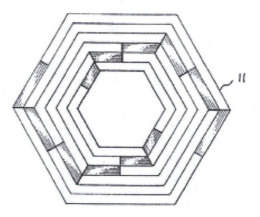

Figure 12.11.   End view of multisized nut driver showing nested hexagonal sockets (Layaou, 2004).

tential? Can a person learn to be more creative by better exploiting their creative potential? Santamarina stated that, "There are skills that can be learned … every student can be creative, better at problem solving and invention if they are aware of their own creativity and how to improve it" (McGraw, 2004, p. 30). Associations between an increase in comfort level and a rise in exploitation of creative potential can be found in the literature. For example, a personality instrument that has been used to loosely measure an individual's creative potential is the Herman Brain Dominance Instrument. The scores and profiles from using the instrument reveal four different ways of thinking and "knowing:" A = analytical-logical-quantitative, B = sequential-organized-detailed, C = interpersonal-sensory-kinesthetic, and D = innovative-holistic-conceptual thinking.

A longitudinal study at the University of Toledo conducted on first-year engineering students from 1990 to 1993 revealed a decrease in the extent of B thinking (corresponding to plug-and-chug problem solving) and a corresponding increase in D thinking (creative) from tests conducted before and after the students went through a newly introduced first-year creative problem-solving course (Lumsdaine & Lumsdaine, 1995). The authors of the study suggest that the shift may have been due to the very plastic nature of the brain that undergoes change with each use, and can therefore result in thinking preferences changes. Preferred thinking modes require less energy in the brain and are usually more enjoyable. Students who enjoyed the design experience in the first-year course may have therefore shifted their thinking preferences to D (Lumsdaine & Lumsdaine, 1995).

This and other studies, such as Wilde (1993), suggest that an increased level of creative activity in the engineering curriculum with an associated comfort level among the students may indeed change the way they think, and thereby increase the exploitation of their creative potential. Comfort level within a course has some correlation to the extent to which teaching styles, methods, and activities match the learning styles and preferences of the students. Ogot and Kremer (2006b) looked into the relation among different stages of the TRIZ problem-solving process and student learning preferences as captured by the Myers-Briggs Type Indicator (MBTI; Briggs-Myers, 1979) personality instrument to determine if a broader segment of the student population would experience comfort in at least one stage of the process as compared to the sole use of traditional ideation methods such as brainstorming.

The MBTI personality instrument is based on Jungian typology of personality types. It tries to measure in what ways people process information and make decisions, that is, their cognitive style. Four dimensions in this typology form continuous scales (Briggs-Myers, 1979; Felder & Brent, 2005): (a) introvert (try things out, focus on ideas) to extrovert (think things through, focus on people), (b) intuitive (imaginative and concept oriented) to sensing (practical, detailed oriented, focus on facts and procedures), (c) feeling (make decisions based on emotion) to thinking (make decisions based on logic and rules), and (d) perceiving (adapt easily to changing conditions, wait for complete data to reach conclusions) to judging (follow agendas, can reach conclusions with in-complete data). The first two dimensions relate more to ways of behaving and approaching problems, whereas the latter two relate more to emotional and personal responses. Combined they can describe 16 different learning styles.

Looking at the dominant personality trait along each of the four MBTI dimensions during the four stages of ideation with TRIZ reveals the following (Ogot & Kremer, 2006b).

Step 1—Problem Clarification

Problem clarification seeks to find the true nature and cause of the problem. It ensures that ideation efforts are directed at solving the right problem. It involves performing needs assessment, external search for what has been done to solve the problem, in this or similar contexts, determination of what the competition has done, and may include product dissection and reverse engineering, and so forth. Visual aids such as black-box modeling and EMS models may be used to clarify the true nature of the design problem. In the context of the MBTI model, this step could be said to be most comfortable with individuals whose dominant personalities are Extrovert, Sensing, Thinking, and Perceiving (ESTP; Fig. 12.12).

Step 2—Abstraction to General Theory of Inventive Problem Solving Problem

The details will change depending on the TRIZ tool employed, but the general approach is the same. For technical contradictions and the contradiction matrix, the designer first determines from the list of 39 general TRIZ parameters that can be used to describe engineering systems, which ones best capture their design problem abstracting the specific problem(s) to a general TRIZ problem(s). In the context of the MBTI model, this step could be said to be most comfortable with individuals whose dominant personalities are Introvert, Intuitive, Thinking, and Perceiving (INTP; Fig. 12.12).

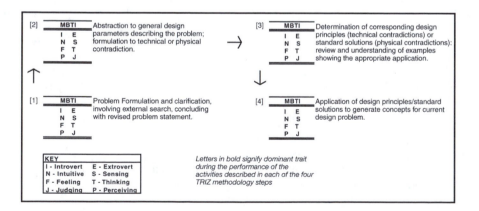

Figure 12.12. Dominant learning style dimensions in each of the four general Theory of Inventive Problem Solving problem-solving steps using technical contradictions and the 40 design principles in the context of the MBTI models.

Step 3—Determination of Corresponding Design Principles

A better understanding of design principles is facilitated by reviewing application examples. One of the design principles recommended by the contradiction matrices in Example 4 was 1 (segmentation). To get a better understanding of the principle, the design team would be able to bring up several examples illustrating how the principle was used. A sample illustrative example for segmentation is shown in Figure 12.13. In the context of the MBTI model, this step could be said to be most comfortable with individuals whose dominant personalities are Extrovert, Sensing, Thinking, and Judging (ESTJ; Fig. 12.12).

Step 4—Application of Design Principles to Concept Generation

Concept generation based on identified design principles follows using traditional ideation techniques such as brainstorming. In the context of the MBTI model, this step could be said to be most comfortable with individuals whose dominant personalities are Introvert, Intuitive, Thinking, and Perceiving (INTP; Fig. 12.12).

Alternatively, looking at the sole use of traditional idea methods such as brainstorming, method 6–3–5, C-sketch, and so forth, the designer goes directly from step 1 problem formulation and clarification to step 4 concept generation, touching on fewer preferred MBTI learning styles. It is important to see these in the context of engineers' work, and their personality

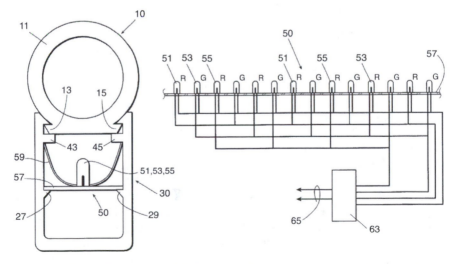

Figure 12.13. Presentation of design principle 1, segmentation, as an abstract principle in conjunction with concrete examples to aid in understanding (Slayden, 2002).

types. In a typical set of engineering students, there is a higher percentage of ISTJ (19%) and ESTJ (11%) than any other type, and that there is much more INTJ and INTP types than estimated in the general population (Capretz, 2002). Further, Capretz (2002) predicted work-related implications of these results as

> ... NTs are heavily represented in R&D organizations. In most companies NTs will be attracted to areas engaged in major design activities. However, once all of the conceptual work on a project has been done, many NTs prefer to start working on something new. ... NTs always seem to be looking for new challenges, whereas STs are comfortable with applying previous experience in order to solve new problems, they are realistic, investigative, but conventional. (p. 171)

Given this information, and because TRIZ provides tools for STs to combine conventional approaches to new problems, and for NTs to generate ideas on how TRIZ design principles can be applied to the problem at hand, in comparison to the application of traditional methods as the sole creative problem-solving tool, providing TRIZ knowledge might mobilize idea generation by everybody in a student design team.

CASE STUDY—IMPLEMENTATION OF A REDUCED TOOLSET ALGORITHM AT THE FIRST YEAR

The previous sections have suggested that significant gains can be obtained in students' ability to solve engineering design problems through the use of TRIZ as part of an existing design course. The main benefits brought on by TRIZ are through (a) embedded design knowledge, and (b) increase in student learning comfort through broader matching of learning styles, as compared to sole use of traditional methods. The case study that follows was able to show ideation gains by using TRIZ. However, it was not designed to discern the extent to which each of the two factors mentioned earlier contributed to those gains.

Although there has been anecdotal evidence that TRIZ can help increase ideation in engineering design problem solving among students, no formal studies could be found in the literature. The case study presents a brief summary of results from a formal ideation assessment of two cohorts of first-year students in the same introductory engineering design course. Each cohort was in different sections and worked on the same engineering design problem over a 6-week period. One set of students was exposed to TRIZ and the other was not. Details of the study can be found in Ogot and Kremer (2006a). The TRIZ cohort consisted of two course sections of 32 students each for a total of 64 students. Three sections totaling 96 students formed the non-TRIZ cohort. Each section was divided into teams of four students each totaling 16 and 24 TRIZ and non-TRIZ teams, respectively.

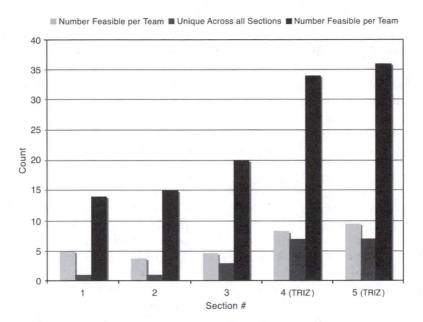

Figure 12.14. Comparison of ideation divergence among Theory of Inventive Problem Solving and non-Theory of Inventive Problem Solving student cohorts.

Although there are numerous metrics for comparison of ideation effectiveness such as quantity, novelty, variety, and quality (Shah, Vargas-Hernandez, & Smith, 2003), the study focused on the first two: (a) quantity—how many feasible ideas each team produced, and (b) novelty—how many of those ideas are unique to that team only. These metrics were embodied in the following results:

1. How many unique feasible ideas were generated per course section.
2. How many unique feasible concepts each team generated.
3. How many feasible design concepts were unique to each experimental cohort (TRIZ teams vs. non-TRIZ teams).

The fume hood design problem, on which the comparison was based, was focused on the regulation of the airflow through the hood to produce a redesigned, cost-effective, efficient, and safe way to offer reliable protection from harmful vapors. Maintaining accurate and constant airflow velocity at the face of the fume hood requires an effective design to account for the changing of the size of the open face area. A comparison along the three measures for TRIZ and non-TRIZ teams is presented in Figure 12.14. From the data in the figure, each TRIZ section generated an average of 35 unique solutions, a 115% increase over non-TRIZ sections that averaged 16.3 solutions per section. A comparison of the number of unique feasible concepts produced per team reveals that TRIZ teams averaged 8.94 feasible concepts per team, a 102% increase over non-TRIZ teams that averaged 4.42 feasible concepts. Finally, TRIZ teams generated 14 design concepts unique among all teams (including other TRIZ teams) as compared to 5 from non-TRIZ teams. If one takes into account the fact that there were 24 non-TRIZ students teams as compared 16 TRIZ teams, the effectiveness of TRIZ as a tool in engineering problem solving is significant.

CONCLUDING REMARKS

Engineering design typically involves the solution of a series of interrelated complex problems that do not have a unique solution. Their solution requires design teams to have the ability to pool knowledge from diverse fields including mathematics, the basic and applied sciences, as well as engineering fundamentals. Solutions to most engineering problems are based on solutions to previous similar problems in the same or different field. The ability to effectively synthesize and transfer this knowledge from the solution of a previous problem and then apply it to the current one comes with experience and knowledge amassed over a period of time. For undergraduate students, both the knowledge and experience are lacking. Systematic creativity methods, such as TRIZ, that have built-in information, can therefore be used to increase their creative output—and therefore their capacity to solve complex problems. TRIZ's structured approach makes it easy to follow and implement. Although it provides a vast and powerful set of tools, this chapter has presented a reduced toolset that is easy to learn and can be incorporated into an existing design course. Our experience at The Pennsylvania State University has shown that the approach can lead to a significant increase in generation of solution concepts to complex engineering design problems.

REFERENCES

Accreditation Board for Engineering and Technology. (2002). *Criteria for accrediting engineering problems*. Retrieved April 10, 2003, from http://www.abet.org/Images/Criteria/E1%200304%20eac%20criteria%2011–15-02.Pdf

Ahmed, S., Blessing, L., & Wallace, K. (1999). The relationships between data, information and knowledge based on a preliminary study of engineering designers. *ASME 12th International Design Theory And Methodology Conference, 3*, 121–130.

Altshuller, G. S. (1988). *Creativity as an exact science: The theory of the solution of inventive problems*. New York: Gordon & Breach.

Altshuller, G. S. (2002). *40 principles: TRIZ keys to technical innovation*. Worcester, MA: Technical Innovation Center.

Baya, V. (1996). *Information handling behavior of designers during conceptual design: Three experiments*. Palo Alto, CA: Stanford University.

Bouchard, C., & Aoussat, A. (2003). Design process perceived as an information process to enhance the introduction of new tools. *International Journal of Vehicle Design, 31,* 162–175.

Briggs-Myers, I. (1979). *Introduction to type*. Gainesville, FL: Center for Applications of Psychological Type.

Capretz, L. F. (2002). Is there an engineering type? *World Transactions on Engineering Technology and Education, 1,* 169–172.

Court, A. W. (1995). *The modeling and classification of information for engineering designers*. Bath, England: University of Bath.

Court, A. W., Culley, S. J., & McMahon, C. A. (1994). The importance of information transfer between the designer and the manufacturer. *International Conference on Flexible Automation And Integrated Manufacturing, X,* X.

Dewulf, S., Mann, D., Zlotin, B., & Zusman, A., (2003). *Matrix 2003*. Leper, Belgium: Creax.

Dym, C. (Ed.). (1999). Designing design education for the 21st century. *Proceedings of a Workshop, Harvey Mudd College, X,* X.

Felder, R. M., & Brent, R. (2005). Understanding student differences. *Journal of Engineering Education, 94,* 57–72.

Günther, J., & Ehrlenspiel, K. (1999). Comparing designers from practice and designers with systematic design education. *Design Studies, 20,* 439–451.

Huang, C.-C., & Kusiak, A. (1998) Modularity in design of products and systems. *IEEE Transactions on Systems, Man, and Cybernetics Part A: Systems and Humans, 28,* 66–77.

Kannapan, S. M., & Marshek, K. M. (1991) Design synthetic reasoning: A methodology for mechanical design. *Research In Engineering Design, 2,* 221–238.

Kryssanov, V. V., Tamaki, H., & Kitamura, S. (2001) Understanding design fundamentals: How synthesis and analysis drive creativity, resulting in emergence. *Artificial Intelligence In Engineering, 15,* 329–342.

Lang, S. Y. T., Dickinson, J., & Buchal, R. O. (2002). Cognitive factors in distributed design. *Computers In Industry, 48,* 89–98.

Layaou, R. E. (2004). Multiple-Size Nut Driver, *U.S. Patent No. 6,732,615*. Washington, DC: U.S. Patent and Trademark Office.

Lumsdaine, M., & Lumsdaine, E. (1995). Thinking preferences of engineering students: Implications for curriculum restructuring. *ASEE Journal of Engineering Education, 84,* 194–204.

Maher, M. L., & Tang, H. H. (2003). Co-Evolution as a computational and cognitive model of design. *Research In Engineering Design—Theory Applications and Concurrent Engineering, 14,* 47–63.

Majumder, D. (1994). *Towards enhanced information support for engineering design tasks (direct manipulation)*. Atlanta: Georgia Institute of Technology.

McGraw, D. (2004). Expanding the mind. *ASEE Prism,* 30–36.

Noel, F., & Brissaud, D. (2003). Dynamic data sharing in a collaborative design environment. *International Journal of Computer Integrated Manufacturing, 16,* 546–556.

Ogot, M. (2005). Problem clarification in TRIZ using energy-material-signal models. *Journal of TRIZ in Engineering Design, 1,* 27–39.

Ogot, M., & Kremer, G. (2004). *Engineering design: A practical guide*. Victoria, British Columbia: Trafford Publishers.

Ogot, M., & Kremer, G. (2006a). Integrating systematic creativity into first year engineering design curriculum. *International Journal of Engineering Education, 22,* 109–115.

Ogot, M., & Kremer, G. (2006b). Systematic creativity methods: A learning styles perspective. *International Journal of Engineering Education, 22*(3), 556–576.

Okudan, G., & Medeiros, D. (2005). Facilitating collaborative design: A review on design representations and workstations. *Proceedings of the ASME Design Automation Conference,2A,* 71–79.

Orloff, M. (2003). *Inventive thinking through TRIZ: A practical guide.* Berlin, Germany: Springer.

Otto, K., & Wood, K. (2001). *Product design: Techniques in reverse engineering and new product development.* Upper Saddle River, NJ: Prentice Hall.

Pahl, G., & Beitz, W. (1996). *Engineering design: A systematic approach* (2nd ed.). New York: Springer-Verlag.

Rantanen, K., & Domb, E. (2002). *Simplified TRIZ: New problem-solving applications for engineers and manufacturing professionals.* Boca Raton, FL: CRC Press.

Royzen, Z. (1999). Tool, object, product (TOP) function analysis. *TRIZ Journal, 9.*

Salzberg, S., & Watkins, M. (1990). Managing information for concurrent engineering: Challenges and barriers. *Research in Engineering Design—Theory Applications and Concurrent Engineering, 2,* 35–52.

Savaransky, S. D. (2000). *Engineering of creativity: Introduction to TRIZ methodology of inventive problem solving.* Boca Raton, FL: CRC Press.

Shah, J. J., Vargas-Hernandez, N., & Smith, S. (2003). Metrics for measuring ideation effectiveness. *Design Studies, 24,* 111–143.

Sim, S. K., & Duffy, A. H. B. (2004). Evolving a model of learning in design. *Research in Engineering Design, 15,* 40–61.

Slayden, J. (2002). Simulated neon light using LEDs. *U.S. Patent No. 6,361,186.* Washington, DC: U.S. Patent and Trademark Office.

Smith, E. (2003, March). From Russia with TRIZ: An evolving design methodology defined in terms of a contradiction. *ASME Mechanical Engineering Magazine, 125,* 20–23.

Terninko, J., Zusman, A., & Zlotin, B. (1998). *Systematic innovation: An introduction to TRIZ.* Boca Raton, FL: St. Lucie Press.

Ullman, D. (2003). *The mechanical design process.* New York: McGraw-Hill.

Wilde, D. J. (1993). Changes among ASEE creativity workshop participants. *Journal of Engineering Education, 82,* 167–170.

Wood, K. L., Jensen, D., Bedzek, J., & Otto, K. (2001). Reverse engineering and redesign: Courses to incrementally and systematically teach design. *Journal of Engineering Education, 90,* 363–374.

Yashima, H., Ito, T., & Kawada, H. (2002). Innovative product development process integrating QFD and TRIZ. *International Journal of Production Research, 40,* 1031–1050.

Yen, S. J., Fruchter, R., & Leifer, L. J. (1999). Facilitating tacit knowledge capture and reuse in conceptual design activities. *Proceedings of the 12th International Conference on Design Theory and Methodology* [CD-ROM]. New York: American Society of Mechanical Engineers.

Chapter 13

Preparing Students to Work Effectively as Members of Interdisciplinary Design Teams

Alok Bhandari, Larry E. Erickson, and E. Marie Steichen
Kansas State University

William A. Jacoby
University of Missouri–Columbia

Many significant achievements have resulted from interdisciplinary teams working cooperatively to design and build new instruments, equipment, structures, manufacturing plants, and public infrastructure systems. From turbo jets to nanotech bandages used to treat burn victims, the projects and products that engineers in industry work on today are created in multidisciplinary teams. However, as any experienced engineer will tell you, the differences between disciplines are much more distinct in engineering education than in engineering practice. Today's engineering graduates need to have the ability to apply the principles of engineering design and solve new problems while working cooperatively as members of interdisciplinary teams. Successful engineering professionals approach new problems with a positive attitude, a creative mind, a willingness to study the problem and related literature, and the ability to listen and learn from their coworkers.

Multidisciplinary teams with a systems perspective are able to draw on the expertise of cooperating individuals to develop new approaches (Haythornthwaite, 2005; Leiffer, Graff, & Gonzalez, 2005). Learning that may be essential for innovation often takes place as interdisciplinary teams meet, ask questions, suggest solutions, and share their knowledge about the design problem. The group dynamics that leads to innovative solutions by multidisciplinary teams includes regular meetings with effective communication of technical information (Smith, Sheppard, Johnson, & Johnson, 2005).

The importance of multidisciplinary teams in industry has prompted accrediting bodies, industry advisory boards, and professional societies to place as much importance on developing communication and interpersonal skills as on technical knowledge and abilities (Fornaro, Heil, & Peretti, 2001). Industry seeks to employ new graduates who are able to begin contributing to teams with a minimum amount of training and some familiarity with "real-world" situations (Dvorak & Dunning, 1994). Additionally, multidisciplinary teams have been identified in industry as a critical feature which provides "better results, shorter decision cycle times, reduced costs and increased profits" (Sutton & Thompson, 1998, p. 1).

Engineering students often work in teams on engineering laboratory experiments and in design classes. In some assignments, one report from the team is requested. This requires students to work cooperatively and accept changes in content or format as the report is prepared. Interaction among students in a group setting is reported as a primary predictor of academic development (Smith et al., 2005). Students also cite that interaction with other students is a dominant factor in personal development and learning satisfaction (Dvorak et al., 1994).

The importance of interdisciplinary teams in engineering education has been recognized and strongly advocated in recent reports and publications (Accreditation Board for Engineering and Technology [ABET], 2005; National Academy of Engineering [NAE], 2004, 2005). Dym, Agogino, Eris, Frey, and Leifer (2005) provided a recent review of design education and learning in design classes and Griffin, Griffin, and Llewellyn (2004) demonstrated that the size of design teams impacts the learning experience. From a broader perspective, it can be argued that the cultural diversity of the American population created a societal dynamic that helped the United States to become the world leader in technology and innovation in the 20th century. Advances in transportation and communication have facilitated exchange of ideas and collaboration worldwide, so this inherent advantage is diminished. More formalized approaches toward providing multicultural competency development and harnessing diversity may be beneficial. This chapter explores the learning science associated with the education of engineering students as members of interdisciplinary design teams.

LEARNING OBJECTIVES

A number of important learning objectives have been articulated for students who enroll in design courses and participate as members of interdisciplinary teams (Ellis, 2003; Miller & Olds, 1994; Steichen et al., 2006). Although some differences are expected from one degree program to the next, after completing a sequence of one or more design courses, the student should be able to do the following:

1. Apply science and engineering principles to understand, evaluate, and design products, processes, and systems.
2. Research and use nontextual resources to solve problems.
3. Communicate progress and results in the form of written reports and oral presentations.
4. Participate as an effective member of a multidisciplinary design team.
5. Learn about and use models, software, published data, and technical publications in the design process.
6. Include consideration of issues relating to environmental health, safety, and sustainability in the design process.
7. Appreciate the importance of team chartering, scheduling, and coordination, and meeting deadlines.

In some educational programs, the methods and approaches of project management are considered sufficiently important to be included as a course in the engineering curriculum (Leiffer et al., 2005). Paul (2005) included legal and ethical issues, contractual relationships, liability, and professional registration in a civil engineering capstone course. Ochs, Watkins, and Booth (2001) included entrepreneurial education in an Integrated Product Development Program which consisted of multidisciplinary teams of students in engineering, business, and design arts. Although a focus on invention and innovation is important in engineering design, it is not typically included in the learning objectives of courses (Wang & Kleppe, 2001).

INTERDISCIPLINARY TEAMS IN INDUSTRY

The growing complexities of modern "real-world" problems faced by industry, government, and universities have given rise to the need for interdisciplinary teams (Miller & Olds, 1994). Most engineering design in industry is carried out by members of interdisciplinary teams who make use of design software and the past experience of the team members and other professional consultants. Often several disciplines are represented on the team because of the knowledge needed for the project.

Because of the importance of teams, Tau Beta Pi, the engineering honor society, includes team chartering and defining a team's own charter in the Engineering Futures program that is delivered to engineering students throughout the United States (Tau Beta Pi, 2005). Some universities use case histories to teach students about interdisciplinary design processes in industry (Chinowsky & Robinson, 1995). Recruiters from industry prefer to hire graduates with experience in working on design problems in teams because these individuals are better prepared to be members of industrial teams (Dym et al., 2005). Walker, Cordray, King, and Fries (2005) found that multidisciplinary teamwork was mentioned often by design experts when considering interpersonal skills that are important for design work.

Miller and Olds (1994) reported the results of an industrial questionnaire sent to 177 companies and government agencies to gain a better understanding of industrial needs. About 75% of design teams were multidisciplinary in nature. Six attributes (technical knowledge, communication skills, ability to work in small teams, ability to self educate, ability to consider nontechnical constraints, and ability to accommodate a multidisciplinary approach to problem solving) were all considered to be important by all of the 67 respondents. One of the positive aspects of being assigned to an interdisciplinary team is the new knowledge that is gained by the individuals. Engineers with 10 years of service with considerable experience working on teams have become more versatile and have greater ability to contribute to projects because of their past experiences. The importance of multidisciplinary teams in industry is well established, and such teams are very common for addressing real problems.

McMasters (2004) stated that the most significant design developments have been the invention of integrated product teams and systems engineering. He reported that bringing together interdisciplinary groups of the right people (including customers) and insisting that they work as fully cooperative teams has turned out to work rather well for the design of new airplanes.

Levi and Slem (1995) have examined professional level teams in research and development organizations and the role of management in promoting teamwork. They reported that the complexity of new products makes teamwork a necessity in research, development, and design. The authors concluded that team leadership should be appropriate for the situation. For significant interdisciplinary projects, teams with an appropriate leader performed better than self-managed teams. A corporate culture which encourages participation in teams and employee empowerment is beneficial. In selecting team members, it is important to consider the ability of the individuals to work effectively on a team as well as the professional skills that are needed for the assignment.

DESIGN EDUCATION WITH TEAMS

Design teams have been common in engineering education for more than 10 years (Dutson, Todd, Magleby, & Sorensen, 1997; Dym et al., 2005; Todd, Magleby, Sorensen, Swan, & Anthony, 1995). However, because design courses, which are taught for a particular major, do not have students from other majors, the teams are often composed of individuals with similar disciplinary preparation. In this environment, students can accomplish all of the learning objectives except for the ability to work effectively on an interdisciplinary team. Design education with real problems in a team environment involves active learning, and it includes interaction among team members as well as interaction with other professionals. Learning science professionals continue to emphasize the importance of active learning in engineering education (Martinazzi & Samples, 1997).

The ABET's third accreditation criterion highlights the importance to industry of developing teamworking skills in engineering education. Universities are approaching this curricular challenge in a variety of ways including "training in team functioning" integrated into the curriculum (Welker & Tymon, 2004). Other strategies include working in teams on projects and providing learning objectives that address components of effective multidisciplinary team functioning (Felder & Brent, 2003; Lovgren & Racer, 2000; Steichen et al., 2006).

In many capstone design courses, efforts are made to challenge students with real problems. The Sunrayce solar car competition involves teams of students designing and building a solar powered automobile for a competitive race (Carroll & Hirtz, 2002; Catalano & Tonso, 1996). The Engineering Projects in Community Service (EPICS) program provides a service-learning experience (Coyle, Jamieson, & Oakes, 2006; Jamieson, Coyle, Harper, Delp, & Davies, 1998; Laeser, Moskal, Knecht, & Lasich, 2003; Oakes, Coyle, & Jamieson, 2000). Many universities have industrial partners that supply real problems for student design teams (Amon, Finger, Siewiorek, & Smailagic, 1996; McDonald et al., 1996; Farrell, Hesketh, Slater, & Savelski, 2004; Knox et al., 1995; Myszka, 2003). In some cases, "real-world" design problems are developed by faculty based on research or consulting needs. Some of the aforementioned problems come with beneficial professional expertise that is provided because of the potential useful information in the final design report. Bhandari, Reddi, Erickson, Hutchinson, and Steward (2004) described the development of a geo-environmental engineering capstone design course for a 12-credit-hr geo-environmental certificate program. This course was cotaught by three instructors from civil engineering, chemical engineering, and biological and agricultural engineering departments. The course was structured around "real-world" design problems that were solved by multidisciplinary teams of students. Students enrolled in this course represented biochemistry, chemical engineering, and civil engineering disciplines (Steichen et al., 2006). Schrader and Koelliker (1996) described a capstone experience for a secondary major in Natural Resources and Environmental Sciences where student teams representing different disciplines, background experiences, expertise, and viewpoints collaborated to solve natural resource problems in the context of watershed management. Design education, where teams work on "real-world" projects, is enhanced when professionals volunteer their services as mentors or consultants (Knox et al., 1995). In some cases, graduate students are members of design teams along with undergraduate students (Schultz & Johnson, 2005). Ollis (2004) has reported that the universities participating in the National Science Foundation (NSF)-funded SUCCEED program have developed a variety of multidisciplinary design courses. The environment needed for creating an effective multidisciplinary design course is described.

Multidisciplinary design teams may include students from more than one course (Fornaro et al., 2001; King, El-Sayed, Sanders, & El-Sayed, 2005). The size of teams varies from about 3 students up to more than 10 (Brickell, Porter, Reynolds, & Cosgrove, 1994; Laeser et al., 2003; Schultz & Johnson, 2005). In their study of methods to select teams of students, Brickell et al. (1994) found that teams that are selected to be heterogeneous with respect to grade point average and homogeneous with respect to their interest were the most effective based on group performance, attitude, and efficiency in use of time. Laeser et al. (2003) examined the effects of gender composition of engineering design teams. At the freshman level, mixed gender teams displayed the lowest level of performance. Laeser et al. (2003) suggested that students may need to learn to work effectively in mixed gender teams, and that some instruction may be needed. Ingram and Parker (2002) argued that factors other than gender and independent of a team's gender composition exert a greater influence on collaborative learning. Dym et al. (2005) reviewed gender and other diversity factors and concluded that maximizing diversity is beneficial.

The first of the learning objectives listed earlier is to be able to design products, processes, and systems. Woods et al. (1997) reviewed 25 years of research on problem-solving skills, including those needed for engineering design, and they developed core units of courses in the curriculum to provide instruction for more than 30 targeted problem-solving skills. Examples related to engineering design include "defining real problems, coping with ambiguity, simplifying and generalizing, 'optimum sloppiness', effective teams and team building, reasoning, and drawing conclusions" (p. 79).

Marin, Armstrong, and Kays (1999) presented their concepts of an optimal capstone design experience and provided constructive ideas with respect to mentoring design teams. Frequent interaction is needed for good mentoring. This can include team meetings, oral progress reports, written progress reports, and individual meetings.

Dym et al. (2005) presented their work on teaching engineering design in a team environment. They examined design thinking and multidisciplinary design discourse that should occur at team meetings and found that students should be encouraged to raise questions and discuss alternatives.

Koen (1994) described a strategy for teaching engineering design that is consistent with the theory of behavior modification. He presented some heuristics that can be used to improve design education. For example, the strategy, "attack the weak link," advocates looking for a single change that will cause the greatest improvement.

Proactive subsets of the student population practice all seven of the educational objectives stated earlier as members of teams competing with other engineering schools. In addition, team leaders emerge and are afforded opportunities to hone all-important leadership skills. Student teams design, build, and race solar cars (American Solar Challenge) and formula cars (Society of Automotive Engineers). Robotics is also an effective vehicle for this type of learning experience (Robotic Technology and Engineering Challenge, American Society of Mechanical Engineers), as are a wide variety of process technologies.

INTEGRATING MULTIDISCIPLINARY TEAMS

When team members have different disciplinary education, there is a greater chance of communication failure because of the difficulty associated with special terms that may not be understood by all members of the team (Fornaro et al., 2001; Miskimins, 2003). There is a greater need to define notation and provide clear oral presentations with appropriate visual aids (Martinazzi & Samples, 1997; Todd et al., 1995). If team members provide portions of a complex design, one or more team members must work to integrate the parts into a complete design, which can be reviewed by all participants.

Where the design addresses a multidisciplinary problem, there is often a need to have several members of the team jointly define the problem, find important literature, and share ideas on proposed designs. Peer learning among team members helps overcome technical language barriers and retention of subject matter from other disciplines (Schmuck & Schmuck, 1997). This increases understanding of terminology essential to interdisciplinary communication, often leading "to the discovery of expressions which have dual meanings" (Miskimins, 2003, p. 1).

Marchman (1998b) has reported that international experiences are beneficial to design teams. Travel to another country for design meetings with students and faculty from that country gave the students a better understanding of the importance and complexity of the international dimensions of the aircraft industry and marketplace. The international travel experience helped to unify the team and build the ability of members to work as a team. Foreign exposure may also include innovative educational approaches. For example, at the Universitat Rovira i Virgili in Tarragona, Spain, upper division students supervise teams of lower division students involved in design projects.

As leadership, supervisory, and delegatory skills are vital to practicing engineers, this is a useful learning experience. International activities also contribute to multicultural competency development.

INTEGRATING DESIGN SOFTWARE

In the past 40 years, advances in computer-aided design software have enhanced the ability of engineers to do design and simulation. Most graduates have learned to use one or more computational programs either in their design classes or in another class. Computations and data analysis using the Excel Spreadsheet Program from Microsoft has become extremely prevalent among engineers and scientists. This greatly facilitates interdisciplinary communication, collaboration, and teamwork. In many applications, there is more specialized design software that can be used. All members of the team need to understand how software is being used and the quality and characteristics of the results that are produced by the software. Diefus-Dux, Samant, Johnson, and O'Connor (2004) have used the evaluation methods of Kirkpatrick (1998) to assure that the students are able to use a specific computer-aided process design tool. Kirkpatrick's Level 1 evaluation measures whether students are satisfied with the instruction and encourages written comments and suggestions. Level 2 evaluation measures student learning. Diefus-Dux et al. used the Level 1 evaluation to improve instructional methods and their implementation to enable students to better use a computer simulation tool for design work.

When design results are obtained with computer-aided design software, it is important to evaluate the results and make sure all of the calculations, equations, and results are appropriate. Communication with respect to the work being done, range of acceptable values for design variables, and methods of arriving at the optimum design usually include a need to understand the software and outputs it provides.

CASE STUDIES IN TEACHING DESIGN

A conventional engineering curriculum often guides students through a sequence of courses expecting students to connect the scientific and design principles taught in these courses during a capstone experience, usually near the end of the curriculum. The design process, however, is best learned through practice and through exposure to "real-world" situations. "Real-world" design experiences can be effectively brought into the classroom by incorporating case studies as an instructional alternative throughout the engineering curriculum (Chinowsky & Robinson, 1995).

Although case studies and capstone experiences are both problem-based learning alternatives, there are significant differences among the two. In most engineering curricula, a capstone experience is a real-world and real-time design experience during the final year or final semester of an undergraduate degree. In a capstone course, the application of design principles is taught through immersion in a project experience that is often set in a real-life context. A case study, on the other hand, typically narrates the execution of an actual engineering project with all its splendor and faults. In these narratives, the successful implementation of design principles and practices is communicated alongside errors and lapses experienced during project execution. The case study allows the students a virtual experience of shadowing a project engineer at a job site. Because cases are about real engineering activities, students are able to compare their judgment and decisions with those made by practitioners and explore the differences and the reasons.

Case studies can serve as highly effective pedagogic tools for preparing a modern engineering workforce, especially if the presentation is made by one of the engineers who participated in the design and project. In addition to presenting a taste of real-life engineering, case studies can help students develop higher level thinking skills needed to solve complex problems, and interpersonal skills to work effectively as members of design teams.

Well-developed and effectively implemented case studies can utilize synthesis of knowledge and applied problem solving to illustrate how engineering works in a societal context. For example, scholars at the University of Virginia used case studies in a course titled "Invention and Design" that focused not only on design concepts but also on engineering ethics and environmental issues (Richards & Gorman, 2004). Goldberg et al. (2002) developed and used a case study in a sophomore-level engineering course to illustrate the concept of inclusive design. Students evaluated the design of accessible automated teller machines by identifying the broadest possible range of users, and designing performance criteria and adaptable interfaces to enable access to people from diverse cultures and with varying physical capabilities.

Kardos and Smith (1979) have made several important recommendations for developing and using design case studies. For example, a good case study exercise describes a real-life situation, consists of well-defined sections followed by a set of exercises or points for discussion, and includes sufficient data for a student to develop or evaluate reasonable solutions. Some effective uses of case studies in teaching design are summarized in Table 13.1.

ENVIRONMENTAL AND SUSTAINABILITY ASPECTS

Teams of engineers and scientists must lead the way to a sustainable global society. The alternative is an uncontrolled Malthusian adjustment in the

TABLE 13.1

Some Effective Uses of Case Studies in Teaching Design
(Kardos & Smith, 1979)

- As reading assignments to familiarize students with the "big picture" or to relate engineering history
- As reading to acquaint students to various aspects of the design problem
- As background reading for class discussion
- As background reading for an in-class active-learning session
- As background reading for a field trip
- As practice in formulating problems
- As motivational material for design laboratories
- As background and source of design projects

human population at some point in the future. Research, design, and deployment of technologies must be considered in an ethical context and costs to society must be calculated accurately. These considerations are necessarily interdisciplinary in nature.

Environmental health and safety must be included in making decisions for new designs. Environmental management systems that include pollution prevention and sustainable development are becoming common. Beloff, Lines, and Tanzil (2005) provided guidance that can be followed to include sustainability strategy in design. Life cycle analysis provides one approach to making decisions when there are clear alternatives to consider. The U.S. Green Building Council's Leadership in Energy and Environmental Design (LEED) rating system is another.

LEED is a voluntary, consensus-based, national standard for developing high-performance, sustainable buildings (see http://www.usgbc.org/leed/). The principles of green engineering and green chemistry (Beloff et al., 2005) may also be used in efforts to include environmental health, safety, and sustainability in designing a product, process, or system. Brennecke and Stadtherr (2002) have described their design-oriented, senior-level course in environmentally conscious chemical process engineering and Nair (1998) has integrated life cycle analysis into design education.

The availability and price of the raw materials for a plant is an example of a sustainability issue. In 2005 and 2006, plants previously constructed to produce electricity with natural gas as the fuel source became uneconomical to operate as base load plants because of large increases in the price of natural gas. When a new plant is being considered, there is a need to carefully estimate the useful life of the plant.

COMMUNICATION AND COORDINATION

Learning to work in teams should be viewed as a process to be practiced and refined in the same way that problem solving is taught as a process. Traditionally, communication and team skills were expected to be the natural consequence of assigning students to work together; the process of teaming was among "the things we expect our students to learn but never teach" (Pimmel, 2001). Teaming processes were integrated in a geo-environmental engineering course through real-world engineering projects to build workforce readiness in problem-solving and effective team performance (Bhandari et al., 2004; Steichen et al., 2006).

Effective communication among team members is essential for interdisciplinary design teams. All members of each team need to grow in their ability to communicate effectively because of the importance of communication in the work environment (Vest, Long, Thomas, & Palmquist, 1995). Several written progress reports accompanied by oral presentations during the quarter or semester mirror industry work settings and prepare students to transition from school to industry. Students should also prepare a draft final report, which is reviewed by a faculty member and returned with constructive comments to allow for corrections and improvements to be made when preparing the final report (Fornaro et al., 2001; Steichen et al., 2006). Hanzevack and McKean (1991) have reported work on teaching effective oral communication as part of a senior design course. Vest et al. (1995) found that design courses are appropriate for teaching good technical communication skills, including proper documentation of the team's design work (Fentimen & Demel, 1995). These skills can be effectively incorporated into current curricula without adding additional courses provided course content and evaluation of student work emphasize the importance of these skills. In this way, communication skills in careers are reinforced to students.

The coordination of tasks and the development of a time schedule to complete project deliverables are necessary (Fornaro et al., 2001). Value is added by making this a reviewed and graded written assignment because students need to learn to coordinate and schedule their meetings and design work. When multidisciplinary teams are working on interdisciplinary projects, more time is needed to define the project and learn about the science and engineering that pertains to it. Creating interactive procedures requires designated time where all participate. Procedures might include establishing a common technical language, setting a decision-making matrix, structuring design project methodology, and iterating designs to reflect the contribution of all team members (Fornaro et al., 2001). This process forces students out of their "comfort zone" (Humphrey, Lovelace, & Hoppes, 1999) and contributes to successful team identification and functioning (Fornaro et al., 2001). Marchman (1998a) recommended creating a group Web site to facilitate teaming and communication, particularly with teams geographically distributed across national and international borders reflecting today's global marketplace.

Tonso (2006) has reported her extensive study of design teams in an engineering design program at a university. She described two teams in detail and presented information on how each student participates in and contributes to each design project. She found that teams of five and six contain some students that are the technical and scientific heart of the team and others that contribute much less to the project. The coordination of tasks and completion of the project are impacted when one or more team members do not complete their part of the project in a timely manner.

EVALUATION OF TEAM PERFORMANCE

Teams that improve continuously have been shown to be the highest performers in engineering and manufacturing environments (Bailey, 1998). The effectiveness of cooperative learning exercises can be significantly enhanced through timely evaluation of team performance followed by information feedback to team members. Evaluating the contributions of individual team members or the performance of a design team as a unit can help students and instructors assess the functioning of a team and mitigate potentially destructive conflicts.

It is important that the assessment techniques and the rationale behind their adoption be clearly communicated to students soon after the creation of structured groups (Angelo & Cross, 1993). While preparing a performance evaluation form, an instructor should have a clear idea about the type of information sought and the extent to which the collected information would benefit a design team in improving its performance. Members of the design team may also be encouraged to contribute questions that help assess group performance. Performance evaluation may be interspersed throughout the duration of a design project and assessed after completion of the activity. Burtner (2000) suggested use of team-readiness self-assessment essays and periodic team assessment reports to monitor effective teaming of classroom engineering design teams.

Tables 13.2 and 13.3 illustrate two examples of performance evaluation forms that can be used as assessment tools to evaluate the success of cooperative learning exercises. Alternately, assessment forms can be developed to specifically evaluate the five elements of group success as defined by Johnson and Johnson (1989): (a) positive interdependence, (b) face-to-face promotive interaction, (c) individual accountability and personal responsibility, (d) social skills, and (e) group processing.

TABLE 13.2

An Example of a General Team Performance Evaluation Form

1. How would you describe the overall effectiveness of teamwork in this project?
Poor   Fair   Good   Very   Good
2. How many group members participated actively most of the time?
None   One   Two   Three   Four All
3. How many group members were fully prepared for the activity?
None   One   Two   Three   Four   All
4. What did you learn from participating in the team that you probably would not have learned working alone? Give one example.
5. What did your team members learn from you that they probably would not have learned working alone? Give one example.
6. What could have been done to improve the performance of your group? Give one example.

Note.   From *Classroom assessment techniques: A handbook for college teachers* (2nd ed., p. 350) by T. A. Angelo & K. P. Cross, (1993), San Francisco: Jossey-Bass. Copyright © 1993 by Jossey-Bass. Reprinted with permission from John Wiley & Sons, Inc.

Davis, Gentili, Trevisan, and Calkins (2002) reported their work on assessment processes and scoring scales for use in engineering design. These scholars developed an integrated assessment plan for engineering design education that is integrated into the curriculum. They included the assessment of the design process, teamwork, and communication with an assessment instrument for each aspect.

ASSESSMENT OF DESIGN COURSES

Efforts to improve engineering education following processes recommended by ABET have been greatly enhanced through the use of formal evaluation for both program development and instructional activities. High-quality assessment of student performance has advanced the field of engineering (Olds, Moskal, & Miller, 2005). ABET Engineering Criterion 3, which describes the competencies graduates of engineering programs must demonstrate, creates some assessing challenges. Meeting this criterion is frequently achieved through one or more multidisciplinary engineering design courses. However, as Davis et al. (2002) pointed out, design in engineering is difficult to assess "due to its creative and iterative nature" (p. 211). Multiple methods are being used to assess students' competencies with respect to engineering design. Included in the methods are portfolios (Olds & Pavelich, 1996), using panels of engineering faculty or practicing engineers to "score the quality of design products" (Davis et al., 2002, p. 211), and "verbal protocol analysis" (Altman & Bursic, 1998; Altman,

TABLE 13.3

An Example of a Performance Evaluation Form Designed to Assess the
Contribution of Individual Team Members

A team member's participation in the group was "Very Good" if
- She/he showed leadership
- She/he attended all group meetings
- She/he always treated all group members with respect
- She/he always performed her/his share of tasks
- Her/his contribution to the design project was top quality

A team member's participation in the group was "Good" if
- She/he attended most meetings
- She/he had valid explanations for missed meetings
- She/he treated group members with respect
- She/he generally performed her/his share of tasks
- Her/his contribution to the project was of good quality

A team member's participation in the group was "Fair" if
- She/he missed some meetings without notifying the group
- She/he was occasionally disinterested and detached
- She/he generally treated group members with respect
- She/he was inconsistent in completing her/his share of tasks
- Her/his contribution to the project was of acceptable quality.

A team member's participation in the group was "Poor" if
- She/he missed several meetings without notifying the group
- Her/his actions adversely affected the group's performance
- She/he was disrespectful of team members
- She/he did not perform her/his share of tasks
- Her/his contribution to the project was of poor quality

Chimka, Bursic, & Nachtamm, 1999; Smith & Leong, 1998; Smith & Tjandra, 1998; Tang & Leifer, 1990). Davis et al. (2002) advocated the use of an integrated assessment strategy and a standardized scoring system. Olds et al. (2005) presented a survey of traditional program evaluation methods and "promising techniques that have rarely been reported in engineering education" (p. 15), and provided a comparison of types of assessment designs, their characteristics, benefits, and drawbacks.

Empowerment Evaluation has been adopted in numerous education-re-lated spheres (Baggett, 1994; Cambourne & Turbill, 1994; Fetterman & Bow-man, 2002; Fetterman et al., 1999; Fetterman, Kaftarian, & Wandersman,

1996; Frank & Walker-Moffat, 2001; Lee, 1999; Martino, 1994; Miller-Whitehead & Abbott, 2001; Patrick, 1995; Smith, 1999). However, the use of Empowerment Evaluation to assess the efficacy of innovative teaching strategies for improving engineering education in geo-environmental engineering programs is a new application (Steichen et al., 2006).

At Kansas State University, Empowerment Evaluation was used to do the following: (a) identify the concepts and applications that would frame a new NSF-supported Geo-Environmental Certificate Program, and (b) assess the effectiveness of the interdisciplinary design course as a teaching strategy to equip engineers to solve complex environmental problems (Steichen et al., 2006).

Empowerment Evaluation is an innovative approach to evaluation which "aims to increase the probability of achieving program success by (a) providing program stakeholders with tools for assessing the planning, implementation, and self-evaluation of their program, and (b) mainstreaming evaluation as part of the planning and management of the program/organization" (Fetterman & Wandersman, 2005, p. 28).

Significant outcomes from engaging in reflective processes of Empowerment Evaluation process were as follows:

- Continuous program improvement through feedback loops (systems approach).
- Fostering of a community of scholars and learners among students and faculty around issues related to engineering design quality.
- Fostering a culture of evidence or evidence-based decision making among emerging professionals.

CONCLUSIONS AND RECOMMENDATION

Engineering design education is present in Colleges of Engineering in a variety of forms. Presently, most capstone design courses are populated by majors in the same discipline; however, many universities have one or more engineering design courses and team competition opportunities where the students work in a multidisciplinary team environment. In industry, it is very common to have multidisciplinary teams that work on engineering designs as well as other problems. The value of forming interdisciplinary teams is well established.

Several important learning objectives associated with interdisciplinary design education were presented in this chapter, and educational progress to advance learning science related to these objectives was reviewed. The ability to work effectively in an interdisciplinary team environment can be taught through review of case studies and by assigning students to multidisciplinary design teams. The importance of effective communication and frequent communication needs to be emphasized when students begin working together. Regular team meetings should include the presentation and discussion of technical issues and design options.

Good design education should include effective mentoring and monitoring of team activities. This requires considerable faculty time. Sometimes the educational environment can be structured to include mentoring by industrial practitioners or other professionals who have an interest in the final design product or educational process by selecting design problems that are real problems. The students and mentors have more interest in working on problems that are new and in need of an innovative solution. They appreciate the opportunity to interact with design engineers with professional experience.

Although there is considerable literature on multidisciplinary engineering design, there is a need to conduct additional learning science research related to effective instruction where the composition of the team includes discipline diversity.

ACKNOWLEDGMENT

We thank Bethany Steichen for reading the manuscript and assisting with the preparation of the manuscript. The idea of developing this manuscript grew out of the opportunity to attend the NSF supported "Center for the Study of Collaborative Problem Solving Workshop" in Breckenridge, CO, September 15 to 18, 2004. This work was partially supported by award EEC-0203133 through the National Science Foundation Combined Research and Curriculum Development Program.

REFERENCES

Accreditation Board for Engineering and Technology. (2005). *Criteria for accrediting engineering programs.* Retrieved October 18, 2006, from http://www.abet.org/criteria_eac.html

Altman, C. J., & Bursic, K. M. (1998). Verbal protocol analysis as a method to document engineering student design processes. *Journal of Engineering Education, 87,* 121–131.

Altman, C. J., Chimka, J. R., Bursic, K. M., & Nachtamm, X. (1999). A comparison of freshmen and senior engineering design processes. *Design Studio, 20,* 131–152.

Amon, C. H., Finger, S., Siewiorek, D. P., & Smailagic, A. (1996). Integrating design education, research and practice at Carnegie Mellon: A multidisciplinary course in wearable computers. *Journal of Engineering Education, 85,* 279–285.

Angelo, T. A., & Cross, K. P. (1993) *Classroom assessment techniques: A handbook for college teachers* (2nd ed.). San Francisco: Jossey-Bass.

Baggett, D. (1994, July). *Using a project portfolio: Empowerment evaluation for model demonstration projects.* Paper presented at the Illinois Evaluation Technical Assistance Workshop, Champaign, IL.

Bailey, D. E. (1998). Comparison of manufacturin gperformance of three term structures in semiconductor plants. *IEEE Transaction on Engineering Management, 45,* 20–32..

Beloff, B., Lines, M., & Tanzil, D. (2005). *Transforming sustainability strategy into action: The chemical industry.* Hoboken, NJ: Wiley.

Bhandari, A., Reddi, L. N., Erickson, L. E., Hutchinson, S. L., & Steward, D. R. (2004). Research integrated curriculum in geoenvironmental engineering. *Proceedings of the 2004 ASEE Annual Conference and Exposition, American Society for Engineering Education, 1,* 1–8.

Brennecke, J. F., & Stadtherr, M. A. (2002). A course in environmentally conscious chemical process engineering. *Computers and Chemical Engineering, 26,* 307–318.

Brickell, J. L., Porter, D. B., Reynolds, M. F., & Cosgrove, R. D. (1994). Assigning students to groups for engineering design projects: A comparison of five methods. *Journal of Engineering Education, 83,* 259–262.

Burtner, J. A. (2000). Teaching freshmen students to assess team performance. *Proceedings of the 2000 ASEE Annual Conference and Exposition, 2793,* 1–5.

Cambourne, B., & Turbill, J. (1994). *Responsive evaluation: Making valid judgments about student literacy.* Portsmouth, NH: Heinemann.

Carroll, D. R., & Hirtz, P. D. (2002). Teaching multidisciplinary solar car design. *Journal of Engineering Education, 91,* 245–253.

Catalano, G. D., & Tonso, K. L. (1996). The Sunrayce '95 idea: Adding hands-on design to an engineering curriculum. *Journal of Engineering Education, 85,* 193–199.

Chinowsky, P. S., & Robinson, J. (1995). Facilitating interdisciplinary design education through case histories. *ASEE/IEEE Frontiers in Education 95 Conference.* Retrieved October 17, 2006, from http://fie.engrng.pitt.edu

Coyle, E. J., Jamieson, L. H., & Oakes, W. C. (2006). Integrating engineering education and community service: Themes for the future of engineering education. *Journal of Engineering Education, 95,* 7–11.

Davis, D. C., Gentili, K. L., Trevisan, M. S., & Calkins, D. E. (2002). Engineering design assessment processes and scoring scales for program improvement and accountability. *Journal of Engineering Education, 91,* 211–221.

Diefes-Dux, H. A., Samant, C., Johnson, T. E., & O'Connor, D. (2004). Kirkpatrick's level 1 evaluation of the implementation of a computer-aided process design tool in a senior level engineering course. *Journal of Engineering Education, 93,* 321–331.

Dutson, A. J., Todd, R. H., Magleby, S. P., & Sorensen, C. D. (1997). A review of literature on teaching design through project-oriented capstone courses. *Journal of Engineering Education, 86,* 17–28.

Dvorak, S., & Dunning, S. C. (1994). Easing the transition from academia to industry: The benefits of industry exposure for students and faculty. *Proceedings of the 1994 Frontiers in Education Conference, 433,* 184–188.

Dym, C. L., Agogino, A. M., Eris, O., Frey, D. D., & Leifer, L. J. (2005). Engineering design thinking, teaching and learning. *Journal of Engineering Education, 94,* 103–120.

Ellis, M. W. (2003). Multi-disciplinary teaching and learning in a senior project course. *Proceedings of the 2003 American Society for Engineering Education Annual Conference & Exposition, 2366,* 1–16.

Farrell, S., Hesketh, R. P., Slater, C. S., & Savelski, M. J. (2004). Industry and academia: A synergistic interaction that enhances undergraduate education. *Proceedings of the 2004 American Society for Engineering Education Annual Conference and Exposition, 1413,* 1–10.

Felder, R. M. , & Brent, R. (2003). Designing and teaching courses to satisfy the ABET engineering criteria. *Journal of Engineering Education, 92*, 7–25.

Fentiman, A. W., & Demel, J. T. (1995). Teaching students to document a design project and present the results. *Journal of Engineering Education, 84*, 329–333.

Fetterman, D. M., & Bowman, C. (2002). Experiential education and empowerment evaluation: Mars Rover educational program case example. *Journal of Experiential Education, 25*, 286–295.

Fetterman, D. M., Conners, W., Dunlap, K., Brower, G., Matos, T., & Piak, S. (1999). *Report to the President: Stanford teacher education program, 1997–1998*. Retrieved October 18, 2006, from http://www.stanford.edu/~davidf/PresidentReport.pdf

Fetterman, D. M., Kaftarian, S., & Wandersman, A. (Eds.). (1996). *Empowerment evaluation: Knowledge and tools for self-assessment and accountability*. Thousand Oaks, CA: Sage.

Fetterman, D. M., & Wandersman, A. (Eds.). (2005). *Empowerment evaluation principles in practice*. New York: Guilford.

Fornaro, R. J., Heil, M., & Peretti, S. W. (2001). Enhancing technical communication skills of engineering students: An experiment in multidisciplinary design. *Proceedings of the 2001 ASEE/IEEE Frontiers in Education Conference, 52G*, 1–6.

Frank, M. W., & Walker-Moffat, W. (2001). *Evaluation of urban after-school programs: Effective methodologies for diverse and political environments*. Paper presented at the annual meeting of the American Educational Research Association. Retrieved October 18, 2006, from http://www.eric.ed.gov/contentdelivery/servlet/ERICServlet?accno=ED458239

Goldberg, L., Jolly, E., Moeller, B., Rothberg, M., Stamper, R., Wollowski, M., et al. (2002). Teaching diversity through inclusive design case studies. *Proceedings of the 2002 Frontiers in Education Conference, 15*.

Griffin, P. M., Griffin, S. O., & Llewellyn, D. C. (2004). The impact of group size and project duration on capstone design. *Journal of Engineering Education, 93*, 185–193.

Hanzevack, E. L., & McKean, R. A. (1991). Teaching effective oral presentations as part of the senior design course. *Chemical Engineering Education, 25*, 28–32.

Haythornthwaite, C. (2005). Knowledge flow in interdisciplinary teams. *Proceedings of the 2005 Hawaii International Conference on System Sciences*.

Humphrey, W. S., Lovelace, M., & Hoppes, R. (1999). *Introduction to the team software process*. Reading, MA: Addison-Wesley.

Ingram, S., & Parker, A. (2002). The influence of gender on collaborative projects in an engineering classroom. *IEEE Transactions on Professional Communication, 45*, 7–20.

Jamieson, L. H., Coyle, E. J., Harper, P., Delp, E. J., & Davies, P. N. (1998). Integrating engineering design, signal processing, and community service in the EPICS program. *Proceedings of the 1998 IEEE International Conference on Acoustics, Speech and Signal Processing*, 1879–1900.

Johnson, D. W., & Johnson, R. T. (1989). *Cooperation and competition: Theory and research*. Edina, MN: Interaction Books.

Kardos, G., & Smith, C. O. (1979). On writing engineering cases. *Proceedings of ASEE National Conference on Engineering Case Studies, 1*, 1–6.

King, L., El-Sayed, M., Sanders, M. S., & El-Sayed, J. (2005). Job readiness through multidisciplinary integrated systems capstone courses. *Proceedings of the 2005 American Society for Engineering Education Annual Conference and Exposition, 1*, 9145–9157.

Kirkpatrick, D. L. (1998). *Evaluating training programs—The four levels.* San Francisco: Berrett-Koehler Publishers.

Knox, R. C., Sabatini, D. A., Sack, R. L., Haskins, R. D., Roach, L. W., & Fairbairn, S. W. (1995). A practitioner-educator partnership for teaching engineering design. *Journal of Engineering Education, 84,* 5–11.

Koen, B. V. (1994). Toward a strategy for teaching engineering design. *Journal of Engineering Education, 83,* 193–201.

Laeser, M., Moskal, B. M., Knecht, R., & Lasich, D. (2003). Engineering design: Examining the impact of gender and the team's gender composition. *Journal of Engineering Education, 92,* 49–56.

Lee, L. E. (1999). Building capacity for school improvement through evaluation: Experiences of the Manitoba School Improvement Program, Inc. *Canadian Journal of Program Evaluation,* Retrieved January 6, 2006, from http://eric.ed.gov/ERICWebPortal/home.port.

Leiffer, P. R., Graff, R. W., & Gonzalez, R. V. (2005). Five curriculum tools to enhance interdisciplinary teamwork. *Proceedings of the 2005 American Society of Engineering Education Annual Conference and Exposition.* Retrieved October 19, 2006, from http://www.asee.org

Levi, D., & Slem, C. (1995). Teamwork in research and development organizations: The characteristics of successful teams. *International Journal of Industrial Ergonomics, 16,* 29–42.

Lovgren, R. H., & Racer, M. J. (2000). Group dynamics in projects: Don't forget the social aspects. *Journal of Professional Issues in Engineering Education and Practice, 126,* 156–165.

Marchman, III, J. F. (1998a). International, multidisciplinary design education. *Proceedings of the 1998 Frontiers in Education Conference, T3G,* 365–370.

Marchman, III, J. F. (1998b). Multinational, multidisciplinary vertical integrated team experience in aircraft design. *International Journal of Engineering Education, 14,* 328–334.

Marin, J. A., Armstrong, J. E., & Kays, J. L. (1999). Elements of an optimal capstone design experience. *Journal of Engineering Education, 88,* 19–22.

Martinazzi, R., & Samples, J. (1997). Using active learning to teach technical and non-technical skills in the same course. *Proceedings from the 1997 ASEE/IEEE Frontiers in Education Conference, TIE,* 211–213.

Martino, L. R. (1994). Peer tutoring classes for young adolescents: A cost-effective strategy. *Middle School Journal, 25*(4), 55–58.

McDonald, D., Devaprasad, J., Duesing, P., Mahajan, A., Qatu, M., & Walworth, M. (1996). Re-engineering the senior design experience with industry-sponsored multidisciplinary team projects. *Proceedings from the 1996 Frontiers in Education Conference, 9A2,* 1–4.

McMasters, J. H. (2004). Influencing engineering education: One (aerospace) industry perspective. *International Journal of Engineering Education, 20,* 353–371.

Miller, R. L., & Olds, B. M. (1994). A model curriculum for a capstone course in multidisciplinary engineering design. *Journal of Engineering Education, 83,* 311–316.

Miller-Whitehead, M., & Abbot, G. (2001). *Efficacy, outcomes, and empowerment evaluation of a school district NET project, Part III: Theoretical model.* Retrieved October 18, 2006, from http://www.tvee.org.

Miskimins, J. L. (2003). Peer learning: Observation of the cluster effect in multidisciplinary team settings. *Proceedings of the 2003 American Society for Engineering Education Annual Conference and Exposition, 3125,* 1–13.

Myszka, D. (2003). Capstone projects that are industry sponsored, interdisciplinary, and include both design and build. *Proceedings of the 2003 American Society of Engineering Education Annual Conference and Exposition, 3447,* 1–9.

National Academy of Engineering. (2004). *The engineer of 2020: Visions of engineering in the new century.* Washington, DC: National Academy Press.

National Academy of Engineering. (2005). *Educating the engineer of 2020: Adapting engineering education to the new century.* Washington, DC: National Academy Press.

Nair, I. (1998). Life cycle analysis and green design: A context for teaching design, environment, and ethics. *Journal of Engineering Education, 87,* 489–494.

Oakes, W. C., Coyle, E. J., & Jamieson, L. H. (2000). EPICS: A model of service-learning in an engineering curriculum. *Proceedings of the 2000 ASEE Annual Conference and Exposition: Engineering Education Beyond the Millennium, 3630,* 2623–2636.

Ochs, J. B., Watkins, T. A., & Booth, B. W. (2001). Creating a truly multidisciplinary entrepreneurial educational environment. *Journal of Engineering Education, 90,* 577–583.

Olds, B. M., Moskal, B. M., & Miller, R. L. (2005). Assessment in engineering education: Evolution, approaches and future collaborations. *Journal of Engineering Education, 94,* 13–25.

Olds, B. M., & Pavelich, M. J. (1996). A portfolio-based assessment program. *Proceedings of the Annual ASEE Conference, 2313,* 1–8.

Ollis, O. F. (2004). Basic elements of multidisciplinary design courses and projects. *International Journal of Engineering Education, 20,* 391–397.

Patrick, J. (1995). *Systemic change: Touchstones for the future school.* Palatine, IL: IRI/Skylight Publishing, Inc.

Paul, M. J. (2005). Carving a capstone: Senior design at the University of Delaware. *Journal of Professional Issues in Engineering Education and Practice, 131,* 90–97.

Pimmel, R. (2001). Cooperative learning instructional activities in a capstone design course. *Journal of Engineering Education, 90,* 413–421.

Richards, L. G., & Gorman, M. E. (2004). Using case studies to teach engineering design and ethics. *Proceedings of the 2004 ASEE Annual Conference and Exposition, 1,* 1–7.

Schmuck, R. A., & Schmuck, P. A. (1997). *Group processes in the classroom.* Boston: McGraw Hill.

Schrader, C., & Koelliker, J. (1996). A multidisciplinary course for environmental professionals. *Proceedings of Watershed '96—A National Conference on Watershed Management,* 1039–1041.

Schultz, R. R., & Johnson, A. F. (2005). Practicing real world design, teamwork, and communications through multidisciplinary systems engineering projects. *Proceedings of the 2005 American Society for Engineering Education Annual Conference and Exposition, 1,* 1–25.

Smith, K., Sheppard, S., Johnson, D., & Johnson, R. (2005). Pedagogies of engagement: Classroom-based practices. *Journal of Engineering Education, 94,* 87–101.

Smith, N. L. (1999). A framework for characterizing the practice of evaluation with application to empowerment evaluation. *Canadian Journal of Program Evaluation, 14,* 39–68.

Smith, R. P., & Leong, A. (1998). An observational study of design team process: A comparison of student and professional engineers. *Journal of Mechanical Design, 120,* 636–642.

Smith, R. P., & Tjandra, P. (1998). Experimental observation of iteration in engineering design. *Research in Engineering Design, 10,* 107–117.

Steichen, E. M., Bhandari, A., Hutchinson, S. L., Reddi, L. N., Steward, D., & Erickson, L. E. (2006). Improving interdisciplinary geoenvironmental engineering education through empowerment evaluation. *International Journal of Engineering Education, 22,* 171–182.

Sutton, J., & Thompson, R. (1998). Multidisciplinary integration: A decision methodology and procedure for instruction. *Proceedings of the 1998 Frontiers in Education Conference, T4D,* 450–455.

Tang, J. C., & Leifer, L. J. (1990). An observational methodology for studying group design activities. *Research in Engineering Design, 2,* 209–219.

Tau Beta Pi. (2005). *Engineering futures curriculum.* Retrieved October 19, 19, 2006, from http://www.tbp.org/pages/whatwedo/EFCurriculum.cfm

Todd, R. H., Magleby, S. P., Sorensen, C. D., Swan, B. R., & Anthony, D. K. (1995). A survey of capstone engineering courses in North America. *Journal of Engineering Education, 84,* 165–174.

Tonso, K. L. (2006). Teams that work: Campus culture, engineer identity, and social interactions. *Journal of Engineering Education, 95,* 25–37.

Vest, D., Long, M., Thomas, L., & Palmquist, M. E. (1995). Relating communication training to workplace requirements: The perspective of new engineers. *IEEE Transactions on Professional Communication, 38,* 11–17.

Walker, J. M. T., Cordray, D. S., King, P. H., & Fries, R. C. (2005). Expert and student conceptions of the design process: Developmental differences with implications for educators. *International Journal of Engineering Education, 21,* 467–479.

Wang, E. L., & Kleppe, J. A. (2001). Teaching invention, innovation, and entrepreneurship in engineering. *Journal of Engineering Education, 90,* 565–570.

Welker, A. L., & Tymon, Jr., W. G. (2004). An integrated plan for improving team functioning. *Proceedings of the 2004 American Society for Engineering Education Annual Conference & Exposition, 1793,* 1–10.

Woods, D. R., Hrymak, A. N., Marshall, R. R., Wood, P. E., Crowe, C. M., Hoffman, T. W., et al. (1997). Developing problem solving skills: The McMaster problem solving program. *Journal of Engineering Education, 86,* 75–91.

Chapter 14

Addressing Gender
in Complex Problem Solving

Barbara Bogue
The Pennsylvania State University

Rose M. Marra
University of Missouri–Columbia

With the launch of the Russian space satellite Sputnik in the 1950s came awareness of the need for a national imperative to educate more engineers and scientists in the United States. Recruiting women, who were grossly underrepresented in engineering and the physical sciences, was a part of this imperative early on. Decades later, the imperative remains, and supporting arguments fall into three broad categories: (a) It is practical and strategic—we need more technology workers to continue technological innovation and progress and to sustain economic growth. Economic studies indicate that technological advances have been responsible for as much as 85% of U.S. income growth (Committee on Prospering in the Global Economy of the 21st Century, 2005). (b) Diversity produces better results—a diverse base for problem solving, management, and product development results in a more diverse output and greater productivity (Catalyst, 2005). (c) It is a moral and ethical imperative. Educators have a responsibility to provide equal access to all disciplines and professions, particularly those that are highly paid, have high employment possibilities, and are key to economic progress (Vest, 2004).

Unfortunately, the goal of attracting more women into science, technology, engineering, and mathematics (STEM) careers where they can engage in complex problem solving has made little progress, particularly in engineering (Bogue, 2005). Although women now make up the majority of college students, they are still the minority in undergraduate study of STEM disciplines (American Society for Engineering Education [ASEE], 2005). In 2000, of women who earned bachelor's degrees, only 1.8% were engineering majors compared to 8.8% men (Muller, 2002). And current statistics indicate a downward trend. Twenty percent of engineering baccalaureate graduates in 2004 were women—a rate that cannot be sustained with current enrollment. (That same year only 18% of the total students enrolled in engineering were women whereas the percentage of first-year students who were women fell to 16.) Although the percentages are better in mathematics (48% among 2001 graduates) and physical sciences (42%), they change dramatically at graduate enrollment, with 26% in both math and physical sciences (National Science Foundation [NSF], 2004). In Computer Science, the percentage of women matriculating and graduating was relatively high in 1986 at 15,000 graduates (comprising approximately 36% of the total) but dropped steadily to 17% in 2003 to 2004 (ASEE, 2005). The disparity is evident in the workforce as well where women comprise 46% of all American workers but only 19% of the technical and 9.5% of the engineering workforce (NSF, 2005a).

This chapter examines the issue of why more women are not attracted to and retained in STEM education from multiple perspectives and situates it in a meaningful context to uncover the potential "paths" to finding solutions for this problem.

Our discussion is framed on two premises: First, that we will not engage women in the complex problem-solving environments that are discussed throughout this volume if we cannot recruit and retain them in underrepresented STEM disciplines. Second and simultaneously, the development and implementation of pedagogically sound complex problem-solving environments can—with an application of gender equity research—be a tool to achieve the first premise as well as be beneficial to all learners.

Specifically, we frame the problem using a wider lens by doing the following:

- Examining the problem broadly from an institutional framework looking at how faculty, administrators, institutional policy, classroom activities, and student skills impact the problem.
- Examining particular classroom strategies that can impact women engaged in STEM problem solving.
- Discussing the need for further research.

KEY CONDITION—FRAMING THE ACHIEVEMENT OF EQUITY IN ACADEME AS A COMPLEX PROBLEM

Understanding why few women enter STEM studies and careers and developing solutions provides a case study of the limitations of working exclusively with well-structured problems. Too often, both individuals and institutions have defined the process of achieving gender equity as a simple or well-defined problem rather than as a complex or ill-defined problem, crippling efforts to make progress toward the goal of achieving gender equity in STEM disciplines.

Because low enrollment was identified as a national problem, the approach to increasing the percentage of women entering STEM has been linear and oriented toward quick fixes. Initial efforts were simply to begin to accept more women into undergraduate programs operating under the premise that if "we accept them, they will come." And come they did; the problem was that they didn't stay (NSF, 1990). Quantification of the problem, incremental changes in how courses were taught, the creation of support groups like Women in Engineering Programs, and dedicated student professional groups plus an awareness of gender equity issues by some administrators and faculty helped to develop more effective interventions (Bogue, 2005), resulting in an increase in the number of women in engineering from 4% in 1965 to approximately 20% today (Commission on Professionals in Science and Technology [CPST], 2004). Unfortunately, this rate represents a plateau where we have stalled and from which we are even losing ground (CPST, 2004).

Most solutions, however, remain simple. There is an argument to be made that the failure to move past 20% is because university administrators, industry and foundation stakeholders, and even researchers continue to formulate the problem on a well-structured model. Programmatic initiatives have been primarily based on formulaic solutions primarily based on personal experience, rather than on existing research and well-developed assessment plans (NSF, 2003). Examples of these include extracurricular mentoring and social activities for women students, high school recruiting of those already interested in engineering and science, identifying and interdicting sources of classroom discrimination, with the focus soundly on changing behaviors rather than institutional culture. What was, and to a great extent continues to be missing, is the following:

- A thorough assessment of organizational climate and student experience of that climate to create a realistic understanding of what works and what doesn't.
- A sophisticated, research-based understanding of the problem by all stakeholders, particularly faculty.

Role of Faculty As Part of the Solution

"White men can't jump" is a popular catch phrase that amuses while it implies underlying truths. It seems harmless, and, as such, is a good example of a micro-inequity or of a building block in an accumulation of disadvantage (for discussion of the latter, see Valian, 1999). Unpacking this phrase leads to a number of questions: What effect does such a "truism" have on little boys who are interested in basketball? Does it mean that white men can't jump at all? This "harmless" phrase can have the result of creating a generation of boys who *know* they cannot succeed in basketball. Citing biological determinants for underrepresentation or underachievement, including the idea of "jump genes" or "math genes" or accepting the status quo of the participation of women in STEM as based on natural abilities rather than preparation and opportunity, can impede diverse participation and achievement.

The underlying issues are complex. Since the 1960s, quantitative and qualitative research has identified reasons why girls and women are not making more progress in STEM. To identify root causes, develop meaningful goals and strategies, and implement programs that successfully increase and develop women in STEM faculty and other key academic institutions, players must become familiar with this research. A complete review of the literature on girls and women in STEM is beyond the scope of this chapter; however, key works include the identification and description of a "chilly climate" (Hall & Sandler 1982; Sadker & Sadker 1994; Sandler, Silverberg, & Hall, 1996; Seymour & Hewitt 1997; Tobias, 1990), development of the concept of "female-friendly science" (Rosser, 1990, 1997), impact on students of stereotypes that underrepresented groups will achieve at lower levels (Steele, 1999) or of people who will not persist (Bowen & Bok, 1998; Lovitts, 2002), a lack of role models in the profession (Brainard & Carlin, 1998; Nair & Majetich, 1995). Virginia Valian (1999) made the impact of bias accessible through her work on the negative impact of the accumulation of disadvantage.

As long as this wealth of research on gender equity remains largely untapped by stakeholders on the front line (faculty, administrators, etc.), achieving gender equity in educational situations will continue to be addressed as a well-structured problem. Too often, faculty and administrators initiate activities, whether in the classroom or in set-aside diversity units (e.g., Women or Minority in Engineering programs), without accessing this growing body of literature or implementing well-designed program assessment. This contributes to an ongoing oversimplification of the problem and can result in well-intentioned but nonproductive or even counterproductive classroom and programmatic experiments.

There is mounting statistical evidence that increasing girls' access to STEM coursework and encouraging participation in problem solving and team-oriented activities is an effective strategy. As girls gain greater access and have more encouragement to study higher level math and science at the precollege level, their participation and achievements improve (Campbell, Hombo, & Mazzeo, 2000; Clewell & Campbell, 2002; National Assessment of Educational Progess [NAEP], 2004, 2005). Gender gaps have been closing over the last few years, with more differences within gender groups than between genders (Barnett & Rivers, 2004; Muller, Stage, & Kinzie, 2001). This explanation is in contrast to one based on girls' and women's ability (or inability) to perform in engineering, math, science, and technology. In fact, the rapid rise in both the scores and in the numbers of girls taking higher level math and science belies the idea that girls lack an innate ability to pursue these studies.

Continuing to frame the underrepresentation of women and minorities as a well-structured problem allows stakeholders to maintain the beliefs that (a) these changes can be handled by dedicated units outside of the classroom without significant participation by faculty and without fundamental institutional change, or (b) that anybody can attack the problem without need for reference to the existing literature and research. If the problem of increasing participation by women were simple, then it could be solved with minimum commitment to change. However, as the theme of this volume states, real-world problems are not generally well-structured and thus require complex solution paths. Faculty are in an ideal position to (a) lead in the development of a complex understanding of the issues involved and creation of inclusive learning environments, particularly as they train the next generations of STEM problem solvers; and (b) transmit that knowledge to students by making them aware of and expecting them to deal with equity and diversity issues as a part of practical application of complex problem solving. The central question is whether faculty and other institutional leaders want to maintain the status quo or foment change.

PROMOTING COMPLEX PROBLEM SOLVING FOR WOMEN IN STEM—CLASSROOM STRATEGIES

As we argue that men and women are much more similar than different in terms of the cognitive traits that may impact their ability to succeed in STEM complex problem solving, we also postulate that success is based on more than cognitive abilities (Barnett & Rivers, 2004; Glazer, 2005; Valian, 1999). The learning environment is equally important and classroom-based strategies can promote the success of all students equally. The underlying premise is that the key to creating a gender equitable classroom environment that promotes success in complex problem solving is identifying and controlling the nature of the interactions in those classes. Classroom strategies focused on how to change classroom environments to improve women's sense of efficacy, interest, and ownership in the classroom are critical—and have been shown to help retain women in STEM fields (Blaisdell, 2000; Marra, Schuurman, Moore, & Bogue, 2005) and thus engage in complex problem solving.

Select Problems or Project Domains That Are Meaningful to Learners

Presenting and selecting problems that are embedded in meaningful contexts can have a positive impact on student interest in those problems. STEM content and problems are often presented out of context, as "word problems" at the end of a chapter. Tobias (1990), after extensive research in college-level math classrooms, concluded that math subject matter was presented as discrete facts, without a background of how the facts were discovered—a methodology "comfortable and intuitive to only a narrow set of self-selected individuals" (p. 9). Although to faculty it is self-evident that STEM knowledge is fascinating and has important societal impacts, when STEM is presented as a solitary study, aloof from culture and practical application, it translates as irrelevant to students. Because women consistently report lack of relevancy as a major factor in reasons to leave engineering (Brainard & Carlin, 1998; Seymour & Hewitt, 1997), this can have a significant impact on their persistence and educational development.

Narrowly focused lectures devoid of historical and societal context can also turn what is an exciting, forward-looking field into a series of courses that are seen as part of the obstacle course to getting to the real goal—succeeding in a STEM career. "Most students scarcely glimpse the excitement of science, nor do they see scientists as people they could grow up to be" (Nair & Majetich, 1995, p. 26). Recent reports confirm that this is the case for both genders (Lemonick, 2006). In computer science in particular, Margolis and Fisher (2002) argued that lecture-based instruction provides a very narrow view of what computer scientists and related technology workers actually do, unintentionally supporting a stereotype of the field as limited and a preserve of programming jocks rather than as the creative basis of modern problem solving.

Ways to counteract this are to integrate contextual learning into STEM classrooms, leading students to an understanding of the relevancy and continuity of their studies, using gender neutral language (Burack & Franks, 2004), and simply breaking up lectures with more active learning experiences. Many programs and course revisions have been designed to accomplish this, often in the context of first-year engineering design and senior capstone design courses featuring hands-on and real-world design activities (Dally & Zhang, 1993; Diefes-Dux et al., 2004; Finelli, Klinger, & Budny, 2001; Marra, Palmer, & Litzinger, 2000; Prince, 2004). Results from such efforts and related ones include the following:

- Instructors can present material in context through real-world personal experiences of applying STEM content (Finelli et al., 2001).
- Simple strategies such as "pausing" a lecture to allow student reflection and sharing on applications of content (Ruhl, Hughes, & Schloss, 1987) or introducing conceptually challenging applied problems (Mazur, 1996) can improve student learning.
- Introductory physics students in classes with substantial use of interactive-engagement methods scored significantly better on content tests than those in traditional physics courses (Hake, 1998).
- Learning gains can be attributed to the nature of the activities rather than time on task (Redish, Saul, & Steinberg, 1997).
- The application of "problem-based" environments (even accounting for the large variation in how "problem-base" is defined) produces positive changes in student attitudes toward their programs or courses (Prince, 2004).

Sue Rosser (1990, 1997) provided extensive guidelines to achieve this and there are also many resources for historical and cultural context, including Lienhard's (2003) *The Engines of Our Ingenuity* book, Web site, and radio programs; Petroski's (1985) *To Engineer is Human;* or Florman's (1976) *The Existential Pleasures of Engineering.* Feynman's lectures are a good example of using holistic, contextual methods to teach physics (Feynman, Leighton, & Sands, 1963).

These strategies have been borne out recently at Smith college, where researcher D. Riley (2003) has implemented a "liberative" pedagogy that connects class material to life, encourages students to be authorities in the classroom, and take responsibility for their own learning and engaging in reflective critiquing of science and other source materials. Although the instructor does not report assessment results of these techniques, the basis of the strategies is to help participants feel more ownership for the content and the classroom activities. Increasing commitment and feelings of belonging have previously been found to be a mainstay of many effective programs to retain women in engineering (Goodman et al., 2002; Marra, Schuurman, Moore, & Bogue, 2005).

Use Carefully Designed and Monitored Collaborative Teams

Teamwork and collaborative or cooperative learning have become staples of engineering classrooms (Wankat, 2002). Diverse experience and talent can enrich teams, even as they make them more complex to manage. Research indicates that well-mixed populations can result in more innovative solutions to design problems and raise the level of critical thinking and analysis (Handelsman et al, 2005; Meng-Jung, 2002). In engineering, the use of collaborative teams has been spurred by the Accreditation Board for Engineering and Technology (ABET) Engineering Criteria 2000, which stated that graduates must demonstrate an ability to function on multidisciplinary teams (ABET, 2000; Prados, Peterson, & Lattuca, 2005).

Cooperative learning has often been proposed as a solution to the adverse effects of the lecture-based learning environment on women. The work of Carol Gilligan usually provides the research basis for this assertion. In *The Chilly Classroom Climate,* Sandler, Silverberg, and Hall (1996) cited Gilligan's work to indicate that "many more women than men define themselves in terms of their connection to others," and thus suggested cooperative learning is more effective for women than lectures (cited in Sandler et al., 1996, p. 42). However, more recent work has called into question both Gilligan's methods and the interpretations of her work (Barnett & Rivers, 2004; Colby & Damon, 1987; Nails, 1983).

The research on cooperative or team learning is mixed as to whether women prefer such an approach (Felder, Felder, Mauney, Hamrin, & Dietz, 1995; Kaufman, Felder, & Fuller, 2000; Seymour & Hewitt, 1997). Sandler et al. (1996) conceded the following: "While the vast majority of traditional research on collaborative learning is neither gender specific nor race specific, research in women's studies and feminist pedagogy strongly suggests that many women are particularly well served in ... more collaborative educational settings" (p. 44). Moreover, cooperative learning has proven effective for both genders, if not always in greater proportion for girls and women. The results of the meta-analysis conducted by Springer, Stanne, and Donovan (1999) on students in science, technology, engineering, and mathematics (STEM) courses show that various forms of small-group learning are effective in promoting academic achievement, favorable attitudes toward learning, increased persistence in STEM courses and programs, and preparing undergraduate students for the collaborative nature of scientific work. In small groups, students teach and learn from each other (Haller, Gallagher, Weldon, & Felder, 2000), develop more sophisticated forms of communicating technical information (Tonso, 1996b), and, through cooperative interactions, learn to behave as a team of engineers (Mayberry, 1998). Additionally, cooperative learning in academic settings can help prepare learners for workplace STEM problem solving. A recent study of practicing engineers shows that most complex STEM problem solving is done in collaborative teams (Jonassen & Strobel, 2005).

A primary problem with cooperative or team learning is that unless team or group work is carefully designed and managed, the bias or marginalization that underrepresented students can experience in the classroom is magnified (Rosser, 1998; Tonso, 1996a). In particular, students' adherence to traditional gender roles within groups or group work (e.g., men do the experiments, women do the reporting) may perpetuate inequity in a way that causes women to question their sense of competency and belonging in engineering. Instead of transforming the learning environment, collaborative work can reinforce existing patterns (Mayberry, 1998; Mouring et al., 1998; Tonso, 1996a).

Research by Felder, Felder, Hamrin, and Dietz (1995), for example, found that women played less active roles in groups than did men. Men believed the greatest benefit of group work was the opportunity to explain material to others, but this activity also caused them to believe that they were doing more than their fair share of work. Conversely, women felt that having material explained to them was the greatest benefit of group work. This reflected their belief that they needed external help and personal interaction to succeed. Women also felt that their contributions in the group were devalued and discounted by male classmates. Subsequently, their confidence levels decreased as time went by (Felder et al., 1995).

These types of behaviors are also present in hands-on and laboratory sessions. Instead of gaining confidence and expertise in the practice of engineering, Seymour and Hewitt (1997) found that in undergraduate lab classes, men took charge, ordered women, gave help women did not ask for, and took credit for work they had not done. A corollary problem is that organizational work that women do as part of team projects (e.g. calling meetings, taking notes) is often discounted or not recognized, but still supports damaging stereotypes (e.g., "woman can only do organizational work—not technical work"). A 2005 Catalyst study documented the real cost of stereotyping women as "caretakers and networkers" and men as "leaders." "Gender stereotypes portray women as lacking the very qualities that people commonly associate with effective leadership" (p. 1), with profound implications for workplace and for team learning, purported to be training for success in the workplace. For example, although the Catalyst study found there is little difference in the leadership styles of women and men, the perception that there was a difference is identified as a factor in the lack of women at top executive levels. Similarly, women students who lead a team may not only go unrecognized, but may be perceived as noncontributors because "soft" or nontechnical team skills are not recognized or rewarded.

The challenge to educators is to ensure that assigned group work(a) enhances learning, (b) increases feelings of self-efficacy, (c) enhances individual participants' sense of belonging in the engineering classroom, and (d) passes on the positive aspects of the cultures of engineering and science so that students become professionals without also perpetuating another generation of marginalizing behavior. Ensuring that group work is conducted in a truly cooperative manner, as described by the following strategies, creates an atmosphere in which these outcomes can happen (Johnson & Johnson, 1998):

- Positive Interdependence—Each student must perceive that he or she cannot succeed unless all others in the group succeed as well. Tactics include adding joint rewards, dividing resources, and requiring complementary roles.
- Individual Accountability—Individuals perform better as a result of cooperative learning. Giving individual tests, having students explain what they have learned to a classmate, submitting time reports, or observing each group and documenting individual contributions can encourage accountability.
- Face-to-Face Promotive Interaction—Keep the size of the group small so that students may help, support, encourage, and praise one another's efforts. Students should verbally explain how to solve problems, teach each other, and connect past and present learning, as well as challenge one another's reasoning and conclusions, facilitate learning efforts, and provide modeling. In this way, students receive verbal and nonverbal feedback from each other.
- Social Skills—Leadership, decision making, trust building, communication, and conflict management skills must be taught, just as academic skills are taught.
- Group Processing—Students should identify what member actions were helpful in ensuring effective working relationships and that all group members achieved learning goals. They also decide which behaviors to keep and which to change. Successes should be celebrated.

These criteria for effective teamwork underscore the need for the intensive involvement of the instructor, well beyond simply choosing a task that is appropriate for group work. To ensure that team behaviors produce the results conducive to equitable learning environments, team processes must be made an explicit, and assessed, part of the task. These requirements must be addressed directly, before, during, and after the assignment, with corrections made midcourse if necessary. Feedback mechanisms and peer team evaluations should also be part of student assessment. Implementing these basic strategies should help cooperative group work fulfill its promise to female students. Web-based resources such as the Field-tested learning assessment guide (http://www.wcer.wisc.edu/archive/cl1/flag/) or the Foundation Coalition (http://www.foundationcoalition.org/home/keycomponents/collaborative_learning.html) can provide a primer on these techniques.

Rosser (1997) made suggestions that specifically address some of the gender issues in implementing collaborative work:

- Group Composition—Including more than one person of a minority race or gender in each group may lead to less isolation.

- Role Rotation—Initially, group members may be allowed to choose their own roles so that they can develop security within the group. These roles must be rotated, however, so that each individual can gain experience and skills.
- Project Choice—Projects and problems should draw on the experiences and issues significant to the gender of participants.
- Grading—Grades should be assigned to reflect the importance of group work to the goals of the course. Instructors must maintain an awareness of the ways that race and gender can interact with group dynamics to influence student peer assessments. Although the goal of equity oriented group work is to eliminate bias, it is still possible that the communication styles, personality traits, and the culture of the engineering classroom can work against student perceptions of the quality of women's contributions in small groups.

Promote Self-Efficacy Via Delivering a Positive Message About Succeeding in STEM

Another important aspect of encouraging women to persist comes from the small, possibly subtle messages they receive during classroom activities. In addition to their results on authority, Cassidy and Cook-Sather (2003) found that the physics teacher they studied did not see his role as to "recruit" women into physics. Although we recognize that acting proactively to recruit valuable "human capital" is a shift in most faculty members' conceptions of their role, it may be a necessary component of recruiting and retaining women and other potentially marginalized students. Women who positively experience this active recruitment are more likely to be fully engaged in the classroom or laboratory and thus retained in STEM disciplines and careers.

Another study reflects the importance of these "small" messages on the impact on student performance. Male and female self-reported high-performing students ($n = 83$) were split into three groups and given the Fundamentals of Engineering exam with one of three different types of instructions. Results and instructions are shown in Figure 14.1. Bell, Spencer, Iserman, and Logal (2003) found that only the students who received the first instruction—which emphasizes the respondents' limitations—showed significant differences between men and women's scores, with women scoring lower. In contrast, the second instruction de-emphasizes the respondent's total score and emphasizes that results will be used to improve the test, and the third specifically states that the test has been shown to be gender-fair. Such results again provide support for Valian's premise of the importance of micro-inequities. They also point to the importance of such tactics in impacting student self-efficacy.

Instruction	Average Scores (%)	
	Females	Males
This test has been shown to be an excellent indicator of engineering aptitude and ability in a large number of settings across a wide spectrum of students. This test is especially effective at assessing people's engineering limitations in problem areas.		
	9	10
The problem set you will be working on today was specifically designed to present you with problems varying in their degree of difficulty so that we might be able to get an accurate picture of which problems should be included or excluded on our future version of this test. We are not interested in your overall score on the test, and, in fact, the problems are in such an early state of development that we could not say what a particular score would signify.		
	21	21
This test has been shown to be an excellent indicator of engineering aptitude and ability in a large number of settings and across a wide spectrum of students. The test is especially effective at assessing people's engineering limitations in problem areas. Prior use of these problems has shown them to be gender-fair — that is, men and women perform equally well on these problems.		
	36	28

Figure 14.1.   Student performance for each of three different instruction sets (Bell, Spencer, Iserman, & Logel, 2003).

Valian (2005) reported a similar phenomenon that can impact another source of self-efficacy—vicarious experiences. Brown and Geis (1984) found that the way a faculty member introduced a female graduate assistant impacted how she was perceived by students. When a faculty member simply introduced the female graduate assistant by name, students rated her leadership ability lower than when the faculty member introduced her and vouched for her expertise and ability to lead. By recognizing this implicit assumption and addressing it with a simple strategy, faculty members can provide an important role model and a vicarious experience of a female expert in STEM for students.

These results exemplify the concept of "stereotype threat," which is the threat "of being viewed through the lens of a negative stereotype, or the fear of doing something that would inadvertently confirm that stereotype" (Steele, 1999, p. 45). Stereotype threat has been found to negatively impact performance in a variety of settings. Thus the direct statement in instruction 3 shown earlier that the test was gender neutral may serve to neutralize any preexisting stereotypes that exist about women's performance on this test (Steele, Barnett, & James, 2002; Steele, 1999).

Walsh, Hickey, and Duffy (1999) found similar results: university women scored lower than men on the Standardized Achievement Test when women believed that the test had previously shown gender differences. In contrast, there was no gender difference in the performance of the same women and men when they believed that the test was merely comparing Canadian students with American students. The researchers indicate that these results suggest that gender stereotype threat could be a key factor in explaining gender differences in mathematical problem solving.

In STEM coursework, in general, the idea that only people who have "natural talent" can succeed, what Nair and Majetich termed a "call to the priesthood"(1995, p. 29), can be a crippling barrier, particularly if a student comes from a group that is identified as a whole as lacking in talent. When courses are taught to the top of the class, or to only the well-prepared students, the failure or nonpersistence of other students in the class is too often a result of the difference in student preparation rather than real ability. Cohoon (2001, 2002) reported that retention for women in computer science is related to faculty expectations, with lower expectations resulting in lower retention. The impact worsens when foreign-born instructors with different cultural values are on the front line (Bohonak 1995; Breene, 1992), or when instructors are themselves computer anxious or have inadequate preparation for teaching computers (American Association of University Women, 2004).

In contrast, recent research from Johns, Schmader, and Martens (2005) indicated that a positive strategy to counteract stereotype threat may be simply to educate affected groups about this phenomenon. When female participants were informed that the difficult math problems they were solving may have a negative stereotype threat that could impact their performance, they achieved the same performance results as their male counterparts, where as without this information they scored lower than men.

Although not specifically linked in the research literature, the impact of stereotype threat may be related to its impact on an individual's self-efficacy, which has been found to be an important factor in the success of women studying engineering (Blaisdell, 2000; Marra, Schuurman, Moore, & Bogue, 2005). Although efficaciousness applies to any situation, it is particularly important in choosing and executing constructive actions in situations that are perceived as negative or a barrier to success (e.g., lack of a meaningful role in a team project). Given that women are generally underrepresented in engineering classrooms, a strong sense of efficacy can help them to persist in such situations. One can hypothesize that the impact

of the instructions in Bell et al.'s (2003) research may be a result of accumu-
lative negative messages that impact women students' self-efficacy and thus
impact actual performance on important STEM learning outcomes. Likewise, Lim, Chua, and Wee (2003) found that strategies similar to the ones
we have been discussing—such as incorporating subject relevance—did
result in significant changes in self-efficacy and intrinsic motivation.

CONCLUSIONS

The importance of increasing the number of women in STEM fields has
strategic, economic, and ethical bases. Although there has been progress
since the issue of underrepresentation of women in STEM first drew attention, most solutions continue to reflect a simple, well-structured approach
rather than effort to frame and attack the problem as complex and ill-structured. Consequently, the methods applied to solving the problem are generally implemented in activities external to the core curriculum and lack
the following:

- A thorough assessment of organizational climate and student experience of that climate to create a realistic picture of what works and what
  doesn't.
- A sophisticated, research-based understanding of the problem by all
  stakeholders, particularly faculty.

The latter point has been a central focus of this chapter as both faculty
understanding and participation is necessary to systemically implement described classroom-based activities that can change learning environments
and positively impact both male and female students. The result is a failure
to make significant and continuing progress on solving the problem.

A discussion of gender equity in STEM concerning complex problems
begs the question of "when is this problem solved?" Typical of complex
problems, the solution state of this problem is not clearly defined. Are we
aiming for 50% representation of women in STEM classrooms, both as students and as faculty, and working environments? Or for other, yet to be
identified metrics? To those interested in this issue, 50% sounds great—especially when one considers our current, much lower, percentage representation. But, typical of complex problems, the authors recognize the need to
continually revisit our progress toward the solution. To do this, the issue of
gender equity must become a continual focus area for faculty, administrators, and funding organizations. Educational researchers need to consistently address gender (and underrepresented minorities) in their research
designs and data reporting. Faculty, particularly at research-focused institutions, need incentives to understand the research in this domain and to

apply strategies that are known to be effective not only for women but for all students. Administrators must become conversant in the research surrounding this issue and use that knowledge to devise and enforce reward systems for faculty and others who create equitable teaching and learning environments that attract and graduate diverse student populations.

This chapter provides the reader with an initial understanding of this systemic—and necessarily complex—problem, and specific strategies and suggestions for beginning to embark on solution paths. Now, as is often the case, intellectual curiosity coupled with the ethical imperative of this problem can lead to (catalyze) well-founded action.

REFERENCES

Accreditation Board of Engineering and Technology. (2000). *Criteria for Accrediting Engineering Programs: Effective for Evaluations During the 2000-2001 Accreditation Cycle.* Baltimore, MD: Engineering Accreditation Commission.

American Association of University Women Tech Savvy. (2004). *A nation online: Entering the broadband age.* Retrieved January 10, 2006, from http://www.ntia.doc.gov/reports/anol/NationOnlineBroadband04.pdf

American Society for Engineering Education. (2005). *Profiles of engineering and engineering colleges.* Washington, DC: Author.

Barnett, R., & Rivers, C. (2004). *Same difference: How gender myths are hurting our relationships, our children, and our jobs.* New York: Basic Books.

Bell, A. E., Spencer, S. J., Iserman, E., & Logel, C. E. R. (2003). Stereotype threat and women's performance in engineering. *Journal of Engineering Education, 92*, 307–312.

Blaisdell, S. (2000). Social cognitive theory predictors of entry into engineering majors for high school students. Unpublished doctoral dissertation, Arizona State University, Tempe, AZ.

Bogue, B. (2005). U.S. women in engineering programs: Challenge, success and re-focus. *Journal of the Institute of Electronics, Information and Communication Engineers, 88*, 861–867.

Bohonak, N. M. (1995) Attracting and retaining women in graduate programs in computer science. In S. V. Roseer (Ed.), *Teaching the majority: Breaking the gender barrier in science, mathematics, and engineering* (pp. 169–180). New York: Teachers College Press.

Bowen, W., & Bok, D. (1998). *The shape of the river.* Princeton, NJ: Princeton University Press.

Brainard, S., & Carlin, L. (1998). A six-year longitudinal study of undergraduate women in engineering and science. *Journal of Engineering Education, 87*, 369–375.

Breene, L. A. (1992). Women and computer science. *Initiatives, 55*, 167–174.

Brown, V., & Geis, F. L. (1984). Turning lead into gold: Leadership by men and women and the alchemy of social consensus. *Journal of Personality and Social Psychology, 46*, 811–824.

Burack, C., & Franks, S. (2004). Telling stories about engineering: Group dynamics and resistance to diversity. *NWSA Journal, 16*, 79–95.

Campbell, J. R., Hombo, C. M., & Mazzeo, J. (2000). *NAEP 1999 trends in academic progress: Three decades of student performance.* Washington, DC: U.S. Department of Education, Office of Educational Research and Improvement, National Center for Education Statistics.

Cassidy, K. W., & Cook-Sather, A. (2003). Putting the "social" back in "socially con-structed": Revising the teaching of psychology as and in collaboration. *Journal of Women and Minorities in Science and Engineering, 9,* 35–52.

Catalyst, X. (2005). *Women "take care," men "take charge:" Stereotyping of U.S. business leaders exposed.* Retrieved March 20, 2006, from http://www.catalystwomen.org/files/full/Women%20Take%20Care%20Men%20Take%20Charg.pdf

Clewell, B. C., & Campbell, P. K. (2002). Taking stock: Where we've been, where we're going. *Journal of Women and Minorities in Science and Engineering, 8,* 255–284.

Cohoon, J. M. (2001). Toward improving female retention in the computer science major. *Communications of the ACM, 44,* 108–114.

Cohoon, J. M. (2002). Women in CS and biology. *ACM SIGCSE Bulletin, 34 ,* 82–86.

Colby, A., & Damon, W. (1987). Listening to a different voice: A review of Gilligan's "in a different voice." In M. Walsh (Ed), *The psychology of women: Ongoing debates* (pp. 321 – 329). New Haven, CT: Yale University Press.

Commission on Professionals in Science and Technology. (2004). *Engineering and technology degrees, 1997–2004* [data reports derived from Engineering Workforce Commission]. Retrieved November 18–30, 2005, from http://www.cpst.org

Committee on Prospering in the Global Economy of the 21st Century. (2005). *Rising above the gathering storm: Energizing and employing America for a brighter economic future.* Washington, DC: National Academies.

Dally, J. W., & Zhang, G. M. (1993). A freshman engineering design course. *Journal of Engineering Education, 82*(2), 83–91.

Diefes-Dux, H., Follman, D., Imbrie, P. K., Zawojewski, J., Capobianco, B., & Hjalmarson, M. (2004). Model eliciting activities: An in-class approach to im-proving interest and persistence of women in engineering. *Proceedings of the 2004 American Society for Engineering Education Annual Conference & Exposition.* Re-trieved March 31, 2006, from http://asee.org/acPapers/2004-1407_Final.pdf

Felder, R. M., Felder, G. N., Hamrin, C. E., & Dietz, E. J. (1995). A longitudinal study of engineering student performance and retention. III. Gender differences in student performance and attitudes. *Journal of Engineering Education, 84,* 151–164.

Feynman, R. P., Leighton, R. B., & Sands, M. (1963). *The Feynman lectures on physics: Vol. 1. Mainly mechanics, radiation and heat.* Palo Alto, CA: Addison-Wesley.

Finelli, C. J., Klinger, A., & Budny, D. D. (2001). Strategies for improving the class-room environment. *Journal of Engineering Education, 90*(4), 491–497.

Florman, S. (1976). *The existential pleasures of engineering.* New York: St. Martin's Press.

Glazer, S. (2005). Gender and learning: Are there innate differences between the sexes? *CQ Researcher, 15,* 445–468.

Goodman, I. F., Cunningham, C. M., Lachapelle, C., Thompson, M., Bittinger, K., Brennan, R. T., et al. (2002). *Final report of Women's Experiences in College Engineer-ing (WECE) project.* Cambridge, MA: Goodman Research Group Inc.

Hake, R. (1998). Interactive-engagement vs. traditional methods: A six-thousand student survey of mechanics test data for introductory physics courses. *American Journal of Physics, 66,* 64–74.

Hall, R., & Sandler, B. (1982). *The classroom climate: A chilly one for women?* Washing-ton DC: Association of American Colleges. (ERIC Document Reproduction Ser-vice No. ED215628)

Haller, C. R., Gallagher, V., Weldon, T. R., & Felder, R. M. (2000). Dynamics of peer edu-cation in cooperative learning workshops. *Journal of Engineering Education, 89,* 285–293.

Handelsman, J., Cantor, N., Carnes, M., Denton, D., Fine, E., Barbara Grosz, B., et al. (2005). Careers in science: Enhanced more women in science. *Science, X,* 1190–1191.

Johnson, D. W., & Johnson, R. T. (1998). Cooperative learning returns to college: What evidence is there that it works? *Change, 30,* 26–36.

Johns, M., Schmader, T., & Martens, A. (2005). Knowing is half the battle. *Psychological Science, 16,* 175–179.

Jonassen, D., & Strobel, J. (2005). Everyday problem solving in engineering: Lessons for educators. Proceedings of the 2005 American Society for Engineering Education Annual Conference & Exposition. Retrieved March 13, 2006, from http://www.asee.org/acPapers/code/getPaper.cfm?paperID=8561

Kaufman, D. B., Felder, R., & Fuller, H. (2000). Accounting for individual effort in cooperative learning teams. *Journal of Engineering Education, 89,* 133–140.

Lemonick, M. (2006, February, 22–33). Are we losing our edge? *Time, 167,* 13.

Lienhard IV, J. H. (2003).*The engines of our ingenuity: An engineer looks at technology and culture.* New York: Oxford University Press.

Lim, G., Chua, K. S., & Wee, K. U. (2003). Effects of instructional intervention on students at-risk in engineering education. *International Journal of Engineering Education, 1,* 525–531.

Lovitts, B. E. (2002). *Leaving the ivory tower: The causes and consequences of departure from doctoral study.* Lanham, MD: Rowman and Littlefield Publishers, Inc.

Margolis, J., & Fisher, A. (2002). *Unlocking the clubhouse: Women in computing.* Cambridge, MA: MIT Press.

Marra, R. M., Palmer, B., & Litzinger, T. A. (2000). The effects of a first-year engineering design course on student intellectual development as measured by the Perry scheme. *Journal of Engineering Education, 89*(1), 39–46.

Marra, R. M., Schuurman, M., Moore, C., & Bogue, B. (2005). Women engineering students' self-efficacy beliefs—The longitudinal picture. *Proceedings of the annual meeting of the American Society for Engineering Education Annual Conference.* Retrieved July 15, 2006, from http://www.asee.org

Mayberry, M. (1998). Reproductive and resistant pedagogies: The comparative roles of collaborative learning and feminist pedagogy in science education. *Journal of Research in Science Teaching, 35,* 43–459.

Mazur, E. (1996). *Peer instruction: A user's manual.* Englewood Cliffs, NJ: Prentice Hall.

Meng-Jung, T. (2002). Do male students often perform better than female students when learning computers?: A study of Taiwanese eighth graders' computer education through strategic and cooperative learning. *Journal of Educational Computing Research, 26*(1) 67–85.

Mouring, S., Schmidt, L., Mead, P., Natishan, M., Moore, D., & Lahtan, C. (1998). The ESTEAM program: Changing the paradigm on engineering student teams from froming for diversity to training for diversity. In B. Bogue, P. Guthrie, B. Lazarus, & S. Hadden (Eds.), *Tackling the engineering resources shortage: Creating new paradigms for developing and retaining women engineers* (pp. 119–125). Montreal, Canada: The International Society for Optical Engineering.

Muller, C. B. (2002, May). The under-representation of women in engineering and related sciences: Pursuing two complementary paths to parity. Paper presented at National Academies' Government University Industry Research Roundtable Pan-Organizational Summit on the U.S. Science and Engineering Workforce, Washington, DC.

Muller, P. A., Stage, F. K., & Kinzie, J. (2001). Science achievement growth trajectories: Understanding factors related to gender and racial-ethnic differences in precollege science achievement. *American Educational Research Journal, 38,* 981–1012.

Nails, D. (1983). Social scientific sexism: Gilligan's measure of man. *Social Research, 50,* 643, 662–664.

Nair, I., & Majetich, S. (1995). Physics and engineering in the classroom. In S. V. Rosser (Ed.), Teaching the majority: Breaking the gender barrier in science, mathematics, and engineering (pp. 25–42). New York: Teachers College Press.

National Assessment of Educational Progress. (2004). *Nation's report card: Trends in average mathematics scale scores by gender.* Retrieved October 15, 2006, from http://nces.ed.gov/nationsreportcard/ltt/results2004/sub-math-gender.asp

National Assessment of Educational Progress. (2005). *Nation's report card: District mathematics results by gender.* Retrieved October 15, 2006, from http://nces.ed.gov/nationsreportcard/nrc/tuda_reading_mathematics_2005/t0020.asp?printver=Y

National Science Foundation. (1990). *The state of academic science and engineering.* Washington, DC: Author.

National Science Foundation. (2003). *New formulas for America's workforce: Girls in science and engineering* (NSF Document No. nsf03207). Retrieved December 12, 2005, from http://www.nsf.gov/publications/pub_summ.jsp?ods_key=nsf03207

National Science Foundation. (2004). *Women, minorities, and persons with disabilities in science and engineering.* Washington, DC: Author.

National Science Foundation. (2005a). *Advance: Increasing the participation and advancement of women in academic science and engineering careers.* Retrieved December 12, 2005, from http://www.nsf.gov/funding/pgm_summ.jsp?pims_id=5383

National Science Foundation. (2005b). *Science and engineering indicators 2004.* Retrieved January 9, 2006, from http://www.nsf.gov/statistics/seind04/c3/c3s1.htm#c3sl17

Petroski, H. (1985). *To engineer is human: The role of failure in successful design.* New York: St. Martin's Press.

Prados, J. W., Peterson, G. D., & Lattuca, L. R. (2005). Quality assurance of engineering education through accreditation: The impact of engineering criteria 2000 and its global influence. *Journal of Engineering Education, 94,* 165–184.

Prince, M. (2004). Does active learning work? A review of the research. *Journal of Engineering Education, 93*(3), 223–231.

Redish, E., Saul, J., & Steinberg, R. (1997). On the effectiveness of active-engagement microcomputer-based laboratories. *American Journal of Physics, 65,* 45–54.

Riley, D. (2003). Pedagogies of liberation in an engineering thermodynamics class. *Proceedings of the 2003 American Society for Engineering Education Annual Conference & Exposition.* Retrieved March 31, 2006, from http://asee.org/acPapers/2003-180_Final.pdf.

Rosser, S. V. (1990). *Female-Friendly science: Applying women's studies methods and theories to attract students. Athene series in women's studies.* New York: Teachers College Press.

Rosser, S. V. (1997). *Re-Engineering female-friendly science. Athene series in women's studies.* New York: Teachers College Press.

Rosser, S. V. (1998). Group work in science, engineering and mathematics: Consequences of ignoring gender and race. *College Teaching, 46*(3), 82–88.

Ruhl, K. L., Hughes, C. A., & Schloss, P. J. (1987, Winter). Using the pause procedure to enhance lecture recall. *Teacher Education and Special Education, 10,* 14–18.

Sadker, M., & Sadker, D. (1994). *Failing at fairness: How our schools cheat girls.* New York: Touchstone.

Sandler, B., Silverberg, L., & Hall, R. (1996). *The chilly classroom climate: A guide to improve the education of women.* Washington, DC: The National Association for Women in Education.

Seymour, E., & Hewitt, N. M. (1997). *Talking about leaving: Why undergraduates leave the sciences.* Boulder, CO: Westview.

Springer, L., Stanne, M., & Donovan, S. (1999). Effects of small-group learning on undergraduates in science, mathematics, engineering, and technology: A meta-analysis. *Review of Educational Research, 69*(1), 21–51.

Steele, C. M. (1999, August). Thin ice: Stereotype threat and black college students. *The Atlantic Monthly, 284,* 44–47, 50–54.

Steele, J., Barnett, J. B., & James, R. (2002). Learning in a man's world: Examining the perceptions of undergraduate women in male-dominated academic areas. *Psychology of Women Quarterly, 26,* 46–50.

Tobias, S. (1990). *They're not dumb, they're different—Stalking the second tier.* Tuscon, AZ: Research Corporation.

Tonso, K. (1996a). The impact of cultural norms on women. *Journal of Engineering Education, 85,* 217–225.

Tonso, K. (1996b). Student learning and gender. *Journal of Engineering Education, 85,* 143–156.

Valian, V. (1999). *Why so slow? The advancement of women.* Cambridge, MA: MIT Press.

Valian, V. (2005) *Tutorials for change: Gender schemas and science careers.* Retrieved October 15, 2006, from http://www.hunter.cuny.edu/gendertutorial/tutorials.htm

Vest, C. M. (2004). Science, technology and America's future. In S. Malcom, D. E. Chubin, & J. K. Jesse (Eds.), *Sanding our ground: A guidebook for STEM educators in the post-Michigan era* (pp. 73–80). Washington, DC: American Association for the Advancement of Science and National Action Committee for Minorities in Engineering, AAAS Center for Advancing Science and Engineering Capacity.

Walsh, M., Hickey, C., & Duffy, J. (1999). Influence of item content and stereotype situation on gender differences in mathematical problem solving. *Sex Roles, 41,* 219–240.

Wankat, P. C. (2002). *The effective, efficient professor.* Boston: Allyn & Bacon.

Part III

Research Agenda for the Future: What We Need to Learn About Complex, Scientific Problem Solving

David H. Jonassen
University of Missouri

Randall W. Engle
Georgia Tech

Peter C-H. Cheng[1]
University of Sussex

Eduardo Salas
University of Central Florida

The complexity of 21st-century problem solving necessitates a multi-perspectival research agenda. To articulate a science of complex problem solving, we need a combination of basic (laboratory) research on cognitive and social processes related to problem solving; applied (classroom) research applying pedagogical, technological, and curricular methods in science/technology/engineering/mathematics (STEM) classrooms; and workplace (ethnographic) research to ascertain the nature of problem solving in STEM workplaces. To be useful, we see these types of research as integrated and interdependent, so the overall approach to research should be use-inspired re-

[1]Peter Cheng's contribution to this section was supported in part by a UK ESRC/EPSRC/DTI grant through the PACCIT research program (RES-328-25-001).

341

search (Stokes, 1997). Use-inspired research involves the dynamic interplay between basic and applied classroom research to develop coordinated, multidisciplinary models of problem solving, drawing on multiple theories of learning, including information processing, cognitive science, situated learning, everyday cognition, dynamic systems, social psychology, organizational psychology, computational modeling, and gender and equity studies. These theoretical positions should underpin the research as well as provide contrasting theoretical perspectives, foci, and data gathering methodologies. These contrasts provide for the intentional opposition of ideas among research groups that will lead not only to new, integrative theoretical perspectives but also to new methodological approaches to studying problem solving.

To begin the process of developing a 21st-century science of problem solving, multidisciplinary researchers from diverse universities throughout the United States and Europe representing the pure sciences, engineering, mathematics, cognitive science, artificial intelligence, learning science, and cognitive, social, and organizational psychology met at a planning conference in September 2004, supported by a National Science Foundation Scinece of Learning Centers catalyst grant (NSF-0350305). During the planning workshop, multidisciplinary researchers generated 23 theory-driven research questions germane to STEM problem solving that clustered into five research themes: Cognitive Processes from Novice-to-Expert Problem Solving, Mental Models and Conceptual Change in Learning to Solve Problems, Models and External Representations of Problems, Individual Differences in Problem Solving from Novice to Expert, and Novice-to-Expert Collaborative and Distributed Problem Solving. These are the research themes and questions that we recommend for directing research on problem solving in the future.

THEME 1—COGNITIVE PROCESSES
FROM NOVICE-TO-EXPERT PROBLEM SOLVING

Research has consistently shown that experts and novices think about a given domain differently (Hardiman, Dufresne, & Mestre, 1989; Larkin, McDermott, Simon, & Simon, 1980; Schultz & Lochhead, 1988). For example, novices tend to focus on the surface features of problems whereas experts consider a deeper representation. Chi, Glaser, and Reese (1982) found that the novices did generate some qualitative analyses, however, experts generated better quality inferences. When faced with a typical or simple problem, experts can call on precompiled schemas for categorizing it (Chi, Feltovich, & Glaser, 1981) and accessing category-appropriate solution procedures (Schoenfeld & Herrmann, 1982). For more complex or novel problems, experts also posses smaller knowledge chunks that can be applied flexibly to such problems. Larkin, McDermott, Simon, and Simon

(1980) found that physics experts generated new values or inferences based on givens without necessarily using formal equations.

The expert–novice dichotomy has represented a dominant research paradigm in problem-solving research for years. However, we believe that research on problem solving should assume a transitional, developmental process from novice to expert, not a dichotomous one. Rather than comparing novices with experts, research questions should investigate how learners transition from novice to expert in their cognitive abilities to solve different kinds of problems. Because experts and novices' reasoning and problem representations differ so dramatically, it is impossible to map expert thinking onto novices during instruction. So research should examine how cognitive processes develop from novices through intermediate stages (advanced beginner, competent performer, skilled performer) before achieving expertise (Dreyfus & Dreyfus, 1986).

Articulating that transitional process is plagued by two main problems. First, since the pioneering work of Bryan and Harter (1899), most of the research on the acquisition of expertise has been predominantly descriptive rather than explanatory (Ericsson, 1996; Ericsson & Smith, 1991; Sternberg & Frensch, 1991), focusing either on identifying stages of expertise or on investigating the properties of training that optimize the acquisition of expertise (e.g., "prudent practice makes perfect" (Ericsson, 1996, 2003). Although that research convinces us that learning to solve problems, especially complex problems, is developmental, not binary, research is still largely atheoretical and is detached from relevant theoretical ideas and empirical results in related fields of inquiry. For example, theories of problem solving, particularly of complex problem solving (e.g., Funke, 2003) and theories of expertise, are very rarely combined. Also, research in the related areas of cognitive and motor skill acquisition has recently produced a remarkable wealth of specific and empirically testable theories (e.g., Haider & Frensch, 2002; Kruschke, 2003; Logan, 1988, 1992) that have not been applied to expertise research. Therefore, we intend to research the development of reasoning and problem representation in different venues from novice through competent performer to expert and to develop staged models of cognitive skills to provide more reasonable learning targets that are within learners' zones of proximal development (Vygotsky, 1978).

Second, theoretical conceptions of problem solving such as the classic General Problem Solver (Newell & Simon, 1972), the IDEAL problem solver (Bransford & Stein, 1984), and other models (e.g., Greeno, 1978), are based on information-processing theories of learning that describe problem solving as a set of processes, including framing the problem, searching for solutions, and implementing and monitoring solutions. However, problem solving is not a uniform activity. Problems differ in many ways, including degree of structure, abstractness, complexity, and dynamicity (Jonassen, 2000). STEM workplace problems, for example, include decision making, troubleshooting, systems analysis, and design problems, which require different cognitive processes to solve.

To address these research problems and produce more systematic and theory-driven research on the cognitive transition from novice to expert problem solving, the following questions should guide researchers:

1. What are the characteristics of workplace problems that make them ill-structured and therefore more difficult to solve? How do workers develop skills for solving them?
2. What are the cognitive stages in learning to solve problems from novice to expert? How do we sequence the transition from structured to ill-structured problems to enhance learning? Do race or gender impact these processes?
3. What are the mechanisms underlying information reduction in acquiring expertise? How do people learn to distinguish task-relevant from task-irrelevant information in a problem situation and relate it to what they already know?
4. What are the cognitive processes (problem definition, analysis, solution generation, and evaluation) in solving STEM problems? How do these processes evolve from novice to expert (sequence, iteration, and cycling)?
5. What kinds of metacognitive processes are used by learners at different stages in solving different kinds of problems? How should STEM students be prepared to use metacognitive strategies?

THEME 2—MENTAL MODELS AND CONCEPTUAL CHANGE IN LEARNING TO SOLVE PROBLEMS

To be able to transfer problem-solving skills, learners must construct conceptual understanding of how problems relate to domain knowledge. Problem solving often fails because students represent problems in only one way, typically quantitative. Relying exclusively on a quantitative (or any single) form of representation restricts student's understanding of the problem and its relation to domain knowledge. Ploetzner and Spada (1998) showed that "the ability to construct and coordinate qualitative and quantitative problem representations is a precondition for successful and efficient problem solving in physics" (p. 96). Qualitative and quantitative representations are complementary. Ploetzner, Fehse, Kneser, and Spada (1999) showed that when solving physics problems, qualitative problem representations are necessary prerequisites to learning quantitative representations. Qualitative representation is a missing link in novice problem solving (Chi et al., 1981; Larkin, 1983). When students try to understand a problem in only one way, especially when that way conveys no conceptual information about the problem, students do not understand the underlying systems in which they are working.

Theme 2 research examines the ways that problem solvers from novice to expert represent the different kinds of knowledge required to solve problems. Newell and Simon (1972) conceived of the problem space as a set of all states that can be obtained while solving a problem (including the initial and goal states) and a set of valid operations including any constraints on those operations. To solve all problems, learners must construct a mental model of the problem space. For well-structured problems, the problem solver's ideas about the contents of the problem space is strongly influenced by the context in which the problem is posed (Rebello et al., 2005). So, learning to solve problems requires that learners construct robust mental models of the problem space. Students who are able to construct mental models with multiple representations are better able to transfer their problem-solving skills (Ploetzner & Spada, 1998; van Heuvelen, 1991). As learners progress from novice to expert, they integrate and compile these models into problem schemas, which enable them to solve problems effortlessly (Sweller, 1989). Very little is known about problem schemas for ill-structured, workplace problems.

We assume that the development of robust mental models is a conceptual change process. Conceptual change is the evolutionary construction of explanatory frameworks or mental models (Vosniadou, 1992, 1994). As learners construct their conceptual frameworks, they revise their personal framework theories of the world (Vosniadou, 1994). As they learn more, they modify their naïve models and synthesize them into more scientifically accepted models. Conceptual change arises from the interaction between experience and existing mental models during problem solving. When learners' models are inadequate to solve problems, cognitive conflict occurs (Strike & Posner, 1985). To resolve that conflict, learners must revise their conceptual models to understand the problem space. So, problem solving and conceptual change are dynamically interdependent (Dunbar, 1998). Learners cannot learn to solve problems effectively without engaging in conceptual change.

We also assume the centrality of model building in problem space construction and conceptual change (Jonassen, Strobel, & Gottdenker, 2005). Solving a problem simply means representing it so as to make the solution transparent (Simon, 1978). Building models of problems externalizes learners' mental models of the problem space, and they readily reflect conceptual change. The internal mental model and the external model function as equal partners in a representation system, each with separate functions. External models activate perceptual processes whereas internal representations activate cognitive processes (Zhang & Norman, 1994). These external representations cannot function independently without the support of internal perceptions or cognitions. Therefore, technology-mediated model building will be integrated into most research activities to assess conceptual change in learners because these models scaffold and externalize internal, mental representations by providing multiple formalisms for representing conceptual understanding and change.

To better understand the role of mental models and conceptual change in the personal articulation of the problem space when learning to solve problems, the following questions should guide researchers.

Theme 2 Research Questions

1. How does the scope of the problem space and the solution space evolve during the transition from novice to expert? How do solvers' mental models of problems, problem-solving processes, and problem and solution spaces evolve?

2. What kinds of knowledge are critical to solving different kinds of well-structured and ill-structured problems in different STEM domains, and how are they best mentally represented? How are knowledge structures changed by solving different kinds of problems in the transition from novice to expert?

3. What strategies do novices, competent performers, and experts use to coordinate their use of alternative representations or models of domain knowledge to resolve differences between concrete examples and abstract laws and to support the integration of knowledge over different ontologies?

4. How does problem solving and learning in different STEM domains vary when alternative representational systems are used to encode the domain knowledge? What are the principles for the invention of novel representational systems to encode domain knowledge for effective problem solving and learning? Do race and gender impact these representations?

THEME 3—MODELS AND EXTERNAL REPRESENTATIONS OF PROBLEMS

Although the research questions and proposals in Theme 2 focused on the ways that learners mentally represent problems and the domain knowledge required to solve them, the research questions and proposals in Theme 3 focus on the ways in which problems and related domain knowledge are represented to learners. Organizing and displaying problems to learners in ways that enhance their mental model construction and engage appropriate problem-solving processes is the goal of Theme 3 research. Models and external representations are integral to the process of solving problems (Zhang, 1997). The representational system used by learners will determine not only how easily they learn but also what knowledge they acquire, the form of the mental models that develop in their minds, and the problem-solving methods they develop (Cheng, 1999, 2002). As learners progress from novice to expert, representational systems evolve as well, either as elaborations to existing representations or the adoption of new ones.

Despite the research that shows dramatic improvements for different representations of well-structured problems (Kotovsky, Hayes, & Simon, 1985), rather little is known about how ill-structured problems should be represented to and by learners to improve their problem-solving effectiveness and learning. To advance the science of problem solving, we must address how to represent complex, ill-structured problems and how diverse perspectives, differing scales of granularity, and multiple levels of abstraction should be treated by a representation. Real-world problems may involve many interrelated dimensions of information or vast amounts of data. Solutions to a complex problem may require the coordinated application of diverse knowledge-based strategies, heuristics, and even weak methods. Developments in areas such as information visualization (Card, MacKinlay, & Shneiderman, 1999) and the role of multiple representations in learning (Van Someren, Reimann, Boshuizen, & Jong, 1998) address aspects of these issues, but only in limited contexts.

We must also understand the nature of the cognitive processes that underpin the use of such representations. Research on creativity and insight (e.g., Kaplan & Simon, 1990; Ohlsson, 1992) has exposed some of the cognitive processes that are involved in ill-structured problem solving, but such research has typically used toy problems rather than the full complexity of STEM problems. Research on scientific discovery has also revealed how experts may use novice-like approaches when faced with problems at the boundaries of their own domains (Klahr & Simon, 1999) and how finding effective new representations is vital to the making of discoveries (Cheng & Simon, 1995). Such research, however, is only just beginning to address the nature of the cognitive processes in ill-structured problem solving.

Finally, to promote learning and transfer of ill-structured problem-solving skills, we not only must represent a problem to students appropriately but also assess their understanding of the problem as they solve it (Bransford, Brown, & Cocking, 2000). According to problem space theory (Newell & Simon, 1972), this daunting task involves detecting problem states that describe the problem solution at each point in time along with transition operators that together constitute a path from the initial state to the goal, that is, the problem solution. Being able to understand students' thinking in this manner opens the door for meaningful formative assessment (Hunt & Pellegrino, 2002). Accomplishing this in a scalable way will certainly require the application of information technology (Theall & Franklin, 2001).

To examine how problem spaces should be represented to learners to create the most useful mental representations, the following questions should guide researchers.

Theme 3 Research Questions

1. Are some codifications of domain knowledge better for novices than experts or for different genders or races? How can these different representations be sequenced to accelerate the development of expertise? Does the knowledge gained outweigh the extra cognitive load of learning alternative representational systems?
2. What kinds of representations do skilled problems solvers use for representing different problem types? When, why, and how do skilled problem solvers transfer information from one representation to another? How do skilled problem solvers integrate information from different representations?
3. What are effective methods for representing metaproblem spaces to learners?
4. How should we represent different STEM problems? Can we use different representations to construct models of how problems are solved, which can then be used to formulate a problem space theory? What attributes of different kinds of problems should be modeled?

THEME 4—INDIVIDUAL DIFFERENCES IN PROBLEM SOLVING FROM NOVICE TO EXPERT

Individual differences ultimately mediate every kind of learning. Because of the cognitive complexity of problem solving, individual differences are even more pervasive predictors of the abilities to solve problems. There are four classes of individual differences that should provide the research foci in the future: cognitive capacities, cognitive controls, epistemological beliefs, and gender and racial differences among learners.

Cognitive Capacities

Only recently have psychologists begun to discover that a variety of individual difference variables are important to complex cognition. We know almost nothing about these variables with respect to ill-structured workplace problems. The most prominently studied variable that has proven to be critical to performance in a wide range of cognitive tasks is working memory capacity (WMC). Although once thought to reflect a limit on the number of items or representations an individual could keep accessible at one time (Miller, 1956), we now know that WMC is best characterized as a limitation in the ability to control attention and the regulation of cognition (Engle & Kane, 2004). There are abiding individual differences in WMC and these differences are manifest in a wide variety of real-world cognitive tasks. A variety of valid and reliable measures of WMC have been developed and widely studied (Conway et al., 2005) and these measures predict performance on a wide array of cognitive tasks, including reading and listening comprehension (Daneman & Carpenter, 1983), language comprehension (King & Just, 1991), following directions (Engle, Carullo, & Collins, 1991), vocabulary learning (Daneman & Green, 1986), note taking (Kiewra & Benton, 1988), writing (Benton, Kraft, Glover, & Plake, 1984), reasoning (Barrouillet, 1996; Kyllonen & Christal, 1990), bridge playing (Clarkson-Smith & Hartley, 1990), and computer-language learning (Kyllonen & Stephens, 1990; Shute, 1991).

Recent studies have begun to demonstrate the importance of social and emotional influences on state-WMC (Feldman-Barrett, Tugade, & Engle, 2004). For example, high WMC participants are better at suppressing intrusive thoughts about a designated event (Brewin & Beaton, 2001). Likewise, low WMC individuals are less effective at suppressing counterfactual thoughts, that is, those thoughts that are irrelevant or counter to reality. Attentional load studies are another valuable technique to study WMC because a secondary attentional load would reduce WMC (Engle, Kane, & Tuholski, 1999). For example, Goldinger et al (2003) showed that low WMC participants showed more counterfactual thinking than did high WMC participants, but only under conditions of a secondary load. This aspect of WMC should have important consequences for a variety of problem-solving situations.

The ability to either keep task-relevant information active or at least quickly and easily retrievable such that irrelevant task information or interfering information will have less impact on directed thought is essential to problem solving (Engle & Kane, 2004). This has been manifest in exceedingly simple but attention-demanding tasks as well as complex tasks. Where attention and cognitive control become important, the task leads to automatic retrieval of information that is interfering or irrelevant to the current task. In those situations, we should see large effects on problem solving of both WMC and those variables such as stereotype threats.

Cognitive Controls

Various cognitive abilities of individual problem solver (e.g., general intelligence, spatial skills, etc.) have been shown to be inconsistent predictors of success on multiple measures of problem-solving performance (Beckman & Guthke, 1995). The most consistent predictor of well-structured problem solving is the cognitive control, field independence (Jonassen & Grabowski, 1993). Field independent learners, because they find it easier to isolate task-relevant information, are better problem solvers. We hypothesize that other cognitive controls, cognitive complexity and tolerance for ambiguity, will also mediate complex problem-solving performance in workplace settings where individuals work independently and interdependently.

Epistemological Beliefs

Learners' ability to solve complex problems, especially ill-structured problems, is linked to their understanding of the nature of knowledge, that is, their epistemological beliefs. Intellectual or epistemological development is a theory of cognitive development related to the epistemological assumptions that learners make about the knowledge they are constructing (Baxter-Magolda, 1992; Belenky, Clinchy, Goldberger, & Tarule, 1986; King & Kitchener, 1994; Perry, 1970). Learners' development progresses from simple, right–wrong thinking, through an exploration of multiple perspectives, to an understanding of knowledge and knowing that uses contextual, reasoned thinking. Students' epistemologies progress through a view of knowledge as a collection of known facts to a perspective that conceives knowledge as contextually determined and evolving.

Attaining a complex epistemology is a desirable outcome of higher education (Hofer, 2000) and arguably of science and engineering professionals. Complex, ill-structured problems require individuals to seek out and evaluate multiple sources of data, choose and apply multiple calculations and analysis methods that are relevant to the problem, and pursue and evaluate multiple solution paths and potential solutions based on multiple solution requirements. Schraw, Dunkle, and Bendixen (1995) found that epistemic beliefs had a greater effect on ill-structured problem-solving tasks than on well-structured tasks. Students' strong beliefs in the certainty of knowledge prevent a thorough analysis of alternative solutions, whereas belief in omniscient authority may limit the set of viable solutions to those suggested by experts.

Epistemological beliefs have also been linked to conceptual change (Theme 2), an essential process in learning to solve problems. Windschitl and Andre (1998) found that college students with higher levels of epistemological beliefs experience more conceptual change when learning in an exploratory, constructivist learning environment than they did when working in a directed, objectivist learning environment. Conversely, students with lower levels of epistemological beliefs benefited more from working in a controlled environment. Angeli (1999) also found an interaction between epistemic beliefs and situated (immersion) and nonsituated (preteach) instructional treatments. Although STEM students hold multiplist views while working on an open-ended design project, they are shocked that neither the client nor the professor has a definite answer to the problem at hand (Marra, Palmer, & Litzinger, 2000; Pavelich & Moore, 1993).

Gender and Race

Gender and racial identity are other variables that may have consequences for problem solving. Research on the effects of gender on academic performance in STEM domains has been inconsistent, depending on the issues examined and methods used. Although women enroll in engineering programs in much lower numbers than men, female engineering students on average earn higher grade point averages and graduate at higher rates (Huang, Taddese, & Walter, 2000). Racial identity has not received as much attention. Richeson and her colleagues (Richeson & Shelton, 2003) have argued that WMC comes into play in the regulation of automatically activated prejudicial attitudes. Another potentially important individual difference related to both gender and race is stereotype threat in math and science tasks. Women performing a math test do less well on that test if, before the test is given, they are primed with the idea that women and men often perform differently on such tasks. Schmader and Johns (2003) demonstrated that stereotype threat has its effect by reducing state-WMC. Seymour and Hewitt (1997) identified the typical engineering classroom and competitive climate as alienating for women students and a factor in their higher attrition in the engineering curriculum. This could have enormous consequences for gender differences in a wide range of complex, real-world situations.

To examine the roles of individual differences in problem solving, the following questions should guide researchers.

Theme 4 Research Questions

1. Under what conditions are individual differences in WMC important in problem solving? Do conditions of cognitive load and proactive interference interact with WMC in problem solving? Do learners with higher and lower WMC respond the same way to various manipulations to training materials and instructional environments?
2. Do problems in different STEM domains differentially affect the interest of a particular gender or ethnicity theme?
3. What is the effect of individual differences (epistemic beliefs, tolerance for ambiguity, field independence) on problem-solving performance?
4. Which individual differences make a difference for problem-solving teams? How can problem-solving groups achieve an optimal balance of heterogeneity and homogeneity on individual differences? How do

members within problem-solving groups with different representations of the issues achieve consensus regarding how key matters are conceptualized and interpreted?

THEME 5—NOVICE-TO-EXPERT COLLABORATIVE AND DISTRIBUTED PROBLEM SOLVING

We live in a flat world, a world where geographical distances are no longer barriers for interactions, collaboration, and problem solving on organizational issues. A world that is interconnected, interdependent, dynamic, and so complex requires now, more than ever, collaboration and teamwork among all involved. For example, the Accreditation Board for Engineering and Technology (ABET) requires that engineering programs must demonstrate that their students have attained an ability to function on multidisciplinary teams, because these teams continue to be a dominant force in industry (e.g., Guzzo & Salas, 1995). Because of this prevalence of teams in industry today, many are formed without much forethought along with the expectation that productivity gains can result only from teamwork (Hackman, 1990). The reality is that there is little guarantee of success, as many work teams fail for any number of reasons (e.g., Hackman, 1998; Tanskanen, Buhanist, & Kostama, 1998).

Problem-solving teams are typically established for short-term situations which require that relatively rapid action be taken against specific workplace problems. Furthermore, such teams often posses a diverse membership. Problem-solving teams are composed of members with complementary skills who maintain a degree of interdependence that requires cooperative interactions (e.g., Fleishman & Zaccaro, 1992; Katzenbach & Smith, 1993). Problem-solving teams face many challenges. For example, "before a decision can be made, the team must first recognize that a problem exists, determine its nature, and determine the desired outcome" (Orasanu, 1994, p. 256). Research has long demonstrated that teams show little inclination to engage in this aspect of the problem solving (e.g., Hackman & Morris, 1975). Problem identification in teams occurs only when the members realize that other team members are aware of the problem (Larson & Christensen, 1993; Moreland & Levine, 1992). It is essential that the team share the problem space (e.g., Orasanu, 1994). For team problem solving to take advantage of a heterogeneous group composition, team members must first be in agreement as to what is the problem. Some research documents that groups may engage in tacit coordination (e.g., Wittenbaum, Stasser, & Merry, 1996) rather than explicitly coordinate their processes. Within the context of teams engaged in complex problem solving, tacit coordination or a lack of planning could lead to the construction of either an incorrect or incomplete conceptualization of the problem.

From the standpoint of team cognition, without a shared understanding of what the problem is, a team not only may be solving the wrong problem, team members also cannot make full use of their resources; the very reason teams are assembled in the first place.

Another problem that often arises during collaborative problem solving is lack of motivation to collaborate. Lack of collaboration can arise from such issues as goal conflict, ethnic conflict, varied perceptions of the assignment, and retention of power. People in groups can hold widely varying goals, and those goals, when in conflict, can undermine movement toward problem solution. Why? People experience three fundamental needs—need for autonomy, need for competence, and need for relatedness (Deci & Ryan, 2003). Group settings can facilitate or undermine fulfillment of one, two, or all three of those needs. For example, group work exists in a social setting that can fulfill relatedness needs or that can create interpersonal conflict that undermines relatedness needs. For example, studies have shown how group members can exclude each other (Cohen & Lotan, 1995). Such exclusion may be based on race or gender. Intervention techniques, such as multiple ability treatment and assigning competence to low-status students, have been tested with school-age children but have not been tested in workplace settings or college classrooms. We adapt these techniques and investigate their efficacy for workplace and college classroom settings.

Another research perspective that we adopt is collective efficacy, an offshoot of self-efficacy research (Bandura, 1997). It refers to a group's shared perception that it can successfully perform a task. Collective efficacy affects the ways that groups make decisions in problem-solving settings (Tasa & Whyte, 2005). We examine how collective efficacy ebbs and flows during problem solving, and how it affects outcomes like success, personal efficacy, and liking of the process.

The research in Theme 5 focuses on how to facilitate the integration of problem-solving teams. To examine the roles of collaborative team members, the following questions should guide researchers.

Theme 5 Research Questions

1. What are the characteristics of effective members of collaborative, problem-solving teams? How does individual-level, problem-solving effectiveness affect team level performance? What combination of characteristics from individuals create the most effective teams? How do gender and race impact these results and how can appropriate interventions impact these results?
2. How do conflict, success, failure, and related social processes among diverse individuals and individuals from underrepresented groups in

collaborative problem-solving situations affect subsequent collaborative effort, learning performance, and leadership emergence?

3. How is collaborative problem solving impeded or enhanced by distributed teams, and how do they compare to the aspects of localized problem-solving teams? What roles do gender and race play?

4. How can collaborative skills and abilities acquired in STEM classrooms and laboratories be better developed to enhance transfer to workplace collaborative problem solving?

5. How do we optimize the processes or problem identification and generate innovative solutions to STEM design problems by interdisciplinary teams?

6. How do members within problem-solving teams possessing different conceptualizations of the problem achieve consensus on how key matters are interpreted?

ASSESSMENT OF COMPLEX PROBLEM SOLVING

The underdeveloped state of the art in problem-solving research and education is attributable, in part, to the primitive state of problem-solving assessment. Assessment of problem solving usually refers to correct answers to well-structured problems. Because problem solving abilities within domains are attributable to integrated and coherent domain knowledge (Glaser, 1992), Sugrue (1995) argued for assessing three kinds of domain knowledge: knowledge of concepts, knowledge of principles that connect concepts, and principles without procedures. To advance research in problem solving, it is necessary to develop multiple innovative approaches to assessing problem-solving performance and learning. We begin with the assumption that complex problem solving cannot be adequately assessed using any single measure. So, for every research question, we must focus on assessing different kinds of conceptual knowledge required to solve problems, problem-solving performance and processes, and solution artifacts. Therefore, every research question and proposal will address some of five different assessment issues: (a) overall index, (b) unit of analysis, (c) conceptual change, (d) modeling, and (e) transfer.

Overall Index

Problem-solving ability includes multiple factors, including cognitive and social skills, knowledge states and conceptual change, component cognitive skills, and forms of reasoning. The primary assessment goal for each research question is to identify the most efficient and predictive set of measures for assessing the ability of individuals and groups to solve different kinds of problems. This overall index must be able to provide predictive evidence about

cognitive and social skills and conceptual frameworks of the learners. The index needs to be customizable so that predictive factors can be adapted for different contexts or problem types. Finally, these customized overall measures
must be correlated to aggregate findings across studies and settings.

Unit of Analysis

Our research questions focus on individual-level performance and conceptions as well as team performance and conceptions. Therefore, we must assess individual cognition and team cognition and performance (Salas &
Fiore, 2004). We must be able to aggregate individual-level effectiveness
into team-level effectiveness as well as disaggregate team-level effectiveness
into individual-level effectiveness.

Conceptual Change from Novice to Expert

Learning to solve problems requires complex conceptual change processes
from novice to expert. As problem solvers gain experience (the primary metric for expertise), they index their knowledge based on the experiences of
problems they have solved previously with conceptual models being associated with the experiences. Conceptual change from novice to expert involves
a gradual shift from context-independent domain knowledge to personal,
experience-based conceptions. Assessment must be sensitive enough to capture these changes. Preliminary evidence suggests the need for component
conceptual skills and argumentation as potentially strong predictors.

Modeling for Assessment

CSSTEMPS assumes the centrality of model building to problem solving
(Jonassen et al., 2005). Building models of problems externalizes learners'
conceptual models. The internal conceptual model and the external model
function as equal partners in a representation system, each with separate
functions. External models activate perceptual processes whereas internal
representations activate cognitive processes (Zhang & Norman, 1994).
These external representations cannot function independently without the
support of internal perceptions or cognitions. Therefore, technology-mediated model building will be used to assess conceptual change.

Transfer to Workplace

Bransford and Schwartz (1999) expanded the concept of transfer to preparation for future learning. For complex STEM problem solving, the clearest
purpose for learning is preparation for future work, which includes the abil-

ity to solve problems independently and collaboratively. Because solving well-structured problems in science and engineering classrooms does not transfer to solving complex, ill-structured, workplace problems, we must discover the forms of assessment that will best predict workplace problem solving and learning. We must also discover how to best assess individual-level problem-solving skills in classrooms and use those assessments to predict individual skills in the workplace.

REFERENCES

Angeli, C. M. (1999). Examining the effects of context-free and context situated instructional strategies on learners' critical thinking. *Dissertation Abstracts International, 60*(5A), 1447.

Bandura, A. (1997). *Self-efficacy: The exercise of control.* New York: Freeman.

Barrouillet, P. (1996). Transitive inferences from set-inclusion relations and working memory. *Journal of Experimental Psychology: Learning, Memory, and Cognition, 22,* 1408–1422.

Baxter-Magolda, M. B. (1992). *Knowing and reasoning in college: Gender related patterns in students' intellectual development.* San Francisco: Jossey-Bass.

Beckman, J. F., & Guthke, J. (1995). Complex problem solving, intelligence, and learning ability. In P. A. Frensch & J. Funcke (Eds.), *Complex problem solving: The European perspective* (pp. 177–200). Lawrence Erlbaum Associates.

Belenky, M. F., Cinchy, B. M., Goldberger, N., & Tarule, J. (1986). *Women's ways of knowing: The development of self, voice, and mind.* New York: Basic Books.

Benton, S. L., Kraft, R. G., Glover, J. A., & Plake, B. S. (1984). Cognitive capacity differences among writers. *Journal of Educational Psychology, 76,* 820–834.

Bransford, J., Brown, A., & Cocking, R. (Eds.). (2000). *How people learn.* Washington, DC: National Academy Press.

Bransford, J., & Stein, B. S. (1984). *The IDEAL problem solver: A guide for improving thinking, learning, and creativity.* New York: Freeman.

Bransford, J. D., & Schwartz, D. L. (1999). Rethinking transfer: A simple proposal with multiple implications. In A. Iran-Nejad & P. D. Pearson (Eds.), *Review of research in education* (Vol. 24, pp. 61–100). Washington, DC: American Educational Research Association.

Brewin, C. R., & Beaton, A. (2002). Thought suppression, intelligence, and working memory capacity. *Behavior Research and Therapy, 40,* 923–930.

Bryan, W. L., & Harter, N. (1899). Studies on the telegraphic language. The acquisition of a hierarchy of habits. *Psychological Review, 6,* 345–375.

Card, S., MacKinlay, J., & Shneiderman, B. (Eds.). (1999). *Readings in information visualization: Using vision to think.* Mahwah, NJ: Morgan Kaufmann.

Cheng, P. C.-H. (1999). Interactive law encoding diagrams for learning and instruction. *Learning and Instruction, 9,* 309–326.

Cheng, P. C.-H. (2002). Electrifying diagrams for learning: principles for effective representational systems. *Cognitive Science, 26,* 685–736.

Cheng, P. C.-H., & Simon, H. A. (1995). Scientific discovery and creative reasoning with diagrams. In S. Smith, T. Ward, & R. Finke (Eds.), *The creative cognition approach* (pp. 205–228). Cambridge, MA: MIT Press.

Chi, M. T. H., Feltovich, P. J., & Glaser, R. (1981). Categorization and representation of physics problems y experts and novices. *Cognitive Science, 5,* 121–152.

Chi, M. T. H., Glaser, R., & Reese, E. (1982). Expertise in problem solving. In R. Sternberg (Ed.), *Advances in the psychology of human intelligence* (pp. 7–75). Hillsdale, NJ: Lawrence Erlbaum Associates.

Clarkson-Smith, L., & Hartley, A. A. (1990). The game of bridge as an exercise in working memory and reasoning. *Journal of Gerontology, 45*, P233–P238.

Cohen, E. G., & Lotan, R. A. (1995). Producing equal-status interaction in the heterogeneous classroom. *American Educational Research Journal, 32*, 99–120.

Conway, A. R. A., Kane, M. J., Bunting, M. F., Hambrick, D. Z., Wlhelm, O., & Engle, R. W. (2005). Working memory span tasks: A methodological review and user's guide. *Psychonomic Bulletin & Review, 12*(5), 769–786.

Daneman, M., & Carpenter, P. A. (1983). Individual differences in integrating information between and within sentences. *Journal of Experimental Psychology: Learning, Memory, and Cognition, 9*, 561–584.

Daneman, M., & Green, I. (1986). Individual differences in comprehending and producing words in context. *Journal of Memory and Language, 25*, 1–18.

Deci, E. L., & Ryan, R. M. (Eds.). (2002). *Handbook of self-determination research.* Rochester, NY: Rochester University Press.

Dreyfus, H. L., & Dreyfus, S. E. (1986). *Mind over machine: The power of human intuition and expertise in the era of the computer.* New York: Free Press.

Dunbar, K. (1998). Problem solving. In W. Bechtel & B. Grahamn (Eds.), *A companion to cognitive science* (pp. 289–298). Oxford, England: Blackwell.

Engle, R. W., Carullo, J. J., & Collins, K. W. (1991). Individual differences in working memory for comprehension and following directions. *Journal of Educational Research, 84*, 253–262.

Engle, R. W., & Kane, M. J. (2004). Executive attention, working memory capacity, and a two-factor theory of cognitive control. In B. Ross (Ed.), *The psychology of learning and motivation* (Vol. 44, pp. 145–199). New York: Elsevier.

Engle, R. W., Kane, M. J., & Tuholski, S. W. (1999). Individual differences in working memory capacity and what they tell us about controlled attention, general fluid intelligence and functions of the prefrontal cortex. In A. Miyake & P. Shah (Eds.), *Models of working memory: Mechanisms of active maintenance and executive control* (pp. 102–134). New York: Cambridge University Press.

Ericsson, K. A. (1996). *The road to excellence: The acquisition of expert performance in the arts and sciences, sports, and games.* Mahwah, NJ: Lawrence Erlbaum Associates.

Ericsson, K. A. (2003). The acquisition of expert performance as problem solving: Construction and modification of mediating mechanisms through deliberate practice. In J. E. Davidson & R. J. Sternberg (Eds.), *Problem solving* (pp. 31–83). New York: Cambridge University Press.

Ericsson, K. A., & Smith, J. (1991). Prospects and limits in the empirical study of expertise: An introduction. In K. A. Ericsson & J. Smith (Eds.), *Toward a general theory of expertise: Prospects and limits* (pp. 1–38). Cambridge, England: Cambridge University Press.

Feldman-Barrett, L., Tugade, M. M., & Engle, R. W. (2004). Individual differences in working memory capacity and dual-process theories of the mind. *Psychological Bulletin, 130*, 553–573.

Fleishman, E. A., & Zaccaro, S. J. (1992). Toward a taxonomy of team performance functions. In R. W. Swezey & E. Salas (Eds.), *Teams: Their training and performance* (pp. 31–56). Norwood, NJ: Ablex.

Funke, J. (2003). *Problemlösendes Denken* [Problem-solving thinking]. Stuttgart, Germany: Kohlhammer.

Glaser, R. (1992). Expert knowledge and processes of thinking. In D. Halpern (Ed.), *Enhancing thinking skills in the sciences and mathematics* (pp. 63–75). Hillsdale, NJ: Lawrence Erlbaum Associates.

Goldinger, S. D., Kleider H. M., Azuma, T., Beike, D. R. (2003). "Blaming the victim" under memory load. *Psychological Science, 14*, 81–85.

Greeno, J. (1978). Natures of problem-solving abilities. In W. Estes (Ed.), *Handbook of learning and cognitive processes* (pp. 239–270). Hillsdale, NJ: Lawrence Erlbaum Associates.

Guzzo, R. A., & Salas, E. (Eds.). (1995). *Team effectiveness and decision making in organizations.* San Francisco: Jossey-Bass.

Hackman, J. R. (1990). *Groups that work (and those that don't): Creating conditions for effective teamwork.* San Francisco: Jossey-Bass.

Hackman, J. R. (1998). Why teams don't work. In R. S. Tindale (Ed.), *Theory and research on small groups: Social psychological applications to social issues, Vol. 4* (pp. 245–267). New York: Plenum.

Hackman, J. R., & Morris, C. G. (1975). Group tasks, group interaction process and group performance effectiveness: A review and proposed integration. In L. Berkowitz (Ed.), *Advances in experimental social psychology, volume 8* (pp. 45–99). New York: Academic Press.

Haider, H., & Frensch, P. A. (2002). Why aggregated learning follows the power law of practice when individual learning does not: Comment on Rickard (1997, 1999), Delaney et al. (1998), and Palmeri (1999). *Journal of Experimental Psychology: Learning, Memory, and Cognition, 28*, 391–406.

Hardiman, P.T., Dufresne, R. J. & Mestre, J. P. (1989). The relation between problem categorization and problem solving among experts and novices. *Memory & Cognition,17*, 627–638.

Hofer, B. (2000). Dimensionality and disciplinary differences in personal epistemology. *Cotemporary Educational Psychology, 25*, 379–405.

Huang, G., Taddese, N., & Walter, E. (2000) Entry and persistence of women and minorities in college science and engineering education. *Education Statistics Quarterly, 2*(3). Retrieved from http://nces.ed.gov/programs/quarterly/vol_2/2_3/

Hunt, E., & Pellegrino, J. W. (2002). Issues, examples, and challenges in formative assessment. *New Directions in Teaching and Learning, 89*, 73–85.

Jonassen, D. H. (2000). Toward a design theory of problem solving. *Educational Technology: Research & Development, 48*(4), 63–85.

Jonassen, D. H., & Grabowski, B. L. (1993). *Handbook of individual differences, learning and instruction.* Hillsdale, NJ: Lawrence Erlbaum Associates.

Jonassen, D. H., Strobel, J., & Gottdenker, J. (2005). Model building for conceptual change. *Interactive Learning Environments, 13*(1–2), 15–37.

Kaplan, C. A., & Simon, H. A. (1990). In search of insight. *Cognitive Psychology, 22*, 374–419.

Katzenbach, J. R., & Smith, D. K. (1993). *The wisdom of teams: Creating the high performance organization.* Boston: Harvard Business School Press.

Kiewra, K. A., & Benton, S. L. (1988). The relationship between information processing ability and notetaking. *Contemporary Educational Psychology, 13*, 33–44.

King, J., & Just, M. A. (1991). Individual differences in syntactic processing: The role of working memory. *Journal of Memory and Language, 30*, 580–602.

King, P. M., & Kitchener, K. S. (1994). *Developing reflective judgment: Understanding and promoting intellectual growth and critical thinking in adolescents and adults.* San Francisco: Jossey-Bass.

Klahr, D., & Simon, H. A. (1999). Studies in scientific discovery: complementary approaches and convergent findings. *Psychological Bulletin, 125,* 524–543.

Kotovsky, K., Hayes, J. R., & Simon, H. A. (1985). Why are some problems hard? *Cognitive Psychology, 17,* 248–294.

Kruschke, J. K. (2003). Attention in learning. *Current Directions in Psychological Science, 12,* 171–175.

Kyllonen, P. C., & Christal, R. E. (1990). Reasoning ability is (little more than) working-memory capacity?! *Intelligence, 14,* 389–433.

Kyllonen, P. C., & Stephens, D. L. (1990). Cognitive abilities as determinants of success in acquiring logic skill. *Learning and Individual Differences, 2,* 129–160.

Larkin, J., McDermott, J., Simon, D. P., & Simon, H. A. (1980). Expert and novice performance in solving physics problems. *Science, 208,* 1335–1342.

Larkin, J. H. (1983). The role of problem representation in physics. In D. Gentner & A. L. Stevens (Eds.), *Mental models* (pp. 75–98). Hillsdale, NJ: Lawrence Erlbaum Associates.

Larson, J. R., & Christensen, C. (1993). Groups as problem-solving units: Toward a new meaning of social cognition. *British Journal of Social Psychology, 32,* 5–30.

Logan, G. D. (1988). Toward an instance theory of automatization. *Psychological Review, 95,* 492–527.

Logan, G. D. (1992). Shapes of reaction-time distributions and shapes of learning curves: A test of the instance theory of automatization. *Journal of Experimental Psychology: Learning, Memory, and Cognition, 18,* 883–914.

Marra, R. M., Palmer, B., & Litzinger, T. A. (2000). The effects of a first-year engineering design course on student intellectual development as measured by the Perry scheme. *Journal of Engineering Education, 89,* 39–46.

Miller, G. A. (1956). The magical number seven, plus or minus two: Some limits on our capacity for processing information. *Psychological Review, 63,* 81–97.

Moreland, R. L., & Levine, J. M. (1992). Problem identification by groups. In S. Worchel Wood & J. A. Simpson (Eds.), *Group processes and productivity* (pp. 17–47). Newbury Park, CA: Sage.

Newell, A., & Simon, H. (1972). *Human problem solving.* Englewood Cliffs, NJ: Prentice Hall.

Ohlsson, S. (1992). Information-processing explanations of insight and related phenomena. In M. T. Keane & K. Gilhooly (Eds.), *Advances in the psychology of thinking* (Vol. 1, pp. 1–44). Hemel Hempstead, Hertfordshire, England: Harvester-Wheatsheaf.

Orasanu, J. (1994). Shared problem models and flight crew performance. In N. Johnston, N. McDonald, & R. Fuller (Eds.), *Aviation psychology in practice* (pp. 255–285). Brookfield, VT: Ashgate Publishing Company.

Pavelich, M. J., & Moore, W. S. (1993, November). Measuring maturing rates of engineering students using the Perry Model. In *Proceedings of Frontiers in Education Conference, 23rd Annual Conference* (pp. 451–455). Washington, DC: IEEE.

Perry, W. G. (1970). *Intellectual and ethical development in the college years: A scheme.* New York: Holt, Rinehart & Winston.

Ploetzner, R., Fehse, E., Kneser, C., & Spada, H. (1999). Learning to relate qualitative and quantitative problem representations in a model-based setting for collaborative problem solving. *Journal of the Learning Sciences, 8,* 177–214.

Ploetzner, R., & Spada, H. (1998). Constructing quantitative problem representations on the basis of qualitative reasoning. *Interactive Learning Environments, 5,* 95–107.

Rebello, N. S., Zollman, D. A., Allbaugh, A. R., Engelhardt, P. V., Gray, K. E., Hrepic, Z., et al. (2005). Dynamic transfer: A perspective from physics education research. In J. P. Mestre (Ed.), *Transfer of learning from a modern multidisciplinary perspective* (pp. 217–250). Greenwich, CT: Information Age Publishing Inc.

Richeson, J. A., & Shelton, J. N. (2003). When prejudice does not pay: Effects of interracial contact on executive function. *Psychological Science, 14,* 287–291.

Salas, E., & Fiore, S. (2004). *Team cognition: Understanding the factors that drive process and performance.* Washington, DC: American Psychological Association.

Schmader, T., & Johns, M. (2003). Converging evidence that stereotype threat reduces working memory capacity. *Journal of Personality and Social Psychology, 85,* 440–452.

Schoenfeld, A. H., & Herrmann, D. J. (1982). Problem perception and knowledge structure in expert and novice mathematical problem solvers. *Journal of Experimental Psychology: Learning, Memory, and Cognition, 8,* 484–494.

Schraw, G., Dunkle, M. E., & Bendixen, L. D. (1995). Cognitive processes in well-defined and ill-defined problem solving. *Applied Cognitive Psychology, 9,* 523–538.

Schultz, K., & Lochhead, J. (1988, April). *Toward a unified theory of problem solving: A view from physics.* Paper presented at the annual meeting of the American Educational Research Association, New Orleans, LA.

Seymour, E., & Hewitt, N. M. (1997). *Talking about leaving: Why undergraduates leave the sciences.* Boulder, CO: Westview.

Shute, V. J. (1991). Who is likely to acquire programming skills? *Journal of Educational Computing Research, 7,* 1–24.

Simon, H. A. (1978). Information processing theory of human problem solving. In D. Estes (Ed.), *Handbook of learning and cognitive process* (pp. 271–295). Hillsdale, NJ: Lawrence Erlbaum Associates.

Sternberg, R. J., & Frensch, P. A. (Eds.). (1991). *Complex problem solving: Principles and mechanisms.* Hillsdale, NJ: Lawrence Erlbaum Associates.

Stokes, D. E. (1997). *Pasteur's quadrant: Basic science and technological innovation.* Washington, DC: Brookings Institute.

Strike, K. A., & Posner, G. J. (1985). A conceptual change view of learning and understanding. In L. H. T West & A. L. Pines (Eds.), *Cognitive structure and conceptual change* (pp. 211–231). New York: Academic.

Sugrue, B. (1995). A theory-based framework for assessing domain-specific problem-solving ability. *Educational Measurement: Issues and Practice, 14*(3), 2935.

Sweller, J. (1989). Cognitive technology: Some procedures for facilitating learning and problem solving in mathematics and science. *Journal of Educational Psychology, 81,* 457–466.

Tanskanen, T., Buhanist, P., & Kostama, H. (1998). Exploring the diversity of teams. *International Journal of Production Economics, 56–57,* 611–619.

Tasa, K., & Whyte, G. (2005). Collective efficacy and vigilant problem solving in group decision making: A non-linear model. *Organizational Behavior and Human Decision Processes, 96,* 119–129.

Theall, M., & Franklin, J. (2001). Using technology to facilitate evaluation. *New Directions for Teaching and Learning, 88,* 41–50.

van Heuvelen, A. (1991). Overview, case study physics. *American Journal of Physics, 59,* 898.

Van Someren, M. W., Reimann, P., Boshuizen, H. P. A., & Jong, T. D. (1998). *Learning with multiple representations.* Oxford, England: Pergamon.

Vosniadou, S. (1992). Knowledge acquisition and conceptual change. *Applied Psychology: An International Review, 41,* 347–357.

Vosniadou, S. (1994). Capturing and modeling the process of conceptual change. *Learning and Instruction, 4,* 45–70.

Vygotsky, L. (1978). *Mind in society.* Cambridge, MA: Harvard University Press.

Windschitl, M., & Andre, T. (1998). Using computer simulations to enhance conceptual change: The roles of constructivist instruction and student epistemological beliefs. *Journal of Research in Science Teaching, 35,* 145–160.

Wittenbaum, G. M., Stasser, G., & Merry, C. J. (1996). Tacit coordination in anticipation of small group task completion. *Journal of Experimental Social Psychology, 32,* 129–152.

Zhang, J. (1997). The nature of external representations in problem solving. *Cognitive Science, 21,* 179–217.

Zhang, J., & Norman, D. (1994). Representations in distributed cognitive tasks. *Cognitive Science, 18,* 87–122.

Author Index

Subject Index

Note: Page numbers followed by f indicate figures; page numbers followed by t indicate tables.